FIELDBOOK

FOURTH EDITION

This book belongs to ALPHONSE S. ZIMBA JR.
"BIG AL"

BOY SCOUTS **OF AMERICA**®

*Dedicated to Boy Scout, Varsity Scout,
and Venturing leaders who inspire Scouting youth
to plan and carry out adventures in the great outdoors.*

The *Fieldbook* is a comprehensive resource for
those with beginning through advanced outdoor
skills and is based on the experience of the
Boy Scouts of America under the leadership of

Roy S. Roberts, *President*

Roy L. Williams, *Chief Scout Executive*

Copyright © 2004
Boy Scouts of America
Irving, Texas
Printed in U.S.A.
No. 33104

Fourth Edition
Total copies of fourth edition—170,000

Library of Congress Cataloging-in-Publication Data

Fieldbook.— 4th ed.
      p.   cm.
Includes index.
     ISBN 0-8395-3104-4
     1. Outdoor life—United States—Handbooks, manuals, etc. 2. Outdoor
recreation—United States—Handbooks, manuals, etc. 3. Boy Scouts of America.
I. Title: Field book. II. Boy Scouts of America.
     GV191.4.F54   2004
     796.5—dc22

2003024650

From the Chief Scout Executive

From the time I was an 11-year-old Scout and throughout my life, I have enjoyed hiking and camping. Scouting provides countless opportunities for young people to enjoy the outdoors. As an extension of *The Boy Scout Handbook*, the *Fieldbook* will help you plan and prepare for outdoor adventures in a variety of environments. Refer to it often.

Your troop, team, or crew should recognize that we should be good stewards of our natural resources. When we accept the privilege of enjoying the outdoors, we also accept the duty of leaving no trace and carrying out conservation projects that will enable future generations of Scouts and Venturers to enjoy the outdoors.

Good luck and good Scouting!

Roy L. Williams
Chief Scout Executive
Boy Scouts of America

Appreciating Our Environment

Throughout this edition
of *Fieldbook,* this icon
alerts you to further
information—including
books, organizations,
Web sites, periodicals,
and audiovisual
materials—available
online. The *Fieldbook*
Web site,
http://www.bsafieldbook.org,
can be used in
tandem with this book
to help you make
the most of your
outdoor experience.

Introduction

*"Something hidden. Go and find it.
Go and look behind the Ranges—
Something lost behind the Ranges.
Lost and waiting for you. Go!"*

—Rudyard Kipling, *The Explorer*, 1898

GO! When it comes to adventure, there is no more important word. Want to explore the great outdoors? Eager to hike, backpack, paddle, and row? Want to pedal, saddle up, camp out, and ski? Do you dream about wild places and challenging experiences? Then you must do one thing to start making those dreams come true. Go!

The *Fieldbook* you are holding is your personal guide to the outdoors. Intended for Scouts of all ages and levels of experience, it can help you build a foundation of skills that will serve you well on any adventure from an overnight campout near your home to a rugged expedition deep in the backcountry. Older Scouts and Venturers might already have enough experience to set out on many of the

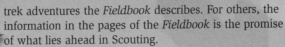

trek adventures the *Fieldbook* describes. For others, the information in the pages of the *Fieldbook* is the promise of what lies ahead in Scouting.

The contents of the *Fieldbook*, based on nearly a century of BSA experience, will help you to become a good leader and to care for the environment with hands-on stewardship efforts. You also will find information about many trek adventures, from backpacking and camping to caving, cross-country skiing, kayaking, rafting, and mountain travel. Chapters on appreciating our environment will give you a deeper understanding of the world around you and of ways to protect our natural resources.

Go! You've taken an important first step by opening the *Fieldbook*. Use it to make thorough trek preparations, then follow a trail, float a river, wander a seashore. Begin looking for adventures and you will find them. Begin learning outdoor skills and they will become your own.

Ahead for you are opportunities to see morning light touching the high peaks, to feel the heat of a desert afternoon, to appreciate the stillness of a winter night when the moon glistens on drifts of snow.

Ahead is the pleasure of a pack on your back and a trail beneath your feet. Ahead is the roar of a river as rafts and kayaks punch through standing waves. Ahead, breezes stir the tall prairie grass, lightning bugs twinkle in the woods, pack horses kick up dust on mountain pathways, and the sails of your boat strain as you lean into the wind.

The more you go, the more you will want to go—in fact, the more you will need to go. You will find yourself eager to reach open country. You will find yourself looking forward to learning all you can about going lightly on, and living in harmony with, the land. Most of all, you will find yourself wanting to see what's over the next horizon, and the horizons beyond that.

Start now. Seek out all that is waiting for you behind the ranges, across the prairies, and on the rivers, lakes, and seas. Discover what is deep in the canyons, the mountains, the forests, and everywhere else that invites you. Lace up your boots. Hoist your pack. Dip your paddle. **GO!**

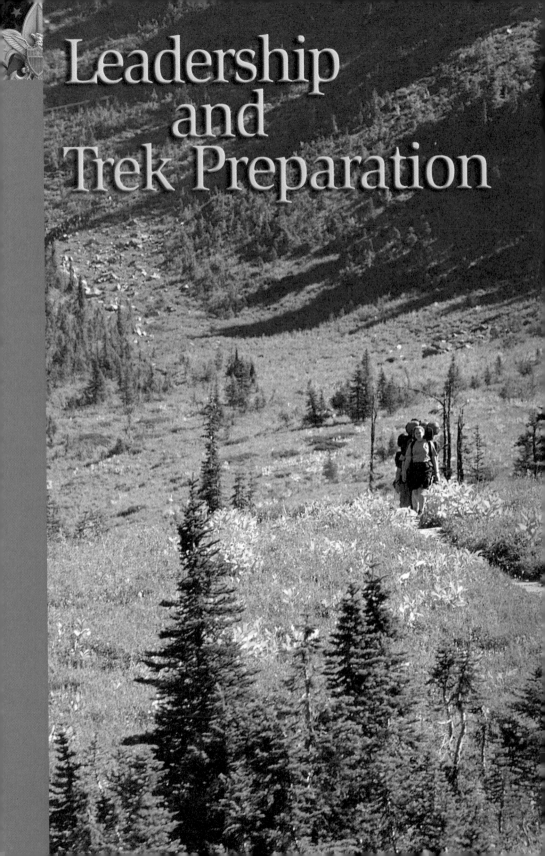

Leadership and Trek Preparation

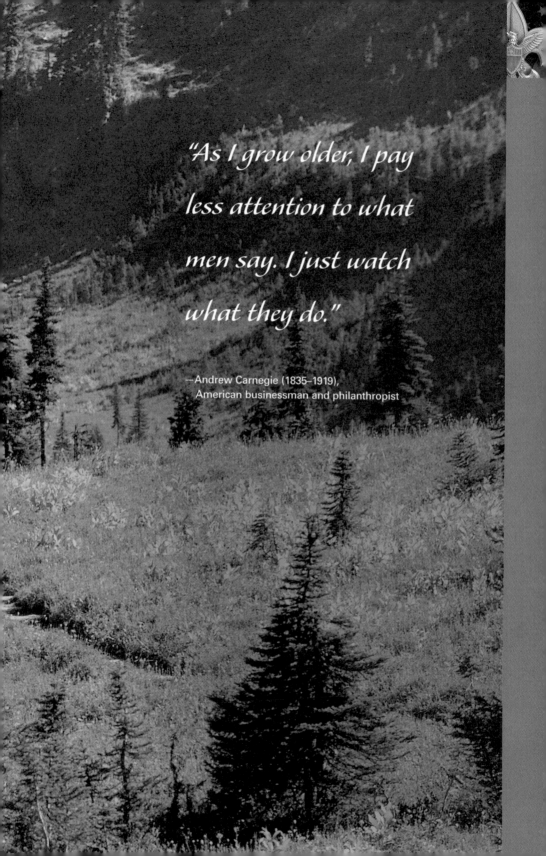

"As I grow older, I pay less attention to what men say. I just watch what they do."

—Andrew Carnegie (1835–1919),
American businessman and philanthropist

CHAPTER
1

Organizing for Adventures

" We strive to create an environment where people are valued as individuals and are treated with respect, dignity, and fairness."

—From *Wood Badge for the 21st Century* (the BSA's premier leadership training course for adult Scouters), Boy Scouts of America, 2001

A mountain travel team pushes toward the summit of a peak. Kayakers and rafters combine their knowledge to find the best routes through a thundering river. Winter campers take turns breaking trail through the drifts. Search-and-rescue team members grab their gear and respond to an emergency. Friends set out for an afternoon of hiking, fishing, or bicycle touring.

Outdoor adventures are better when they are shared. While there is safety in numbers, group dynamics involve more than simple risk management. Groups taking part in trek adventures are usually small, and the challenge of living outdoors is often heightened by weather, distance, and logistical hurdles. Joining with others ensures plenty of brains and brawn for meeting all sorts of situations.

Leadership situations seldom involve one person giving orders and everybody else simply doing what they are told. Instead, all members must take responsibility for the team's success. When the need for direct leadership arises—coping with emergencies or defusing risky situations, for example—group members who shoulder their portion of the load and act in the group's best interests will enhance the probability of success.

Group members working toward common goals can amass a storehouse of experience. As members of a group iron out their differences and build upon their strengths, they become proof that the whole can be greater than the sum of its parts.

1

Group Formation

Groups form in many ways and for many reasons. The 1914 newspaper ad placed by British explorer Ernest Shackleton brought together a team of 27 adventurers for an attempted first crossing of Antarctica. Stranded for nearly two years after their ship, the *Endurance,* was crushed by ice, they worked together so well against overwhelming odds that all of them managed to return home safely. They failed to fulfill their original plan of a trans-Antarctic trek, but in terms of crew behavior and team leadership, the Shackleton expedition can be considered one of the most successful of all wilderness journeys.

"Men wanted for hazardous journey. Small wages. Bitter cold. Long months of complete darkness. Constant danger. Safe return doubtful. Honour and recognition in case of success."

—Ernest Shackleton, 1914

Every group has initial motives for coming together. People might be drawn to the values and opportunities of a Scout unit or a school outdoor club. Family members setting out for a camping trip often act as a team once they hit the trail. A group might be as tightly knit as close friends seeking adventures, or as random as strangers signing up for a commercial trip, a guided wilderness experience, or a training course set in the outdoors.

Those joining an outdoor group might be similar in age and level of experience, or they could represent a broad range of backgrounds. Perhaps they have shared many trek adventures already, or they might be at the beginning of their outdoor explorations. Whatever the case, people are the raw material of every group. Their histories, interests, and abilities are the building blocks for organizing an effective team for the field.

Can a blind mountaineer climb Mount Everest? It's been done. Can hearing-impaired people form trail maintenance crews doing quality work deep in the woods? Of course. Can someone with food allergies, asthma, or diabetes take part in extended backpacking trips? The answer is *perhaps,* depending upon recommendations from the person's doctor and prior arrangements made by the group. The outdoors is open to all who want to enjoy it, bringing with them a variety of experience and possibility that will enrich almost any group.

Group Size

The number of people traveling together in the outdoors must never exceed the limits established by those managing the lands where a trek will occur. The minimum size for a BSA group taking part in outdoor activities is four. That way, if someone becomes injured or ill, one party member can administer first aid while two others go for help.

Members of a trekking group should organize themselves as smaller teams of two each. These buddies share the challenges of a trip, keep track of each other, and alert group leaders to any concerns that may arise. Two people give reassurance to each other and share responsibility for navigating using map and compass.

For more on leadership, see the chapter titled "Outdoor Leadership."

HOW FAR AND HOW FAST?

This general guide can help you plan how far your group will travel in a given time.

Two miles per hour—*the speed of average hikers crossing gentle terrain*

One mile per hour—*the speed of hikers with heavy packs in rugged country*

One hour—*the amount of travel time to add for every thousand feet of elevation to be gained*

Half an hour—*the amount of travel time to subtract for every thousand feet of elevation to be lost*

For more information on determining how far groups can travel in varying terrains, see the chapter titled "Mountain Travel."

Learn From and Share With Other Travelers

Every organization involved in the outdoors has developed its own variations on teamwork, leadership, empowerment, and training. People wishing to be fully aware of a wide range of approaches to outdoor activities will seek out opportunities to learn about other organizations and their ways of doing things. They can take the best of what they learn from each group to incorporate into their own vision of leadership, group dynamics, and the practice of outdoor skills.

Matching Groups With Adventures

Which comes first, the itinerary or the group? It all depends. Ernest Shackleton knew what he wanted to achieve in Antarctica. With a plan in place, he began recruiting the people he felt could accomplish the goals he had set. The same process is the foundation of other extremely challenging treks, especially those requiring extensive specialized experience. Group organizers will, like Shackleton, seek out people qualified as mountain travelers, river runners, or cavers, or possessing other skills they feel will help ensure the success of a particular expedition. (Of course, high levels of expertise are no assurance of a person's ability to fit in as a member of a particular group. The history of wilderness exploration is crowded with accounts of able people whose personalities prevented them from meshing with others to form successful teams, a factor that sometimes led them to make very bad choices in dangerous circumstances.)

Usually, though, a group comes together first—as a Scout unit, for example, or a group of friends, or a school outdoor club. The challenge then is for leaders to help the group develop goals that are appropriate for the abilities of its members. Ideally, these possibilities offer opportunities for members to accept responsibilities of increasing importance and to recognize and celebrate real success.

Seasoned leadership can make up for some group inexperience if leaders manage challenges in ways that encourage the members to expand their knowledge. A group new to kayak touring would not yet have the training to embark on long journeys across open seas. On the other hand, the group could find plenty of satisfaction paddling in sheltered waters while they master kayaking skills that will prepare them for increasingly challenging adventures.

In helping groups shape their adventures, leaders should not overextend a group to the point of compromising safety or creating a high probability of failure. A novice group taking on a hard winter trek might find that they are overmatched by the weather. If they spend too much time being cold, wet, and hungry, they may be unwilling to try future outdoor adventures. When group members begin with manageable trips, though, and build up to more strenuous ones, they can develop confidence and ability along the way. Ideal itineraries have the flexibility to include demanding goals as well as more manageable alternatives should conditions change or the initial plan prove to be too difficult.

In addition to considering the abilities of group members, group leaders must be realistic about their own qualifications, and should accept responsibility only for treks that are within their levels of experience and skill.

Age-Appropriate Guidelines

Many activities described in the *Fieldbook* are ideal for Scouts of all ages. Some of the more challenging trek adventures are better suited for Venturers, Varsity Scouts, and older Boy Scouts. The BSA's Age-Appropriate Guidelines for Scouting Activities publication is useful for matching groups with outdoor activities that are within their capabilities, training, and experience. For more information, see the BSA's Web site at *http://www.scouting.org*.

1

Orienting a Group

Orient a map before a hike and it is set true to the world. Aligned with the compass and square with the North and South poles, the map can make more sense than if it were left flapping in the wind. Likewise, when a group is oriented before a trek, it is squared away for the journey to come. Everybody is aligned with the group's goals, plans, and methods. Members understand what lies ahead, and they know what their roles will be for achieving the most for their group and for themselves.

Orienting a group before a trip can significantly improve the quality of the experience, the safety of the group members, and each person's ability to care for the environment.

The task of orienting a group rests primarily with its leaders. A newly formed or inexperienced group may need lots of pretrip preparation, beginning with members getting acquainted with one another and discovering common points of experience and interest.

Orienting groups of any skill level involves the following steps:

- Setting the tone

- Developing group structure and standards

- Establishing goals

- Determining logistical tasks

"Even in those early days, I was a great dreamer. I used to go for long walks about the area or cut across the paddocks jumping over fences with my mind far away, just thinking about adventurers and exciting things to do."

—Sir Edmund Hillary

Setting the Tone

The chapter titled "Gearing Up" lists clothing and equipment that can be carried to help ensure safe outdoor experiences. Nowhere on those lists, though, is the most important item of all—a positive attitude.

Leaders help set the tone right from the beginning of group orientation. Once a group has left the trailhead, the tone set by its leaders can be even more important. Trek adventures can be tough. There will be times when people are colder or hotter than they would like to be, and when they are hungry and tired. There will be days when headwinds hold them back or trails are rugged and steep. There might be nights when storms batter a camp, when a stove malfunctions, or when a key piece of gear is lost. Discouraging developments are bound to occur, but if a group looks at them in a positive, realistic way, difficulties can melt to a manageable size. When spirits are high, a group can achieve almost anything.

Train yourself and your group to look for answers rather than staying stuck in uncomfortable situations. Cold and wet? Do something about getting dry and warm. Somebody having trouble with a heavy pack? Give them a hand. Not sure which way the route goes? Get out the map and compass, put your heads together, and figure things out.

"Adventure is merely discomfort rightly perceived," goes an old traveler's saying, and there is some truth in that. Choosing to perceive discomfort—and all of adventure—as an opportunity to act in positive, productive ways is a responsibility to be taken seriously by every person in a group.

Group standards, understood from the start, make clear what is acceptable behavior during group activities, and what is not.

Developing Group Structure and Standards

A group's structure is the framework that helps hold it together through good times and bad. A team like Shackleton's crew headed for Antarctica might have a clear hierarchy of command. A group of friends heading for the backcountry might be set up more informally, with each person having a say in many of the decisions and the most experienced member recognized as the leader who will make the call if there is no clear consensus or if options must be considered quickly. With Venturing crews, Varsity Scout teams, and Boy Scout troops, Scouting offers a variety of organizational structures tailored to the ages and experience levels of group members.

The standards established by a group usually are an outgrowth of the beliefs and the shared experience of the organization to which the members belong. The most basic standards are nonnegotiable guidelines intended to enhance the safety of individuals and the quality of the environment—the mandatory use of life jackets during watercraft activities, for instance, or a commitment to follow the principles of Leave No Trace throughout a trek. Anyone who wishes to take part in an adventure with the group must agree in advance to follow these standards. (Nonnegotiable standards should be limited to matters of real importance. Too many rules can dilute the emphasis of those that are vital.)

Group standards also extend beyond matters of risk management and environmental protection to include essentials of how group members will treat one another. Most are commonsense means of interacting with others in any situation and any setting. Each person will be treated fairly and equally. Differences will be respected and harassment will never be tolerated. Everyone will be supported and encouraged.

For more on group safety standards, see the chapter titled "Managing Risk." For more on guidelines that protect the environment, see the "Leaving No Trace" section of this book.

Establishing Goals

Goals provide group members with a shared vision and purpose. The goal of a wilderness trip might seem to be as clear as getting to a distant lake or standing on a mountaintop, but a destination is only part of it. *How* a group reaches a landmark is always a more important goal than *where* it hopes to arrive. Making a good decision about altering an itinerary or turning back might be much smarter, and a far more valuable learning experience, than touching a summit.

Establishing goals is a matter of imagining what you want to accomplish and then determining how to make that vision a reality. No doubt you and the others in your group can see yourselves paddling down a river, sleeping in igloos, hiking across a desert, or taking part in any number of other outdoor adventures. Determining logistical tasks will go a long way toward providing a blueprint for achieving your goals. Go a step further during pretrip meetings, skill sessions, and shakedowns, and enliven your goals with the commitment to ensure that everyone accepts responsibility not only for the group's success, but also for creating a healthy environment in which each person can thrive.

> When people travel the same trails, cook and eat together, and share the challenges and triumphs of outdoor living, they will discover much about practicing patience, respecting others, and developing lasting friendships.

Determining Logistical Tasks

The final part of orienting a group, determining logistical tasks, is a way of mapping out the steps to reach group goals. Many groups use written charts and checklists to delegate responsibilities so that nothing will be overlooked. Group members see to it that they have the gear, clothing, and provisions they will need. They know who has the assignments for cooking certain meals, who will carry first-aid gear, and how other chores will be divided up.

Organizing equipment, putting together menus, repackaging food for the trail, and other pretrip activities are opportunities for group members to work together before a trek begins. Along with the rest of the group orientation process, these activities can help the members fit into their roles and increase group cohesion that will be important to the effective operation of the group once it sets out for the field.

For more on logistical tasks, see the chapter titled "Planning a Trek."

CHAPTER

2

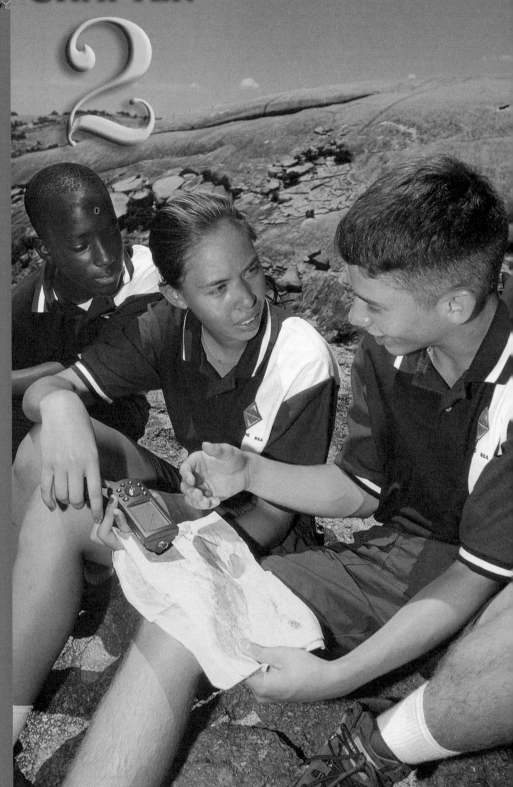

Outdoor Leadership

"Leadership is not just passed on from the more experienced to the less experienced. There are too many people with a lot of experiences who don't know what they're doing."

—Paul Petzoldt, outdoorsman and writer who climbed Wyoming's Grand Teton mountain more than 300 times by the time he died at age 91

Leaders come in all shapes and sizes, and they use all manner of techniques to achieve success. At times they might be in the forefront of outdoor activities, though they are just as likely to allow others to step ahead. They can be determined to reach a mountaintop, run a stretch of white water, and rise to other challenges, but they also find satisfaction in doing whatever they can to ensure that others reach their goals. Many have become famous. Others might be known as leaders only among the groups they have led, but are remembered with fondness and admiration by those with whom they shared adventures. All are women and men who have practiced the art of leadership, a skill as important to trek adventures as any in this book.

Every group going into the backcountry should have a recognized leader, a person who can orient people and then keep them organized, supported, and moving toward their objectives. While much of what occurs in the field can be decided through discussions and mutual agreement, a leader must be ready to provide clear direction when decisions need to be made quickly or when group members are unable or unqualified to determine a realistic course of action.

Leadership comes to life in the outdoors as challenges reveal the true nature of people relating to one another and to their surroundings. Guiding a Venturing crew, Scout troop, or Varsity Scout team when the sky is clear, the nights are

A leader shares group responsibilities by delegating tasks and then providing resources and support so that everyone can succeed. In difficult situations, others will look to a leader for guidance, for wisdom, and for making essential decisions.

pleasant, and everyone is experienced and well-prepared can be easier than when the foul weather settles in or the Scouts' skills are minimal, but that's not always the case. Even seasoned outdoor travelers can suffer an injury or illness, or discover that they are confronted with other unexpected circumstances that will severely test them.

Effective leaders help the others develop trip plans, prepare for the trek adventures, and learn skills to be used during outdoor activities. They delegate responsibilities, providing the tools and information people must have in order to do well. They adapt their leadership styles in response to the needs of individuals and groups, and at times they may modify their own agendas, as the ultimate goal of a leader—establishing an environment in which others can achieve their goal—is of greater importance than summiting any mountain or running any river.

Preparing to Lead

Leadership is more than a set of skills to be mastered. It is about the willingness to listen, to observe, to share, and to serve the interests of others. It also is about using good judgment, making decisions, and putting plans in motion. You can learn much about leading well by reading about leadership, by watching others lead, and by taking part in formal training opportunities. Most important, though, is putting yourself in various positions of responsibility and trying out principles of good leadership in real situations.

From an assistant patrol leader helping to plan a meeting to the president of a Venturing crew preparing for an extended wilderness journey, a hallmark of Scouting is providing settings for people to learn how to lead by being leaders. As your own experience as a leader grows within and beyond Scouting, you can take a number of steps that will help you maintain your readiness to step into leadership roles:

- Keep yourself in good physical condition and your personal equipment set to go.

- Develop your technical competence so that it is sufficient for the demands of upcoming treks. Include training in first aid.

- Increase your understanding of leadership by observing experienced leaders, working with mentors, and encouraging feedback from members of your group.

Leading Responsibly

Outdoor leaders must stay within their abilities, agreeing to lead only those activities for which they have experience and expertise. If your Scout troop, Varsity Scout team, or Venturing crew is considering a whitewater kayaking trip, for instance, and wants you to be its leader, you must have a mastery of kayaking and of watercraft safety. You need to know how to orient your group for an upcoming adventure, how to direct activities during the trip, and how to respond to emergencies.

You also must gain the trust of those you will lead. Through your actions and your words, everyone will know that your decisions are based on the needs, interests, and safety of all.

Preparing Your Group

A leader has important pretrip responsibilities for orienting a group, setting the tone, and clarifying the reasons for guidelines that everyone will follow. Just as leaders can carry out their responsibilities most effectively when they are fully informed, group members are best able to succeed when they have a clear understanding of agreed-upon standards, and when they can share in planning and carrying out activities. Leaders who are enthused about upcoming events set a positive tone that can carry over into the field.

For more on orienting Scout troops, Varsity Scout teams, Venturing crews, or other groups for trek adventures, see the chapters titled "Organizing for Adventures" and "Planning a Trek."

Leadership Qualities

While their styles may vary, effective leaders all share the following qualities:

- They ensure a safe environment for their groups and themselves.

- They establish ground rules ahead of time and insist that they are followed.

- They clearly communicate their expectations.

- They retain for themselves the right and responsibility of ultimate decision-making authority.

—From *Lightly on the Land,* Student Conservation Association, 1996

2

Monitoring Progress

Seasoned outdoor leaders know that an important first step in coping with first-aid situations is this: "Don't just do something; stand there!" The idea is that they must evaluate a situation before they can make good decisions about how to proceed.

Leadership usually is not a response to an emergency, but the approach is similar. To lead well, invest energy in listening and observing so that you can assess what is going on, figure out what a person or a group needs in order to succeed, and then find ways to address those needs.

Individuals and groups seldom will act in exactly the same ways from one trek to another or even on succeeding days of the same journey, and what is true for one situation will not always be true for every other. People preparing for a trek adventure often are excited about the opportunities that lie ahead, but their initial enthusiasm may fade as they realize how much work lies between them and their goals—how far they will have to hike, for example, or the extent of the skills they have not yet mastered. They might even be at odds with one another and with their leaders, but as they begin to experience progress, they often come around to working alongside each other in pursuit of common goals. Successes lead to greater confidence and growing enthusiasm, and that can encourage everyone to focus on the efficient completion of short-term and long-term tasks.

"The adventure begins when you lose the map," goes a tongue-in-cheek traveler's saying. Likewise, it is when the best-laid plans of a Scout troop, Varsity Scout team, or Venturing crew no longer work that leadership will be truly put to the test.

Adjusting Your Leadership Style

Responsive leadership requires that as you are hiking, camping, and enjoying other outdoor activities, you also are observing your group and its surroundings. By developing an evolving picture of group members' attitudes, their progress toward goals, and the nature of the challenges they face, you can adjust your leadership style based on what the others appear to need.

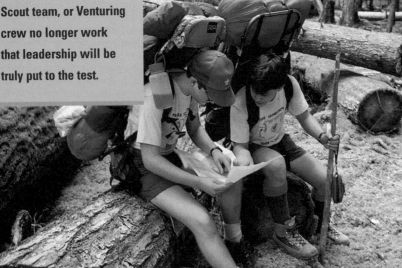

Individuals and groups unaccustomed to a particular kind of outdoor adventure, for example, might require lots of clear direction from you as they learn essential skills and are introduced to new settings and routines. Those who have had plenty of experience probably won't need that kind of hands-on leadership, but can thrive when you provide them with plenty of support and information, then get out of their way and let them figure out on their own how to proceed.

The more you know about those you lead, the better you can provide them with appropriate leadership. The abilities, backgrounds, interests, and personalities of individuals all are factors, and levels of enthusiasm and motivation are key indicators of a group's development. By continually monitoring your group, you can be ready to make adjustments whenever adjustments need to be made.

Be flexible in your approaches, noting not only what works for those you are leading, but also what is comfortable for you. Try different styles in different situations. At its heart, leadership is as much an art as it is a skill. Finding your own effective styles is a matter of doing your best with what you know at the moment, and then using the experience you have gained to do even better the next time.

Empowering Others

The greatest gift a leader can give members of a group is the clear understanding that they are responsible for their own success. Provide everyone with the guidance and resources they need to do well, then give them room to take care of things to the full extent of their abilities. In return, group members can offer their willingness to take on much of the work of making the group go, and to see tasks through to the end.

You can further empower people by striving to maintain an environment that is both physically and emotionally safe. Physical safety is largely a matter of risk management through organizational standards and the good judgment of everyone in the group. Emotional safety is a more elusive concept, but its effects upon the well-being of each person and the group as a whole can be every bit as vital as physical security. For example, there is no place in Scouting for negative peer pressure or harassment in any form.

Maintaining Ultimate Decision-Making Authority

In addition to sharing tasks and empowering others, a leader must retain authority for ultimate decision making. When individuals can't come to an agreement on issues of importance, the leader makes the call. When conflicts arise, a leader does whatever is necessary to find resolution. Most of all, when safety is a concern, a leader finds ways to help a group minimize danger and manage risk.

To a great degree, you will have established your leadership authority by all of your actions that precede the moment when a decision must be made. If you have demonstrated your involvement and have earned the trust of those you are leading, you will find that they can be very willing to support your decisions. Explaining the reasons for your decisions, either beforehand or during debriefings after events, will further increase the quality of the leadership relationship.

At times, your decision-making responsibilities might involve dealing with inappropriate behavior. Most often that will pertain to safety issues— someone's unwillingness to keep a clean camp in bear country, for example, or an individual's habit of going off alone without telling anyone. It also can extend to personality conflicts, questionable language, and other actions affecting the quality of the experience for other members of a Scout troop, Varsity Scout team, or Venturing crew.

Ideally, nonnegotiable standards determined by the group before a trek begins will have outlined what is acceptable and what is not. The structure and tone of a group should provide further guidance for the ways that the members will conduct themselves and treat one another.

When inappropriate situations arise, talk with the people involved out of earshot of others. Discuss the concerns you have about their behavior, and listen carefully to what they have to say. Based on what you hear, you might be able to suggest ways that they can follow the group's guidelines and still get what they want.

Stay Calm

Don't respond in anger to the actions or words of others, even if what they have said or done upsets you. In emergency situations, try not to let fear and uncertainty cloud your judgment. By seeking workable solutions, you also are showing through your actions the way that others can act when they are upset or under stress.

Leadership Tools

Every leader develops his or her own style, though most successful leaders use the following tools:

Be Realistic

Do your best to see things as they are, not as you wish they were. Be a bit of a pessimist in terms of what might go wrong, but an optimist in guiding people toward the effective management of risk.

Be Consistent and Fair

Group members want to know what they can expect from you as their leader, and what you expect of them. Strive to be consistent in word and action, and make it clear that you are working together.

Step In

Cheerfully accept your share of the chores. Lead others by having fun doing whatever needs to be done.

Monitor Yourself

Are you chilly, hungry, sleepy, too hot, or too cold? Upset, angry, or worried? By doing something about personal issues, you can more clearly focus on the leadership needs of the moment. It might simply be a matter of putting on another layer of clothing, having something to eat, or taking a moment to gather your thoughts. You also might discover when you need more information before making a decision, or when it would be wise to talk things over with others in your group as you are making up your mind.

Be Caring

Perhaps the most powerful tool of leadership is this: Care about the people you are leading. Respect and value others, and help each person feel that he or she has important contributions to make. Look for ways to draw on the strengths of every individual to the advantage of the entire group, and let all members know you are pleased to have them along. Say something positive to every person in the group at least once a day.

Communicating Well

The ability to communicate well is an essential skill for leaders of any team. Because the members will be assuming much of the responsibility for the success of their groups and will themselves act as leaders for many activities, they also can benefit from knowing how to share ideas.

Information about a group and its condition often is as close as your ears. "We're getting tired." "What shall we cook for dinner?" "I have an idea for a better way to bear-proof our camp." "Isn't this a bad place to be if that thunderstorm catches up with us?"

As you listen, try to delay making judgments on what you are hearing until you have all the information. "I got it," is a good initial answer to those who have something to say. "Could you explain that to me again?" is an appropriate response when you don't understand.

You can't tailor every situation to be ideal. Now and then you will find yourself in discussions with others when sharing ideas is difficult. Practice communicating effectively, though, and you will find it to be a vital tool for addressing problems, resolving difficulties, and building spirit.

Feedback

People who are warm, dry, well-fed, and enjoying the challenges they face are bound to be upbeat and pleased with the way things are going. From overheard comments, laughter, and body language, you have clear feedback that a trek is going well. If people have become wet, hungry, chilly, or bored, though, you will know from their mood and lack of energy that aspects of planning and carrying out a trek have not been adequate for the journey, and that you might need to adjust your leadership style.

Tips on Receiving Feedback

Seeking out feedback from everyone can further clarify your understanding of what is occurring during a trek, and can help improve the performance of you and your group.

1. Listen carefully. Receiving feedback requires a heightened awareness of yourself and the person offering the feedback.

2. Listen actively. Restate what you are hearing in your own words so that the speaker knows that the message you are receiving is the same as the one the speaker intended to send.

3. Listen emphatically. Put feedback in its proper context by observing the speaker's body language, tone of voice, and emotions. Consider the speaker's reasons for providing feedback.

Communication

The following guidelines can help you in communicating ideas to others:

1. Listen effectively.

2. Convey information to the right person at the right time.

3. Stay consistent in the information you are sharing, but be open to making changes.

4. Be open to the ideas of others.

Feedback

Generate feedback by asking the following:

1. How are we doing?

2. How am I doing?

3. What will make things better?

2

Feedback often is a way of improving the effectiveness of a team while it is in the field. *Debriefing* and *evaluating* can occur after a trek, or at the conclusion of each day and each stage of an extended outdoor activity.

Tips on Giving Feedback

Offering ideas to others can help them improve their performance and expand the group's success.

1. Think about your motives. Unless feedback will be helpful, there is no reason to give it.

2. Find out if people are open to receiving feedback.

3. Deal only with specific behavior that can be changed.

4. Ask recipients of feedback to rephrase what they heard you say so that you can be sure they have understood your message.

Debriefing and Evaluating

Even the best outdoor adventurers can find room for improvement, and groups can always become more effective. After an outdoor activity, and at least daily during an extended expedition, sit down with everyone and discuss what went well and what could have been better.

1. *Debrief* by discussing key events of the day with everyone to get a clear understanding of what happened.

2. *Evaluate* by weighing that understanding against the group's goals, standards, and logistical tasks, then use your findings to improve future outdoor activities.

Among the questions that can guide debriefing and evaluation are these:

- What went well?
- What could have been better?
- What skills do we need to acquire or improve?
- What gear wasn't needed?
- What gear or supplies were we missing?
- Where shall we go next?

Celebrate Success

Every outdoor adventure you have will become a collection of fond memories. Take time during and after a trek to reflect on your experiences together, to celebrate your successes, to reinforce what you learned, and to realize how remarkable it is to be in the great outdoors with a group of friends, all of you doing your best.

The confidence of a Venturing crew, Scout troop, or Varsity Scout team grows as members succeed together—planning and carrying out their first wilderness trip, finishing a rugged hike, or mastering the techniques of winter camping. Success fosters success, and a series of achievements can inspire group members to get in the habit of setting out to do well. Fresh opportunities to succeed can increase their self-assurance and their eagerness to try adventures they know will test them and help them work hard.

A Final Word on Leadership

The excitement and challenge of being a leader should involve you deeply with those you lead, but allow yourself to relax sometimes away from other activities. On extended adventures, you could rise earlier in the morning to enjoy a quiet half hour to yourself—a chance to enjoy a cup of cocoa as you sit under a tree and watch the day beginning to unfold.

Give yourself permission to make mistakes, too. Being a leader is a learned skill. The more you do it, the more effective you will be, but there always will be room to improve. Do the best you can, and next time do even better.

Whatever leadership styles you choose, keep in mind the basics of leadership. Strive to empower others, reach a consensus when making decisions, and provide whatever a group is missing, and you will be well on your way to practicing effective and responsible leadership in the field.

> *"Leadership is the capacity to move others toward goals shared with you, with a focus and competency they would not achieve on their own."*
>
> —John Graham (outdoor leader and president of the Giraffe Project), *Outdoor Leadership,* 1997

Becoming Fit

"Vigorous outdoor living is the key to the spirit of Scouting."

—Robert S. S. Baden-Powell (founder of the worldwide Scouting movement), *Aids to Scoutmastership,* 1919

You're hiking along a rugged trail at a strong, steady pace, the miles rolling beneath your feet. You're canoeing all day, paddling with an almost effortless rhythm. You're bicycling toward the horizon, your legs pushing you along hour after hour with ease and speed.

Maintaining a high level of fitness will help you fully enjoy outdoor adventures. You will have the strength to take on demanding challenges and the endurance to see them through to the end. Rather than struggling to keep up or limiting yourself to short journeys along easy routes, you can set out with the confidence that you possess the power and stamina to accomplish whatever needs to be done.

Getting yourself physically fit for an adventure trek is a terrific goal, but that should be just the beginning. Staying fit means you will be ready for any opportunities for outdoor activities that come along, and prepared for all else that presents itself throughout your life.

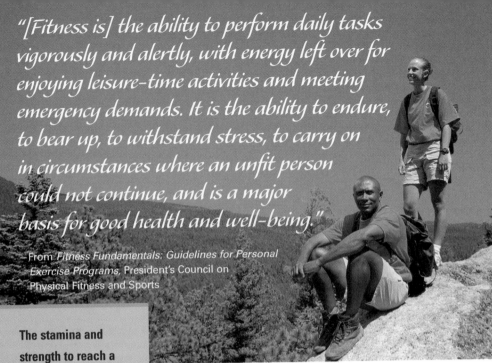

"[Fitness is] the ability to perform daily tasks vigorously and alertly, with energy left over for enjoying leisure-time activities and meeting emergency demands. It is the ability to endure, to bear up, to withstand stress, to carry on in circumstances where an unfit person could not continue, and is a major basis for good health and well-being."

—From *Fitness Fundamentals: Guidelines for Personal Exercise Programs,* President's Council on Physical Fitness and Sports

The stamina and strength to reach a mountain summit, ski a cross-country course, or complete other outdoor journeys often can be found on the playing fields near your home. Enliven your daily fitness routines by focusing on where your efforts to get strong and tough can lead you.

What Is Fitness?

Tall, short, wide, thin—the basic shape of your body is strongly determined by genetics. Your height, bone structure, and general musculature come in large part from your biological ancestors. So do many of the ways in which your body responds to food, to exercise, to stress, and to environmental influences.

Whatever your physical type, you can consider yourself fit when you have the strength and endurance to accomplish all you aspire to do, and when you have made staying in shape over the years a regular part of what you do. That means getting plenty of exercise and enough sleep, regularly brushing and flossing your teeth, and keeping immunizations up-to-date.

Becoming fit also means eating a balance of nourishing food in portions appropriate for you. By themselves, the numbers on a weight scale seldom are a reliable guide for measuring fitness. For one thing, muscle weighs more than fat. If you are thinking of dieting to lose weight to achieve a certain appearance or as part of a fitness routine, consult a physician or nutritionist for guidance.

Whatever your shape and size, celebrate your body, do all you can to care for it, and give yourself every chance to excel. Then focus your energy on positive activities, friends, school, Scouting, family, and all else there is to enjoy in life.

For more on nutrition, see the chapter titled "Outdoor Menus."

3

"Normal" and "fit" are not the same as what many images portrayed in movies, on television, and in magazines would have us believe. The impossibly thin women and unnaturally muscular men often portrayed in advertising and the media might help sell lots of clothing, deodorant, and automobiles, but they are not practical role models for real people.

Being Active

There are many ways to exercise. Among them, you can find fitness activities that keep you interested and challenged so that you will want to do them regularly. You might already take part in sports with friends, in organized athletics, and in physically demanding personal endeavors. Consider what your current activities offer in terms of overall fitness, then adjust what you do to ensure that your body is getting the attention it needs. To prepare for most trek adventures and to increase overall fitness, include a mix of aerobic activities to improve endurance and stamina, and strengthening exercises for increasing power.

Regular physical activities will help keep you fit and ready for trek adventures.

Aerobic Exercises

Aerobic means "with air." Aerobic exercises are continuous, rhythmic activities that require your body to increase its use of oxygen. Brisk walking, jogging, running, jumping rope, swimming, cycling, and cross-country skiing can be aerobic exercises if you do them steadily for prolonged periods—usually 20 minutes or more at a level sufficiently ambitious that you would find it difficult to carry on a normal conversation. The effort you make will cause your heart and lungs to work harder, especially if you maintain an exercise pace that makes it difficult to converse normally. By gradually increasing the intensity and duration of your aerobic exercises over a period of weeks, you can help your cardiovascular system become stronger and more efficient.

Strength Exercises

Physical activities designed to increase muscular strength usually are intense, but of brief duration. Well-planned strengthening routines—including push-ups, abdominal crunches, and workouts with weights—force muscles to perform beyond their current capacities. Over time, the muscles will respond by becoming more powerful.

Before beginning any exercise routine, it's a good idea to have a thorough physical examination. Your physician will give you the green light to undertake the activities you are planning, or explain any limitations you might have. A physician also can help you plan a program of good nutrition and exercise.

Getting Started

Warming up before playing sports or beginning an exercise session loosens your muscles, makes your joints more flexible, and prepares your body and mind to be in motion. Jogging, a game of catch, and a series of stretches all can serve to get you ready for more strenuous activities. Using similar easy activities to cool down after exerting yourself allows your heart rate, respiration, and temperature to return gradually to their normal resting states.

Exercise Notebook

An exercise notebook can be an important tool for making the most of your fitness efforts. Write down the routines you use and the number of repetitions for each exercise, and you'll have a record of your physical progress that can encourage you to keep improving. Over time, a written record will help you to evaluate and adjust your exercise plan.

Date and Time	Exercise	Repetitions or Duration	Other
June 12 3:40 P.M.	Warm-ups	Jogging	
	Lateral raises	3 sets of 15	
	Push-ups	3 sets of 12	Keep back straight.
	Crunches	3 sets of 12	Feet flat, knees bent
	Squats	3 sets of 12	
	Walking crane lunge	5 minutes	Use hallway next to gym.
	Calf raises	3 sets of 20	
	Play basketball	30 minutes	Run hard to keep heart rate up.

An electronic spreadsheet might be a convenient way to track the types, durations, and repititions of your exercises.

Fitness is a lifelong endeavor. Be patient and keep at it, gradually increasing the duration and degree of exertion.

Stretching

Stretching can relax your muscles, increase your flexibility, and help calm and focus your mind. You can stretch anytime, but you might find it especially productive as you are cooling down after exercising. Ligaments and muscles will already be loose, and stretching can be a relaxing way to conclude a workout.

As with any physical activity, learn the correct techniques and then gradually increase the range of each stretch. Breathe slowly and naturally. Stretching should never be painful; pay attention to your body and don't overextend.

3

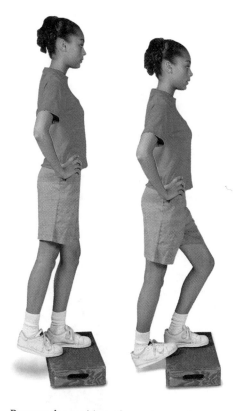

Achilles Tendon and Calf Stretch

Stand with both feet on a ledge or platform that is at least 3 inches tall. Step back with your right foot, placing the ball of your foot on the platform edge. Stretch your calf muscles and Achilles tendon by slowly dropping your right heel toward the floor. Hold the stretch for 15 to 30 seconds, then step up onto the platform and stretch the left leg.

Hip and Lower Back Stretch

Sit tall with one leg extended, the other leg crossed over it, and your elbow against your raised knee. Gently turn your upper body toward your hand on the floor, and hold the stretch for 15 to 30 seconds. Reverse the position of your legs and arms, and repeat the stretch by twisting your torso in the other direction.

Quadriceps Stretch

To stretch the strong muscles in the front of your thighs, start standing, grasping a table or other solid object for balance. Reach back, grasp one of your feet, gently pull it toward your lower back, and hold that position for 15 to 30 seconds. Return to the start position, then perform the stretch with the other leg.

Groin Stretch

Sit on the floor with your legs stretched out in front of you and your back straight. With your right hand, bring the right heel to the groin. With the left hand, bring the left heel to the groin, joining the soles of the feet and bringing them close into your body. With your legs turned out at the hips, slowly press your knees to the floor. Hold for 20 seconds and release.

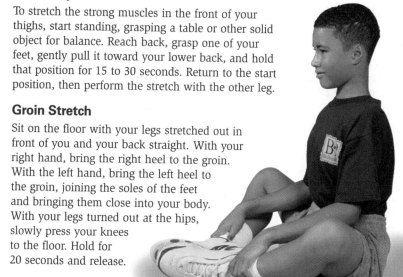

Lower Back Stretch

Lying on your back, bend a leg toward your chest, interlace your fingers around your knee, and gently pull it closer to your torso. After 15 to 30 seconds, release your hold and then perform the stretch with your other leg. (As a variation, you can bend both legs, grasp them together, and hold the stretch for 15 to 30 seconds.)

Hip Flexor Stretch

Kneel on one knee and position your other leg so that your thigh is parallel with the ground. With your hands on that thigh, lean forward until your thigh and calf form a right angle, then let your hips sink down. Hold the stretch for 15 to 30 seconds to loosen the muscles and tendons of your hip, then reverse the positions of your legs and repeat.

Hamstring Stretch

Stand with the right heel forward and place your hands on top of the right thigh to help you balance. Bend your back leg slightly. Bend at the hips and lower your torso toward your bent knee, gently stretching your back and the hamstring muscle in the back of your thigh. After 15 to 30 seconds of stretching, stand upright, reverse leg positions, and perform the stretch in the other direction.

Training for Stamina

The value of stamina training lies in raising your heartbeat and respiration rates, and maintaining those levels for 20 to 30 minutes or more. You can measure your heartbeat as you are exercising by stopping your activities for a moment and taking your pulse; place two fingers on the pulse point of your wrist or against the carotid artery in your neck. For most healthy people, the American Heart Association recommends an exercise target heart rate ranging from 50 percent to 75 percent of maximum heart rate.

- To figure maximum heart rate for a healthy person, subtract his or her age from 220.

- To figure your ideal heart rate for exercising, multiply your target number by your maximum heart rate. If you want to exercise at 70 percent of maximum heart rate, for example, multiply your maximum heart rate by .70:

  (220 – your age) × .70 = target exercise heart rate

"There were no shortcuts, I realized. It took years of racing to build up the mind and body and character, until a rider had logged hundreds of races and thousands of miles of road. I wouldn't be able to win a Tour de France until I had enough iron in my legs, and lungs, and brain, and heart."

—Lance Armstrong, *It's Not About the Bike,* 2000 (He overcame cancer to win bicycle racing's most prestigious event multiple times.)

Cross-training— engaging in a variety of different sports activities and exercises—can eliminate the monotony of a single training routine and can increase the fitness of a wide range of muscle groups.

For someone 17 years old, a target exercise heart rate of 70 percent would be 142 beats per minute.

Many activities lend themselves to stamina training. Playing basketball or soccer, for example, is an ideal way to have a good time and get plenty of exercise, too. The key is to keep moving so that your heart rate stays in the target zone of exertion.

If you are tuning up for a particular trek adventure, you can use specific forms of stamina training to target the muscles you will use the most during your outdoor activities. A few examples follow:

- To prepare for backpacking, climb up and down the stairs at a sports stadium, walk briskly up and down the sidewalks of steep city hills, jog on a treadmill set at an incline, use stair-stepping machines.

- To prepare for mountain biking, mimic mountain conditions on a stationary cycle by alternating periods of intense and easy pedaling.

- To prepare for paddling watercraft, swim to improve both your endurance and the strength of your upper body. Use a rowing machine at a gym.

Training for Strength

Develop a strength-training plan that is safe and effective, and that you can sustain through the months and years. An appropriate program involves exercises that work all of the major muscle groups. You might be able to use exercise equipment and weights at a school gymnasium or a health club, use a few free weights for exercising at home, or complete a thorough exercise routine without using weights at all. School coaches, physical education instructors, and other fitness experts can assist you in planning an exercise program that is right for you. Routines will be most effective when you follow these guidelines:

- Follow a qualified trainer's guidance when using weights or weight machines, and practice proper form throughout the repetitions of each set.

- Engage in strength training two or three days a week. Allow at least 48 hours between exercise sessions so that muscle tissues can recover.

- Include eight to 10 exercises for the large muscle groups of the upper and lower body.

- As you become stronger, gradually increase the intensity and duration of workouts.

- Be consistent. Stick with a good exercise routine for several months and you are likely to see improvements in your level of fitness.

Sample Exercise Routine Without Weights

UPPER BODY

Modified Push-Ups

Begin facedown, your arms bent and the palms of your hands flat against the floor. Keeping your spine and neck straight, let your knees serve as hinges while you push yourself upward until your arms are fully extended. Slowly lower yourself back to the floor, then repeat. As your strength increases, shift to the regular push-up position with your weight on your hands and toes. Keep your spine and legs in a straight line.

3

Lateral Raises and Front Raises

With your elbows slightly bent, stand upright and slowly lift your arms sideways in a smooth arc. When your arms reach shoulder height, slowly lower them and then repeat the motion. For variety, raise and lower your arms in front of your body. (Holding a can of food or other light weight in each hand will increase the workload of these exercises.)

LOWER BODY

Calf Raises

Ensure your balance by putting your hands on a wall, a pole, or the shoulder of a workout partner. Raise yourself on tiptoe as high as you can and hold that position for about three seconds, then lower your heels as far as they will go and again pause briefly. Repeat.

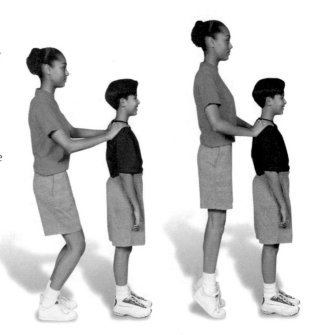

Squat

Keeping your spine straight, gradually bend your hips and legs, sliding down as if you were sitting on an imaginary chair. Lower yourself until your thighs are parallel with the ground. After several seconds in that position, slowly rise until you are standing, then repeat.

Walking Crane Lunge

This exaggerated form of walking is a good exercise for developing the thighs and buttocks. With your hands on your hips, take a wide step forward, leading with your heel and bending the knee until it is at a 90-degree angle. Be sure to keep your knee aligned with your heel. Press down onto the front heel, then bring the body back to an upright position with the legs together. Repeat with the other leg.

ABDOMEN

Crunches

Start by lying faceup in a comfortable position. Reduce stress on your lower back by bending your knees and keeping the soles of your shoes flat on the floor. Place each arm across your chest, then use your abdominal muscles to curl your torso far enough to lift your shoulder blades. Ease your torso back down and repeat.

BACK

Leg Raises

Lying facedown, contract the muscles of one leg, keep it straight, lift it from the floor, and hold that position to the count of 10. Lower that leg, then do the exercise with the other leg, again counting to 10. Repeat.

Exercising With Weights

Used correctly, free weights and weight machines can be a boon to fitness efforts. Qualified fitness experts can help you learn how to use free weights and machines, and they can monitor your form to ensure that you are doing each exercise correctly. They are sure to remind you that beginning with light weights and gradually increasing exercise intensity will allow you to make progress without suffering injury.

3

Note: You should begin a weight-training program under the supervision of a qualified instructor.

Some of the weight-training exercises you might incorporate into your exercise routine include the following:

- Chest/bench press, seated row, overhead/ military press, and overhead pull-down for upper-body strength

Leg extensions (quadriceps)

- Leg curls for hamstring strength

- Leg press and calf raises for lower-body strength

- Crunches for abdomen strength

- Spinal extensions for back strength

Leg curls (hamstrings)

Arm curls

Overhead pull-down

Overhead press (military press)

Chest press (bench press)

3

Mental Fitness

Your body has grace and strength that you can nurture and improve. Likewise, your mind is full of potential. Just as you take positive steps to build your physical strength and stamina, do all you can to enhance your mental fitness, too. Take advantage of opportunities to learn new skills, to engage in positive experiences, and to interact with others in productive ways. Take pride in your accomplishments and strive to do more. Wherever you go and whatever you do, approach life with enthusiasm, with dedication, and with joy.

For more on the importance of attitude, see the chapter titled "Organizing for Adventures."

"Physical fitness is not only one of the most important keys to a healthy body, it is the basis of dynamic and creative intellectual activity."

—John F. Kennedy (1917–1963),
35th president of the
United States

Planning a Trek

"Good planning means living the experience in advance."

—Sir Edmund Hillary (along with Tenzing Norgay, the first to reach
the summit of Mount Everest), 1953

Planning is one of the great joys of an adventure. Anticipation builds when a group pores over maps and plans what to see and do in the out-of-doors. As you form a trip itinerary, you can imagine hiking a woodland trail, casting for catfish in a slow-moving river, or carving turns in fresh snow with cross-country skis. As you gather your gear you can almost see your tent pitched in a deep forest, your pack leaning against the summit marker of a high peak, your canoe paddle dipping into the waters of a quiet lake. As you repackage provisions, you can look forward to tasty dishes cooked outdoors. Once everything is prepared, anticipation will turn to action, and you can enjoy every adventure to the fullest.

Why Plan?

Adventures begin as daydreams. Transforming those dreams into reality requires thoughtful research and a written itinerary. Your goal is to make good estimates of what to expect and then to prepare well enough so that you are ready for the unexpected as well.

The more challenging the trek you consider, the more thorough your planning should be. Anticipating trail conditions, changes in elevation, distances to be traveled, expected weather conditions, the availability of water, and the locations of campsites will help your group plan an appropriate itinerary.

The most useful trek-planning tools may well be a notebook and a sharp pencil. Putting ideas on paper forces you to think them through. Checklists increase the likelihood you won't forget anything. After a trek, you can refer back to your notes to see which aspects of planning worked well and what can be improved the next time around.

4

Planning a trek, whether to a favorite campsite close to home or clear across the continent, is a matter of looking ahead, making realistic predictions of situations that might be encountered, and then preparing to meet them.

Planning Group Adventures

The chapter titled "Organizing for Adventures" discusses some of the ways that people come together to form groups and then to select outdoor activities. Treks should be satisfying for the most experienced group members, yet not so difficult that some in the group are pitted against situations far exceeding their abilities. In a group composed of people with varying levels of skill, part of the challenge for more capable members can be to help those with less experience succeed, ensuring that the entire group reaches its goals.

Planning Well

Backcountry lore is filled with cautionary examples of people going into the woods poorly equipped, lacking outdoor knowledge and skills, or unaware of potential dangers. The result of poor planning is often a dismal experience that leads to entertaining stories after it is over—a night in a wet sleeping bag, a day with no food, a long hike home with blisters and sunburn. Ill-prepared individuals have, in fact, sometimes managed to endure storms, deal with injuries, and become found after having gotten themselves quite lost. Unfortunately, there also are many cases of people whose lack of planning led to disaster.

Plan Ahead and Prepare—The First Principle of Leave No Trace

Trek planning can help you protect the environment. Research the area where you will travel and you'll know if group size is limited, whether campfires are allowed, and where you can pitch your tents. Be realistic as you lay out your itinerary, and you can ensure that everyone will reach appropriate campsites at a reasonable hour each day. You also can prepare for the proper disposal of waste and ways to travel and camp without disturbing others.

For more on planning ways to enjoy the outdoors responsibly, see the "Leaving No Trace" section of this book.

4

Where to Go

America is blessed with terrific places for adventures. Wherever you live, you aren't far from lands that invite exploration and outdoor activities. Parks, forests, seashores, rivers, lakes, wetlands, deserts, and mountains abound. You can find small areas just right for a day hike, and great regions of forests, mountains, deserts, and plains that invite treks of days, weeks, and even months.

Many of America's recreational areas are on public lands administered by land management agencies. Depending on the popularity and condition of a particular area, agencies might regulate outdoor recreation with permits, reservation systems, and other management tools. Regulations exist for a reason, usually to enhance safety, minimize human impact, protect the resource, and ensure that future generations can enjoy visiting the areas, too. In addition to information about regulations, agencies can be valuable sources of information about the terrain, prevailing weather, and the current conditions of trails, rivers, snowfields, and other natural features.

The agencies administering the greatest expanses of public lands are those of the federal government. They include the Bureau of Land Management, the USDA Forest Service, the National Park Service, and the U.S. Fish and Wildlife Service.

The American landscape features a rich variety of places for trek adventures. See the Fieldbook *Web site for a larger version of this map.*

4

USDA Forest Service

Gifford Pinchot, the first chief of the U.S. Forest Service, stated the guiding principle of the agency as "the greatest good for the greatest number in the long run." The mission of the USDA Forest Service is to sustain the health, diversity, and productivity of the nation's forests and grasslands to meet the needs of present and future generations. One of the many public interests served by the Forest Service is providing opportunities for recreation in open spaces and natural environments. The Forest Service manages 191 million acres of America's forests and rangelands, including national forests, experimental forests and ranges, grasslands, and land utilization projects.

Portions of some national forests are set aside as wilderness areas to preserve the unspoiled quality of the environment. The forests also are home to many of America's national trails, national wild and scenic rivers, and national recreation areas.

National Park Service

The National Park Service, established in 1916, is directed by Congress "to promote and regulate the use of the . . . national parks, monuments, and reservations, . . . to conserve the scenery and the natural and historic objects and the wildlife therein . . . by such means as will leave them unimpaired for the enjoyment of future generations." In addition to protecting natural resources, the National Park Service strives to provide the public with opportunities for camping, wilderness exploration, hiking, horseback riding, cross-country skiing, watercraft adventures, and the study of nature and American history.

The National Park Service administers approximately 84 million acres of our natural, historical, and cultural heritage with units in almost every state in the Union and in Guam, Puerto Rico, and the Virgin Islands. Among Park Service areas are Yellowstone (America's oldest national park), Alaska's Wrangell-Saint Elias National Park and Preserve (at more than 13 million acres, the largest park), and the Thaddeus Kosciuszko National Memorial in Pennsylvania (the smallest facility with just .02 acres).

Bureau of Land Management

The territories of the Bureau of Land Management contain rugged desert landscapes, evergreen forests, snowcapped mountains, and an abundance of wildlife. An agency within the U.S. Department of the Interior, the bureau administers 262 million acres of America's public lands, located primarily in 12 western states. The bureau sustains the health, diversity, and productivity of the public lands for the use and enjoyment of present and future generations. Its areas are managed under multiple-use principles that encourage outdoor recreation as well as fish and wildlife production, livestock grazing, timber harvesting, industrial development, and watershed protection.

U.S. Fish and Wildlife Service

The mission of the Fish and Wildlife Service is to conserve, protect, and enhance fish, wildlife, and plants and their habitats for the continuing benefit of the American people. Its primary responsibilities are for migratory birds, endangered species, freshwater and migratory fisheries, and certain marine mammals. The Fish and Wildlife Service manages more than 500 national wildlife refuges stretching from the Arctic Ocean to the South Pacific, and from Maine to the Caribbean. Varying in size from half-acre parcels to thousands of square miles, the National Wildlife Refuge System encompasses well over 90 million acres of the nation's wildlife habitats, making up the world's largest and most diverse collection of lands set aside specifically for wild animals.

The National Trails System

Trails provide travelers access to the heart of the outdoors. Most are open to hikers and backpackers. Certain trails also are designated for use by horses and pack animals, and a few can be accessed by mountain bikes. More than 12,000 miles of trails thread their way through national parks, a hundred thousand miles of trails are in national forests, and thousands of miles more can be found on lands administered by other agencies. Some of the more well-known trails include:

- Appalachian National Scenic Trail—2,158 miles
- Continental Divide National Scenic Trail—3,100 miles
- Florida National Scenic Trail—1,300 miles
- Ice Age National Scenic Trail—1,000 miles
- Iditarod National Historic Trail—2,350 miles
- Juan Bautista de Anza National Historic Trail—1,200 miles
- Lewis and Clark National Historic Trail—3,700 miles
- Mormon Pioneer National Historic Trail—1,300 miles
- North Country National Scenic Trail—3,200 miles
- Nez Perce (Nee-Me-Poo) National Historic Trail—1,170 miles
- Oregon National Historic Trail—2,170 miles
- Pacific Crest National Scenic Trail—2,638 miles
- Potomac Heritage National Scenic Trail—700 miles
- Santa Fe National Historic Trail—1,203 miles
- Trail of Tears National Historic Trail—2,052 miles

Finding out who manages the land through which you want to travel is crucial to planning a trip. Private and public lands often have restrictions and regulations, usually designed to protect the environment and the outdoor experience for all users.

LOCAL TOUR PERMIT APPLICATION

BOY SCOUTS OF AMERICA

FOR TRIPS AND CAMPS UNDER 500 MILES

State, County, and City Agencies

Most states, counties, and cities have agencies dedicated to the management, preservation, and maintenance of the natural resources within their jurisdictions. Their names indicate the scope of their responsibilities—for example, departments of ecology, state park and forestry departments, county forestry commissions, fish and game management agencies, departments of natural resources, and offices of parks and recreation. Many have Web sites explaining their functions and recreational opportunities.

BSA Local Council High-Adventure Bases

High-adventure bases operated by Boy Scouts of America local councils can drop you right into the middle of terrific action. Whitewater kayaking, extended backpacking, and sailing are just a few of the activities that groups can enjoy. (Links on the BSA Web site describe these and other high-adventure opportunities. See *http://www.scouting.org/boyscouts/directory.)*

BSA National High-Adventure Bases

For real excitement beyond your council, it's hard to beat the national high-adventure bases of the BSA. Designed for Venturers, older Boy Scouts, and Varsity Scouts, each base offers the training, equipment, and support needed to set out on wilderness treks that will challenge your skills, knowledge, and willpower.

Philmont Scout Ranch

Wander the rugged high country of northern New Mexico on a backpacking trek, as a member of a conservation work crew, or by taking part in an advanced wilderness adventure. Philmont is a backpacker's paradise, covering more than 137,000 acres of mountains, forests, meadows, and streams. Staffed camps offer program opportunities including rock climbing, black-powder rifle shooting, living history, horseback riding, archaeology, environmental awareness, and many others.

Florida National High Adventure Sea Base

Explore the clear waters of the Florida Keys and the Bahamas by watercraft. Snorkel and scuba dive among schools of brilliantly colored tropical fish. Investigate a primitive island, search for the wreckage of galleons, fish the Gulf Stream waters, practice windsurfing, and study the marine life of North America's only living coral reef.

Northern Tier National High Adventure Program

The Sioux and Chippewa once traveled this northern lake country. French-Canadian trappers followed, their canoes loaded with furs. Headquartered in the beautiful Superior-Quetico boundary waters of Minnesota, Ontario, and Manitoba, the Northern Tier offers wilderness canoeing expeditions and programs featuring fishing and winter camping.

4

Planning How Long

Where you can go in the out-of-doors and what you can do will be strongly influenced by how much time you have for a trek. A group's weekend outing nearly always will be fairly close to home and involve a limited number of options. With several weeks to travel, the same group can greatly extend the range of its wanderings. The longer or more distant a trek will be, the more important the planning process becomes, both to cover all the details of the trek and to explore all the possibilities.

Include in your plans sufficient time to travel to and from the points at which your adventure will begin and end. If necessary, also include time to acclimatize to significant changes in elevation.

Good planning has been at the heart of many successful treks. The Lewis and Clark expedition, for example, set out in 1803 on a three-year journey of exploration that would take them across North America and back. As he prepared for the expedition, Meriwether Lewis tried to think

of everything that 33 men would need for a trip of several years in uncharted terrain. His long list of items included 193 pounds of dried soup and three bushels of salt. The expedition eventually ran out of nearly all of

their supplies except for two items—gunpowder and the lead to make bullets. Lewis knew that as long as they could hunt, the men would be able to feed themselves. To that end, he had arranged to bring along three times the amount of gunpowder and lead that the expedition actually used.

Planning How Far

The distance a group can cover depends on weather, terrain, physical conditioning, and the weight of the gear. Is the country rugged? In terms of time, a mile of flat trail is far different from a mile that gains a thousand feet in elevation. Paddling across a lake will take longer than guiding a watercraft down a fast-flowing river. Are group members lean and strong or a bit out of shape? As a group, do you walk with a fast, steady stride or at a leisurely pace with frequent pauses to examine vegetation, watch wildlife, and take photographs?

Plan the distances of your first treks conservatively. It is better to have too much time to reach a destination than too little. By not rushing, you might enjoy yourself more, be less apt to make mistakes, and have time for activities other than traveling and setting up camp.

For more on determining travel distances, see the chapter titled "Mountain Travel."

Even the best-prepared group should allow extra time for unforeseen events. Give yourselves anywhere from a few hours' to several days' leeway in case headwinds kick up during trips by watercraft or bicycle, bad weather moves in, or the terrain is more rugged than you had expected. A layover day during a longer trek allows group members to rest and relax, enjoy side trips, or prepare a lavish meal.

Planning Alternatives

Trek plans should include plenty of flexibility. Cover the basics, ensuring that you have the right people, gear, food, and a decent itinerary, but try not to set anything else in stone. That way you will be better able to adapt to changing circumstances in the field. It also is a good idea to devise an alternate itinerary in case your original plans are disrupted by unforeseen events.

Planning What to Carry

The amount of food and equipment you will need is a crucial consideration in planning any trek adventure. Most groups find that taking five or six days of food is about the maximum weight they can reasonably carry and the maximum bulk that will fit in backpacks or in panniers on bicycles or pack animals. If your group requires cold-weather clothing or other extra gear, pack space will be even more limited. One solution for longer treks is to arrange to be resupplied along the way with additional provisions.

For more on equipment, see the chapter titled "Gearing Up." For more on food, see the chapter titled "Outdoor Menus." For more on resupplying a group, see the chapter titled "Backpacking."

Planning How to Get There

As you design a journey, don't overlook the means by which your group will reach the starting point of the trek. Public transportation can be a possibility, though traveling by private motor vehicle is often more convenient. It might be possible for your group to be dropped off at one trailhead and picked up at another, allowing you to complete a route without backtracking. Find out where vehicles can be safely parked and whether parking permits are required. Land management agencies and local guidebooks often have that information.

4

Writing a Trip Plan

When your group arrives at a consensus of what your itinerary and alternate plans will be, write them down. Include a description of your intended route, where you want to camp, and what time you will return. Leave copies with several responsible adults. A written itinerary lets support people know where you are going and when you intend to return, but only if you stick to it.

Trip Plan

Trip plan of _____

Where
Destination _____
Route going _____
_____

Route returning _____
_____

When
Date and time of departure _____
Date and time of return _____

Who
Names of participants _____
_____

Why
Purpose of the trip _____
_____

What
☑ Gear and other items to be taken:
☐ Outdoor Essentials
☐ Other clothing and gear _____
_____

Permits required _____
Special equipment needs _____
Special clothing needs _____

How
List the principles of Leave No Trace that relate to your trip. For each one, write a sentence explaining what the patrol will do to follow that principle. _____
_____
_____
_____

"Our belief at the beginning of a doubtful undertaking is the one thing that assures the successful outcome of any venture."

—William James (1842–1910), American psychologist and philosopher

Being Prepared for Emergencies

Perhaps the most critical test of a group's level of preparation will occur if emergencies arise. Precious time needed for response to a crisis can be added by having on hand emergency contact information and an emergency action plan. This is true on a day hike, an overnight or longer unit camp, and all other activities, including high-adventure treks.

Emergency Response Plan

An emergency response plan informs group members of an approach to be taken in case of injuries or illnesses. It is strongly recommended that the group members practice this plan before setting out. Along with your trip plan, copies of the emergency response plan should be provided to those persons in the frontcountry who can assist your group.

If you are delayed for a nonemergency reason, make every effort to notify your contacts so that an emergency response is not activated. And when you return, be sure to notify everyone with whom you have left a trip plan so they won't report you missing or worry unnecessarily.

Sample Emergency Response Plan

Trip Location and Description   Date _____
(Attach a copy of the trip plan.)

Group Information
Group leaders _____
_____

Medical training level of leaders _____
_____

Group members _____
_____
_____
_____

Medical training level of members _____
_____

Resources
Locations of nearest public telephones _____
_____

(If a mobile telephone will be carried, ensure that batteries are
fully charged.)

Group first-aid kit: Are contents up-to-date? _____
                             Who will carry it? _____

Emergency Contacts
Telephone numbers of people and organizations to notify
_____
_____

(Land management agency, BSA council officials, emergency response
system, and/or search-and-rescue alert numbers)

Driving instructions from trailhead or activity area to clinics, hospitals,
and other health-care facilities _____
_____

Action
Steps to be taken in the event of an emergency
_____
_____
_____

4

Emergency Contact Information

Each person planning to go on a trek should provide emergency contact information to group leaders and support personnel, either through official organization forms or a card such as this one:

Sample Emergency Contact Information Card

Name _____   Date _____

Primary Emergency Contact

Name _____

Relationship _____

Telephone numbers

Home _____

Work _____

Mobile _____

Secondary Emergency Contact

Name _____

Relationship _____

Telephone numbers

Home _____

Work _____

Mobile _____

For more on planning ahead to maximize the safety of a trek, see the chapter titled "Managing Risk."

The process of planning can enliven the days and weeks leading up to a trek by focusing your group's attention on the possibilities ahead. Preparing well for a trip also can ensure that you have considered the gear and provisions you will need, the itinerary you will follow, and the actions you will take if an emergency arises. That will leave you free to enjoy all that you discover along the way.

Outdoor Menus

"Happiness is a good camp meal."

—From *Fieldbook,* 2nd edition, Boy Scouts of America, 1967

A camp cook stirs a pot of stew bubbling over the flame of a backpacking stove. Rafters resting in the eddy of a rushing river reach into their pockets for handfuls of dried fruit and trail mix. Long-distance hikers deep into a journey dig through their packs to see what's left of a 10-day supply of provisions. Winter campers brush the evening snow from their hats and enjoy a hearty meal that will help them stay warm through the night.

If you've spent much time in the outdoors, you know that eating is a constant necessity. Meals can be among the great pleasures, too—fun to prepare and a highlight of a trek. Food will brighten a stretch of stormy weather, energize trekkers striving toward a destination, and revive many a weary soul.

As you plan your menus, you also have the opportunity to shape the sort of experience you have during a trek. When simplicity is important, the provisions in your pack can be basic as well—bags of flour, beans, dried vegetables, powdered milk, jerky, nuts, and a few other items from which to make your meals. When convenience is higher on your list of priorities, or when cooking gourmet meals is an activity you anticipate with pleasure, there is a tremendous range of ingredients you can take along to prepare dishes that will be as memorable as any other aspect of a journey.

Some travelers are content to eat the same foods day after day. Others crave variety. Whatever your food interests, plan well and then choose your provisions with care. Once you hit the trail, you can turn your attention to the adventure unfolding around you, confident that the food you need is in your pack and that there will be plenty to go around.

5

Emergency food is one of the 10 Scout Outdoor Essentials to be carried on every trek. A small bag of trail mix, some fruit, and a couple of energy bars will ensure that you will always have something to eat regardless of delays, emergencies, or other challenges.

For more on the Scout Outdoor Essentials, see the chapter titled "Gearing Up."

Planning Menus

The length of a trip and the manner in which you will move your gear and provisions are factors in determining the nature of a trek menu:

- On trips of just a few days, you can take any foods that will stay fresh and that you are willing to carry.

- As trek distances and durations increase, the weight of provisions will become a concern of increasing importance. Careful food selection should allow you to eat well with about 1^1/$_2$ to 2^1/$_2$ pounds of ingredients a day for each person. Decide at home what to prepare for each camp meal, then bring ingredients specifically chosen for each dish. For convenience, measure meal ingredients and carry them in plastic bags marked to identify the contents, the meal for which the ingredients are intended, and instructions for preparation.

- For extended journeys, trek provisions planning might be the most practical method of food selection. Instead of separately bagging ingredients for each meal, pack staples in bulk (so many pounds of cheese, so much trail mix, so many packets of sauce mix, etc.), then draw on them each day as you would the contents of a kitchen cupboard at home. Eating the berries you picked or the fish you caught can provide a welcome change from the monotony of trail food.

With good planning, Scouts and other outdoor travelers should be able to manage backpacks with enough food, stove fuel, and gear for about a week on the trail. Longer treks will require resupplies of provisions. Methods include prearranged trailhead rendezvous and mail drops.

For more on resupplying, see the chapter titled "Backpacking."

The Nuts and Bolts (and Fruits and Grains) of Nutrition

Food is fuel for the body. The harder your body works, the more calories it burns and the more you need to eat. Those calories come from three primary sources—carbohydrates, proteins, and fats. For healthy, active people, a balanced diet includes about 50 percent to 60 percent carbohydrates, 20 percent to 30 percent proteins, and 15 percent to 25 percent fats.

Following nutrition guidelines can help you develop healthy lifelong eating habits. While these guidelines might also be useful for ensuring variety in your menus, any nutritional deficiencies that might occur during treks can be made up when you get home.

Carbohydrates

Carbohydrates provide both quick and long-term energy. Whole-grain bread, bagels, crackers, and cereals are loaded with carbohydrates. So are bulgur, lentils, rice, and other grains, and pastas including noodles, spaghetti, and macaroni. Fruits and vegetables are sources of carbohydrates, and also contain high levels of vitamins and minerals.

Proteins

Proteins are essential for building and repairing muscle and bone, and are sources of calories. Beef, poultry, fish, nuts, eggs, and dairy products all are protein-rich foods.

Fats

Fats contain about twice the calories per ounce as do carbohydrates or proteins. Cheese, margarine, vegetable oil, and other foods with a high fat content can keep you going for hours. Since you burn calories to stay warm, eating high-fat foods before going to bed on cold evenings will help you enjoy a comfortable night's sleep.

Vitamins, Minerals, and Nonnutrient Dietary Essentials

In addition to carbohydrates, proteins, and fats, your body needs water, fiber, and a sufficient supply of vitamins and minerals.

Water

The human body is made up of 70 percent water. Drinking plenty of water will help you digest food, stay energized, and better cope with the challenges of heat and cold.

For information on dehydration, see the chapter titled "Managing Risk." For guidelines on treating drinking water, see the chapter titled "Hygiene and Waste Disposal."

Fiber

Fiber is roughage that is not absorbed by the body. It helps move food products through the digestive tract, reducing the likelihood of constipation. Many grains, fruits, and vegetables close to their natural forms are high in fiber.

Vitamins and Minerals

For all but the most extensive treks, a diet composed of a variety of foods that includes fruits and vegetables is likely to provide the vitamins and minerals you need to maintain good health.

Shopping for Trek Adventure Food

Adventurers a century ago had a limited choice of provisions compact enough to carry and stable enough not to spoil. Wilderness travelers relied on grains, flour, pemmican, and jerky. Trekkers today can still build their menus around simple staples, but they also have other forms of food from which to choose.

Dry Foods

Nuts, pasta, flour, beans, rice, seeds, powdered milk, and other dry foods form a large portion of a diet for active people. They usually are less expensive when purchased in bulk and then repackaged for the trail. Protect them from moisture, and they are unlikely to spoil.

5

Fresh Foods

Fresh foods typically are more nutritious than highly processed forms of the same items; they contain more vitamins and minerals, as well as provide roughage. Many won't keep long without refrigeration, but if you don't mind carrying the weight you can take fresh fruits, vegetables, and certain meats for meals during the first days of a trek. River rafters sometimes stock insulated chests with ice to preserve a wide range of perishable food.

Cheese

Cheese is a high-calorie fresh-food favorite of many outdoor travelers. It can be eaten by itself or used as a recipe ingredient. Jack, cheddar, mozzarella, Parmesan, and other harder varieties of cheese will stay fresh for a number of days without refrigeration, especially if the weather is cool. Cheese sealed in plastic when purchased also might last longer if the airtight wrapping is left unopened. Should a layer of mold appear on a piece of hard cheese, pare it away with a knife and use the unaffected portion underneath.

Canned Foods

Many foods are available in cans. If weight is an issue, though, you'll want to be very selective about which canned products, if any, you decide to carry. Small cans of tuna or boned chicken, for example, weigh just a few ounces and will add protein, calories, and flavor to pastas, soups, and other dishes. Wash and flatten empty cans, then carry them home for proper disposal.

Convenience Foods

Every supermarket offers dozens of convenience foods that are ready to eat or can be prepared quickly. Those you might want to try include gravy and pasta sauce mixes, biscuit and pancake mixes, jerky, energy bars, and main courses that require only the addition of hot water.

Dehydrated/Freeze-Dried Foods

Dehydrating and freeze-drying remove most of the moisture from a food item. The result is a product that weighs ounces rather than pounds and that won't take up much room in your pack. The serving sizes listed on packaged foods often are optimistic—a freeze-dried entrée that says it contains food for four might, in fact, be just enough to feed two hungry backpackers.

Dehydrating Your Own Foods

A dehydrator designed for home use might be a worthwhile investment for Scouts interested in cutting costs and increasing the variety and appeal of their outdoor meals. For best results, follow the instructions that come with the dehydrator. Many can be set up to dehydrate fresh produce, herbs, sauces, meats, eggs, and even dairy products.

A kitchen oven also can be used as a dehydrator. Here's a good way to dry vegetables and fruit:

1. Begin with fresh, ripe produce. Wash it well; remove cores, stems, and bruised or brown spots; and thinly slice.

2. Apples, peaches, and other soft produce can be dehydrated without further preparation. Tougher vegetables such as broccoli and cauliflower should be steamed briefly before dehydrating. Place slices in a vegetable steamer inside a large pot containing an inch of water and bring to a boil, or microwave them in an appropriate container after sprinkling them with water and putting on the lid. Steam or microwave for half the time normally used for cooking.

3. Remove an oven rack, then set the oven at its lowest temperature. Tightly stretch cheesecloth or muslin over the rack and secure it with safety pins. Spread produce slices on the cloth, put the rack in the oven, and leave the door open a few inches. (If necessary, prop the door open.)

4. Sample a few slices now and then. When they are dry but not brittle (a process that might take eight hours or more), pack them in plastic bags, then store in a refrigerator or freezer until you need them for a trek. Dehydrated fruits and vegetables can be eaten as they are, added to dishes you are cooking, or soaked in water for a few hours to restore their original sizes and shapes.

Breakfast

A good breakfast gives you a foundation of energy to power you through the morning. Include something to drink (nothing beats a hot cup of cocoa on a chilly morning), some fruit (fresh, dried, or a juice mix), and a main course. If you are eager to get out of camp, a bowl of granola with nuts, fruit, and some reconstituted powdered milk can hit the spot. On more leisurely mornings you might prepare hot cereal, pancakes, hash browns, or scrambled eggs.

Eggs

Eggs are a campground treat, both as breakfast items and as recipe ingredients. Fresh eggs will stay that way for a couple of days without refrigeration. (Pack three or four in an empty cardboard potato-chip tube, separating and cushioning them with loosely wadded newspaper.) Many outdoors or camping supply stores and catalogs offer dried eggs in a convenient powdered form.

Trail Food

Food to snack on throughout the day plays such an important role in outdoor nutrition that it is almost a meal in itself. Maintain energy reserves between meals by eating frequently, especially whenever you start to feel hungry. Fruit, cheese, and trail mix are ideal. Make your own mix by combining nuts, raisins, and candy-coated chocolate bits, then store the mix in a plastic bag. Experiment by adding other ingredients—shredded coconut, for example, or granola.

"Cooking and eating in the outdoors present exciting challenges, and when you're properly prepared, can provide a pleasant experience."

—From *Fieldbook for Canadian Scouting,* Boy Scouts of Canada, 2000

Lunch

Plan lunch foods that can be eaten without much preparation. Bagels, pita bread, and tortillas pack well without crumbling, while bread and crackers require more care to prevent them from being smashed in your pack. Round out a lunch menu with peanut butter, cheese, and meats that keep without being refrigerated—summer sausage and salami, for example. Add some fresh or dried fruit and, for dessert, dip into your bag of trail mix.

Dinner

Dinner is a chance for you to catch up on nutrients your other meals might have lacked, and to consume the calories you will need to keep you warm through the night. Evening menus are limited only to your imagination and the amount of weight you are willing to carry on a trek. In general, though, travelers out for more than a few days usually settle into a routine of preparing one-pot specials.

One-Pot Specials

To prepare a one-pot main course, choose an ingredient from each column in the One-Pot Special Chart and combine in proportions appropriate for the number of people in your cooking group. Give some thought to the preparation time for each ingredient to determine the order in which you will add the items. Dried vegetables, for example, might require soaking before being added to the pot, and some sauce mixes dissolve more readily in cold water than in hot. Complete the meal with a beverage and, if you wish, something for dessert.

5

The One-Pot Special Chart

(Select one item from each column.)

Pastas and Grains[1]	Sauces[2]	Protein[3]	Extras[4]
Noodles	Soup mixes	Canned meats	Cheese
Macaroni	Gravy mixes	(chicken, tuna)	Nuts
Ramen-style	Spaghetti	Jerky	Coconut
noodles	sauce mix	(beef, turkey)	Raisins
Rice (white, instant,		Nut burger mix	Sunflower seeds
or brown)		Summer	Bacon bits
Bulgur		sausage	Fresh or dried
Couscous		Dried	vegetables
		chipped beef	Fresh or
		Textured	dried fruit
		vegetable	Fresh potatoes
		protein (TVP)	or potato flakes
			Onion flakes
			Margarine

[1]Notes on pastas and grains:

- White rice—$1/2$ cup dry rice and 1 cup of water per person per meal. Combine rice and cold water in the pot and bring to a boil. Cover and let simmer until done—about 8 to 10 minutes.

- Instant rice—1 cup dry instant rice and 1 cup of water per person per meal. Stir the instant rice into boiling water, remove from the stove, and let the pot sit for a few minutes.

- Brown rice—$1/2$ cup dry rice and 1 cup of water per person per meal. Prepare as you would white rice, but allow 30 to 45 minutes of cooking time. (The extended cooking time makes brown rice impractical on many treks.)

- Pasta—4 ounces per person per meal. Bring a pot of water to a boil. If you have it, add a tablespoon of cooking oil or margarine, then stir in the pasta. Allow to boil until pasta is done (cooking time will vary according to the type of pasta). Drain.

- Ramen-style noodles—one package per person per meal. For a stewlike consistency, add 1 cup of water per packet; 2 cups of water per packet makes a soup. Measure the water into a pot, bring it to a boil, add the noodles, and cook until done—about 3 to 5 minutes. (The noodles will be easier to eat with a spoon if you break them up before adding them to the pot.)

- Packaged entrées—Convenience-food versions of macaroni and cheese and many dishes featuring pasta and rice come with several or all of the one-pot ingredient columns covered. For best cooking results, follow the instructions on the package.

[2]Notes on sauces:

- Powdered sauce mixes in a variety of flavors can be purchased in packets that are easy to carry and convenient to prepare.

- Instant soup and powdered gravy mixes also can be used as sauces for pasta and rice dishes.

[3]Notes on protein:

- A 6-ounce can of tuna or boned chicken is a good amount for two people.

- As a meat substitute, textured vegetable protein (TVP) is lightweight, easy to pack, and nutritious.

[4]Notes on extras:

- Vegetables and fruit—Green beans, corn, tomatoes, apples, peaches, pears, and other fruits and vegetables are available in freeze-dried or commercially dehydrated forms. Many can be dehydrated at home, too. On short trips, consider carrying fresh fruit and vegetables.

- Soaking dried fruits and vegetables for an hour before preparing a meal will reconstitute them and hasten cooking.

- Fresh potatoes can be sliced and boiled, then eaten as a side dish or added to one-pot specials. Reconstitute potato flakes according to the product directions.

- Margarine adds fat and flavor to recipes. Liquid margarine comes in plastic squeeze bottles just right for backpacking. Stick or semisolid margarine can be stored in a plastic jar with a secure screw-on lid.

Trek Provisions Planning

For many shorter trips, you can plan each meal then purchase and repackage the ingredients for it. That strategy will become increasingly cumbersome if a trek will extend beyond three or four days. When that's the case, trek provisions planning is a more effective and time-efficient means of organizing food. Instead of having each meal in one package, carry bulk quantities of menu ingredients and then draw on them to prepare one-pot specials and other recipes throughout a trek. As a trip winds down, there are bound to be more of some ingredients left than others. That's when you can use your imagination to devise meals from what is still available.

Here is one way that trek provisions planning works:

❶ Calculate the total amount of food that can reasonably be carried on the trek—usually between 1½ and 2½ pounds per person per day. For example, five people on a weeklong trek would need a total of 70 pounds of provisions, as shown below:

7 (days) X 5 (people) X 2 (pounds of food per person per day) = 70 pounds of food

❷ Develop a checklist similar to the one at right that organizes the foodstuffs you want into categories.

❸ Calculate how many pounds of food you will need in each category. Based on the food lists of many groups packing provisions for extended treks, the approximate percentage of the total food weight assigned to each category is as follows:

General staples—40 percent

Breakfast foods—10 percent

Trail foods—25 percent

Dinner foods—25 percent

(Feel free to adjust the percentages if your experiences in the field suggest that your group's preferences are different from those listed here.)
Calculate the pounds for each category by multiplying the total trek food weight by the percentages: general staples X .40, breakfast foods X .10, trail foods X .25, dinner foods X .25.

Use the checklist as a general guideline for selecting trek provisions. As you determine amounts, consider the sorts of recipes you will want to prepare, the likes and dislikes of those traveling with you, experiences you've had with food on other treks, and the importance of a balanced diet.

Trek Provisions Planning Checklist

General Staples

(Ingredients for use with any meal)
Percentage of the total food weight—40 percent

_____ **TARGET WEIGHT** for this category

ITEM WEIGHT

_____ Fruit drink mixes (lemonade, apple cider, etc.)
_____ Cocoa mix
_____ Brown sugar
_____ Honey
_____ Cheese (cheddar, jack, mozzarella, Parmesan)
_____ Meat (jerky, summer sausage, salami, pepperoni, and other unrefrigerated varieties)
_____ Peanut butter
_____ Cornmeal
_____ Biscuit mix
_____ Tortillas
_____ Bagels
_____ Pita bread
_____ Powdered milk
_____ Dried eggs
_____ Oil
_____ Margarine
_____ Seasonings
_____ **WEIGHT** of general staples

Breakfast Foods

(Ingredients for morning meals)
Percentage of the total food weight—10 percent

_____ **TARGET WEIGHT** for this category

ITEM WEIGHT

_____ Oatmeal and other hot cereals
_____ Granola and other cold cereals
_____ Pancake mix
_____ **WEIGHT** of breakfast foods

Trail Foods

(Ingredients to combine into trail mix, to eat alone, or to add to other dishes)
Percentage of the total food weight—25 percent

_____ **TARGET WEIGHT** for this category

ITEM WEIGHT

_____ Fruit, dried (apricots, apples, cranberries, pineapple, banana chips, etc.)
_____ Peanuts
_____ Mixed nuts
_____ Sunflower seeds
_____ Raisins
_____ Coconut
_____ Crackers
_____ Energy bars
_____ Hard candy
_____ Candy-coated chocolate bits
_____ **WEIGHT** of trail foods

Dinner Foods

(Ingredients primarily for one-pot specials and other evening meals)
Percentage of the total food weight—25 percent

_____ **TARGET WEIGHT** for this category

ITEM WEIGHT

_____ Pasta (noodles, macaroni, ramen-style noodles)
_____ Rice
_____ Beans (refried, black, lentils)
_____ Potato flakes
_____ Couscous (steamed semolina pasta)
_____ Vegetables (dried)
_____ Onion flakes
_____ Falafel (spicy vegetable patties)
_____ Hummus (pureed chickpeas)
_____ Sauce and gravy mixes (powdered)
_____ Instant soup
_____ Brownie mix
_____ Cake mix
_____ Instant pudding mix
_____ **WEIGHT** of dinner foods

_____ **COMBINED TARGET WEIGHT** of all categories

_____ **COMBINED ACTUAL WEIGHT** of all categories

5

Seasonings

Seasonings will enhance your meals by bringing variety and interest to even the most ordinary recipes. Small plastic bags are good containers, as are thoroughly cleaned plastic aspirin bottles with secure lids. Label containers so you will know what's inside, and use each seasoning with care—it's easy to add flavor to a dish, but you can't remove it if you put in too much. A basic kit might contain the following seasonings. Add others if you wish.

- ☐ Salt
- ☐ Black pepper
- ☐ Garlic powder
- ☐ Basil
- ☐ Chili powder
- ☐ Other

Repackaging Foods

Most foods on grocery store shelves are sealed in cardboard, foil, paper, plastic, or glass. Most of that packaging is useless on the trail. Eliminate it as you organize food for a trek, and you'll rid your pack of excess weight and clutter. Here's one way to get it done:

Divide food supplies into piles, one for each meal you'll prepare during a trek. Beginning with the first meal of the trip, measure the amount of each ingredient that a recipe calls for and put it into a plastic bag.

For example, you might be planning a quick dinner of tuna-and-rice casserole, bagels, instant pudding, and cocoa. To feed yourself and three companions, you calculate that you will need 2 cups of white rice, 2 packets of gravy mix, two 6-ounce cans of tuna, and 3 ounces of dried vegetables.

Measure the rice into one bag and the vegetables into another, then stow them in a larger bag along with the gravy packets and cans of tuna. Write the cooking instructions on a slip of paper and include that in the bag, too. Close the bag and label it with the name of the entrée. Place all the ingredient bags for each meal in a larger bag labeled with the name of the meal.

In camp, pull out the bag for a particular meal and find inside all the ingredients in the right proportions.

Plastic Bags and Food Containers

Repackaging food for a trek of even just a few days can involve lots of plastic bags. Heavy-duty freezer bags with sturdy plastic zip seals come in 1-quart and 1-gallon sizes. Bread wrappers and other simple plastic bags are good, too—close each by tying the neck with a loose overhand knot.

Many camping supply stores sell refillable squeeze tubes and plastic jars with screw-on lids for carrying peanut butter, jelly, margarine, honey, and other sticky, oily, and potentially messy foods. Guard against leakage by carrying each jar or squeeze tube in a plastic bag of its own.

Cooking Gear

Decide which meals you want during a trip and then determine the cooking gear needed to prepare them. If you are backpacking with all your food and equipment, you will want to keep everything as light as possible. On treks that involve watercraft or pack animals, weight probably won't be such an issue; you can bring along a greater variety of menu items and the cooking gear to make more complicated meals.

Check outdoors and camping supply stores and catalogs for pots, pans, and utensils designed especially for outdoor use. Some kits include pots that nest together and lids that double as frying pans. As an inexpensive alternative, look for lightweight pots and pans at garage sales, surplus outlets, and discount stores. Some pot handles can be removed simply by removing a screw. They might not nestle together as tightly as camp cook kits, but cheap pots will boil water just as well as pricier cookware.

Most treks are best undertaken by small groups of people, so you'll need only a camp stove and a couple of pots to prepare meals that will satisfy everyone. Split larger groups into cooking teams of three to four people, each with its own stove, cook kit, and provisions. Winter campers might want to add a larger pot with a lid so that they can melt snow to replenish water bottles and provide plenty of hot drinks.

Depending on the menus they intend to prepare, three or four people cooking together will manage well with the following cooking gear:

- [ ] 1 backpacking stove with fuel
- [ ] 1 large pot and lid (2½- or 3-quart size)
- [ ] 1 small pot and lid (1½- or 2-quart size)
- [ ] 1 lightweight frying pan (10 to 12 inches in diameter)
- [ ] For melting snow, add 1 large pot and lid (6- to 10-quart size)
- [ ] Hot-pot tongs

Hot-pot tongs allow you to move pots and pans onto and off of a stove, and to stabilize them while adding ingredients or stirring. You can use your personal spoon and pocketknife as your primary cooking utensils, or you might want to carry a lightweight ladle or spatula for stirring, flipping, and serving.

At the end of a trip, review the cooking gear you used, what you lacked, and what proved to be unnecessary. Make a similar assessment of your food choices and recipes. Use your reviews to refine your menu planning and gear selection so that they mesh exactly with the journeys on which you are embarking.

For information on selecting stoves, see the chapter titled "Using Stoves and Campfires." For more on personal gear for eating, see the chapter titled "Gearing Up." For guidelines on sanitary handling and preparation of food, see the chapter titled "Hygiene and Waste Disposal." For information on bear bags and other means of protecting food in camp, see the chapter titled "Traveling and Camping in Special Environments."

Baking

Peach cobbler, cornbread dripping with honey, biscuits right out of the pan—the results of baking enliven any meal. If you are camping in areas where campfires are appropriate, fashion an oven out of two frying pans: Use one as the lid of the other, and add a layer of coals on top to provide heat. Reflector ovens and cast-iron or aluminum Dutch ovens offer a world of baking opportunities, especially for horse packers and other travelers able to manage the weight of the ovens.

A number of manufacturers market ovens for use with camp stoves. These ovens, lightweight and ingenious in design, allow heat to circulate around and over cooking food, enabling trekkers to enjoy baked goods wherever they go.

5

Basic Biscuits

You can buy biscuit mix at a grocery store and prepare according to directions on the box, or use a good biscuit recipe to make your own.

In a sturdy plastic bag, combine these dry ingredients:

2 cups flour

I level teaspoon salt

4 level teaspoons baking powder

5 level tablespoons powdered milk

Carry separately in a plastic jar or bottle with a leak-proof lid:

4 tablespoons (1/4 cup) margarine, cooking oil, or shortening

When you are ready to make biscuits, thoroughly mix the margarine, cooking oil, or shortening into the dry ingredients, then add enough water (about 1 cup) to form a stiff dough. Pat the dough flat (about 1/2 inch thick), then use the rim of a camp mug to cut the dough into biscuits. You can cook the biscuits in one of several ways:

- Bake them in a camp stove oven, a Dutch oven, or a reflector oven.

- Cook them in a frying pan lightly oiled with cooking oil, shortening, or margarine. Arrange biscuit dough in the pan, then cover it and brown the biscuits over low heat (about 8 minutes). Turn the biscuits over, replace the lid, and brown the other side.

- Make dumplings by dropping spoonfuls of dough into boiling soup or stew. Cover and cook for about 10 minutes, then take out one dumpling and cut it open to see if it is done inside. If the dough is still sticky, return the dumpling to the pan, replace the cover, and cook for another 2 to 3 minutes.

A Final Word on Menus

Choosing food for a trip presents more opportunity and challenge than almost any other aspect of trek preparation. Success is a matter of trial, error, and an element of bravery—building on the menu successes of past outings and learning from the occasional culinary mishaps that are bound to occur. You also can learn about menu possibilities and tricks of the outdoor kitchen from books devoted to camping recipes and cooking methods. Master a few simple meals, then begin branching out with dishes that will delight your taste buds, satisfy your hunger, provide the energy you need, and amaze those who are traveling and dining with you.

"Food is always on our minds. We seem to be constantly hungry. As soon as one meal is finished we begin planning what to have at the next."

—Cindy Ross, *A Woman's Journey*, 1982 (She hiked the entire Appalachian Trail from Georgia to Maine, and the Pacific Crest Trail from Mexico to Canada.)

Managing Risk

"I say we have a great chance to get to the summit, but we may also have to turn back, and I want all their support if we have to do that."

—Peter Whitaker, climber/guide

An injury that doesn't happen needs no treatment. An emergency that doesn't occur requires no response. An illness that doesn't develop demands no remedy. The best way to stay safe in the outdoors is to avoid getting into trouble in the first place. That requires planning, training, leadership, good judgment, and accepting responsibility—in short, risk management.

We manage risk in almost every aspect of our lives. There is risk involved in stepping out of our homes in the morning, but we go anyway. There are risks in crossing a street, catching a bus, and taking part in sports, but we find ways to minimize these risks and maximize our safety and well-being.

Risk management is so much a part of outdoor adventures that often we hardly notice we are doing it. When we fill bottles with water from streams and lakes, we deal with the risk of parasites by treating the water with a filter or chemicals, or by boiling it. When we share the outdoors with bears, we protect them and ourselves by hanging our food out of their reach, eliminating odors from our sleeping areas, and keeping campsites spotless. When foul weather blows in, routes become uncomfortably exposed, streams swell, or snow loads make avalanches a possibility, we consider all the available information and then make decisions that keep risks at acceptable levels.

Perceived risk can energize outdoor activities by bringing to them an immediacy that is sharper than what we normally experience. The actual risk on a well-managed ropes course, for example, is relatively low, but participants experiencing the

6

events of the course might perceive that the risk is much higher than it actually is. That heightened awareness can take them beyond their usual comfort levels and encourage them to accept challenges that will stretch their abilities and build their confidence.

The only way to eliminate risk completely in the out-of-doors is to give up the pleasures, challenges, and satisfaction of taking part in an adventure. Rather than attempting to do away with it, group members and leaders can manage risk by identifying its sources, understanding its boundaries, and tailoring their behavior to minimize exposure to danger.

"If there is a common thread to adventure across the millennium, it is risk. And risk is its greatest asset."

—Richard Bangs (Eagle Scout, river guide, and founder of Sobek Travel), *Adventure Without End*, 2001

Shared Management of Risks

Many outdoors-oriented organizations have guidelines to address certain hazards they believe to be of particular concern to their members. This chapter, for example, will discuss hypothermia, lightning, and several other potential risks of great interest to the Boy Scouts of America. A truly effective approach to risk management, though, is found not just in the details, but also in the willingness of everyone in a group to take an active role in maximizing his or her own safety and the safety of others.

A leader who empowers group members with resources, training, and responsibilities for conducting successful treks often will find that they also can be trusted to do their part to manage risk. When each person has a part to play in the success of a trek, everyone has a stake in risk management. Group members are far better prepared to deal with illnesses or injuries if they are versed in response plans and if they know where they are, what resources are at their disposal, and what skills they can draw upon. On the other hand, leaders who expect group members simply to obey rules and instructions—to be followers rather than thinkers and problem solvers—might discover that their groups aren't able to deal effectively with the changing nature of risk.

Risk Management

Here are three keys to effective risk management:

- Everyone in the group commits to having a safe experience.

- Everyone understands and follows group guidelines established to minimize risk.

- Everyone has a say in recognizing and dealing with risks that arise during a trek.

Personal Risk Management Behavior

The more responsibility every member of your group takes for personal health and safety, the more each of you can contribute to a successful trek. You also will be in a stronger position to provide assistance if an emergency does arise. Among the ways you can increase your role in risk management are these:

- Stay in good shape so you are ready for the physical demands of a trek.

- Know where you are going and what to expect.

- Adjust clothing layers to match changing conditions.

- Drink plenty of water.

- Protect yourself from exposure to the sun, biting insects, and poisonous plants.

- Take care of your gear.

A critical aspect of risk management is letting others know when you are having difficulties or are aware of a concern that might affect you or the group. Many people have a tendency to keep things to themselves. They don't want to slow down the group, or are worried about what others will think of them. But stopping for a few moments to deal with a hot spot on a heel can help avoid bringing the group to a long halt later in the day

6

Take care of yourself, and you will be far less likely to have trouble on the trail. You also will be much better able to help others deal with difficult situations.

when blisters break out. Voicing concern about changing weather or questionable route decisions can bring important matters to the attention of the rest of your group.

Outdoor-Oriented First Aid

We often go to remote areas to get away from it all, but among the things we are getting away from is quick access to emergency support and care. If someone has an accident in an American city, dial 911 and an emergency team will probably be on the scene in minutes, ready to treat injuries and to provide transport to a medical center.

The farther that group members are from medical facilities, the more important is their ability to deal with emergencies on their own. Responding to incidents during trek adventures can involve not only immediate treatment, but also evacuating ill or injured persons to the frontcountry, or stabilizing them and maintaining their safety for hours or even days until medical assistance arrives.

Those who intend to travel in the backcountry should prepare themselves with first-aid training, ideally including training in caring for injured and ill persons in remote settings. Among the training courses available in various parts of the country are Red Cross Wilderness First Aid Basic, Wilderness First Responder, Wilderness Emergency Medical Technician, and Mountaineering Oriented First Aid.

Preparing a Group to Manage Risk

Risks associated with the outdoors can involve rain, wind, heat, cold, avalanche, water, wildlife, vegetation, and falling. Human elements affecting risk include lack of physical preparation, improper training, poor judgment, and unreasonable expectations by group members, leaders, parents, and others. Many of these concerns can be addressed by leaders helping group members decide upon activities that are appropriate to their skills, experience level, and interests. Preparing a group to manage risk also involves a certain amount of pretrip paperwork and development of an emergency response plan.

For more on matching groups with appropriate activities, see the chapters titled "Organizing for Adventures," "Outdoor Leadership," and "Planning a Trek."

Rescue team professionals and trained volunteers responding to backcountry calls can be exposed to considerable risk. Never hesitate to summon help when you need it, but minimize the need for assistance by preparing well and doing your best to proceed in ways that maximize your safety and that of others.

Paperwork

The policies of a given organization will determine the paperwork that must be completed before a trek begins—releases for medical treatment, for example, proof of health insurance, tour permits, and any forms required by land management agencies. Leaders also should be fully informed in writing if a group member requires medications, has any medical issues, or deals with allergies. Always prepare a written itinerary of where you plan to be on each day and night of a trek. Leave copies with several responsible people who will take appropriate action if you haven't returned according to schedule.

Emergency Response Plan

Developing a written emergency response plan requires group members to figure out the steps to be taken during trek emergencies and to write down contact information for agency personnel, law enforcement authorities, and medical response networks. The plan should outline strategies for contacting help, if help is needed. Along with your group's roster, itinerary, intended route, and expected time of return, give copies of the emergency response plan to support persons in the frontcountry.

For more on itineraries and emergency response plans, see the chapter titled "Planning a Trek."

GPS receivers and wireless phones are sometimes useful during outdoor emergencies.

Wireless Telephones and Risk Management

Global positioning system (GPS) receivers allow travelers to pinpoint locations, but they are no substitute for mastering the use of maps and compasses. Likewise, wireless telephones can be a convenient means for groups to contact emergency response personnel, but phones are useless if they malfunction, the batteries are exhausted, or distance and terrain prevent clear reception of signals.

Frivolous use of wireless phones can seriously diminish solitude, independence, and challenge in the outdoors. If you carry a portable telephone, stow it deep in your pack and bring it out only for emergency calls. Most of all, never assume that having a portable telephone grants you any protection to attempt activities beyond your levels of skill and experience, especially if you are far from emergency support.

Managing Risk in the Field

The degree of risk in a situation depends on a host of factors that can change from one moment to the next. Take, for example, a log that, a few feet above a stream, offers an inviting route for hikers to reach the far bank. On a warm day in a BSA local council camp, the risk involved in walking across the log might be very low. Even if you fall, it's not far to the water. If you get wet, you can go to your tent and change clothes. If you sprain your ankle, you are close to medical assistance. Do you walk over the log? Probably.

During a backpacking trip, you come upon a similar log lying across a stream, but this one is located miles up a trail and the day is windy and cold. If you slip off the log, you have only the clothing you are carrying to replace wet garments. If your pack is submerged, the clothes, food, and gear stowed in it could become soaked. If you hurt your ankle, you might be stranded miles from a road. Do you use the log to cross the stream? Perhaps, but you might decide to lessen the risk by straddling the log and scooting across in a sitting position, or you might wade if the stream is calm and shallow, or you might seek out a better place to cross. Each option will take longer than walking the log, but not nearly as long as dealing with the possible results of a fall.

Managing risk often is a matter of considering the "what if" of a situation. What if I fall? What if I lose my pack? What if I sprain my ankle? Other considerations that might be factors are the time of day, your group's level of fatigue, hunger, or anxiety, and the amount of experience you've had with similar situations.

Put lots of faith in your gut feeling about a situation. If it doesn't seem right but you're not sure why, your instincts might be telling you something you need to know, but have not yet fully understood. Take plenty of time to consider your options.

Anyone in a group should feel empowered to call a halt to group activities whenever he or she perceives a risk that should be addressed. In turn, group leaders and other members must respect those concerns and give them full consideration.

While the tone of a group is best when it is upbeat and members strive to see the positive in every situation, it's good to be a pessimist about hazards, erring on the side of too much caution rather than not enough. The risk management portion of your brain should be focused on what could go wrong so that you can act in ways that increase the likelihood of things going right.

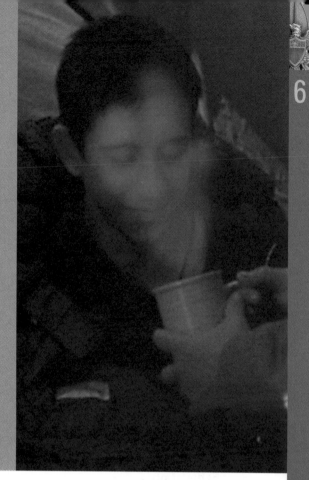

"The only reasonable rule in remote regions anywhere is not to take unnecessary chances, weighing always the possible loss against the potential gain, and going about life with as wide a safety margin as practical."

—Bradford Angier (seasoned outdoorsman and author of many books on woodlore), *Living Off the Country,* 1966

Incident Response

Risk management is not built on a list of rules, but rather on good judgment and a willingness to accept responsibility for one's own safety and that of others. Incident response is what happens when an injury or illness has occurred during a trek and a group must decide how to handle it.

Accounts of injuries and illnesses in the outdoors often try to pinpoint a specific cause. Hypothermia, for example, often is blamed on chilly weather, cotton clothing, and precipitation. Of course, the steps that led to poorly dressed travelers shivering in the rain can be traced back to decisions that might easily have prevented that dangerous situation from occurring at all. With qualified leadership, personal responsibility, and effective planning, those travelers would have had warm clothing and rain gear. They would have been well-hydrated and have had energy food in their packs. They would have kept an eye on the weather and made timely decisions about where to go, when to camp, and whether to turn around and go home.

The following pages discuss ways to prepare for and manage certain risks, and also the basics of how groups can respond to incidents brought about by these concerns. (Watercraft adventures and some other trek activities present specific risk management issues that will be addressed in the chapters discussing those activities.)

6

Dehydration

Water is essential for nearly every bodily function, including brain activity and temperature control. We lose moisture through breathing, sweating, digestion, and urination. A person who gives off more water than he or she takes in risks becoming *dehydrated.* The first sign of dehydration usually is dark urine. Other signs can include weariness, headache and body aches, and confusion.

> Dehydration can play a significant role in a number of maladies including heat exhaustion, heatstroke, hypothermia, and frostbite.

Help keep your body in balance by eating enough throughout the day. The importance of drinking plenty of fluids cannot be overemphasized. Don't wait until you feel thirsty—that's an indication that you are already becoming a bit dehydrated. Replenish your water supplies at every opportunity and drink often in warm weather and cold alike.

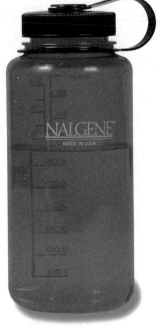

Incident Response for Dehydration

A person showing any indications of dehydration should rest in the shade and sip water until the symptoms subside.

Heat Exhaustion

Heat exhaustion can be brought on by a combination of dehydration and a warm environment. The condition is not uncommon during sports activities and trek adventures conducted in hot weather, especially if participants are not fully acclimated to the conditions. Symptoms can include the following:

- Skin that is pale and clammy from heavy sweating

- Nausea and tiredness

- Dizziness and fainting

- Headache, muscle cramps, and weakness

Incident Response for Heat Exhaustion

To treat heat exhaustion, have the victim lie in a cool, shady place with the feet raised. Remove excess clothing. Cool the victim by applying cool, wet

cloths to his or her body and by fanning. If the victim is fully alert, let him or her sip from a glass of water and take bites of salted food, such as nuts. Recovery should be rapid. If symptoms persist, call for medical help.

Heatstroke

Heatstroke occurs when a person's core temperature rises to a life-threatening level (above 105 degrees). Causal factors include dehydration and over-exertion in hot environments. Symptoms can include hot, red skin that can be either dry or sweaty; confusion; and a rapid pulse.

Incident Response for Heatstroke

A heatstroke victim must be cooled immediately. He or she is in danger of dying. To quickly lower the body temperature and begin restoring hydration, move the victim to a cool, shady spot and cool him or her any way you can. Keep the victim lying down and comfortable, with head and shoulders slightly raised. Remove outer clothing and sponge the victim with cold water. Cover the victim with wet towels, wet clothing, or whatever else is handy, and fan him or her. Place the victim in a stream, in a tub filled with cool (not ice-cold) water, or in front of an air conditioner running full blast in a house or car. Use combinations of all available treatments.

Get emergency medical help as soon as possible. The victim's temperature might go up again, or he or she might vomit or require rescue breathing.

For more on conducting trek adventures when temperatures are warm, see the chapter titled "Hot-Weather Travel and Camping."

6

Hypothermia

Hypothermia occurs when a person's body is losing more heat than it can generate. It is a danger for anyone who is not dressed warmly enough, though simple exposure to cold is seldom the only cause. Dehydration is a common factor. Wind, damp clothing, hunger, and exhaustion can further compound the danger. The temperature doesn't have to be below freezing, either—a lightly dressed hiker caught in a cool, windy rain shower can be at great risk. So is a swimmer too far out in chilly water or immersed too long.

A person experiencing hypothermia might feel cold and numb; become tired, anxious, irritable, and increasingly clumsy; have slurred speech; shiver uncontrollably; make bad decisions; and lose consciousness.

A group that knows how to treat hypothermia should be well enough aware of the risk that its own members will seldom, if ever, need to be treated for it.

Incident Response for Hypothermia

Treat a victim of hypothermia by preventing him or her from getting colder and, if necessary, by using any or all of the following methods to help the body warm again to its normal temperature.

❶ If the person is fully conscious and can drink, offer plenty of warm liquids (cocoa, soup, fruit juices, water).

❷ Move the person into the shelter of a building or a tent and get him or her into dry, warm clothes.

❸ Zip the person into a dry sleeping bag. Cover the head with a warm hat or sleeping bag hood.

❹ Provide water bottles filled with warm fluid to hold in the armpit and groin areas.

❺ If hypothermia is advanced, help the person to breathe warm, moist air to aid in rewarming.

❻ Monitor closely and be ready to administer other first aid.

❼ Seek medical care.

While one person is being treated for hypothermia, the rest of a group also might be at risk. Protect yourself and others by taking shelter, putting on layers of dry, warm clothing, and having something to eat and drink. Look after one another.

6

Frostbite

Flesh exposed to low temperatures or cold wind can freeze. Far from the warmth of the body's core, toes and fingers are especially vulnerable, as are the nose, ears, and cheeks. A frostbite victim might complain that his or her ears, nose, fingers, or feet feel painful and then numb, but some victims won't notice anything. Grayish-white patches on the skin are signs of frostbite. Since dehydration increases the danger of frostbite, cold-weather travelers must be every bit as diligent about drinking fluids as they are when the temperature is high.

Incident Response for Frostbite

Only superficial frostbite—frostnip—can be treated in the field. If you suspect that frostbite is deep (extending below skin level), wrap the injured area in a dry blanket and get the victim under the care of a physician as soon as possible. Don't rub the injury.

To treat frostnip, move the victim into a tent or building, then warm the injured area and keep it warm. If an ear or cheek is frozen, remove a glove and warm the injury with the palm of your hand. Slip a frostnipped hand under your clothing and tuck it beneath an armpit. Treat frostnipped toes by putting the victim's bare feet against the warm skin of your belly.

For more on conducting trek adventures in chilly conditions, see the chapter titled "Cold-Weather Travel and Camping."

Sunburn

Although skin appears to recover from sunburn, damage to its cellular structure accumulates. That can lead to premature wrinkling and is a primary cause of skin cancer. Use sunscreen to protect exposed skin, giving special attention to your face, ears, nose, and neck. To be effective, sunscreen should have a sun protection factor (SPF) of at least 15. Apply it liberally before sunlight exposure, and reapply if you are sweating and after immersion in water. Hats with large brims, long-sleeved shirts, and long pants will provide further protection.

Sunlight reflected by water or snow can intensify the damaging effects of solar radiation. Zinc oxide offers total blockage of the sun's rays, and might be what you need for your face and ears during watercraft adventures and treks at high altitudes or on snow. Wear sunglasses to prevent eyestrain, and shield your lips against chapping and sun injury by applying a lip balm with an SPF of 15 or higher.

Incident Response for Sunburn

Prevent further injury by getting out of the sun, either by seeking shade or by putting on a hat and clothing that affords protection. Treat painful sunburn with damp cloths. Remedies containing aloe vera also might provide relief.

Lightning

Open water, mountaintops, the crests of ridges, the bases of tall or solitary trees, and large meadows can be hazardous places during lightning storms. Plan to be off peaks and other exposed locations before afternoon when thunderstorms are more prevalent. If you are caught in a dangerous area, quickly move to shore or descend to a lower elevation, ideally away from the direction of the approaching storm. A dense forest located in a depression offers the greatest protection. Stay clear of shallow caves and overhanging cliffs—ground currents might arc across them. Avoid bodies of water and metal fences, too, and anything else that might conduct electricity. In a tent, stay as far as you can from metal tent poles.

If a lightning storm catches your group in the open, spread out so that people are at least 30 feet from one another. Further minimize your risk by crouching low with only the soles of your shoes touching the ground. You can use your sleeping pad for insulation by folding it and crouching upon it.

30 OR MORE FEET APART

Incident Response for Lightning Strikes

Persons struck by lightning might suffer varying degrees of burns. Of more immediate concern is the likelihood that their hearts have stopped beating and they are no longer breathing. Treat by checking their circulation and respiration; if necessary, perform CPR (cardiopulmonary resuscitation). Once they are stabilized, attend to burns or other injuries, treat for shock, and closely monitor their vital signs until they are under a physician's care.

For more on lightning and its causes, see the chapter titled "Monitoring Weather."

6

Flash Floods

In arid regions of the country, dry streambeds and small creeks can become raging rivers in just a few minutes. The rains causing the flood might be falling right where you are, or they could be coming down miles upstream of your location. When traveling in areas where flash floods are possible, make it a point to always know how to reach the safety of higher ground. Pitch your tents above the high-water marks of past floods. In flowing streams, watch for an increase in the speed or volume of current and for other indicators of imminent flooding. Moving water can be extremely powerful; stay clear of areas that have become flooded.

Incident Response for Flash Floods

If you are caught in a flood, assume a position with your feet aimed downstream, then use them to absorb impact against objects. Should you manage to get to an island or into the branches of a tree, stay calm and wait for assistance.

For more on surviving a fall into moving water, see the chapter titled "Watercraft Adventure Safety." For more on safely crossing streams, see the chapter titled "Mountain Travel."

Avalanches

Avalanches are a serious concern for all travelers whose outings take them into snowy, mountainous regions. An avalanche occurs when snow breaks loose on a slope, or when a cornice of snow collapses and tumbles down. Large avalanches can carry away trees and tents, and even a small snowslide can bury a person caught in its path.

Your greatest protection against avalanches is knowing where, how, and when they are likely to happen and then planning routes that take you elsewhere. Indicators of danger include the following:

- Signs of previous avalanches—conditions that were right for past avalanches might well come together again to cause future snowslides.
- Steep terrain—avalanches usually happen on slopes of 40 to 60 degrees.
- Accumulations of new snow—it takes a while for fresh snowfall to consolidate enough to stabilize.
- Variations in the quality of snow layers, especially if one or more layers are airy, granular, or in slabs—a weak layer in the snowpack can allow layers above to break loose and slide.
- Air temperature rising to near or above freezing, causing changes in snowpack stability.
- Sounds that suggest cracking or settling of the snowpack.

Falling rocks pose a danger to unwary backcountry travelers. Loose stones at the base of a cliff might indicate a likelihood of rockfall. If you hear a rock clattering down, or if you accidentally kick one loose, shout "Rock!" to warn those below to take cover.

Travel in areas with significant risk of avalanche is beyond the scope of this book and calls for more specialized training.

As with any trek adventure risks, don't be reluctant to change your plans or postpone a trip when avalanche danger is high. The mountains will still be there for you after conditions have improved.

In addition to understanding the basics of avoiding avalanche zones, the following steps will help you prepare for travel in steep, snowy terrain:

- Complete an avalanche-safety training course taught by qualified experts.

- Check local avalanche-forecasting networks (operated by weather bureaus and land management agencies) before setting out. The most useful networks are updated at least once a day.

- Choose travel companions who understand the danger of avalanches and will do their part to manage the risk.

- Carry avalanche safety equipment and know how to use it. Battery-powered beacons worn by each group member emit a radio signal that can be picked up by the beacons of others.

Incident Response for Avalanches

If, despite your preparations and judgment, you see an avalanche roaring toward you and you can't get out of its path, jettison your pack. Get rid of skis, too, if you are wearing them. When the snow hits, move your arms and legs in a swimming motion to keep yourself upright, and try to keep your head above the surface. As the avalanche slows and begins to settle, push away any accumulation of snow from your face to form an air pocket that will allow you to breathe.

Should others in your party be caught in an avalanche, keep your eye on them as long as you can, and note the exact place you saw them last. Hopefully, they'll be wearing avalanche beacons so that you can recover them quickly. If not, listen for their voices, probe the area with ski poles from which you've removed the baskets, and don't give up hope. Sturdy short-handled shovels made of plastic or metal can prove invaluable for freeing avalanche victims. People have survived under the snow for 30 minutes before being rescued. Treat avalanche victims for shock and hypothermia. For more on snow shovels, see the chapter titled "Cold-Weather Travel and Camping."

Poisonous Plants

Vegetation greatly enriches outdoor experiences, but there are a few species of plants that outdoor travelers will want to avoid. Poison ivy, poison oak, poison sumac, and nettles can cause skin inflammation and itching. Don't eat wild plants, including mushrooms, unless you are positive that you can identify them and know that they are safe for human consumption. For more on vegetation, see the chapter titled "Plants."

Poison ivy

Incident Response for Exposure to Poisonous Plants

The irritants in poison ivy, poison oak, and poison sumac can take up to 10 minutes to bond with the skin. Thoroughly washing with soap and water, or with water alone, soon after exposure to these plants can minimize their effects. The same is true of nettles. Hydrocortisone cream might reduce itching. Avoid scratching affected skin, as that can increase the size of the irritated area.

Poison oak

If someone has ingested poisonous plants, induce vomiting. Save some of the vomit in a plastic bag for medical analysis, and get the person to a physician.

Asthma

Poison sumac

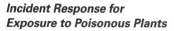

The symptoms of an asthma attack can be similar to those of a person suffering anaphylactic shock—a constriction of the throat and increasing difficulty in breathing. Conditions that might trigger an asthma attack include dust, physical exertion, changes in

The foliage of poison sumac stays green from spring through summer (left), then turns red in the fall (above).

6

humidity, and changes in elevation. Many people coping with asthma use inhalers and other forms of medication to treat asthma episodes. Before a trek begins, they should fully inform group leaders of their health histories, treatment regimens, medications, and the locations of those medications.

Anaphylactic Shock

In rare cases, stings or bites of insects can cause *anaphylactic shock,* a condition that restricts breathing passages and requires immediate treatment by a physician or a person trained in emergency first aid. People who are allergic to peanuts, shellfish, and certain other foods can have similar reactions if they ingest those items.

Travelers who know they are susceptible to anaphylactic reactions (and anyone dealing with asthma) should consult with their physicians to prepare themselves for the outdoors with strategies and treatment kits, and should share that information with the leaders of their groups. For example, the emergency kits carried by people who know they might suffer from anaphylactic shock often include an EpiPen® for injecting a measured dose of epinephrine.

EpiPen®

Animals

Seeing animals in their natural habitat is always a pleasure, but it's wise to remember that they are the permanent residents of the backcountry while we humans are the visitors. Treat animals with respect, give them enough space so they won't feel threatened by your presence, and properly manage your food storage, and they seldom will present a risk to your safety.

When it comes to insects, accept the fact that there are lots more of them than there are of us, and that some will be delighted to take a bite out of you. Reduce the likelihood of that happening by applying repellents or by wearing long pants, long-sleeved shirts, and head nets.

For more on wildlife, see the "Leaving No Trace" section of this book, and the chapters titled "Observing Nature" and "Wildlife." For more on insect repellents, see the chapter titled "Hot-Weather Travel and Camping."

Incident Response for Animal-Caused Injuries

In the event that you are scratched or bitten by an animal, seek medical attention; a physician must determine whether antibiotic, rabies, or other treatment will be necessary.

Bears

For guidelines on managing risk in bear country, see the chapter titled "Traveling and Camping in Special Environments."

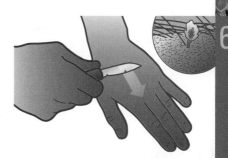

Bee and Wasp Stings

Scrape away a bee stinger with the edge of a knife blade, but don't squeeze the sac attached to the stinger—that might force more venom into the skin. An ice pack or cool compress might reduce pain and swelling. Watch for any indications of anaphylactic shock.

Tick Bites

Ticks are small bloodsucking arthropods that bury their heads in the flesh of their hosts. Protect yourself whenever you are in tick-infested woodlands and fields by wearing long pants and a long-sleeved shirt with snug cuffs and collar. Button your collar and tuck the cuffs of your pants into your boots or socks. Inspect yourself and other group members daily, especially the hairy parts of the body, and immediately remove any ticks you find.

If a tick has attached itself, grasp it with tweezers close to the skin and gently pull until it comes loose. Don't squeeze, twist, or jerk the tick, as that might leave its mouthparts in the skin. Wash the wound with soap and water, and apply antibiotic ointment. After dealing with a tick, thoroughly wash your hands. If a tick has been embedded more than a day or poses difficulties in removal, see a physician.

Lyme disease is an illness carried by some ticks. A red ringlike rash might appear around the bite. A victim might feel lethargic and have flulike symptoms, fever, a sore throat, and muscle aches. Anyone experiencing these symptoms in the days and weeks following a trek adventure, especially activities in areas where ticks are known to carry Lyme disease, should be checked by a physician.

Chigger Bites

Almost invisible, chiggers burrow into skin pores where they cause small welts and itching. Try not to scratch chigger bites. You might find some relief by covering chigger bites with hydrocortisone cream or by dabbing them with clear fingernail polish.

Spider Bites

The bite of a female black widow spider can cause redness and sharp pain at the wound site. The victim might suffer sweating, nausea and vomiting, stomach pain and cramps, severe muscle pain and spasms, and shock; breathing might become difficult.

The bite of a brown recluse spider might not hurt right away, but within two to eight hours there can be pain, redness, and swelling at the wound. An open sore is likely to develop. The victim might suffer fever, chills, nausea, vomiting, joint pain, and a faint rash.

Victims of spider bites should be seen by a physician as soon as possible.

Scorpion Stings

Scorpions might startle you if you find them underneath your tent or ground cloth, or shake them out of your boots first thing in the morning. They usually are more imposing than they are dangerous, and scorpions that can cause humans serious injury are uncommon. Ordinary scorpion stings usually are not as dangerous as bee stings; they can cause severe, sharp pain, swelling, and discoloration, but generally have no lasting ill effects. If you are stung, cool the wound area with cold water or ice and seek medical attention.

Snakebites

Snakes are found in many parts of the country, but bites from them are rare. Snakes try to avoid humans, usually striking only when cornered or surprised. Use a hiking stick to

poke among stones and brush ahead of you when you walk through areas where snakes are common. Watch where you put your hands as you collect firewood or climb over rocks and logs. Snakebites seldom result in death.

The bite of a nonpoisonous snake causes only minor puncture wounds and requires only ordinary first aid for small wounds—scrubbing with soap and water, then treating with an antiseptic.

A poisonous snakebite might cause the victim to feel sharp, burning pain. The area around the bite might swell and become discolored. However, a poisonous snake does not inject venom every time it bites. Know which poisonous snakes are native to the area you plan to hike, and know how to identify them.

Snakes are not warm-blooded and so cannot carry rabies, though any bite that breaks the skin has the potential of causing infection.

Incident Response for Poisonous Snakebite

Get the victim under medical care as soon as possible so that physicians can neutralize the venom. A person who has been bitten by a poisonous snake might not be affected by the venom for an hour or more. Within that time, the closer to medical attention you can get the victim, the better off he or she will be. The victim might be able to walk; carrying him or her also might be an option. Before setting out, do the following:

❶ Encourage a frightened victim to remain calm, and give reassurance that he or she is being cared for.

❷ Remove rings and other jewelry that might cause problems if the area around a bite swells.

❸ If available within three minutes of the bite, apply a Sawyer Extractor® directly over the fang marks and leave in place for no more than 10 minutes. Properly used, the extractor can remove up to 30 percent of the venom. *Do not* make any cuts on the bite— that's an old-fashioned remedy that can cause the victim much more harm than help.

❹ Immobilize a bitten arm with a splint and a sling, keeping the wound lower than the level of the victim's heart.

❺ *Do not* apply ice to a snakebite. Ice will not help the injury, but could cause damage to skin and tissue.

If the victim must wait for medical attention to arrive, add these treatment steps:

❶ Have the victim lie down and remain still. Position the bitten part lower than the rest of the body. If you have not done so already, immobilize the bitten limb with a splint.

❷ Put a broad constricting band (a bandanna or a strip of cloth at least 1 inch wide) around the bitten limb 2 to 4 inches above the bite (between the heart and the bite) to slow the spread of venom. This is not a tourniquet; it is intended to impede the lymphatic system but not the circulation of blood. The band should be snug, but loose enough to slip a finger under easily. Periodically check for a pulse on both sides of the band. You must not cut off blood circulation entirely. Do not use a constriction band around a finger, a toe, the head, or the trunk.

❸ Treat for shock, but keep a bitten extremity lower than the heart.

When helping victims of bites or stings, do whatever you must to avoid being bitten or stung yourself. A rescuer who becomes injured could greatly complicate any emergency situation.

Shark Attacks

Though rare, shark attacks on humans create dramatic headlines in the media. Many more people die each year from the effects of bee stings than from shark bites. Reduce even that remote likelihood of a shark attack by avoiding areas where sharks are known to congregate. Don't enter the water alone. Blood, fish bait, and human waste in the water might attract sharks, as can bright objects such as jewelry. If sharks are sighted, return to shore quickly but with a minimum of splashing.

Jellyfish Stings

Your trips along shorelines and on the open sea can bring you within proximity of a variety of animals you will enjoy observing from a distance. The Portuguese man-of-war and jellyfish have stinging cells on their tentacles. When touched, the toxins in those cells may attach to the skin and cause a sharp, burning pain.

Do not wash affected skin with fresh water, as that can cause the release of more toxin. Instead, soak the injury for 30 minutes in alcohol or vinegar, then use tweezers to remove the remaining tentacles. Quickly get the victim under medical care. People who are allergic to jellyfish stings might go into deep shock.

Keeping Risk in Perspective

Perhaps the greatest risk to be managed during trek adventures is also one of its real attractions—the simple matter of distance. The farther you travel from clinics, physicians, and rescue squads, the more you must rely upon yourself and your companions to maintain your safety. Of course, the best response to risk is to stay out of trouble in the first place. That requires planning, leadership, and an awareness of your surroundings so that you can make good decisions every step of the way. Add the first-aid training you need to respond effectively to an illness or injury that might arise, and you can make the management of risk second nature on every outdoor adventure.

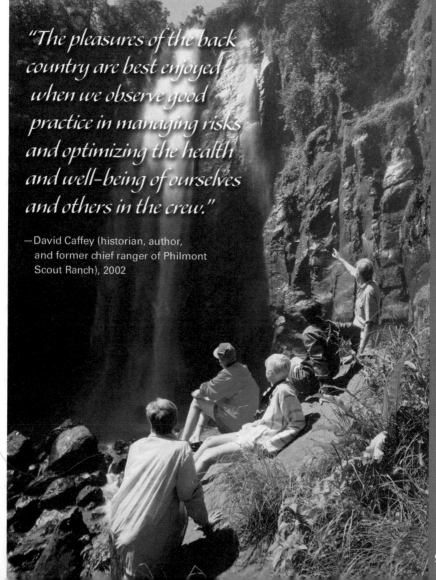

"The pleasures of the back country are best enjoyed when we observe good practice in managing risks and optimizing the health and well-being of ourselves and others in the crew."

—David Caffey (historian, author, and former chief ranger of Philmont Scout Ranch), 2002

Leaving
No Trace

"The mission of
Leave No Trace
is to promote and
inspire responsible
outdoor recreation
through education,
research, and
partnerships."

—From the mission statement of the
Leave No Trace Center for Outdoor Ethics

CHAPTER
7

Implementing Leave No Trace

"We should all realize that every right implies a responsibility, every opportunity an obligation, every position a duty, and that the most effective sermon is expressed in deeds instead of words."

—Waite Phillips (1883–1964), whose gift of property
  to the BSA became Philmont Scout Ranch

Until a few hundred years ago, nearly all of North America was wilderness. Human impact on the land was relatively minor. To start with, there weren't very many people. Their lifestyles tended to be compatible with their surroundings. Even when those early Americans did scar the land with fire or overuse, often the environment recovered soon after their activities ceased.

By about 1900, though, so much of the North American landscape had been settled and developed that many believed the era of the frontier was over, that wilderness was no longer in unlimited supply.

North Americans also began to realize the importance of wild lands as ecosystems for wildlife and vegetation. Watersheds provided clean water. Forests purified the air and provided food and shelter for many animals. Open territory allowed wild animals the space and resources they needed to survive.

Urban dwellers started looking to the backcountry as an escape from the demands of life in the cities. They gradually came to realize that mountains, forests, prairies, waterways, and deserts had recreational value. The outdoors attracted people of all walks of life. In canoes, kayaks, and rafts, they set off on lakes and rivers. They swung packs on their shoulders and headed up the trails. They climbed mountains, explored caves, and snowshoed and skied across landscapes buried in snow.

Just as backcountry travelers know that a few basic essentials carried in their packs and pockets can enhance their safety (a pocketknife, a water bottle, rain gear, etc.), outdoors enthusiasts can carry in their heads and hearts the principles of Leave No Trace to help ensure the well-being of the land.

With so many visitors, the environment began to suffer. Campsites were beaten down and trails eroded. Pressure on wildlife caused species to abandon areas that had long been important places for finding food and raising young. In short, the outdoors was in danger of being loved to death.

Today, caring for the environment has become a key aspect of enjoying the outdoors. The ability to travel and camp without leaving any sign of one's passing is among the most admired skills of outdoors experts. The principles of Leave No Trace can help you to attain that level of skill and to enjoy your adventures even more fully by knowing that, in every way possible, you are doing what's best for the environment.

Leave No Trace

Protecting the environment is a cooperative effort involving those who use the outdoors and those who manage it. Members of Scout units bring with them a clear understanding of responsible behavior. They want to take good care of the areas where they travel and camp, and will gladly do so if they know how that can be done.

Those who manage public and private lands try to balance the needs of the environment with the wishes of its users. To that end, agencies and landowners develop management plans identifying how and when various areas may be used. Their intent is to encourage people to enjoy the outdoors in ways that have little negative impact upon the land.

Leave No Trace principles provide a common base for users and managers of public and private lands to work with one another toward the goal of enjoying and protecting the land. The reward for everyone is a healthy environment that can be enjoyed today and by generations to come.

Innovations in outdoor equipment have helped change many camping habits. Efficient backpacking stoves allow wilderness travelers to cook without campfires. Secure tents with waterproof floors make lean-tos and ditching unnecessary and allow hikers to camp on durable surfaces where they will not harm vegetation. Lightweight cooking gear and group equipment allow backpackers to travel in groups that are small and compatible with a wilderness experience.

Frontcountry outings—car camping, camporees, jamborees, and the like—also can be conducted in ways that are environmentally sound while still affording a maximum of enjoyment. A goal of Leave No Trace is that *every outdoor activity,* from an afternoon gathering in a city park to a monthlong expedition in a remote wilderness, is planned and carried out in ways that provide the greatest satisfaction for participants and the highest level of protection for the environment. The guidelines for making that happen are the principles of Leave No Trace.

Everybody's Leaving No Trace

Leave No Trace—it's what the experts do. Mountaineers climbing the highest peaks in the world nearly always plan to bring down with them more pounds of trash than they create. River guides make it their business to help people camp comfortably with little impact on fragile shorelines. Long-distance hikers, desert travelers, professional trail maintenance crews, and others who live for long periods of time in the backcountry take pride in their skill at protecting the environment.

Scouts today have the knowledge and the equipment to pack light, wander far, and leave no sign of themselves as they go. Outdoors enthusiasts everywhere are embracing this as the new standard for enjoying the backcountry. They thrive on the challenge and accept the responsibility of mastering forms of outdoor recreation that leave no trace upon the land.

Leave No Trace is a national education program designed to promote practical skills and an outdoor code of ethics that preserves the integrity of protected lands and high-quality recreational experiences. The Boy Scouts of America has adopted Leave No Trace as an important tool for guiding its members in appropriate ways to enjoy and protect the outdoors.

For more information, see the *Fieldbook* Web site links to Leave No Trace.

Leave No Trace

Plan Ahead and Prepare

- *Know the regulations and special concerns for the area you'll visit.*

- *Prepare for extreme weather, hazards, and emergencies.*

- *Schedule your trip to avoid times of high use.*

- *Visit in small groups.*

- *Repackage food to minimize waste.*

- *Use a map and compass to eliminate the use of rock cairns, flagging, or marking paint.*

You would almost never set out on an adventure without first figuring out the gear you would need and the food you would carry. As part of your preparations, it should be just as automatic to plan the most effective means for conducting your outdoor activities without leaving a trace.

Thinking through the Leave No Trace principles is a good way to start. As you begin organizing an outdoor trip, ask yourself how you can apply each of the principles. Will you need any equipment? Should you alter the size of your group or change your activities to match the area you will visit? Is there a less popular time to go when you can have the area more to yourselves?

Well before your departure, contact the land management personnel of the area you intend to visit. Explain the journey you have in mind and ask how you can best implement Leave No Trace. Many agency staffers are familiar with the principles and can advise you how to use them to make the most of your time in the outdoors.

For more about planning ahead and preparing, see the chapters titled "Organizing for Adventures," "Planning a Trek," and "Outdoor Menus."

Travel and Camp on Durable Surfaces

- *Durable surfaces include established trails and campsites, rock, gravel, dry grasses, or snow.*

- *Protect riparian areas by camping at least 200 feet from lakes and streams.*

- *Good campsites are found, not made. Altering a site is not necessary.*

In popular areas:

- *Concentrate use on existing trails and campsites.*

- *Walk single file in the middle of the trail, even when it is wet or muddy.*

- *Keep campsites small. Focus activity in areas where vegetation is absent.*

In pristine areas:

- *Disperse use to prevent the creation of campsites and trails.*

- *Avoid places where impacts are just beginning.*

Some surfaces are better able than others to withstand human impact. Trails and designated campsites can increase your pleasure in the outdoors by making it easier for you to go from one place to another and to find convenient places to pitch your tents at the end of the day. When you stay on existing pathways and campsites, the surrounding landscapes will be protected from being trampled, eroded, and compacted.

Disperse use in pristine areas. When traveling off-trail, use durable surfaces such as rock, gravel, sand, bare soil, ice, snow, and dry grass. Hike abreast rather than in single file to avoid creating a new trail. When camping in pristine areas, locate your kitchen and concentrate your activities on durable surfaces. Vary your route to get water and to go to the bathroom to prevent new trails from being formed. When leaving, help return a pristine site to its natural condition by replacing any rocks that were moved and scattering leaf litter or pine needles to make the site look as natural as possible. Be sure to consult local land managers before planning to travel and camp in pristine areas.

For more about traveling and camping on durable surfaces, see the chapters titled "Planning a Trek" and "Traveling and Camping in Special Environments," and the "Trek Adventures" section of this book.

Dispose of Waste Properly

- *Pack it in, pack it out. Inspect your campsite and rest areas for trash or spilled foods. Pack out all trash, leftover food, and litter.*

- *Deposit human waste in catholes dug 6 to 8 inches deep at least 200 feet from water, camp, and trails. Cover and disguise the cathole when finished.*

- *Pack out toilet paper and hygiene products.*

- *Carry water for washing dishes or for bathing 200 feet away from the source; use only small amounts of biodegradable soap. Strain dishwater, then scatter the water when you are finished.*

"Pack it in, pack it out" is a tried-and-true guideline for responsible outdoor travel. That's easiest to do when you limit the amount of potential trash you take with you and refine your food lists so that you will eat most of your provisions during your trip.

Even more important are the ways you dispose of human waste and washwater. You can do that effectively even in fragile environments if you have learned ahead of time what to do.

For guidelines on properly disposing of waste, see the chapters titled "Hygiene and Waste Disposal" and "Traveling and Camping in Special Environments," and the "Trek Adventures" section of this book.

Leave What You Find

7

- *Preserve the past: Observe but do not touch cultural or historic structures and artifacts.*

- *Leave rocks, plants, and other natural objects as you find them.*

- *Avoid introducing or transporting nonnative species.*

- *Do not build structures or furniture, or dig trenches.*

A cluster of flowers beside an alpine trail. A few bricks from a historic farmstead. A bird nest on the low branch of a tree. A rack of elk antlers in a meadow. Petrified wood in a desert. The discoveries you can experience in the outdoors are rich and varied. Every journey will bring with it something new for you to see and enjoy. With every discovery, you can make the choice of leaving what you find. Here are some reasons why:

- Future outdoor visitors will have the excitement of discovering for themselves what you have found.

- Plant communities and wildlife environments will not be negatively impacted.

- Researchers can make the most of archaeological and biological sites.

- Archaeological, cultural, and historic artifacts preserve a record of our country's past. Some artifacts and locations are sacred to American Indians; others might contain clues to the past that anthropologists and archaeologists can help us interpret.

For more on ways to enjoy what you see and leave what you find, see the "Appreciating Our Environment" section of this book.

A disturbed artifact has been taken out of context, and this can remove chapters from important stories. So important is this concern that on public lands these resources are protected by law.

See the *Fieldbook* Web site for links to more information about resources like the Archaeological Resources Protection Act of 1979 and the National Historic Protection Act of 1966.

7

Minimize Campfire Impacts

- *Campfires can cause lasting impacts on the land. Use a lightweight stove for cooking and enjoy a candle lantern for light.*

- *Where fire is permitted use an established fire ring, a fire pan, or a mound fire lay.*

- *Keep fires small. Only use sticks from the ground that can be broken by hand.*

- *Remove partially burned garbage, including that left by others.*

- *Burn all wood and coals to ash, put out campfires completely, then scatter cool ashes.*

Today's outdoor travelers have a wide range of options for cooking without an open fire and for staying warm and creating a focus of evening activities. They also have a much greater understanding of when a campfire can be kindled and when a fire could have a lasting impact on the land.

Choices concerning campfires are among the most important made in both the frontcountry and the backcountry. Where open fires are appropriate, Leave No Trace guidelines offer clear direction for the best ways to collect firewood, establish fire lays, and manage open flames.

For more on minimizing campfire impacts, see the chapter titled "Using Stoves and Campfires."

Camp stoves enable outdoor travelers to heat water and cook meals quickly and efficiently. They can be used almost anywhere and will not blacken rocks, leave ashes, or scar the land.

Respect Wildlife

- *Observe wildlife from a distance. Do not follow or approach wild animals.*

- *Never feed animals. Feeding wildlife damages their health, alters their natural behaviors, and exposes them to predators and other dangers.*

- *Protect wildlife and your food by storing rations and trash securely.*

- *Leave pets at home.*

- *Avoid wildlife during sensitive times: mating, nesting, raising young, or wintertime.*

Among the great pleasures of Scout adventures is sharing the environment with wildlife. In fact, it goes beyond sharing. We are the visitors in most outdoor settings, while wild animals are the real residents. We are, in effect, visiting their homes.

An important aspect of Leave No Trace is to reduce the impact we might have on wildlife. Travel quietly and give animals the space they need to feel secure. Avoid nesting areas, calving sites, and other areas critical to wildlife. Picking up wild animals, chasing them, or otherwise altering their normal activities can be stressful and could compromise their ability to survive. You are too close if an animal changes its activities because of your actions or presence.

Bears, moose, raccoons, and other animals can become aggressive and dangerous if they feel provoked or threatened by people. Failure to protect your food supplies might attract bears and other animals to your camp in search of a meal, and that, in turn, can lead to their destruction.

Respect wildlife. Photograph, observe, and enjoy from a distance the permanent residents of the backcountry, and do your part to help keep wild animals wild.

For more on respecting wildlife, see the "Appreciating Our Environment" section of this book. For guidelines on traveling and camping in bear habitat, see the chapter titled "Traveling and Camping in Special Environments."

7

Be Considerate of Other Visitors

- *Respect other visitors and protect the quality of their experience.*

- *Be courteous. Yield to others on the trail.*

- *Step to the downhill side of the trail when encountering horseback riders or pack animals.*

- *Take breaks and set up camp away from trails and other visitors.*

- *Let nature's sounds prevail. Avoid loud voices and noises. Respect other visitors who might be seeking solitude.*

Extending courtesy to other hikers and campers is a natural inclination of outdoor travelers. Remember, though, that everyone in camp and on the trail is seeking a certain balance of socialization and solitude. Enjoy the company of those you encounter on the trail and at campsites near yours, but respect their desires for quiet and space.

Leave portable radios and sound systems at home. You will find it much easier to appreciate the outdoors, and you are far less likely to disturb other outdoor travelers and wildlife. A cellular telephone may be carried as

a means of emergency communication, but stow it deep in a pack until it is really needed. If you must make calls, do so out of the sight and sound of others.

For more on being considerate of other visitors, see the "Leadership and Trek Preparation" section of this book.

Erasing the Traces That Exist

The principles of Leave No Trace are intended to help people enjoy the outdoors in ways that leave no sign of their passing. Using these principles is a tremendous way to show your concern for the health of the environment and your dedication to visiting the outdoors in ways that are appropriate for you and for the land.

With the freedom to use the outdoors for recreational purposes come the responsibilities and opportunities to roll up your sleeves and help repair damage done by others. You can do a lot to help repair damage and to shield the environment from further harm. In cooperation with land management agencies, Scouts can take on projects to repair trails and campsites and to restore wildlife habitats. Effective projects require thorough planning and guidance from knowledgeable experts.

For more on caring for the environment, see the "Appreciating Our Environment" section of this book.

LEAVE NO TRACE AWARENESS AWARD
Youth and adults who master and practice responsible outdoor ethics may be eligible to receive the BSA's Leave No Trace Awareness Award. Visit the *Fieldbook* Web site for more information and applications for this award.

Using Stoves and Campfires

"Our mountaineering equipment was very simple and extremely light. . . . For fuel we had wood alcohol to be burned in aluminum stoves and also petroleum to be burned in a Primus stove. The latter proved by far the more successful."

—Frederick A. Cook, *To the Top of the Continent,* 1908 (Among the first to attempt a climb of Mount McKinley, he reminds us that decisions concerning stoves and fires have confronted campers for a very long time.)

There was a time when campers could build fires wherever they wished. The skill with which they could kindle a blaze was a mark of their woodland expertise, and the fires they created became the centers of their camp activities. They cooked over them, dried wet clothing next to them, warmed themselves by them, and gazed into the embers. Few could imagine an evening without a fire, and even so thoughtful a wilderness advocate as Henry David Thoreau saw nothing wrong with building a bonfire in the Maine woods and leaving the glowing coals behind as he moved on.

We live in a much different age from that of Thoreau. There are still times when a campfire is appropriate and even desirable. If it is built in the wrong place or in the wrong manner, however, a campfire can leave scars on the ground that will take a very long time to heal. The mark of experienced campers has become not just the ability to build a fire, but also the wisdom to know when not to light one.

Reliable, lightweight stoves offer today's campers a reasonable alternative to open fires. By considering the advantages and disadvantages of campfires and stoves and then using the heat source that's right for a given situation, you will find that your own outings will be enhanced and that you will have one more means available in your quest to travel the outdoors without leaving a trace.

8

Minimizing Campfire Impacts by Using Camp Stoves

The most effective way to minimize campfire impact is to not build a fire at all. Camp stoves make that possible. They also extend the range of outdoor travelers by giving them a reliable means of generating heat anywhere, anytime, and in any weather.

Reliabilty, ease of use, and minimum impact make stoves a good choice for most backcountry journeys.

Advantages of Camp Stoves	Disadvantages of Camp Stoves
• They will not scar the ground or damage trees. • They burn nothing native to the backcountry. • They operate reliably under adverse conditions. • They create steady heat that won't blacken rocks or cooking gear. • They are quick and convenient. • They make travelers more self-sufficient and able to camp high on a rocky mountain, deep in a treeless desert, and in the drifts of a snowy forest.	• They have to be carried. • They require the handling of flammable liquid or gaseous fuels. • Empty fuel canisters must be packed out for disposal or recycling.

Choosing a Stove

Of the many stoves on the market, those burning the following fuels are most useful. Always read and follow the manufacturer's instructions for carrying, fueling, using, and storing camp stoves.

White-Gas Stove

White gas, a refined naphtha petroleum product commonly used in lightweight stoves in North America, is available at most camping stores. Choose only white gas specifically approved by stove manufacturers. White gas is very volatile and must be carried, stored, and used with the utmost caution. Legal restrictions often prohibit transporting white gas on aircraft, ferries, and other means of public transport. Scouts planning adventures that will involve travel on boats or airplanes should research their options well in advance to determine how best to get their stove fuel to the trailhead.

Fill outdoors. Never loosen cap or fill tank near flame, pilot lights, or while stove is hot.

Carefully follow stove manufacturers' instructions when selecting fuel. Some stoves operate only with white gas, while others also burn unleaded gasoline, kerosene, or even jet fuel.

More advanced white-gas stoves are equipped with pumps to pressurize their fuel tanks, which can be a real advantage in cold weather.

Kerosene Stove

Kerosene is a hot-burning, nonexplosive fuel available almost anywhere in the world. While kerosene camp stoves are unusual in North America, they are a familiar sight on international expeditions. A kerosene stove must be preheated before it can be lit.

Cartridge Stove

Simplicity, safety, and convenience are features of butane and propane cartridge stoves. Cartridge stoves need no pumping or preheating; simply attach a fuel canister, turn the control knob, and light the burner. Cartridge stoves work well in warm weather and at high altitudes, but they lose efficiency as the temperature drops.

8

Propane Tank Stove

Two-burner propane stoves are too heavy for backpacking but can be just right for larger groups on river rafting expeditions, frontcountry camping close to a road, or remote base camps of conservation work crews supplied by pack animals.

KNOW AND FOLLOW CAMPFIRE RESTRICTIONS AND ALWAYS CARRY A STOVE

Before setting out on an adventure, check with the land managers of the area you intend to visit for current campfire regulations. Fires may be banned in sensitive environments where high use has caused excessive impact, and during dry or windy periods when there is an increased danger of wildfires. Carrying a stove allows you to cook meals even if you discover at the last minute that you can't kindle a campfire.

Using Stoves Safely

Stoves of different designs operate in different ways. Read and understand the manufacturer's instructions before lighting any stove, and then follow them exactly. In addition, *always* heed these stove safety rules:

- Position the stove in a stable location.

- Use pots appropriate in size for your stove.

- Always attend a lighted stove.

- Let a stove cool completely before you put it away. (If storing for a month or more, empty the fuel tank.)

- Never attempt to open or refuel a hot stove.

- Store liquid fuel in well-marked bottles designed for that use.

- Even if they are empty, keep fuel bottles and canisters away from sources of heat.

- Reduce fire danger at home by storing all fuel containers in a shed, detached garage, or other uninhabited structure.

- Never use a stove inside or near a tent.

8

Minimizing Campfire Impacts

An open fire creates heat, and that can be good. You can use a campfire for warmth, for cooking meals, and for the sheer joy of a fire in camp. Unfortunately for the environment, the heat of a campfire radiates not only upward, but also down into the soil where it can kill organisms that enrich the soil. Without a long period of recovery, that soil will not be able to support plant life, and the scar on the land caused by a fire might be visible for many years to come.

Advantages of Campfires	Disadvantages of Campfires
• They create heat suitable for cooking food, drying gear, and warming chilly campers. • They require no special equipment. • They provide a psychological lift on cold, stormy days and can be the focus of fellowship and contemplation.	• Fires can char the ground, blacken rocks, and sterilize the soil. Vegetation can have a hard time growing again where a fire has burned. • Fires consume dead branches, bark, and other organic material that could have provided shelter and nutrition for animals and plants. • Firewood collection can create new trails and damage trees. • Campfires must be closely watched to prevent them from spreading into surrounding vegetation. • Fire sites mar the natural appearance of an area.

Appropriate Fires

A good way to think about a campfire is to consider it a tool to be used for specific and important uses. If you are prepared to use a stove, too, or to go without an open flame at all, you can make appropriate choices about when and how to kindle a campfire.

Selecting and Preparing a Leave No Trace Campfire Site

A Leave No Trace campfire site has the following advantages:

- Fire will cause no further negative impact on the land.

- Fire cannot spread from it, and the area surrounding the site will not be further degraded by the concentrated trampling of people cooking and socializing.

The best places for your campfires are sites designated by the land managers. Many of these sites have metal rings, grills, or stone fireplaces that should be used where you find them. Otherwise, shield durable surfaces (exposed rock, for example) and more fragile earth (the forest floor or a meadow) from heat damage by using a *mound fire* or a *fire pan.*

Leave No Trace Campfire Checklist

Ask yourself the following questions before building a campfire. A *yes* answer to every question indicates a fire might be appropriate. If any of your answers is *no,* don't build a fire.

✓	YES	NO	
			Do current land management regulations permit open fires?
			Will the fire be safe?
			Will having a fire cause little or no damage to the environment?
			Is firewood plentiful?
			Can signs of the fire be erased?

8

Mound Fire

To make a *mound fire,* collect a good supply of *mineral soil*—silt, clay, or sand that does not contain organic matter that could be harmed by heat. Among the places you can find mineral soil are streambeds, gullies, beaches, and within and beneath the roots of toppled trees. Use a pot or stuff sack to carry the mineral soil to the fire site. Pour the soil onto a tarp, ground cloth, or trash bag, then form the soil into a mound 4 to 5 inches thick and 18 to 24 inches in diameter. Build your fire on top of the mound. After burning the wood to ash, extinguish any remaining coals. Crush the ashes and spread them over a wide area, then return the mineral soil to the site from which you borrowed it.

Fire Pan

A *fire pan* is a metal tray with sides high enough (more than 3 inches) to contain burning wood and ashes. Backyard barbecue grills and clean oil-drain pans can be used as fire pans on river trips, horse-packing journeys, frontcountry camp-outs, and other trips when the weight and bulk of gear are not great concerns. For backpacking, a lightweight aluminum pan designed for roasting turkeys can be folded to fit under the top flap of your pack. Protect the ground from heat by elevating fire pans on rocks or by lining them with several inches of mineral soil.

8

NO PIT FIRES

Removing sod and digging a hole to contain a blaze is no longer considered an acceptable method for reducing campfire impact. Even if the pit is carefully refilled, the replaced sod often dies and the soil beneath it settles, leaving a noticeable scar on the land. Rely instead on a fire pan or mound for open fires, or use a light-weight camp stove.

Gathering Firewood

Fire building requires three types of flammable material—*tinder, kindling,* and *fuelwood.*

Tinder

Tinder is fine, dry material that will burst into flame at the touch of a match. Pine needles, the inner bark of dead branches, weed fluff, dry grasses, and slivers shaved with a knife from a stick all make effective tinder. Gather a double handful.

Kindling

Kindling is material that will burn with a little encouragement. Twigs no thicker than a pencil are the easiest to find. You'll need a small armload.

Fuelwood

Fuelwood is dead and downed wood no thicker than your wrist that you'll use to keep your blaze burning. Since you want to keep the fire small, you almost always can gather what you need without using an ax or saw. Place fuelwood near the fire lay and, if bad weather threatens, protect it with a ground cloth or dining fly.

Limiting the Impact of Gathering Firewood

Gathering tinder, kindling, and fuelwood for a fire is not as simple as picking up the first sticks you find. Standing and downed timber can serve many purposes in an ecosystem, some of them critical to wildlife. The visual impact caused by removing wood also can be a factor in where and how you collect fuel for your fire.

Build campfires only where you can find plenty of dead wood. Avoid scouring every last stick from a campsite by walking a few minutes to areas where wood is more abundant. Use only sticks from the ground of a size that can be broken by hand—don't snap branches off of living or dead trees or strip the bark. On backcountry treks, plan to leave axes, hatchets, and saws at home. For camporees and other frontcountry campouts, consider bringing bundled firewood or bags of charcoal from home. Always be prepared to use a stove instead of a fire.

Laying and Lighting a Fire

Heat rises. That's the secret to successfully building a fire. Take advantage of that fact by placing a handful of tinder on your fire site, then arranging kindling above that and the fuelwood over that. Light the base of the tinder and make sure that your fire gets plenty of air. Flames forming in the tinder will make their way up into the kindling. As they gain strength, they will ignite the fuelwood, too. That's really all there is to starting a fire, though there are dozens of ways to organize tinder, kindling, and fuelwood into a fire lay. Here are two:

Tepee fire lay

Tepee Fire Lay

Mound plenty of small kindling over a big, loose handful of tinder in the center of your fire site. Arrange several pieces of fuelwood above the kindling to form the shape of a tepee. Leave an opening in the "tepee" to allow air in to the fire. Light the tinder, and the flame should rise through the tinder and crackle up into the kindling and fuelwood above.

Add larger pieces of fuelwood as the flames grow stronger. When the fire is strong enough for the tepee to collapse, use a stick to push the embers into a compact bed.

Lean-to Fire Lay

Push a stick at a 45-degree angle into the fire site, the upper end of the stick pointing into the wind. Place tinder beneath the stick and lean kindling against both sides of the stick. When the kindling is burning well, add fuelwood. Air drawn into the lean-to will help keep the flames going.

Extinguishing a Fire

One of the most important moments in tending a campfire occurs when you are finished using it.

Allow a fire to burn down to ash or very small coals by tossing all partially burned sticks into the fire and letting them burn to ash. Extinguish the fire by dousing the embers with plenty of water. Stir the ashes to moisten them thoroughly. Don't stop until you can *safely* place your hand on the extinguished coals. Remove any litter and scatter unused firewood where you found it.

When a fire ring or other designated fire site is full, or if you have used a fire pan or mound, broadcast cold ashes over a wide area of vegetated ground well away from camp. Return mineral soil to the location from which it was borrowed. Finally, replace any ground cover you disturbed, and do whatever else you can to restore the fire site to the condition in which you found it.

A Final Word

The ability to generate heat can enrich your outings, but with fire comes the responsibility to use it wisely. Do your part by carrying a lightweight stove on all your camping trips and using it whenever an open fire might harm the environment. You will have the convenience of a stove when you need it, the pleasure of an open fire when you want it, and the satisfaction of traveling the backcountry cleanly, responsibly, and well.

Hygiene and Waste Disposal

"Nowhere is the line between good and bad or right and wrong drawn more distinctly than in the question of the sanitary facilities of a camp."

—From *Camp Sanitation*, Boy Scouts of America, 1928

In the outdoors there seldom is much in the way of plumbing. There is no on-demand hot water for washing dishes or for bathing, and no flush toilet for getting rid of human waste. There are no garbage disposals for leftover food. Doing without those conveniences can be one of the more interesting delights of outdoor adventures. So, too, can practicing good hygiene and waste disposal as a means of protecting both the health of the outdoors and the health of you.

Maintaining good hygiene in the outdoors ensures that you are doing all you can to protect yourself, your companions, and your surroundings for the duration of every adventure. Your ability to do that increases dramatically if you have prepared yourself before a journey by getting in shape, eating well, and getting plenty of rest. Have a yearly physical checkup and keep your immunizations up-to-date.

For more on personal health and fitness, see the chapters titled "Becoming Fit" and "Outdoor Menus."

When expedition leaders and members of their groups do all they can to practice good hygiene, others in their groups are likely to follow their example.

9

What Can Make You Sick in the Out-of-Doors

The causes of illness during outdoor adventures include microscopic organisms and chemical residue.

Protozoa

Protozoa

Protozoa are single-celled organisms found in nearly every kind of habitat, but most are found in aquatic habitats. *Giardia,* a parasitic protozoan, is commonly spread from hand to mouth. Thoroughly washing your hands after using a cathole is one of the most effective ways to avoid it. *Giardia* sets up residence in your intestines, where it can cause diarrhea, nausea, and vomiting.

Bacteria

Bacteria

Bacteria are single-celled microorganisms, some of which can be passed from one person to another. They also can be contracted from streams and lakes, and can be present in the soil. Avoid bacterial infections by keeping your tetanus immunizations current, by washing your hands frequently, and by thoroughly disinfecting any cuts or scratches you might suffer.

Viruses

Viruses are submicroscopic infective agents, many of which can spread easily from one person to another. Fortunately, most viruses do not survive long when exposed to the environment.

Virus

Chemicals

Residue of agricultural pesticides and fertilizers can endure a long time in the outdoors. Heavy metals can leach into streams from mines and construction sites. Avoid still water, especially if it has a sheen of unnatural color.

Most outdoor travelers do not have the means to treat water contaminated with chemicals or heavy metals.

9

Personal Cleanliness

According to the U.S. Centers for Disease Control, the human hand is the most likely source of infectious microbes. Washing your hands is especially important after bowel movements and just before handling food.

Handwashing Stations

Encourage everyone in your Scout unit to wash regularly by setting out a pot of water and a small plastic bottle of biodegradable soap. Dispose of washwater by broadcasting it at least 200 feet away from any campsites, trails, and sources of water.

Waterless Hand Cleansers

Waterless hand cleanser, often in the form of alcohol-based gel, is available at many grocery stores and drugstores. It can be an ideal aid for maintaining hygiene in camp and on the trail. A small dab rubbed on the hands will kill most harmful germs and then evaporate, leaving hands dry without the need of a towel. A small plastic pump bottle set out in camp can be used by those about to handle food or returning from having relieved themselves. Waterless cleanser is also convenient to use on the trail, during water-craft trips, and in other situations where washing with soap and water is not a convenient option.

THREE IMPORTANT THINGS YOU CAN DO TO KEEP YOURSELF AND OTHERS HEALTHY

❶ Wash your hands.

❷ Wash your hands.

❸ Wash your hands.

Bathing

Bathing while camping usually is more important psychologically than it is from the standpoint of health. If you do want to bathe, you'll need a couple of pots of water. Carry them at least 200 feet from springs, lakes, or streams. Use biodegradable soap and the water from one pot to give yourself a thorough scrubbing. Use water from the second pot for rinsing by dipping it out with a cup. In the summer, you can let the pots of water warm in the sun before you use them, while chilly weather might call for heating the water over a stove. After your bath, broadcast the used water over a large area.

Water used to wash dishes does not need to be treated, though it is wise to allow everything to air dry before using it again. Most harmful microorganisms that exist in water cannot survive in a dry environment.

Safe Drinking Water

The safest water to use on a Scout outing is that which you have carried from home. Always start out with one or more full water bottles and replenish your supply from tested public systems whenever you can. On adventures of longer duration, streams, lakes, springs, and snowfields are potential sources of water, but be sure to treat all water you get in the wild, no matter how clean it appears to be.

Three effective ways to treat water are *boiling, chemical treatment,* and *filtering.*

Boiling

The surest means of making your water safe is to heat it to a rolling boil—when bubbles 1/2 inch in diameter are rising from the bottom of the pot. (According to research conducted by the Wilderness Medical Society, simply reaching the boiling point is sufficient to kill any organisms that water might contain.) If water used for food preparation comes to a boil at least once, it requires no further treatment. Cooking pasta noodles, for example, will kill any germs that might have been in the water when you first filled the pot.

Advantages of Boiling	Disadvantages of Boiling
• 100 percent effective • Simple to do	• Requires a stove and fuel or a campfire, as well as a pot • Takes time

Chemical Treatment

Chemical treatment tablets employ iodine or chlorine to kill waterborne bacteria and viruses.

Advantages of Chemical Treatment

- Effective against viruses and bacteria
- Simple to use
- Inexpensive, lightweight, and convenient to pack
- A good backup to carry in case you can't boil or filter water

Disadvantages of Chemical Treatment

- Not always effective against all protozoa
- Requires a waiting period before water can be considered safe to drink
- Can leave a chemical taste in the water
- Can lose potency over time

Filtering

Most portable filters are simple handheld pumps used to force water through a screen with pores so small that bacteria and protozoa cannot get through. The finer the screen, the more effective the filter. Information provided with new filters describes their use and maintenance, and the degree of filtration they can provide.

MUDDY WATERS

Allow muddy water to stand in a pot until the silt settles to the bottom. Dip the clear water off the top and remove any remaining organic debris by straining the water through a bandana into a clean container. Ensure its safety by using a filter or chemical treatment tablets, or by bringing it to a boil.

Advantages of Filtering

- Effective against protozoa and bacteria. Filters equipped to add chemical treatment might also kill some viruses.
- Filters come in a range of capacities and designs to fit the needs of groups according to their size and the duration of their journeys.

Disadvantages of Filtering

- Filters can be expensive.
- Filtering elements must be cleaned or replaced frequently.
- Pump mechanisms of filters might malfunction.

Food Handling and Storage

Caring for provisions is important both for your palate and for your health. The ways in which you store food can affect the well-being of wildlife, too.

- Plan meals around ingredients that need no refrigeration.

- Estimate portion sizes to minimize leftovers.

- Keep all food items out of the reach of animals.

For more on food handling and storage, see the chapters titled "Outdoor Menus," and "Traveling and Camping in Special Environments."

Washing Dishes in Camp

Start a trip with clean utensils, pocketknives, and kitchen gear. Larger groups at base camps or on extended journeys can set up a three-step dishwashing system:

- *Wash pot*—contains hot water with a few drops of biodegradable soap

- *Cold-rinse pot*—cold water with a sanitizing tablet or a few drops of bleach to kill bacteria

- *Hot-rinse pot*—clear, hot water

If each person washes one pot, pan, or cooking utensil in addition to his or her own personal eating gear, the work will be finished in no time. Use hot-pot tongs to dip plates and spoons in the hot rinse. Some travelers also dip their plates, cups, and utensils in boiling water before a meal to ensure they are sanitary. Lay clean utensils on a plastic ground cloth to dry, or hang them in a mesh bag or lightweight net hammock.

Smaller groups in more extreme settings can devise variations on the basic dishwashing theme, starting with menu planning. Meals that require no cooking or that can be prepared by boiling just a few cups of water can minimize cleanup chores. Scour pots and pans with a small scrub pad, sand, or snow. Managed with care, a couple of pots of hot water are all you need to clean up after most meals.

Hygienic First Aid

9

Modern first-aid training teaches important methods for protecting care providers from pathogens potentially carried in blood and other bodily fluids.

Boy Scouts of America Recommendation

Treat all blood as if it were contaminated with blood-borne viruses. Do not use bare hands to stop bleeding; always use a protective barrier, preferably latex gloves. Always wash exposed skin areas with hot water and soap immediately after treating the victim. The following equipment is to be included in all first-aid kits and used when rendering first aid to those in need:

- Latex gloves, to be used when stopping bleeding or dressing wounds

- A mouth-barrier device for rendering rescue breathing or CPR

- Plastic goggles or other eye protection to prevent a victim's blood or other bodily fluids from getting into the rescuer's eyes in the event of serious arterial bleeding

- Antiseptic for sterilizing or cleaning exposed skin areas, especially if there is no soap or water available

Thoroughly wash your hands before and after treating a sick or injured person.

Soiled bandages, dressings, and other used first-aid items should be burned completely in a hot campfire or stored in double plastic bags and discarded in the frontcountry.

"It is very important that perfect cleanliness be observed in camp, as it adds much to health and comfort."

—M. Parloa, *Camp Cookery*, 1878

All trash that is packed in should be packed out.

In a nutshell, here is what you need to know about getting rid of trash. Plan a trip carefully and you will create very little that needs to be disposed. As for the rest, if you pack it in, then pack it out. That includes the nutshell.

Proper Waste Disposal

No matter how heavy your pack feels at the beginning of a trip, it will be lighter on your way home. You will have eaten most of your food, and that should leave plenty of space for your trash and that left by others—a few flattened cans, some food wrappers, a small plastic bag containing orange peels and leftover macaroni, perhaps a broken tent pole. Anything you leave behind is trash to the next person who sees it, so don't leave anything behind.

Disposing of Human Waste

Does a bear poop in the woods? Yes, it does, and so do we. The difference is that bear scat is compatible with the outdoors, while human waste has the potential of introducing lots of nasty bacteria and protozoa. There also are strong aesthetic differences. Finding wildlife droppings can add to our appreciation of the identities, diets, and activities of animals. Finding piles of human waste, especially flagged with shreds of soiled toilet paper, will add nothing to your outdoor experience except disgust for those who care so little for the out-of-doors and its visitors.

Here, then, are the basics of how to dispose of human waste in ways that minimize contamination of the environment and limit the risk to wildlife and people.

9

Urine

If toilet facilities are available, use them. Otherwise, urinate away from trails, camps, and places where people gather. Choose rocks or bare ground; animals may defoliate vegetation in their efforts to absorb the salts left by concentrations of urine.

Solid Waste

Nobody wants to come across a pile of human waste on a trail or near a campsite. It's unsightly, it's an immediate health hazard, and it can be a major contributor of pathogens seeping into springs, lakes, and streams.

Dispose of human waste in one of three ways:

- Use existing toilet facilities.
- Use a cathole.
- Pack it out.

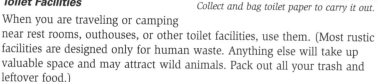

Toilet Facilities

Collect and bag toilet paper to carry it out.

When you are traveling or camping near rest rooms, outhouses, or other toilet facilities, use them. (Most rustic facilities are designed only for human waste. Anything else will take up valuable space and may attract wild animals. Pack out all your trash and leftover food.)

Cathole

Where no toilet facilities exist, dispose of human waste in a cathole. Choose a private spot at least 200 feet from camps, trails, water, and dry gullies.

With a trowel or the heel of your boot, dig a hole 6 to 8 inches deep, but no deeper than the topsoil (humus). Take care of business, then cover the hole with soil and camouflage the site with leaves or other ground cover. Organic material in the topsoil will break down the waste over time and render it harmless.

Packing It Out

In certain pristine environments—deserts, canyons, caves, alpine tundra, snowfields and glaciers—waste might not easily decompose. The leavings of large numbers of people would negatively impact the health of the environment and the quality of everyone's experience. The best way to deal with human waste in those settings is to carry it out. That requires a few simple preparations and a supply of *pack-it-out kits*.

Land managers of areas requiring you to carry out human waste will give you guidance on how to dispose of it at the end of a trip, usually by placing it in special receptacles near trailheads. Do not toss pack-it-out kits into outhouses, trash cans, or any other trash receptacles; that can create a health hazard and in many places is prohibited by law.

MAKING A PACK-IT-OUT KIT

- 1 1-gallon self-sealing plastic bag
- 1 paper bag
- 1/4 cup of cat litter
- 1 81/2-by-11-inch sheet of typing paper to use as a target

Assemble each kit by putting the cat litter in the paper bag, folding it closed, and placing the paper bag inside the plastic bag. Slip the sheet of target paper into the plastic bag, too, and seal the bag shut. Your Scout unit will need one kit per person per day, plus a few extras just in case. You should also have several sturdy plastic trash bags.

Using a Pack-It-Out Kit

❶ In an out-of-the-way place, put the target paper on the ground and secure the corners with small rocks or snow. Take careful aim and accomplish the task at hand.

❷ Put the target paper, its contents, and any toilet paper you might have used into the paper bag. The cat litter will control odors.

❸ Roll the paper bag closed and seal it inside the plastic bag.

❹ Place all used pack-it-out kits in one or more trash bags that can be packed to the frontcountry for proper disposal.

Wash your hands with soap and water or disinfect them with waterless hand cleanser.

Emvironmentally friendly human waste kits are commercially available to make carrying out your waste even easier. These kits are lightweight and can be disposed of in a trash receptacle.

Disposing of Dishwater and Washwater

The dishes are done, faces are washed, laundry is drying on a line. How best can you dispose of soapy water so that it doesn't harm the environment?

The most important step was the one you took before you began—selecting a wash site at least 200 feet from any streams, lakes, or other sources of water. Next is straining any food particles out of dishwater, using a strainer, a sieve, or a piece of fiberglass screen. Put the particles in a plastic bag along with other bits of leftover food to be packed out to the trailhead. (Water used for personal washing or for laundry does not need to be strained.) Finally, broadcast the water over a wide area.

Disposing of Leftover Food

By planning well, you should have few leftovers to manage. When you do, though, stow them in double plastic bags, along with any food particles strained from dishwater, to pack out to a trailhead.

From planning menus to carrying home leftovers, use a Leave No Trace approach to food management.

CHAPTER
10

Traveling and Camping in Special Environments

"Our camp in the cool mountain air banished the fatigues of weary miles; night, under the mountain stars, gave us refreshing sleep; and, from the morning we crossed Pitt Ferry, we dated a new life."

—Clarence King (American explorer, scientist, and, from 1879 to 1881, the first director of the U.S. Geological Survey), *Mountaineering in the Sierra Nevada*, 1872

An evening in the desert, a tent above tree line, a night under the stars. Camping in special environments can be just what the word suggests—special. Taking you far from home, removing you from the usual routines and distractions of modern life, journeys into special environments can be filled with discovery and adventure.

Of course, every environment is special in its own way, and each deserves your best effort to treat it well. The principles discussed in the chapter titled "Implementing Leave No Trace" outline the basic means you can use to enjoy any outdoor setting responsibly. The unique qualities of certain environmental areas demand that visitors make additional preparations and apply specific methods in order to use Leave No Trace most effectively. The following guidelines can help you minimize your impact when traveling or camping in the deserts, in alpine tundra regions, along shorelines, and in bear habitat.

With the freedom to enjoy the outdoors comes the responsibility to pitch in now and then to help repair damaged landscapes. The chapter titled "Being Good Stewards of Our Resources" explores many opportunities for volunteers to help the environment.

Deserts

Treks into arid regions of the continent can be among the most rewarding and challenging of journeys. The rewards come from finding yourself in the midst of magnificent scenery, difficult terrain, and complex ecosystems. The challenge is twofold. First, you must keep yourself safe in an environment not always suited to human comfort. Second, you must see to it that you do no harm to an environment that is sensitive to human impact.

Most desert landscapes consist of scattered islands of life and fertility surrounded by rock and inorganic mineral soil. Because of the general scarcity of water and organic soils, arid lands lack the capability to recover from damage caused by careless visitors. For example, slow-growing desert plants, once they have been injured, will take longer to repair themselves than those in a lush environment.

Traveling and Camping

Plants and *cryptobiotic soil crusts* that have been trampled beneath boot soles, bicycle wheels, or tents can take years to recover. Avoid disturbing desert vegetation and crusts by using existing trails and campsites whenever you can.

Where there are no trails, travel in dry washes, along bedrock, and across other areas where not much grows. Choose similar sites for camping, but avoid dry watercourses; these can flood with little warning even when storms are some distance away.

An obvious feature of deserts is the lack of water. Where it does exist, protect its purity and access, and take only what you need. Camp well away from pools and streams to reduce chances of polluting them and to allow wildlife to approach them.

Protect desert cultural heritage by viewing but not altering ancient dwellings, rock art, or other artifacts. Leave everything where you find it and camp well away from these areas.

Sanitation

Dispose of human waste in catholes 4 to 6 inches deep that are located at least 200 feet from permanent and temporary water sources, trails, or campsites. The sun's heat will desiccate waste and kill harmful microorganisms. Where land managers expect it, use pack-it-out kits.

For more on sanitation, see the chapter titled "Hygiene and Waste Disposal."

Campfires

Desert vegetation grows very slowly, and the debris from dead, decaying wood can provide critical nutrients to ensure soil fertility. Plan ahead so that you can do your cooking over backpacking stoves rather than relying on open fires.

10

Cryptobiotic soil crusts **are a unique feature of some arid ecosystems in the American West. The crusts are self-sustaining biological communities formed by living organisms, such as lichens, and their by-products. Many have the appearance of tiny, black, irregular pedestals. They reduce erosion, fix nutrients in the soil, and increase water absorption, thus creating a hospitable environment for plants.**

10

Protecting Riparian Zones

Some arid regions are broken by lush vegetation growing along the sides of streams. These *riparian zones* can be essential to the survival of wildlife and vegetation. They also can be a magnet to outdoor travelers seeking water and shade. Protect riparian zones by concentrating your impact on rock, sand, and other durable surfaces.

Alpine Tundra

The gorgeous tundra of high mountains is windy, treeless, and covered much of the year by snow. Scattered with rocks and covered in places by a thin mantle of soil, tundra can support communities of vegetation that have adapted specifically to endure the harsh conditions of cold, wind, intense sunlight, and brief growing seasons. While able to thrive on its own, tundra vegetation is especially vulnerable to damage from trampling or from poorly located tent sites.

Traveling and Camping

Stay on existing trails and use established campsites. Where no pathways exist, travel and camp on rock or snow. Spread out as you hike, going abreast rather than in single file.

Sanitation

Decomposition of human waste in alpine areas can be extremely slow. When using a cathole, find a private site where you can make the hole in organic soil. If local regulations require that you carry out your waste, use pack-it-out kits.

Campfires

Wood is extremely scarce in tundra regions and of much greater importance as a component of soil nutrition than as campfire fuel. Carry a backpacking stove on trips into the high country and save campfires for more appropriate locations.

Shorelines

Kayaking, canoeing, rafting, sailing, and other adventures on water often bring outdoor travelers to shorelines for campsites, rest areas, and portages. The recreational use of certain watercourses means that many popular stopping points and layover sites can receive a heavy amount of use. That use often is concentrated in areas important to wildlife and vegetation.

Traveling and Camping

Unnecessary impact in river corridors can be avoided by carefully preparing for your trip. For example, if river runners fail to bring proper clothing to stay warm and dry, they might be forced to build large fires that can have a negative impact on the land. Proper preparation includes knowing what to expect, repackaging food supplies, having the proper equipment, and having knowledge of the river you plan to visit.

Limit your camping to established sites. When that is not possible, seek out durable surfaces such as gravel bars and sand beaches with little or no vegetation. Otherwise, a good rule of thumb is to camp at least 100 feet from the shoreline, and 200 feet from side streams and springs.

Along ocean coastlines, camp between the highest daily tide mark and the seasonal high-tide/storm-wash line. Check with local land managers to learn where this is.

Sanitation

Travel by watercraft generally makes it easy to carry the necessary facilities to pack out human waste. Otherwise, use catholes located at least 200 feet from open water, trails, and campsites, and well above high-water lines.

Campfires

The capacities of most watercraft allow you to carry the stoves, fuel, and provisions you need to make cooking a high point of each evening's entertainment. Consider building a fire only when driftwood is plentiful or when you have packed in a supply of charcoal, and then use fire pans or mound fire lays.

Bear Habitat

One principle of Leave No Trace is to respect wildlife. That applies to animals in any setting, though it can take on added significance in special environments. These often are critical wildlife habitats—nesting areas, feeding grounds, travel corridors, haul-out sites for marine mammals. Wherever your adventures take you, enjoy wildlife from a distance and do nothing that might cause animals to alter their natural behavior. When it comes to bears, that can require added preparation, knowledge, and diligence.

Bears have come to symbolize the wildness of the outdoors. Their size, power, range, and intelligence have allowed them to thrive for eons in many regions of North America. The pressures of land development and urban expansion have reduced bear habitat.

Left to themselves, bears eat a wide range of food, including berries, grubs, fish, and small mammals. Wild bears typically are shy and try to avoid people. However, bears that get easy meals from campsites can lose their fear of humans, and that can lead to the animals' destruction.

Ensuring your own security and that of all others in your group is very important. Protecting the safety of bears is a high priority, too. Follow the principles of Leave No Trace and you will be well on your way to traveling and camping responsibly in bear country.

The following recommendations are intended to minimize bear-human encounters, but no one can guarantee that an individual will not be injured by a bear even if these recommendations are followed. Bears are wild animals. It is ultimately your responsibility to be cautious and respectful when traveling and camping in bear habitat.

Traveling and Camping

10

Do the following before going into bear country:

- Check with local land management personnel for current information on bear activity and the best ways to keep yourself and the bears safe.

- Find out what gear you will need to "bear-proof" your camp—nylon cord and food bags for *bear bags,* for example, or food storage canisters (discussed later in this chapter). Learn how to use those items, and include them on your list of bear country essentials.

- Plan menus with ingredients that won't create unnecessary odors. Avoid strong cheeses, cans of tuna fish and sardines, grease, and other smelly food items.

Do the following while you are on the trail:

- *Stay alert.* Study the terrain ahead. Be on the lookout for bears or signs of bears. Almost the only occasions for problems with bears on the trail occur when people startle a bear or come too close to a bear's cubs or sources of food.

- Make noise so that bears can hear you coming and get out of your way. Sing, whistle, clap your hands, and talk loudly. Some hikers hang small bells on their packs.

- Never leave packs or food items unattended, even for short periods of time.

Do the following while camping:

- Be especially cautious where there are signs of recent bear activity. Moist bear droppings, newly overturned rocks, and fresh claw marks on tree trunks all are indications that the bears, rather than you, have already reserved the spot.

- Accept the fact that bears will investigate your camp. Your goal is to make camp completely uninteresting to them. Bears that find nothing to eat will sniff around and then move on.

> *"Your best weapon to minimize the risk of a bear attack is your brain. Use it as soon as you contemplate a trip to bear country, and continue to use it throughout your stay."*
>
> —Dr. Stephen Herroro (professor of biology and environmental science, University of Calgary, and a leading authority on ecology and bear behavior), *Bear Attacks: Their Causes and Avoidance*, 2002

10

- Set up your sleeping tents 200 feet or more away from your camp cooking area. Allow nothing in the tents except sleeping bags and pads, flashlights, and perhaps a book or two. Since the clothing you wear during the day can pick up odors from food, sunscreen, and toiletries, change into clean sleeping clothes before going to bed. Store your day clothes along with your other gear under a rain fly near the cooking area. (Clothing that smells of spilled food should be hung in a bear bag.)

- At night and whenever you leave the cooking area unattended, put every bit of food, trash, and smellables in a bear bag at least 300 feet from your campsite, or stow them in bear canisters or in the bear boxes provided at some campgrounds. Canisters and bear boxes might have insufficient capacity to store more than a couple days' food.

- Clean up any spilled food or crumbs and store them with your trash.

- Thoroughly wash and rinse pots, plates, utensils, and other kitchenware after meals. Strain washwater and scatter it over a wide area at least 200 feet from camp. (Place any bits of food in a plastic bag and store it with the trash.)

If a bear approaches your campsite, make loud noises to discourage it from coming closer. If a bear enters your campsite, leave the area and stay away until the bear is gone. Don't risk injury by attempting to save your food or gear; it would be much easier to replace provisions and equipment than it would be to replace you.

Follow any other advice provided by the land management agencies of the bear habitat you are visiting.

How to Protect Your Food and Other Smellables

Wherever you camp, it's a wise practice between meals to stow your food beyond the reach of wildlife. If there are bears around, it is extremely important that you get all the smellables out of your tent and pack whenever you will be away from camp or are bedding down for the night. Even in the absence of bears, ground squirrels, mice, raccoons, and other animals can create havoc with unprotected provisions.

Three effective means of bear-proofing your provisions are *bear bags, bear boxes,* and *bear canisters.*

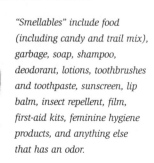

"Smellables" include food (including candy and trail mix), garbage, soap, shampoo, deodorant, lotions, toothbrushes and toothpaste, sunscreen, lip balm, insect repellent, film, first-aid kits, feminine hygiene products, and anything else that has an odor.

10

Bear Bag

While there is still plenty of daylight, find a tree with a sturdy horizontal branch about 20 feet above the ground. Put a couple of handfuls of soil in a bandanna and secure it to the end of a 50-foot length of nylon parachute cord. Toss the weighted cord over the branch. Stash your provisions in a sturdy plastic trash bag or in a waterproof stuff sack. Twist it closed and secure it to one end of the cord with a clove hitch. Pull the other end of the cord to raise the bag until the bottom of the bag is at least 12 feet off the ground and 8 feet away from tree trunks—well beyond the reach of any bears that might stand beneath it, climb the tree, or venture out onto a branch. Secure the free end of the cord to a tree.

Never leave food unattended. Hang food and all smellables well out of the reach of bears, or store them in bear-proof containers.

A second bear-bag technique requires two 50-foot cords. Toss the end of one over a high branch. Toss the second cord over a branch of equal height on a second tree at least a dozen feet away from the first. Secure one end of each cord to the bear bag. Pull on the free ends of the cords to hoist the bag, centering it between the trees. Tie off the cords.

Some designated campsites are equipped with a wire cable or pole secured horizontally between two trees at a height of 16 feet or more. Toss a cord over the center of the cable or pole and use it to hoist bear bags out of the reach of animals.

Bear boxes are most often found at frequently used campsites.

Bear Box

Some popular campgrounds in bear territory, especially those in state or national parks and forests, have metal containers that can be used for storing food and other smellables. Follow the instructions to close and lock the lids.

Bear Canister

Much of North America's bear habitat includes tundra and other regions with few trees tall enough to make bear bags effective, and so remote that bear boxes are few and far between. An effective solution to the problem of protecting food and other smellables is to carry bear canisters with you. These canisters are made of a very strong, lightweight plastic and have lids that cannot be pried open by animals. Simply place food and smellables in the canisters and leave them on the ground at least 200 feet from the tents where you intend to sleep. Relying upon canisters demands careful planning to ensure that provisions, toiletries, and all other odoriferous items carried on a trip will fit inside.

Bear canisters are ideal for protecting provisions in treeless terrain.

Sanitation

Avoid using scented lotions, soaps, deodorants, and shampoos while in bear habitat. Wash early enough in the day that residual aromas will have time to dissipate before bedtime.

10

Bear Safety Checklist

Review this list before setting out on a bear country trip. Go through it again each morning and each evening while you are in bear habitat.

✓ YES	
	While hiking, alert bears to your approach by making noise. Never approach or provoke a bear.
	Set up your sleeping area at least 200 feet away from where you will cook and eat.
	Ensure there are no smellables in sleeping tents.
	Clean up any spilled food, food particles, and campsite trash.
	Use a bear bag, bear box, or bear canister to protect all unattended smellables.
	Dispose of strained dishwater at least 200 feet from your campsite and sleeping area.
	Clean fish far from campsites. Toss entrails in flowing water, or pack them out.
	Wash early in the day. Avoid using scented lotions, soaps, deodorants, or shampoos.
	Change into clean sleeping clothes before going to bed.

Trek
Adventures

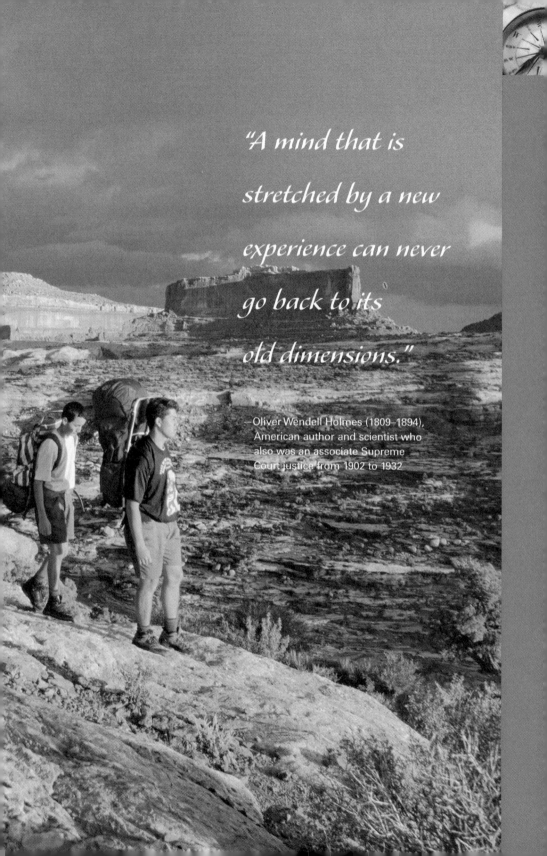

"*A mind that is stretched by a new experience can never go back to its old dimensions.*"

—Oliver Wendell Holmes (1809–1894), American author and scientist who also was an associate Supreme Court justice from 1902 to 1932

Gearing Up

"Go light; the lighter the better, so that you have the simplest material for health, comfort and enjoyment."

—Nessmuk (George Washington Sears, whose writings about his canoe adventures in the Adirondack Mountains encouraged many readers to set off on treks of their own), *Woodcraft,* 1884

As a boy wandering the Cascade Range of Washington State, future Supreme Court Justice William O. Douglas rolled his provisions inside a blanket, lashed on his frying pan and hatchet, and hiked with the bundle draped over his shoulder. Author Henry David Thoreau used a 10-foot square of white cloth for shelter on a trip into the wilds of Maine. Naturalist John Muir sometimes explored California's High Sierra carrying little but a blanket, some bread, and a bag of tea. When Scouts hit the trail in the early years of the Boy Scouts of America, many pinned together the edges of blankets to make bedrolls, kept warm with bulky woolen clothing, and set up their camps using heavy military surplus tents and gear.

While food, clothing, and shelter are still the basic needs of outdoor travelers, equipment and clothing for the outdoors have become tougher, lighter, and more versatile than ever before. Surplus gear and inexpensive clothes can still form the bulk of a group's outfit, while groups with specific requirements can find items designed to fit the most demanding activities. Add what you need for safety and comfort, and you'll be prepared for any trek.

Whatever you take probably will ride in a pack on your shoulders, or be loaded onto livestock, or be stowed aboard a sled, kayak, raft, or canoe. The lighter the load, the easier it will be to carry. The more you can do without, the less complicated your camps and the greater your ability to enjoy the outdoors without leaving a trace. John Muir's blanket, tea bag, and crust of bread is too little for most of us today, but he had the right idea—keep it light, keep it simple, but include all the essentials.

"Simplicity in all things is the secret of the wilderness and one of its most valuable lessons. It is what we leave behind that is important."

—Sigurd Olson, American nature writer and influential 20th-century conservationist

Shakedown

Get together several days before you depart on a trek and conduct a *shakedown*. Spread all your equipment, clothing, and provisions on the floor or on a ground cloth outdoors, then consider each item. Is it essential? If so, place it beside your pack. If not, put it in a separate pile. Can you cut down on weight by sharing small containers of some items with others (sunscreen, insect repellent, etc.)? Check off each item on your lists of food and gear to be sure you have all the basics and your portion of the group equipment and provisions, but nothing more.

Next, take a look through the pile of nonessentials. Some of the items could make your trip more pleasant, but you'll have to decide whether they are worth the extra weight. In the case of a plant identification book, binoculars, or a camera, the answer might well be yes. Ounces add up quickly, though; the more thorough your shakedown, the lighter your load will be. A review *after* a trip can make you aware of items you didn't use and might want to leave at home next time.

For more on deciding what foodstuffs to carry on a trek, see the chapter titled "Outdoor Menus."

Outdoor Essentials

11

The outdoor essentials form the core of gear and provisions for any outdoor journey. While you might go on many trips without using some of the essentials, you will find them of tremendous value when situations develop that you must manage using only what you have on hand.

The Outdoor Essentials

- Pocketknife

- First-aid kit

- Extra clothing

- Rain gear

- Water bottle

- Flashlight

- Trail food

- Matches and fire starters

- Sun protection

- Map and compass

A Timely Piece of Gear

Many outdoor travelers consider a watch another basic essential. Knowing the time of day allows you to note your progress and calculate when best to start back or begin making camp. A watch with an alarm can be vital if you intend to get up early to set out on the next leg of a journey.

Pocketknife

Why: Cut a cord, trim a bandage, slice some cheese, whittle a tent stake, tighten a screw on a camp stove—a pocketknife is the all-purpose tool for the out-of-doors.

What: Choose a quality knife that includes among its tools one or two cutting blades, a can opener, and a screwdriver. Keep it sharp and clean.

First-Aid Kit

Why: Carrying a few first-aid items on treks will allow you to treat scratches, blisters, and other minor injuries, and to provide initial care if more serious emergencies arise.

What: Each member of the group should carry basic first-aid items in a self-sealing plastic bag.

11

Personal First-Aid Kit

- Adhesive bandages—6
- 3-by-3-inch sterile gauze pads—2
- Adhesive tape—1 small roll
- Tweezers

- 3-by-6-inch moleskin—1
- Soap—1 small bar
- Antiseptic—1 small tube
- Roller bandage

Patrol/Crew First-Aid Kit

Each patrol or crew should carry a first-aid kit commensurate with the type of outdoor activity, the location of the outing, and the level of training of the assigned first-aider. This kit should include items for protection against blood-borne pathogens including latex gloves, a mouth-barrier device (for rescue breathing), and goggles or other eye protection. Symptoms and treatment given, along with the time and date, should be recorded using a crew first-aid log. For more on being prepared for emergencies, see the chapter titled "Managing Risk."

Extra Clothing and Rain Gear

Why: Weather conditions in the outdoors can change, sometimes with surprising quickness. Have the clothing you need to deal with extremes of weather—heat, cold, and storm.

What: See the discussion of outdoor clothing later in this chapter.

Water Bottle

Why: The amount of water you need to carry depends on the activities of the day and the sources of water you will encounter. While heat and humidity can make you more thirsty, it is very important to drink plenty of fluid in cold weather, too.

What: Water containers should be light, unbreakable, and secure.

- **Disposable water bottle.** A recycled plastic soda or water bottle is cheap and available at any grocery store. Secure a piece of parachute cord to the bottle with duct tape to form a carrying loop.

- **One-liter, widemouthed plastic water bottle.** Easy to fill and to clean; available at most outdoors or camping supply stores.

- **Collapsible water jug.** If you will be camping in a site where water must be carried some distance, a collapsible one-gallon plastic jug can be very convenient. It also protects stream and lake banks from excessive damage due to frequent trips to get water.

For information on treating water you collect outdoors, see the chapter titled "Hygiene and Waste Disposal."

Flashlight

Why: Even the best-planned trips sometimes take longer than expected. A flashlight will help you set up camp in the dark or find your way home after the sun has gone down. Carry spare batteries and an extra bulb for your flashlight.

What: Several types of flashlights are useful during treks.

- **Headlamp.** By keeping your hands free, a headlamp is terrific for night-time hiking and mountain travel, and for dealing with nighttime emergencies.

- **Penlight.** A rugged penlight designed for the outdoors casts a narrow, bright beam, takes up little space, and doesn't weigh much. It is best suited for use in camp rather than for lighting your way on the trail.

- **Regular flashlight.** A regular flashlight can serve all of your trek needs, but some are heavy. Regular flashlights are most helpful on trips when you are not limited as to how much you carry.

Trail Food

Why: You'll burn a lot of energy in the outdoors. A stash of trail food will keep you going through planned activities and is especially important if a trip lasts longer than expected.

What: Choose high-energy foods. Make your own trail mix with nuts, raisins, and diced dried fruits. Bring along a small bag of granola and an apple or an orange.

For more about food for the outdoors, see the chapter titled "Outdoor Menus."

Matches and Fire Starters

Why: Plan your clothing, shelter, and meals well enough so that you can conduct your activities without relying on an open fire, but be prepared to build one in an emergency.

What: Carry several fire starters that are reliable, durable, and protected from the elements.

- **Butane lighters.** Stow them in self-sealing plastic bags.

- **Matches.** Store these in plastic bags or in empty plastic medicine bottles with secure lids. Matches can be further protected from moisture by dipping them one by one in melted paraffin.

- **Stubby candles, pitch pine, lint,** and other personal favorites for starting fires in difficult circumstances can be sealed in plastic bags.

For guidelines on deciding when a fire is appropriate and how best to build one, see the chapter titled "Using Stoves and Campfires."

Sun Protection

Why: Sunburn is a common injury among people who enjoy being outdoors. Repeated burns can cause long-term damage and the potential for skin cancer. People with lighter skin are most at risk, though others are not immune.

What: Discourage sunburn by using plenty of sunscreen with a *sun protection factor* (SPF) of at least 15. (An SPF of less than 15 provides insufficient protection; an SPF greater than 30 adds little extra safety from the sun.) Reapply sunscreen after swimming or if you are perspiring. A broad-

Sunscreens with zinc oxide provide extra protection against the sun's harmful rays and can be applied to areas—like the nose—that burn easily.

brimmed hat, a long-sleeved shirt, and long pants provide even more protection. For travels across snowfields, in deserts, and on open water, wear sunglasses for your comfort and safety.

For more on dealing with the sun, see the chapter titled "Hot-Weather Travel and Camping."

Map and Compass

Why: The deeper you travel into the backcountry, the more important a map and compass become. Use them to find your way through unfamiliar terrain, when visibility is poor, and where expected trail signs are missing. Even when a map and compass aren't essential for route finding, practicing with them is fun and will help prepare you for times when you must rely on them.

What: You will need a compass with a good-sized baseplate, a topographic map of the area in which you intend to travel, and the knowledge to use them both separately and together.

For more on selecting and using compasses and maps, see the chapter titled "Navigation."

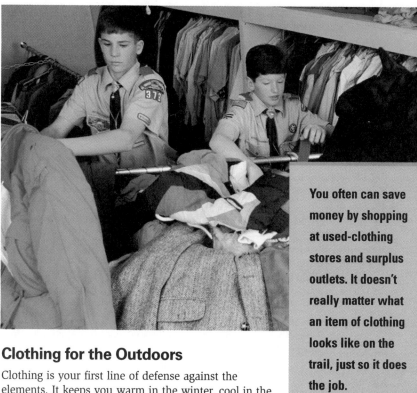

You often can save money by shopping at used-clothing stores and surplus outlets. It doesn't really matter what an item of clothing looks like on the trail, just so it does the job.

Clothing for the Outdoors

Clothing is your first line of defense against the elements. It keeps you warm in the winter, cool in the summer, dry in storms, and protected from insects, sun, and wind. To help decide what you need, learn about the materials from which clothing is made.

Wool

For generations of outdoor travelers, wool was the fabric of choice. Of course, that's about all there was for making warm clothing. Wool still is terrific for many cold-weather adventures because it is durable and water resistant, and will help you stay warm even when the fabric is wet. A wool shirt or sweater will ward off the chill of summer evenings, too. Wool also is an excellent choice in hiking socks, hats, and mittens. If wool irritates your skin, you might be able to wear wool blends or wear woolen layers over clothing made of other fabrics.

Cotton

Cotton clothing is cool, comfortable, and a good choice for hot-weather shirts and shorts in dry climates. If cotton becomes wet, though, it loses its ability to insulate, and it can be slow to dry in cold weather. In hot weather, the evaporation from wet cotton gives a cooling effect. Wearing cotton clothing can be a real danger on cool days, especially when mist, rain, and wind bring with them the threat of hypothermia. (For more information on hypothermia, see the chapter titled "Managing Risk.")

Synthetics

Outdoor clothing made of fleece, polypropylene, and other manufactured fabrics can be sturdy and comfortable, and can maintain warmth even when wet. Look for synthetics in underwear, shirts, sweaters, vests, jackets, pants, mittens, and hats. Lightweight nylon shorts and shirts are ideal for hot weather because nylon dries quickly. Waterproof and breathable synthetic fabrics are used in parkas and rain gear, and in the shells of mittens and gloves.

Layering System

For the most comfort in the outdoors with the least weight in your pack, use the layering system. Choose layers of clothing that, when combined, will meet the most extreme weather you expect to encounter. On a chilly autumn day, for example, you might set out from the trailhead wearing long pants, a wool shirt, a fleece sweater, mittens, and a stocking hat. As you hike, the effort will cause your body to generate heat. Peel off the sweater and stuff it in your pack. Still too warm? Loosen a few buttons on your shirt or slip off your mittens and hat.

When you reach your campsite and are no longer exerting yourself, stay warm by reversing the procedure, pulling on enough layers of clothing to stay comfortable. After the sun goes down, you might want to add an insulated parka and fleece pants or long underwear.

You also can use the layering system to keep cool in hot climates by stripping down to hiking shorts, a T-shirt, and a brimmed hat. Lightweight long pants and a long-sleeved shirt will shield you from insects, brush, and the sun.

For more on managing your clothing to stay comfortable in challenging weather, see the chapters titled "Cold-Weather Travel and Camping" and "Hot-Weather Travel and Camping."

The WWW of Layers

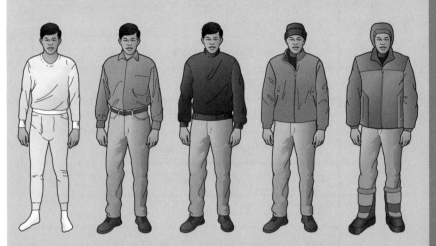

*A wicking layer, warmth layers, and a windproof layer make up
the WWW of an outdoor clothing system.*

Versatility in your clothing is the heart of a successful layering
system. Several shirts, a sweater, and a jacket will allow you
to adjust your clothing in many more ways than would a
single heavy coat. The *kinds* of layers matter, too:

Wicking layer. The layer closest to your body is made of
synthetics that can *wick,* or draw, moisture away from
your skin.

Warmth layers. Intermediate
layers have effective insulating
properties to trap the warmth
your body generates.

Windproof layer. An outer layer
prevents wind from blowing away
the heat trapped in the other layers
of your clothing.

*Wool gloves with water-repellent
shells are ideal for cold weather.*

11

✓ Basic Cold-Weather Clothing Checklist

	Long-sleeved shirt
	Long pants (fleece or wool)
	Sweater (fleece or wool)
	Long underwear (polypropylene)
	Socks (wool or synthetic blend)
	Warm hooded parka or jacket
	Stocking hat (fleece or wool)
	Mittens or gloves (fleece or wool) with water-resistant shells
	Wool scarf
	Rain gear

✓ Basic Warm-Weather Clothing Checklist

	T-shirt or short-sleeved shirt (lightweight)
	Hiking shorts
	Underwear
	Socks
	Long-sleeved shirt (lightweight)
	Long pants (lightweight)
	Sweater or warm jacket
	Brimmed hat
	Bandannas
	Rain gear

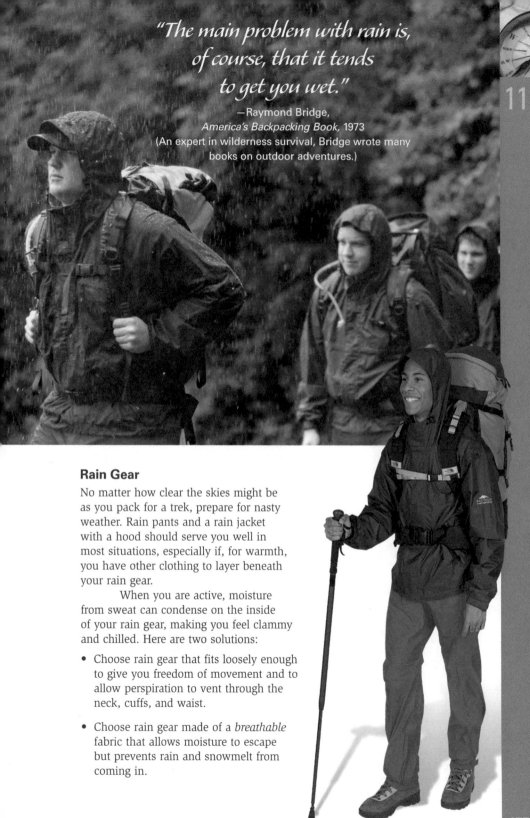

"The main problem with rain is,
of course, that it tends
to get you wet."

—Raymond Bridge,
America's Backpacking Book, 1973
(An expert in wilderness survival, Bridge wrote many
books on outdoor adventures.)

Rain Gear

No matter how clear the skies might be
as you pack for a trek, prepare for nasty
weather. Rain pants and a rain jacket
with a hood should serve you well in
most situations, especially if, for warmth,
you have other clothing to layer beneath
your rain gear.

When you are active, moisture
from sweat can condense on the inside
of your rain gear, making you feel clammy
and chilled. Here are two solutions:

- Choose rain gear that fits loosely enough
  to give you freedom of movement and to
  allow perspiration to vent through the
  neck, cuffs, and waist.

- Choose rain gear made of a *breathable*
  fabric that allows moisture to escape
  but prevents rain and snowmelt from
  coming in.

Footwear for the Field

Many outdoor treks involve miles of trail hiking. Other treks, including kayaking, rafting, mountain travel, and cross-country skiing, require specialized shoes or boots, but even then you might find that you need to walk some distance to reach a river, a mountain, or a snowfield. No matter how you spend your time in the outdoors, you'll probably want to have a pair of good, durable hiking boots. In most cases, that will mean boots made of leather or trail shoes composed primarily of nylon.

Leather Boots

Your feet and ankles can take a pounding when you are traveling over rugged terrain, especially if you are carrying a backpack. Most leather boots have a steel shank between the upper and the sole for stiffness and lateral stability—important factors when you are toting heavy loads or traveling cross-country. Leather boots also can shed water and insulate your feet in cold weather.

A drawback of leather boots can be their weight. For serious mountaineering, you might want stiff, rugged boots. For most trail hiking and camping, though, flexible leather boots at half the weight and cost should be just right.

Conventional wisdom holds that a pound of weight on your feet is equal to about 5 pounds in your pack. Don't buy more boot than you need.

Trail Shoes

A wide range of lightweight footwear builds on the technology of athletic shoes beefed up for use on trails. Combining nylon uppers with rugged soles, some trail shoes are cut higher like hiking boots, and some are cut below the ankle like running shoes. They offer varying degrees of stability, durability, and protection from the elements. This type of shoe is best suited for treks when you are carrying a day pack or a lightweight backpack.

Trail shoes

Trail running shoes

Selecting Footwear

Trek adventure footwear must fit extremely well. Boots or shoes that are too tight or too loose are an invitation to blisters. Spend as much time as you need to find the footwear that is right for you and for the activities you intend to enjoy.

When you go to a store to try on trekking footwear, put on the socks you will use in the outdoors. Find a clerk who is knowledgeable about the activities you will be doing, and who also knows a lot about how to fit shoes. Lace up a pair of boots or shoes, then walk around the store. Kick your toes forward—they should not jam against the front of the boot. Kick your heel back into the heel pocket—your foot should feel secure. The widest part of your foot should not slip, nor should it feel squeezed. Try several other models, giving each the same careful tests.

Breaking In Boots

Regardless of the design and material of your new boots or shoes, wear them several times before using them in the field. Gradually extend the length of the walks on which you wear them, and soon they'll feel like a natural part of your feet.

Caring for Outdoor Footwear

Clean your boots or shoes after every outing. Use a stiff brush to remove mud, or wash them off with water and mild soap, then allow footwear to dry at room temperature. (Placing shoes too close to a campfire can dry out leather and damage nylon.) The manufacturers of leather boots might recommend treatment with a boot dressing or waterproofing agent; follow their instructions.

Socks

Hiking socks made of wool or a blend of wool and nylon are terrific. Synthetic liner socks worn underneath them increase comfort and reduce the chances for blisters to occur by wicking moisture away from your skin.

Gaiters

Gaiters shield your feet and lower legs from rain, dew, dust, and mud; help keep gravel and snow out of your boots; and help prevent spreading seeds of noxious plants.

SPECIALIZED FOOTWEAR

Outdoor sports and activities can best be enjoyed when your footwear matches your challenges. Ski touring, horseback riding, canoeing, kayaking, rafting, caving, and cold-weather camping all benefit from the right boots or shoes.

11

Sleeping System

For the best possible rest, put together a sleeping system keyed to the temperatures and weather conditions you expect to experience.

Sleeping Bag

The cloth part of a sleeping bag is called the *shell*. The shells of most modern sleeping bags are made of nylon. Some use a breathable fabric that fends off mist and light rain. *Fill material* inside the shell traps your body heat and holds it close to you. Choices of fill materials are *goose down* and *synthetic fibers*.

Goose Down

Down is the fluffy feathers geese grow next to their skins. It provides the most warmth for the least weight of any fill material used in sleeping bags and insulated clothing. Its major drawbacks are its expense and the fact that it loses its loft and can no longer keep you warm when it becomes wet. Although down must be sheltered from the elements, usually with a good tent, it can be the best choice for cold-weather camping in relatively dry conditions and for treks requiring very light gear.

The key to camping comfort is to carry a good sleeping bag that will help you keep warm at night but not become a burden to carry during the day.

Synthetic Fibers

Synthetic fill is made of polyester fibers spun in various ways to provide warmth-trapping loft even when wet. The disadvantages of some synthetic-filled bags are their weight and bulk.

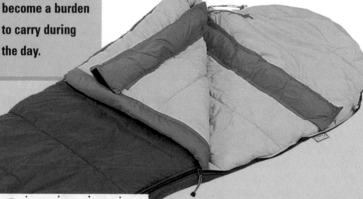

Simple quilting. *Loses heat where the stitching passes through the fabric.*

Double quilting. *Two quilts fastened together in an offset way to eliminate cold spots. Material tends to be heavy.*

Box wall. *Prevents the filling from moving about.*

Slant wall. *Prevents down from moving about and gives it room to expand.*

Overlapping tube or V-baffle. *Very effective, but because it uses a lot of material, it tends to be heavy.*

Packing and Caring for Your Sleeping Bag

Stow your sleeping bag in a stuff sack lined with a plastic trash bag. That will protect your sleeping bag even in bad storms or the capsizing of a kayak, canoe, or raft.

Air out your sleeping bag at the end of a trip. Keep it in a large cloth laundry sack or hang it in a dry, out-of-the-way spot until your next adventure.

Don't store a sleeping bag in its stuff sack; fill that is compressed for a long time loses some of its loft and insulating capacity.

With ordinary use, a sleeping bag should not need to be cleaned very often. If it has become excessively soiled or has lost a good deal of its loft, though, you might be able to restore it by laundering. per the manufacturer's directions. Some bags can be laundered using a mild, fragrance-free detergent, and washing the bag in cold water in a commercial-sized washing machine. Run the rinse cycle a second time to remove any soap residue. A wet bag is heavy and prone to damage; support its full weight as you move it from the washer to a drier. Dry it on the coolest setting and expect the drying process to take from two to five hours.

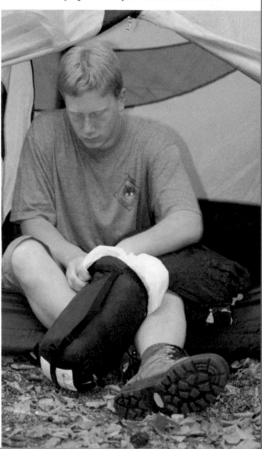

Sleeping Bag Comfort Ratings

Manufacturers often assign a *comfort rating* to a new sleeping bag— an estimate of the lowest temperature that bag is designed to address. People differ in the amount of insulation they need to stay warm, so use comfort ratings as a general, rather than absolute, guide. Sleeping inside a tent can enhance a sleeping bag's insulating power. A fleece *bag liner* can add another 10 degrees to the warmth of a bag and help keep it clean.

Bags shaped to be snug against your body tend to be warmer than looser bags. Added features, such as collars, hoods with drawstrings, and tubes of fill material backing the zippers, will further slow the loss of body heat.

Sleeping Pad

What you have beneath you at night is as important in keeping you warm and dry as what's on top. A *sleeping pad* will prevent the cold ground from drawing away body heat, and gives you a comfortable surface on which to sleep. Your best choices are *foam pads* and *self-inflating pads*.

Foam Pad

Foam pads vary in the degree of insulation and comfort they provide. *Closed-cell* foam pads tend to be effective at preventing heat loss, but at the expense of comfort. *Open-cell* foam pads are softer, but might not be as warm or as durable. Though lightweight, bulky foam pads can be challenging to stow in a pack.

Self-Inflating Pad

The choice of many outdoor travelers, a *self-inflating* sleeping pad is an airtight nylon shell covering open-cell foam. It provides maximum insulation and warmth. Self-inflating pads often are more expensive and heavier than other kinds of pads, and they should be accompanied by a small repair kit for patching punctures.

Unroll your sleeping bag early on dry days so it can fluff up as much as possible. In humid or rainy weather, however, leave the bag in its stuff sack until bedtime so it won't absorb moisture from the air.

Using Your Sleeping System

Just as you wear layers of clothing that can be adjusted to meet changing weather conditions, you can set up your sleeping system for night temperatures any time of the year. Start with a good general-use sleeping bag and leave the zipper open on warm evenings. If the night is cold, zip the bag to your chin and pull the hood snugly around your head. For more warmth, put on long underwear, a stocking hat, dry socks, and mittens. Add a fleece sweater or jacket, too, or wrap it around your hips and thighs.

Make a pillow in any weather by arranging some extra clothing (in bear country, clean clothing only) in a stuff sack or inside a sweater with the sleeves tied together.

Cross Section of the Sleeping System

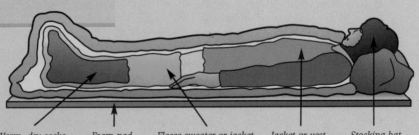

Warm, dry socks   Foam pad   Fleece sweater or jacket   Jacket or vest   Stocking hat

"A good tent is a luxury, a poor tent an abomination."

—Francis H. Buzzacott, *Complete Campers Manual: Or How to Camp Out and What to Do,* 1903 (His expeditions as an outdoor guide for 40 years included treks to the Arctic Circle and Antarctica.)

Shelter

Desert campers need shelters that are open and airy yet will shade them from the sun. Long-distance hikers, kayakers, and cyclists need shelters that are lightweight yet appropriate for many variations in the weather. The safety of mountaineers and winter campers can depend largely on tight, strong tents that will withstand the force of wind-driven snow and sleet.

Fortunately, there are shelters available for almost every traveler. Among the options for modern outdoor adventurers are tarps, bivouac bags, and tents.

Tarp

A tarp is the simplest of outdoor shelters; it weighs just a few pounds and can be set up in dozens of ways. Use it as your primary shelter or as a dining fly to protect your group's gear or cooking area from sun and storm. Rig it the way you want with lengths of parachute cord at the corners and as a ridgeline. A tarp has no floor, which can pose challenges in soggy terrain, nor does it have netting to keep insects at bay. Still, for a flexible shelter in mild or hot climates, a tarp is hard to beat.

Bivouac Bag

The *bivouac bag,* originally intended as an emergency refuge for mountain climbers forced to spend nights on cliffs far from their camps, is a waterproof envelope that slips over a sleeping bag. Most bivouac bags are made of fabrics that shed rain, dew, and snowmelt, yet allow body moisture to pass through into the night air.

Bivouac bags are very light, but they also are confining. That's something to consider if you intend to travel where you might need to stay inside for a day or two waiting out a storm.

Tent

Most campers rely on tents for their shelters. The great variety of tents on the market allows you to select one matched to your adventures. In addition to noting a tent's weight, among the factors to consider when comparing tents are *season, size,* and *shape.*

Season

Three-season tents are intended for use in the spring, summer, and autumn. Many have mosquito-netting panels to allow plenty of warm-weather ventilation.

Four-season tents are built to withstand the strong winds and snow loads of winter. Some have extra poles for added stability, and they tend to be heavier than three-season tents.

Convertible tents have panels that can be zipped closed over mosquito-netting vents. Leave them open for ventilation on warm nights, then close them to block the wind and spindrifts of snow during cold-weather trips.

Size

Tents are marketed as suitable for one, two, three, or four sleepers. Consider the way you will most often travel and the sort of group with whom you will camp.

Shape

The *A-frame* tent, essentially a pup tent made light and strong with modern materials and engineering, is roomy and usually has a waterproof floor and mosquito-netting vents and doors. Breathable fabric allows moisture to escape from inside the shelter, while a waterproof rain fly protects the tent from exterior moisture. A two-person A-frame tent weighs 5 to 9 pounds and will keep a couple of hikers and their gear dry.

Flexible poles have allowed tent makers to develop *dome*-shaped tents. These tents stand up well in rain, wind, and snow, and the spaciousness of their interiors makes them great for two to four campers. A dome tent can be flipped upside down in the morning to dry the bottom of the tent floor.

A-frame tent

Tent designers are constantly trying to improve their products by altering or combining basic tent shapes, adding features, and even removing basic features. The resulting *hybrid* tents sometimes look odd, but occasionally there are real advances that make tents lighter, roomier, stronger, and more functional. One of these tents might be exactly what you need.

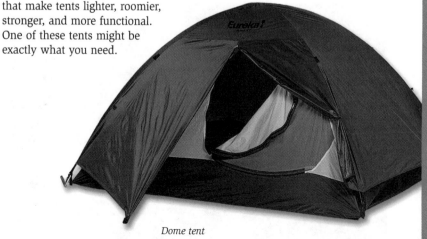

Dome tent

Choosing a Tent

With so many tents on the market, you'll want to shop around until you find the shelter that is just right for you. If you can, borrow or rent different tents and use them on overnight treks to see what they are like. Ask a salesperson to help you pitch tents in the showroom, then crawl inside and check them for size, comfort, quality of construction, and ease in setting up and taking down.

If possible, choose a tent that will blend in with the outdoor surroundings. Earth-toned shades of green, brown, gray, or blue help reduce the visual impact of a campsite.

Guidelines for Choosing a Tent

Answer the following questions before you shop for a tent to help you think through your needs:

1. In what weather extremes will you be using your tent?

2. How will you transport your tent? (Carry it yourself, split the load with others, haul it by pack animal or watercraft, etc.)

3. Do your adventures involve a base camp or do you plan to move to a new campsite every day or two?

4. How many people will share the tent?

Ground Cloth

A sheet of plastic under your tent will protect the floor from rocks and twigs and keep moisture from seeping through. Prevent rain from running between the tent floor and the ground cloth by placing the cloth so that it doesn't extend beyond the area covered by the tent, or by using the cloth to line the interior of the tent.

Gear for Cooking, Eating, and Drinking

The gear you need for cooking, eating, and drinking depends upon what you intend to cook, eat, and drink. Expect to carry personal utensils, a cook kit, and one or more stoves.

Personal Eating Gear

An insulated mug cup that won't burn your lips is just the thing for hot and cold drinks. A large plastic cereal bowl or a kitchen storage bowl is all you need for most meals, and you can dig your way through the majority of trail dishes with nothing more than a spoon.

Cooking Gear

As you plan the menus for an outdoor adventure, match your meals to your cooking gear. One or two lightweight pots will form the foundation of your kitchen. Add another pot or frying pan for more complicated meal preparations. Don't forget the lids; they hold in heat, shorten cooking times, and prevent dust and insects from blowing into your food.

Stoves

Backpacking stoves are easy to carry and convenient to use regardless of the weather. Stoves also make it easier for you to leave no trace as you are camping.

For more on cooking gear, see the chapter titled "Outdoor Menus." For more on stoves, see the chapter titled "Using Stoves and Campfires."

Water Treatment System

Any water taken from untested sources must be treated. Your options include boiling, treating with chemicals, and filtering. Each method requires planning before you leave home and carrying a few items once you embark on a trail.

For more about treating water, see the chapter titled "Hygiene and Waste Disposal."

Toiletry Kit

When it comes to toiletries, a small amount will go a very long way. You can, for example, buy the smallest tube of toothpaste you can find, or save a nearly empty tube to carry in your pack.

The following are basic toiletry items to take with you:

- Toothbrush and toothpaste
- Dental floss
- Soap
- Waterless hand cleanser
- Small towel
- Toilet paper
- Trovel for digging cathole latrines

For more on personal cleanliness, see the chapter titled "Hygiene and Waste Disposal."

Other Gear

Specific outdoor activities can be enhanced with specialized gear. Depending on what you will be doing, you might wish to carry some or all of the following items:

- Whistle
- Nylon cord
- Insect repellent
- Notebook and a pen
- Repair kit
- Hiking stick or trekking poles
- Camera
- Binoculars
- Fishing gear
- Animal identification books, plant keys, geological studies, star charts, or other guides

Journal

Much like Lewis and Clark did while exploring more than two-thirds of the American continent, many outdoor enthusiasts carry a small notebook and pen to record the events of their travels, to note unusual flora or fauna discovered along the way, to compose a bit of poetry, or to record the distance and time spent traveling each day. A journal offers an opportunity to relive the experience years later and to share it with others.

Packs, Panniers, Dry Bags, Duffels, and Saddlebags

Many journeys require special gear for transporting food and equipment. Bicyclists and horse packers might need panniers or saddlebags to hold their supplies, while winter campers might choose to haul their gear on sleds. Waterproof *dry bags* will protect the equipment and provisions of canoeists, rafters, and kayakers even if they capsize. Backpackers carry a wide range of both internal- and external-frame packs.

More information on packs, bags, and duffels can be found in other chapters of this "Trek Adventures" section.

"I never knew a camper who did not burden himself, at first, with a lot of kickshaws that he did not need in the woods; nor one who, if he learned anything, did not soon begin to weed them out; nor even a veteran who ever quite attained his own ideal of lightness and serviceability."

—Horace Kephart, *The Book of Camping and Woodcraft*, 1906
(An encyclopedia of living in the open, Kephart's popular book was a favorite of Scouts during the BSA's early years.)

Navigation

"No, I can't say as I was ever lost, but I was bewildered once for three days."

—Daniel Boone (1734–1820), frontiersman

Nature has provided many of its creatures with keen senses of direction. Species of birds migrate thousands of miles between warm southern climes and northern breeding grounds. Some butterflies also are migratory, and animals as diverse as honeybees, bats, whales, and reindeer seem to move with great certainty about where they are and where they wish to go.

Humans do not have the gift of strong directional instinct. What we do possess, however, is the ability to think clearly. By supplementing our reasoning with a few navigational instruments, we can make our way through even the most complicated wilderness terrain.

Navigation is problem solving of the highest order. It demands that you pay attention to details and make sense out of many bits of information. As with most outdoor skills, navigational competence can be developed only with practice. Increase your awareness of topography by observing your surroundings on outdoor trips and noting the lay of the land. Imagine the most likely locations for trails, campsites, portages, and summit routes, and then see if your guesses are right. Hone your ability to use maps and compasses by referring to them from the time you leave the trailhead. Before long you will seldom find yourself confused.

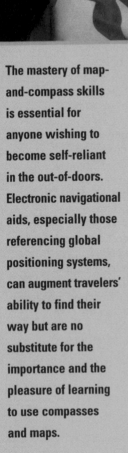

The mastery of map-and-compass skills is essential for anyone wishing to become self-reliant in the out-of-doors. Electronic navigational aids, especially those referencing global positioning systems, can augment travelers' ability to find their way but are no substitute for the importance and the pleasure of learning to use compasses and maps.

Maps

Maps are written records of places. Featuring both natural and constructed features, *planometric maps* offer an artistic representation of an area. *Topographic maps* go a step further by including three-dimensional representations of the shape of the terrain. The most useful maps for trek adventures are those based upon data prepared by the U.S. Geological Survey (USGS) of the Department of the Interior. Sporting goods stores often carry maps of nearby recreational areas. Maps for many parts of the country can be downloaded from Internet sites or ordered directly from the USGS.

For more on the U.S. Geological Survey and on downloading maps, see the *Fieldbook* Web site.

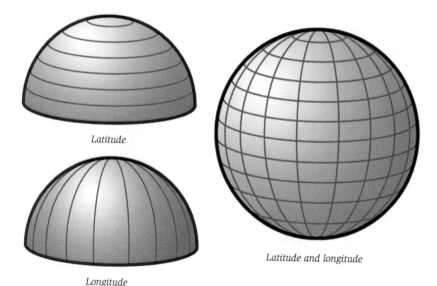

Latitude

Longitude

Latitude and longitude

Latitude and Longitude

As a means of pinpointing geographic locations, *cartographers* (those who make maps) have overlaid the globe of Earth with a grid of numbered, intersecting lines. The north-south lines—*meridians of longitude*—are drawn from the North Pole to the South Pole. Just as there are 360 degrees in a circle, there are 360 lines of longitude. The *prime meridian*—the line passing through the Royal Observatory at Greenwich, England—is *zero degrees longitude.* The numbering of meridians proceeds both westward and eastward from the prime meridian, meeting in the Pacific Ocean at 180 degrees longitude. (This 180th meridian also serves as the *international date line.*)

The east-west lines of the grid are *parallels of latitude.* The equator serves as *zero degrees latitude.* Lines running parallel with it are numbered sequentially to the poles. The North Pole is 90 degrees of latitude north of the equator; the South Pole is 90 degrees south. In a manner similar to that by which an hour of time is divided into smaller units, each degree of longitude and latitude is divided into 60 *minutes,* and each minute of longitude and latitude is divided into 60 *seconds.*

A downloaded map that you print out at home might not stand up very well to moisture. Ink can run when exposed to rain or snow, and the paper might disintegrate when wet. Fold a map so that the critical information shows, then keep the map in a self-sealing plastic bag.

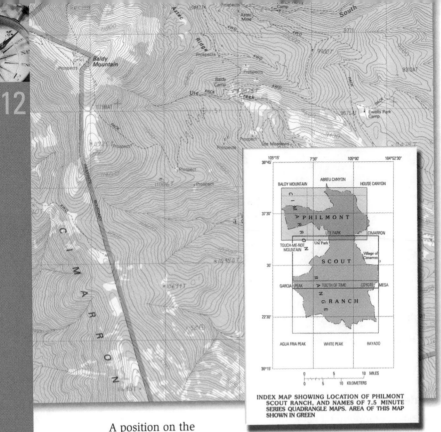

INDEX MAP SHOWING LOCATION OF PHILMONT
SCOUT RANCH, AND NAMES OF 7.5 MINUTE
SERIES QUADRANGLE MAPS. AREA OF THIS MAP
SHOWN IN GREEN

A position on the globe is stated latitude first, followed by longitude. For example, the coordinates of latitude and longitude for the summit of Baldy Mountain, the highest point on Philmont Scout Ranch in New Mexico, are *36º37'45" N* and *105º12'48" W.* That means that hikers standing atop Baldy are 36 degrees, 37 minutes, 45 seconds north of the equator, and 105 degrees, 12 minutes, 48 seconds west of the prime meridian.

The UTM Grid

Often used by search-and-rescue teams, the *universal transverse macerator (UTM)* grid is a metric coordinate system designed to pinpoint any location on Earth, with the exceptions of north and south polar regions. UTM grid lines are always 1 kilometer apart (about six-tenths of a mile) and are aligned with true north (discussed later in this chapter). Numerical notations for the UTM grid appear in the margins of many topographic maps.

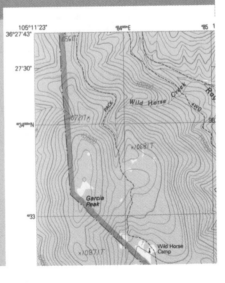

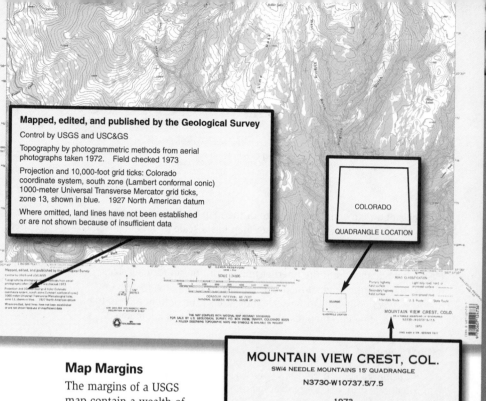

Mapped, edited, and published by the Geological Survey

Control by USGS and USC&GS

Topography by photogrammetric methods from aerial photographs taken 1972. Field checked 1973

Projection and 10,000-foot grid ticks: Colorado coordinate system, south zone (Lambert conformal conic) 1000-meter Universal Transverse Mercator grid ticks, zone 13, shown in blue. 1927 North American datum

Where omitted, land lines have not been established or are not shown because of insufficient data

COLORADO

QUADRANGLE LOCATION

MOUNTAIN VIEW CREST, COL.
SW/4 NEEDLE MOUNTAINS 15' QUADRANGLE
N3730-W10737.5/7.5

1973

AMS 4459 II SW—SERIES V877

Map Margins

The margins of a USGS map contain a wealth of useful information:

Date

Time is the enemy of map accuracy. The newer a map, the more precisely it can portray the current appearance of an area and the more exactly it will note the declination of magnetic north (discussed later in this chapter). The date printed in a map's margin indicates the year the map was created or most recently revised.

Location and Size

The geographical area covered by a topographic map is indicated by the coordinates of latitude and longitude printed in the map's corners. (Each map also will bear the name of a prominent geographic feature appearing somewhere within its boundaries—Knox Bluffs, for instance, or Waubonsie Peak.) The size of that area can be cited in the margin in terms of minutes. The maps most useful for backcountry travelers are *7.5-minute* maps and *15-minute maps:*

- *7.5-minute maps* encompass an area that is 7.5 minutes of latitude south to north, and 7.5 minutes of longitude east to west. (Since 1 minute of latitude on the ground is 6,200 feet, a 7.5-minute map will cover about 9 miles, north to south. The area covered by a 7.5-minute map ranges from 49 to 71 square miles, depending upon its latitude. The width of a minute of longitude, and thus the width of the map, will vary depending on the map's distance from the equator.)

- *15-minute maps* enclose an area that is 15 minutes of latitude south to north, and 15 minutes of longitude east to west.

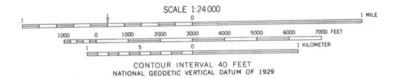

SCALE 1:24 000

CONTOUR INTERVAL 40 FEET
NATIONAL GEODETIC VERTICAL DATUM OF 1929

Scale

The *scale* of a map compares the size of the map itself to the dimensions of the land it represents. A 7.5-minute map has a scale of 1:24,000 (1 inch on the map representing 24,000 inches on the land; thus, a mile is about $2^{1}/_{2}$ inches on a map). A 15-minute map features a scale of 1:62,500. (Maps downloaded from the Internet might print out in formats sized differently from the original maps. To ensure accuracy, always use the *distance rulers* printed near the scale indicator in the bottom margin to translate the scale into map distances of feet, miles, and kilometers.)

Map Colors

Cartographers rely on different colors of ink to indicate the various landscape features of a topographic map:

■ **BLUE** *is used for aquatic features—streams, lakes, oceans, wetlands, etc. Contour lines of glaciers and permanent snowfields are also blue. Aquatic landmarks such as rivers and lakes are further denoted by having their names written in* italics.

■ **GREEN** *indicates vegetation, usually forests sufficiently dense to hide a group of travelers.*

□ **WHITE** *signifies land such as meadows and boulder fields with little or no tall vegetation. A group of travelers would be visible from the air.*

■ **BLACK** *ink is used for anything that is the work of humans—buildings, railroads, trails, etc. Names of geographical features are always written in black.*

■ **RED** *ink can be applied to certain survey lines (township and range, for instance) and to highlight primary highways and other significant constructed features.*

■ **PURPLE** *overlays revisions to a map that are based on aerial photos but have not yet been fully verified in the field.*

■ **BROWN** *is reserved for contour lines and elevations.*

Contour Lines

A topographic map is a two-dimensional model of the three-dimensional world. The sense of three dimensions is portrayed through the use of *contour lines,* which are drawn with brown ink. Each contour line represents a specific elevation above sea level. The vertical difference between adjacent lines is indicated in the margin of a map as that map's *contour interval—* anywhere from 10 feet to 200 feet, depending on the scale of the map and the ruggedness of the terrain.

Each contour line forms a loop. Hike a line and, because you will stay at exactly the same elevation, you eventually will return to your starting point. Lines close together indicate steeper areas than regions with contour lines far apart. Maps with few contour lines signify relatively flat territory such as that forming a prairie or wetland.

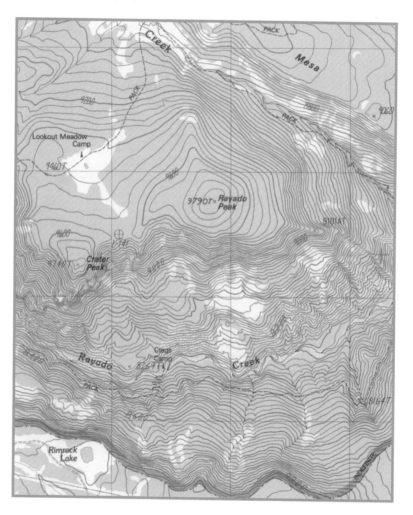

Map Symbols

For more information on map symbols, see the *Fieldbook* Web site.

TOPOGRAPHIC MAP SYMBOLS

Roads, Railroads, and Other Features

Primary highway		Railroad: single track	
Secondary highway		Railroad: multiple track	
Light-duty road		Overpass; underpass	
Unimproved road		Power transmission line	
Trail		Landmark line	Telephone

Land Surface Features

U.S. mineral prospect		Distorted surface	
Quarry; gravel pit		Gravel beach	
Mine shaft		Glacier	
Mine dump		Woodland	
Tailings		Orchard	
Tailings pond		Vineyard	
Dune area		Mangrove	
Sand area		Scrub	
Levee			

Buildings and Related Features

Buildings		Airport, paved landing strip, runway, taxiway, or apron	
School			
House of worship		Campground; campsite	
Cemetery	Cem	Winter recreation area	
Tanks	Water Tank	Ranger district office	
Wells	Oil Gas	Guard station or work center	
Picnic area			
Landmark			

Water Features

Dam with lock		Rapids		
Canal with lock		Falls		
Exposed wreck		Intermittent lake		
Rock or coral reef		Dry lake bed		
Rock: bare or awash		Marsh (swamp)		
Wide wash		Submerged marsh		
Narrow wash		Wooded marsh		
Perennial streams		Aqueduct tunnel		
Intermittent streams		Channel		
Water well; spring		Sounding; depth curve		

Elevation

Horizontal control station		Index contour	
Vertical control station	BM $\times_{671}$ $\times$ 672	Supplementary contour	
Checked spot elevation	$\times$ 5970	Intermediate contour	
Unchecked spot elevation	$\times$ 5970	Depression contours	

Boundary

Federally administered park, reservation, or monument (internal)	

Meaning of Map Colors

Green	Major vegetation (forest, brush, orchard)
Blue	Water (lake, stream, spring, marsh, water tank)
Red	Highways or boundaries
Black	Human-made structures and place names (buildings, roads, trails, bridges, railroads)
White	Absence of major vegetation, (prairie, meadow, tundra— above timberline)
Brown	Contour lines and standard elevations

Determining Distance

A compass bearing can point you in the direction you wish to travel, but it can't tell you how far along that route you will need to go in order to reach your destination. For that, you can refer to the distance rulers in the map's margin.

❶ Place one end of a piece of string on the map at your starting point.

❷ Lay out the string on top of the route you plan to use, bending the string to conform with any twists and turns of the route.

❸ Pinch the string where it touches the map symbol for your destination.

❹ Stretch the string on the bar scale in the bottom margin of the map and measure it to the point where you are pinching it. That's the approximate length of your route.

Compasses

For directional guidance, early explorers relied on the North Star, the prevailing winds, the movements of ocean currents, the migrations of birds, and other observations of the natural world. When they could, they followed sketchy maps and the reports of fellow wanderers. Then came the compass, appearing a thousand years ago in Asia and a century later in Europe. At first it was nothing more than a magnetized bit of metal floating on a piece of wood in a bowl of water. By Columbus's time it had evolved into an instrument

The sextant is a navigational device used since Columbus' time.

sufficiently reliable to guide the explorer's three ships across the Atlantic. Today, the liquid-filled compass is an indispensable navigational tool.

Celestial Navigation

Before compasses, people who needed to move from one place to another often guided their travels by looking to the stars. Perhaps you can already identify the North Star and prominent northern constellations, such as Ursa Major and Cassiopeia. Maybe you know how to find Orion and Scorpius in the southern sky. Whenever they are visible, these and other skymarks can serve as reliable references of direction.

For more on stars and constellations, see the chapter titled "Watching the Night Sky."

The compass most useful for adventure-trek navigation consists of a magnetized needle balanced inside a circular, rotating housing mounted atop a baseplate. The plate is etched with a *direction-of-travel arrow*. The floor of the compass housing is engraved with an *orienting arrow* and, parallel with it, several north-south *orienting lines*.

The circumference of the housing is divided into directions—north, south, east, and west—and further divided into 360 degrees, just as in any circle: $0°$ coincides with north, $90°$ with east, $180°$ with south, $270°$ with west, and $360°$ is again north ($0°$ and $360°$ overlap as they close the circle). Any direction can be expressed in degrees. For example, $95°$ is a little south of straight east, while $315°$ is midway between west and north.

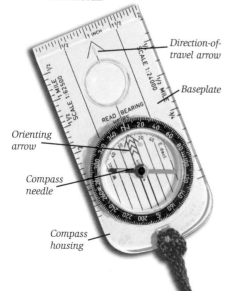

Direction-of-travel arrow

Baseplate

Orienting arrow

Compass needle

Compass housing

"There has always been a romantic fascination to persons who could find their way through the wilderness and over hidden trails—the Indian, the pioneer scout, the guide, the tracker, the explorer."

—Bjorn Kjellström, orienteering enthusiast and founder of the Silva compass company

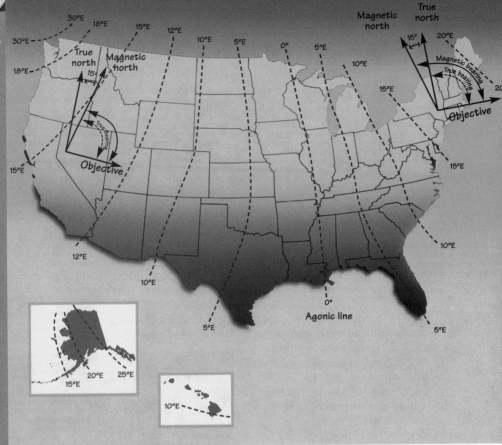

Because magnetic north continually drifts westward across the United States, declination for a particular area is always changing. The National Geographic Data Center's Web site (http://www.ngdc.noaa.gov/seg/potfld/geomag.shtml) provides up-to-date declination information to help you determine your true bearing.

Declination

Somewhere north of Canada's Hudson Bay lies the center of a natural magnetic field strong enough to pull the tip of a compass needle toward itself. This area is called *magnetic north,* and it is toward magnetic north that all compass needles point. Magnetic north is more than a thousand miles away from the North Pole, or *true north.* (You can find the approximate location of magnetic north on a globe or other map of the world at latitude 78° N, longitude 104° W.)

Draw an imaginary line from the North Pole to the point where you are standing. Draw a second line from magnetic north to your position. The difference between those two lines, expressed as the degrees of the angle they form, is the *declination* for a particular location.

In the American Midwest, the lines drawn from the two norths will be close to one another and the declination small. In fact, a line drawn northward through Mississippi and Wisconsin will intersect both the magnetic and geographic North Poles. Along that *agonic line,* a compass needle pointing at magnetic north will also be pointing at true north.

However, if you move west of the agonic line, the angle between a line drawn from your location to the geographic North Pole and a line from your location to magnetic north will gradually increase. At Philmont Scout Ranch in New Mexico, the magnetized compass needle will point about 10 degrees to the right of true north, while in Seattle it will point about 18 degrees to the right. Take the compass east of the agonic line to New York City, and the needle will swing about 14 degrees to the left of true north. On the coast of Maine, the declination will have increased to 18 degrees or more.

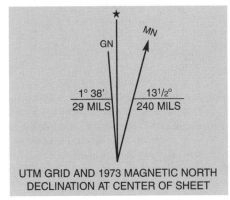

UTM GRID AND 1973 MAGNETIC NORTH DECLINATION AT CENTER OF SHEET

Citations in the margins of many USGS maps indicate the declination of an area.

On older USGS maps, a margin diagram of two arrows indicates the declination for that map's area. The arrow representing true north may be labeled *True North,* or topped by a representation of the North Star. The arrow indicating magnetic north will probably be labeled *Magnetic North* or *MN.* The angle formed by the two arrows is the declination for that map. (Newer maps might include degrees of declination, but not the arrows, in their margins.)

Dealing With Declination

Where declination is greater than a few degrees—that is, anywhere except in a narrow corridor near the agonic line through the center of North America—failing to account for declination can lead to errors in navigation that could render a compass and a map almost useless. Over the course of a mile's travel, an error of just a few degrees can pull you off your intended route by hundreds of yards.

Most maps are drawn with true north as their reference and can be said to "speak the language of true north." (Remember those lines of longitude extending to the North Pole? They form the left and right borders of the majority of maps.) Compasses, however, rely on a magnetized needle and thus have magnetic north as their native language. To use a map and compass together, you must resolve this difference, either by changing the compass or by changing the map.

Magnetic north is drifting westward at a rate that changes declination in much of the United States by about one degree each decade. Note the date of a map; the older the map, the less accurate its stated declination.

Marking a Compass for Declination

A basic baseplate compass can be marked to help travelers adjust for declination. On the compass housing, place a tiny *declination dot* of indelible ink, brightly colored enamel paint, or fingernail polish at the degree reading that matches the declination of the area where you intend to travel. For example, if the declination is 15 degrees to the east of true north, place the dot at 15 degrees on the circumference of the compass housing. If the declination is 15 degrees to the west of true north, place the dot at 345 degrees— that is, 360 degrees (true north) minus 15 degrees. A careful look at the declination information in the map margin should make it clear whether magnetic north is to the left or to the right of true north.

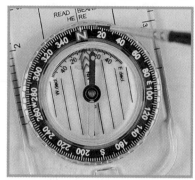

Marking a compass for declination

When your adventures take you to a region with a different declination, remove the original declination dot of ink, paint, or polish with a cotton swab dipped in denatured alcohol. Replace the dot with a fresh one correctly positioned on the compass housing.

Turn the compass housing so that *N* (true north) touches the direction-of-travel arrow. Then, holding the compass in the palm of your hand, turn your body until the red tip of the magnetic needle points at the declination dot. The needle is pointing to magnetic north, but the rest of the compass is speaking the language of true north.

Adjusting a Compass for Declination

For a few dollars more than the price of a basic compass, you can purchase a compass that can be corrected for declination. Follow the manufacturer's instructions to make the adjustment, usually by turning a small screw or gently twisting an inner portion of the compass housing to change the position of the orienting arrow etched on the housing floor.

Adjusting a compass for declination

After you have adjusted it, turn the entire housing of the compass so that north on the circumference of the housing (indicated by *0°* or the letter *N*) is aligned with the direction-of-travel arrow on the baseplate. For the moment, think of that as the line drawn to true north. The angle the true-north line forms with the newly adjusted orienting arrow should be the same as the angle formed in the map margin by the true-north and magnetic-north lines.

Changing the Map for Declination

Another way to deal with declination is by teaching a map to understand the language of magnetic north. Use a protractor (and the skills you learned in geometry class) to transfer the angle of declination to the map, then use a straightedge ruler to extend a magnetic-north line across the map. Draw additional lines parallel with the first line, a ruler's width apart. Use these *magnetic-north lines* as your references when using an unadjusted compass (that is, one that is also speaking the language of magnetic north) to orient the map and find your way.

(*Note:* The margin arrows indicating the angle of declination of older maps might not be drawn to scale. Though good for suggesting the general aspect of declination, they are not a reliable guide for extending magnetic-north lines across a map.)

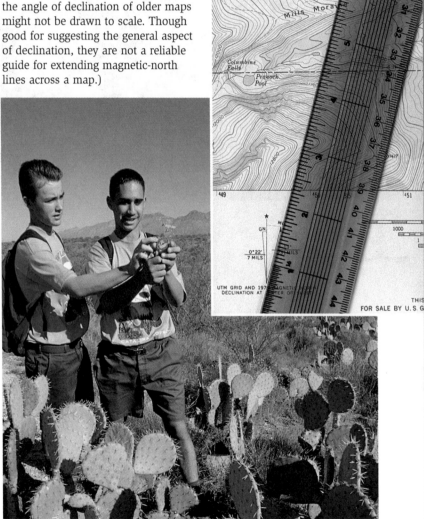

Draw magnetic-north lines on a map with the help of a protractor and a straightedge.

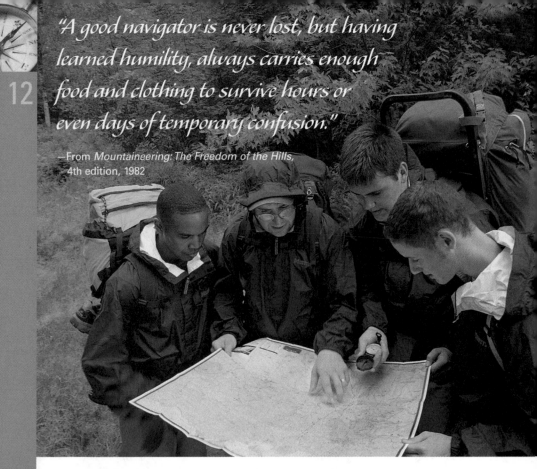

Using Maps and Compasses Together

Maps and compasses used together serve as a much more powerful navigational aid than either a map or a compass alone.

Orienting a Map

A map that is *oriented* is aligned with the topography it represents. North on the map points toward the North Pole. Landscape features in the real world have the same directional relationships to one another as are indicated on the map.

To orient a map, first rotate the compass housing until *N* lines up with the direction-of-travel arrow on the baseplate. The *compass bearing* is north.

Next, place the long edge of the compass baseplate alongside any true-north line on the map—the left or right border, any line of longitude, township boundaries, etc. Turn the compass and the map as a unit until the red tip of the compass needle points toward the declination dot (for declination-marked compasses) or the compass needle settles inside the orienting arrow on the floor of the compass housing (for declination-adjusted compasses). When that happens, the map is oriented. (If you have adjusted the *map* for declination but not the compass, line up the baseplate with any magnetic-north lines you have extended across the map and allow the compass needle to settle inside the orienting arrow.)

True-North Lines

True-north lines on a map are any lines that parallel meridians of longitude—most notably the map's vertical boundaries. Based on longitude meridians, north-south township lines and UTM grid lines also can be used as true-north lines. In the field, a map without many true-north lines can prove difficult to use with a compass. Prepare the map ahead of time by using a straightedge and a pencil to scribe lines on the map running parallel with the map's north-south borders.

Identifying Landmarks

Have you ever seen a mountain range and wondered what each summit was called? With a compass and a sharp eye, you can identify any landmark prominent enough to appear on your map. Here's how:

Hold the compass in the palm of your hand, and point the direction-of-travel arrow on the baseplate at the landmark in question. Turn the compass housing until the red end of the needle points at the declination dot (for declination-marked compasses) or until the needle is aligned with the orienting arrow (for declination-adjusted compasses). That will give you the *bearing* from your position to the landmark.

Next, place the compass on your map with the long edge of the baseplate touching the spot that represents your present location. (The map does not need to be oriented.) Ignoring the needle, rotate the compass baseplate around that point on the map until the orienting arrow and orienting lines are parallel with any true-north lines on the map. Beginning from the map symbol for your location, draw an actual or imaginary line *away from yourself* along the edge of the baseplate. The line should intersect the point on the map representing the landmark.

To identify landmarks with a compass that has not been adjusted for declination, use the *magnetic-north lines* you have drawn across the map instead of the *true-north lines*. The same is true of other map-and-compass procedures, including pinpointing your location and finding your way.

Take a bearing on the landmark.   Orient the map.   Identify the landmark.

Avoiding Obstacles

To avoid an obstacle such as a lake or rock outcropping, take a 90-degree reading to both sides of your course of travel and count your paces as you go. When you have cleared the obstacle, continue on your original bearing until you completely bypass the obstacle. Then take a reverse 90-degree reading and take the same number of paces as you did previously. At that point, continue on your original course of travel.

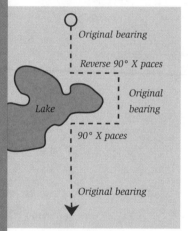

Pinpointing Your Location

If you're not sure where you are but you can see a couple of features on the land that are also indicated on your map, it's easy to determine your location. First, point the baseplate direction-of-travel arrow on your compass at one of the landmarks—a mountaintop, the outlet of a lake, a building, etc. Then, holding the baseplate still, turn the compass housing until the red tip of the needle points at the declination dot (for declination-marked compasses) or until the needle lines up in the outline of the orienting arrow (for declination-adjusted compasses). You've just taken a bearing on the landmark.

Now place the compass on your map with the edge of the baseplate touching the symbol representing the landmark. (The map does not need to be oriented.) Ignoring the needle, rotate the entire compass around that point on the map until the orienting lines on the floor of the compass housing are parallel with any true-north lines on the map. Lightly pencil a line *toward yourself* along the baseplate edge from the landmark symbol.

Find a second landmark and repeat the process of taking a bearing, placing the compass on the map, and drawing a line toward yourself. The spot on the map at which the two lines intersect indicates where you are. To confirm your readings, repeat the procedure with another landmark.

Finding Your Way

Assume you know where you are. On the map you see a lake you would like to reach by the most direct route. Place the long edge of your compass baseplate on a real or imaginary line connecting the map points representing your present location and that of the lake. Turn the compass housing until the orienting lines in the compass housing parallel any true-north lines on the map.

Hold the compass at waist level with the direction-of-travel arrow on the baseplate pointing *away from you*. Without changing the compass setting, turn your body until the compass needle aligns itself with the orienting arrow (for declination-adjusted compasses) or the red tip of the needle points to the declination dot (for declination-marked compasses). When that happens, the direction-of-travel arrow will be aimed at the lake. You have just taken a bearing for the route to your destination.

Look up along the direction of travel. If you can see the lake, you need make no further use of the compass. If the lake is out of sight, though, locate an intermediate landmark toward which the direction-of-travel arrow is pointing—a tree, boulder, or other feature—and walk to it. Take another bearing, identify the next landmark in line with the direction-of-travel arrow, and go to it. Continue until you reach your destination.

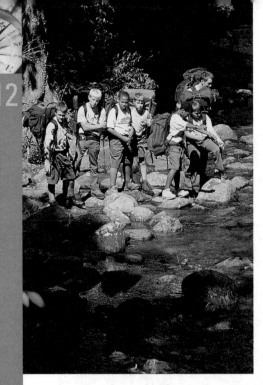

Offset Technique

Hiking uphill, crossing streams, ducking under brush, and scratching bug bites as you navigate your way through the backcountry can cause *lateral drift,* an accumulation of small errors in taking and following compass bearings that can throw you off your intended course. Compensate for lateral drift by using *offset technique*—deliberately aiming a little to the left or right of your destination.

For instance, assume the lake you want to reach is very small. You notice on the map that a creek flows from it to the left, perpendicular to your line of travel. Rather than take a bearing on the lake itself and risk missing it by passing too far to the right, set a course for a point on the creek a few hundred yards below the lake. When you reach the creek anywhere along its length, all you need to do is follow it upstream until you arrive at the lake. (Streams, power lines, fences, drainage ditches, trails, roads, and ridges all make good *backstops* or *handrails* for offset technique.)

Measuring Distances in the Field

Counting your steps is a good way to estimate distances as you travel. Learn the length of your step this way:

1. Using a tape measure, mark a 100-foot course on the ground.

2. Walk at a normal speed from one end of the course to the other, counting your steps as you go.

3. Divide the total number of steps into 100 and you'll know the length of one step.

For example, if you used 50 steps to go 100 feet, your step length is 2 feet. If it took you 40 steps, figure 2½ feet per step. In the field, you can measure distances by counting every step along the way, or by counting each time your right foot touches the ground. (A 2½-foot *step* becomes an easier-to-count 5-foot *pace.*)

Global Positioning Systems (GPS)

Modern technology has provided travelers with a powerful electronic means of navigation—the global positioning system. A GPS receiver accurately calculates the latitude and longitude of any spot on the globe by taking bearings on satellites orbiting 12,000 miles above Earth. Small enough to carry in the pocket of a pack, a GPS receiver can be used to

- Identify precise locations.

- Note elevations above sea level.

- Chart routes by inputting coordinates of latitude and longitude, or by downloading entire maps.

- Plot the record of a trek, creating a history that can guide a group retracing its steps.

Electronic navigational instruments surely will continue to improve in accuracy, versatility, and ease of use. But just as having a calculator does not eliminate the need to know how to add and subtract, a GPS receiver (especially one with dead batteries) is no substitute for being able to navigate with traditional tools. Develop confidence in your ability to use maps and compasses and then, if you wish, augment them with a GPS receiver.

For more on augmenting navigational skills with the global positioning system, see the *Fieldbook* Web site.

CHAPTER 13

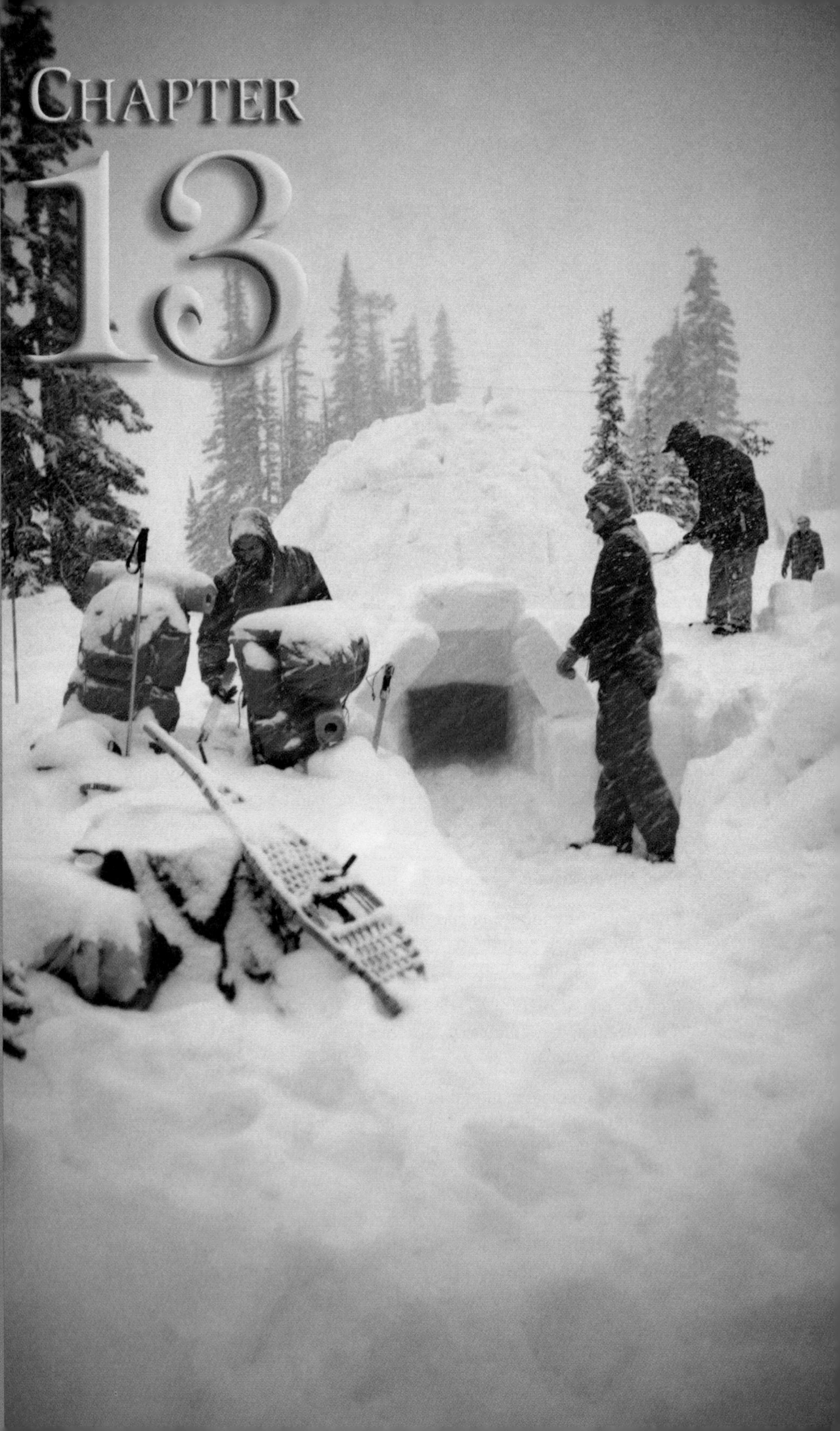

Cold-Weather Travel and Camping

"Those hours spent monitoring the skies taught me a lot about the weather and have literally saved my life during my explorations, when I've been trapped in snowstorms thousands of miles from the nearest weatherman."

—Will Steger, writer, photographer, polar explorer, and member of the BSA Northern Tier National High Adventure committee

Cold-weather camping is among the most challenging and rewarding of outdoor activities. In northern latitudes and at higher elevations, camping in the cold can happen almost any time of the year. As temperatures drop and winter conditions move in, the familiar meadows, campsites, and trails of summer disappear beneath the drifts and can become a wonderland sparkling with ice and snow. A day of traveling by snowshoes or skis, a hot meal cooked over a backpacking stove, steaming mugs of soup made from melted snow, and a camp beneath a frosty sky are pleasures reserved for those willing to learn how to thrive when even the thermometer seems to be in hibernation.

Living well in the cold requires planning and experience. You can do the planning with others in your group and master the skills you need on short trips and journeys when conditions are not so severe. As for experience, you'll gain plenty of that when you pack up your winter gear, pull on your warm clothing, and head for the chilly outdoors to see how well your plans play out. It won't be long before you discover the satisfaction of being in the outdoors year-round, staying comfortable no matter what the weather throws your way.

Many outing clubs, colleges, and universities sponsor public classes in winter camping, as do some sporting goods stores and military units. A number of BSA local councils conduct cold-weather camping programs. Philmont Scout Ranch and the Northern Tier National High Adventure Program bases offer courses in the best techniques of winter camping. The *Fieldbook* Web site can lead you to plenty of online resources exploring winter gear, books, and training for cold-weather adventure.

Staying Warm in Cold Weather

To function well, your body must maintain a core temperature of a little higher than 98 degrees. Chief among the sources of that heat are the conversion of food and water to energy, and warmth absorbed from external elements such as the sun, the earth, and campfires.

Heat can be transferred away from your body in several ways:

- *Radiation*—body heat dissipating into cooler surrounding air (from bare hands and head, for example)

- *Evaporation*—sweating

- *Convection*—wind stealing away the layer of warmth next to your skin

- *Conduction*—direct contact with cold surfaces, such as sitting or lying on snow, ice, or frozen earth

- *Respiration*—exhaling

The challenge of staying warm in cold weather is a matter of maximizing heat generation and minimizing heat loss. That can be done with a threefold approach—*cold-weather clothing, food and fluids,* and *shelter.*

13

Cold-Weather Clothing

The clothing you wear and carry should be made of materials such as wool and fleece that can insulate even when damp. Do not wear cotton, even for inner layers, because it will retain body moisture. There should be several layers so that you can better regulate your body temperature—peeling off a sweater as you generate heat during exertion, for example, or pulling on a hat, mittens, and a parka as you are beginning to cool down. Various layers also should wick away moisture, insulate for warmth, and block the wind, as discussed earlier in this section of the *Fieldbook*.

Clothing insulates by trapping dry, warm air inside the fabric and between layers of garments. Perspiration can crowd out that warmth by filling fabric with moisture-laden air that conducts heat away rather than maintaining it. Cut down on sweating during periods of exertion by loosening or removing clothing layers *before* you become overheated. Try to stay comfortably cool by resting now and then as you travel. Replace damp clothing with items that are clean and dry.

For more on selecting outdoor clothing, see the chapter titled "Gearing Up."

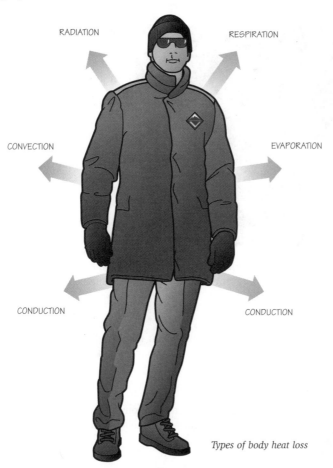

RADIATION

RESPIRATION

CONVECTION

EVAPORATION

CONDUCTION

CONDUCTION

Types of body heat loss

Staying Warmer by Keeping *COLDER*

Keep the word *COLDER* in mind when assembling your clothing system for outings in winter conditions. Each letter in the word stands for an important guideline to follow in order to maximize warmth:

CLEAN. Clothing free of grime insulates best.

OVERHEATING. Avoid it. Clothes will stay drier and warmer.

LAYERS. Rely on loose, light layers for the greatest range of adjustment.

DRY. Use protective layers to shield clothing from external moisture.

EXAMINE REGULARLY. Pay attention to the condition of your clothing.

REPAIR QUICKLY. Take care of tears, broken fasteners, frayed edges, and other damage as soon as you notice them. Duct tape is ideal for temporary patches in the field.

Cold-Weather Headgear

Heat loss by radiation from an uncovered head can be enormous, much greater than from any other area of the body. Experienced winter travelers know that when hands and feet begin to chill, it's time to put on a hat.

Stocking Hat

Hats made of wool or fleece will insulate your head even if the material becomes damp.

Balaclava

A *balaclava* is a stocking hat that can be pulled completely over your head and neck, leaving only a small portion of your face exposed.

Hood

A parka for winter wear should have a permanently attached hood to block the wind and provide insulation. A ruff encircling the face will protect it from harsh winds and gather frost from your breath rather than allowing it to saturate the hood's shell.

Scarf

Wrap a wool or fleece scarf around your neck for warmth. Pull it up beneath your eyes to shield your face from the wind. Tuck the ends inside the front of your clothing.

Neck Warmer

A fleece or knit-wool neck warmer has enough stretch for you to pull it over your head, and enough insulating power to slow the loss of heat from your neck and lower head.

13

Cold-Weather Footwear

The keys to warm feet in the winter are keeping them dry, keeping them insulated, and keeping the blood circulating through them. Thin liner socks will wick moisture away from your skin. Winter-weight socks made of wool, synthetics, or blends of both materials insulate well as long as they stay dry, and will retain some insulating power even when damp. Boots and other winter footwear should fit well enough so that circulation is not constricted even when your socks are bulky.

Mukluks

Layers of insulation between your feet and the cold ground slow the rate at which heat is drawn away from your feet. The rubber soles of hiking boots provide some protection from the cold ground. Even better are foam insoles. Buy them at sporting goods stores or make your own by cutting pieces of an old closed-cell foam sleeping pad and shaping them to fit inside your footwear.

Plastic mountaineering boots

Leather hiking boots might be the most frequent choice for winter camping trips, snow-shoeing, and mountain travel. (Follow manufacturers' instructions to waterproof your boots, giving special attention to the seams.) Other winter footwear choices to consider, especially as the temperature drops, are mukluks, shoepacs, plastic mountaineering boots, insulated cross-country skiing boots, and vapor-barrier boots.

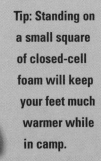

Tip: Standing on a small square of closed-cell foam will keep your feet much warmer while in camp.

Shoepacs

Cross-country skiing boots

Leather hiking boots

Shoepacs

13

Cold-Weather Handgear

As distant outposts of your body's circulatory system, your hands are likely to feel the chill early and often. Prepare for the worst with cold-weather handgear that is the best.

Gloves and Mittens

Synthetic or wool gloves trap body heat and still allow a maximum of hand flexibility. Mittens will keep your hands warmer than gloves of the same weight because your fingers are together inside mittens and can share warmth through direct contact. The disadvantage of mittens is that they decrease your dexterity for picking up items and manipulating gear.

Mittens and gloves are the clothing items most likely to get wet during cold-weather activities. Stow a backup pair in your pack when your travels will take you into snowy or wet terrain. To keep from losing mittens or gloves, thread a length of parachute cord through your sleeves and use an alligator clip tied to each end of the cord to secure your handgear.

Zippers on clothing, tents, and packs can be a challenge to manage when you are wearing bulky mittens or gloves. Give yourself something larger to grip by tying a loop of nylon cord to each zipper pull.

Shells

Many models of gloves and mittens are sewn into waterproof shells. Separate shells worn over mittens or gloves are a good choice because they serve as a layer that you can remove if you become too warm. Also, mittens and gloves that become damp are easy to remove from shells for drying.

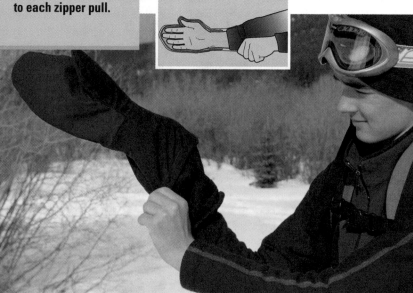

Mittens allow fingers to share warmth through contact.

Cold-Weather Food and Fluids

The most efficient cold-weather heat generator is the one you always carry with you—your own body. Keep it well-fueled by eating plenty of nourishing food. Peanut butter, nuts, cheese, hard sausage, and butter or margarine add fats that provide lots of slow-burning calories. Carry plenty of snack food where you can reach it easily, and eat whenever you feel hungry or chilled. A stick-to-the-ribs evening meal and a bedtime snack will help you stay warm through the night.

Drinking fluids is every bit as important in cold weather as during hot-weather adventures. Thirst is an unreliable measure of your body's need for fluid, especially when conditions are cold. A better gauge is the color of your urine. If it is dark yellow, you aren't getting enough fluid in your system. Drink frequently so that your urine stays light-colored or clear.

For more on fluids and trek menus for any weather, see the chapter titled "Outdoor Menus."

Gathering and Storing Winter Water

A good place to replenish your water supplies is a stream flowing too swiftly to freeze. To dip from a stream without the risk of falling in, hang a widemouthed water bottle by a cord from a long stick or a ski pole.

You also can get water by melting clean snow. If you have a cup of water, add it to a pot full of snow before melting the snow over a stove. That will speed the melting process and prevent the pot from scorching. Ice and slab snow will produce more water than powder snow.

13

A bottle of water won't freeze overnight if you take it with you into your sleeping bag. Fill it with hot water, tighten the lid, slip it into a sock, and use it for a foot warmer. You can also count on the insulating power of snow by burying widemouthed water bottles or a covered pot of water under a foot of snow. Place the bottles upside down, clearly mark the spot, and in the morning when you dig up the cache you'll have water for cooking breakfast.

For information on treating water, see the chapter titled "Hygiene and Waste Disposal."

"Just what causes most people to refrain from outdoor life in winter is the fear of cold."

—Claude P. Fordyce, *Touring Afoot,* 1916

Cold-Weather Shelters

13

Four-Season Tents

Tents for winter camping usually are sturdier than summer-weight tents. Some have an extra pole or two to help them stand up to snow loads and wind, and there might be a vestibule for storing gear. Tents designed for arctic conditions have large vents so that water vapor can escape, and frost liners to trap moisture before it can infiltrate the tent fabric.

Cover the dead man with a generous layer of snow.

Tie loops of cord through the tent loops so you need only cut the cord if you cannot remove the dead man anchor.

Since tent pegs are intended to hold in the ground rather than in snow, staking out a tent on a snowfield can be a challenge. Try tying tent lines to skis, ski poles, or ice axes jammed into the snow, or to trees or large rocks. Another possibility is the *dead man,* made by securing a tent line around sticks buried in a foot or more of snow. Use brightly colored parachute cord instead of white tent cord so that the lines will be visible against the snow. Lines should be longer for snow camping to accommodate a wider range of anchoring options.

13

Snow Structures

Shelters made of snow can be ideal refuges on winter camping trips and a unique part of a cold-weather adventure. With an interior temperature just below freezing, a snow shelter insulates much better than a tent, which will have an inside temperature almost matching that of the outdoors. Unlike tents, snow shelters won't flap in the wind. They do take time to construct—several hours for a snow cave, half a day or more for an igloo—and the right snow conditions must be present. In snow that's not too deep, the best snow structure might be a snow dome.

DRY CLOTHES

Building a snow shelter can be a strenuous effort that might leave you with wet clothing. Plan ahead by bringing dry clothes and mittens to replace those dampened by sweat and snowmelt.

Snow Shovel

An essential tool for building snow caves and other winter shelters is a snow shovel. The shovel you choose should be strong, light, and durable. Those designed to be packed by cross-country skiers, snowshoers, and mountaineers are just right.

Snow Saw

When the snow is deep and well-packed, use a snow saw or an ordinary carpenter's saw to cut blocks for constructing wind breaks, igloos, and snow trenches. Snow saws are available at military surplus stores and at outdoors supply shops specializing in winter adventures. The best carpenter's saw to use has a stiff blade and large teeth. Make a sheath for your saw by cutting a piece of old fire hose to length and tying it in place with short nylon cords secured through holes in the hose.

Snow Dome (Quinzee)

Begin by shoveling up a mound of snow 6 feet high and 10 to 12 feet in diameter at the base. Leave it alone for a couple of hours to give the snow a chance to settle the drier the snow, the longer it will take). If they are readily available or you have brought them from home, push several dozen 18-inch-long sticks into the mound at regular intervals, aiming them toward the center. Do not break branches off trees for this purpose.)

Cut a 24-inch-high entrance into the mound and hollow out the inside of the dome. Dig until you've exposed the ends of all the sticks, or until the snow inside of the dome takes on the light blue color of light refracted through snow. Either way, you should end up with a roomy, secure shelter inside an 18-inch-thick shell. Fashion a door by piling snow on a ground cloth, gathering up the corners, and tying them with a cord. The snow will crystallize into a ball that can be pulled with the cloth against the entryway to trap warm air inside the dome. Punch several ventilation holes in the dome with a ski pole or stick, orienting them at different angles so that drifting snow will not cover them all.

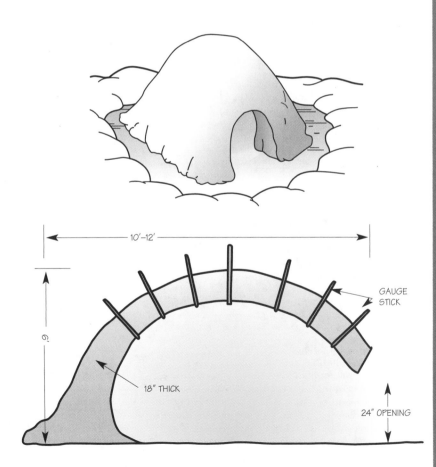

10'–12'

GAUGE
STICK

18" THICK

24" OPENING

T-Front Snow Cave

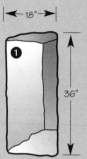

A variation on the classic snow cave design can be quick and efficient:

❶ Dig an entrance about 18 inches wide and as high as your chest.

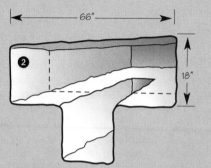

❷ Widen the top to form a T shape.

❸ Dig several feet farther into the drift and excavate the interior of the cave. The floor of the cave will be at about waist level, so much of your digging will be upward and to the sides.

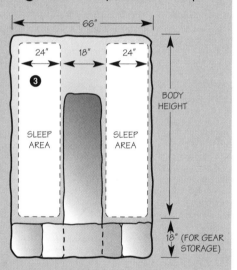

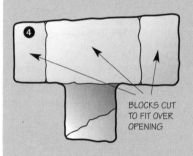

BLOCKS CUT TO FIT OVER OPENING

❹ When the interior space is fully formed, use blocks of snow, bags of snow, or snowballs packed together to seal the top of the T.

❺ Use a ski pole or shovel handle to poke several ventilation holes in the ceiling at a 45-degree angle to the floor.

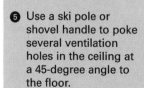

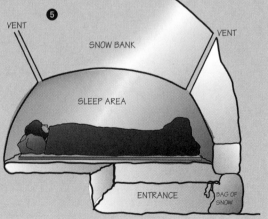

Snow Cave

For terrific protection in the worst winter storms, dig a snow cave into a deep drift or a steep, stable snow slope. Start by burrowing a tunnel into the drift, angling it upward for several feet. Next, excavate a dome-shaped room at the top of the tunnel, judging the thickness of the roof by watching from the inside for a light blue color of the snow that indicates the wall thickness is about right. Smooth the curved ceiling to remove sharp edges that could cause moisture to drip onto your gear. Finally, use a ski pole or shovel handle to punch several ventilation holes in the ceiling at a 45-degree angle to the floor. Since the entrance to the cave is lower than the sleeping area, rising warm air won't escape through the entrance and heavier cold air can't seep in.

Igloo

Although you'll need practice to build an igloo, the finished structure will be as windtight and pleasant to use as it is attractive. The best snow for building an igloo is found on open, gentle, windswept slopes. For the snow to be firm, temperatures must be no higher than 25 degrees Fahrenheit during the day and no higher than 10 degrees Fahrenheit at night—snow hard enough that your boots leave only faint prints. Test the hardness and depth by pushing the handle of a ski pole into it; there should be firm resistance for at least 36 inches.

For an igloo large enough to sleep five campers, first clear away any soft surface snow from an area about 20 by 40 feet. This will be the "quarry" from which you'll harvest snow blocks for the igloo.

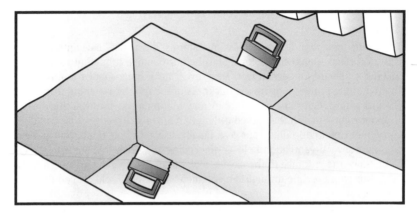

Use a snow saw or a full-sized carpenter's saw to cut from the quarry blocks measuring about 6 by 30 by 36 inches. The first block or two won't come out cleanly; clear away the debris with a shovel until you can hop into the hole left by the removal of the initial blocks. From then on you can cut each block cleanly along its back, sides, and base, and lift it from the quarry. Line up the blocks on the slope above the quarry. Keep the sides of the quarry square as you work, and make the blocks uniform in size. You will need 40 to 50 full-sized, well-shaped blocks.

After the blocks are cut, use a piece of cord and a ski pole to scribe a circle 10$\frac{1}{2}$ feet in diameter. The outside of the circle should be about 8 feet up the slope from the quarry. Tramp down the snow along the outside of the line marking the circle, then set the snow blocks side by side around it to form the first tier of the igloo. Using the saw for precision shaping, taper the base of each block slightly and lean it inward just a little so that all the blocks lock solidly against one another. Pack snow against the outside of the blocks.

Next, remove one of the blocks to create an opening in the tier. Carry as many blocks as possible into the igloo; it's much easier to build with them when both you and the blocks are inside the structure. Replace the entrance block, then use the saw to cut two side slopes in the first tier of blocks. Called *spirals* these slopes are essential to the success of your igloo-building efforts.

Trim the tops of the first tier's blocks with the saw so that they are banked inward toward the center of the igloo. That done, begin the second tier by placing a block at the low point of a spiral. If the spiral rises from left to right, note that the upper left-hand corner and the lower right-hand corner of each second-tier block bear the weight of that block. When those two corners are secure, gravity will lock the block in place on the sloping spiral and banked top of the first tier. Lift the next block into position, again locking the upper left-hand and lower right-hand corners into place. For a perfect fit, trim the edges of the block with the saw.

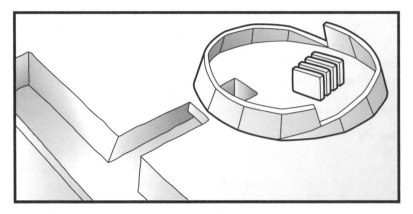

Continue to build your way up the spirals, leaning each successive tier more sharply toward the igloo's center. As the blocks near the top, they will be almost horizontal. Trim every block so that the two critical corners fit properly. The last few blocks might require extensive shaping before you can ease them into place, but the shell of the igloo will be strong by then, and you shouldn't have much trouble securing the blocks. The final block is known as the *keystone*. To get out of the igloo, create a maintenance entrance by removing a block from the first tier on the side away from the quarry, but save the block so that you can replace it later.

Use a saw and shovel to cut a tapered trench from the quarry to the base of the igloo. The trench should be as deep as the floor of the quarry, about 24 inches wide at the top and 36 to 48 inches wide at the base.

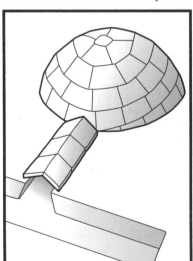

Burrow under the igloo wall and up through the floor to create an entrance, then lean blocks of snow against each other over the trench to form a gabled roof over it. Fill any gaps between the igloo blocks with snow.

Add a few last touches to make your winter house a home. Cut ventilation holes near the top of the roof. Bring in your sleeping bags and pads through the maintenance entrance, and then close it off by replacing the snow block. Stow the rest of your equipment in the entrance tunnel.

An igloo is a very efficient winter shelter, one that can last for weeks if temperatures remain low. If built correctly, it is tremendously strong and, after the snow has settled for several hours, it can easily support the weight of a person standing on top of it. Cold air will drain out of the igloo into the quarry below, and even when the outside temperature is well below zero the interior of an igloo can be a relatively comfortable 25 to 30 degrees Fahrenheit. The quarry also can serve as a patio and kitchen; use your saw to carve benches on which to do your cooking and eating.

Emergency Winter Shelters

While not as comfortable as snow caves or igloos, tree pits and snow trenches have the advantage of quick construction. They are good examples of alternative winter shelters that can serve you well in emergency situations.

Tree Pit

The area beneath the branches of a large evergreen tree can be nearly free of snow. Crawl underneath and form a small living space. Bare earth radiates some heat, so remove the snow from the tree pit floor if you can. Use a foam pad protected by a ground cloth as insulation beneath you. A fir or spruce tree will shed snow outside of the pit.

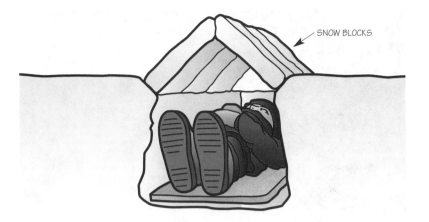

SNOW BLOCKS

Snow Trench

Build a snow trench by using the same method as for an igloo entryway. Insulate the trench floor with a foam sleeping pad if you have one. Cut blocks of snow to shape a 36-inch-deep trench that tapers from 24 inches at the top to 36 to 48 inches at the base. Place the blocks on edge along the sides of the excavation, then lean them against each other to form a pitched roof.

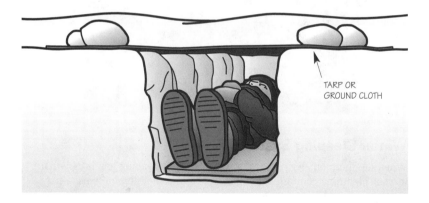

TARP OR
GROUND CLOTH

Snow Pit

Where snow is deep enough, you can dig a long, narrow pit for an emergency shelter. Insulate the floor of the pit with a foam sleeping pad if you have one. Form a roof by stretching a tarp or ground cloth over the top of the trench. Weigh down the edges with snow, stones, or branches, then cover the roof with several inches of snow to provide insulation. Tunnel into one end of the pit and, when you are inside, fill the entry with snow to keep out the cold. Poke a few ventilation holes near the entrance and check them occasionally to ensure that they remain clear.

Winter Sleeping Systems

When the thermometer plunges, a well-insulated sleeping bag is essential to your nighttime comfort. Adding layers—fleece clothing, mittens, a hat, warm socks, and even one or more additional sleeping bags—extends the range of a bag. A fleece liner will keep the bag clean and add a few more degrees of insulating power, as will a bivouac bag. (Liners must not be made of cotton.) Sleeping inside a tent or snow shelter can prevent wind from sapping away warmth, too. Of course, insulation beneath your bag is vital, usually in the form of a foam sleeping pad.

With all the emphasis on insulation, don't become so warm that you perspire during the night. That can rob your sleeping system of its ability to keep you cozy. Ventilate by opening the bag, taking off your hat, or removing other clothing layers.

For more on sleeping systems, see the chapter titled "Gearing Up."

13

Carrying Your Gear

A winter trek requires more gear, provisions, and fuel than a summer trip of equal duration. A large backpack can serve you well if you will be hiking and works fine for mountain travel in rugged terrain. With some practice, you also can snowshoe or cross-country ski with a backpack.

Many snow campers depend on sleds for moving their gear. A smaller sled with a harness is sized for one person to pull, especially while on skis or snowshoes. Larger sleds can carry the bulk of a group's equipment and food with several people hitched to the harness to haul the load. Whether on foot or using skis and snowshoes, cold-weather travelers will find their balance enhanced with the use of ski poles.

Making Camp

Transformed by snow, frost, and cold, a winter camp can be a place of wonder. The campsite itself might be your destination for an adventure, or it might serve as a base from which you can range out each day to ski, snowshoe, and explore. In either case, settle in and make yourself at home with a secure shelter, a convenient cooking area, and an eye toward the weather.

Stowing Your Stuff

Drifts have a habit of swallowing up unattended camping gear. Snowmelt can soak into clothing, equipment, and food. Organize your clothing and provisions in plastic bags before departing from home, and leave your sleeping bag and extra clothing inside your pack until you need them. Tie fluorescent tape or brightly colored nylon cord to knives, compasses, and other small items so that you can find them if they slip away. Keep your mittens and gloves on your hands or tied to a cord threaded through your sleeves. Stash cooking utensils inside pots when you aren't using them. Before going to bed, make sure everything is stored in your pack, on your sled, or in your shelter; items left outside could become buried by snow during the night.

13

Cold-Weather Camping Expertise

Every time you camp out in the winter, you'll figure out a few more ways to make your cold-weather adventures more rewarding. Here are a few hints from the experts:

Carry waterproof matches (in a plastic container), flashlights, and extra batteries in the inside pockets of your clothing, where body heat can help improve their performance.

Fill an unbreakable vacuum bottle each morning with hot drinks or soup to be enjoyed later in the day. Fill it before going to bed, too, so that you'll have something hot to drink when you wake up the next day.

The lids on widemouthed water bottles won't freeze up as quickly as can those on smallmouthed ones. The larger caps also are easier to manage when you are wearing mittens. Insulate a water bottle with a piece of closed-cell foam sleeping pad sized to encircle the bottle and duct-taped in place.

Choose an insulated mug that will retain the heat of soup and drinks, but won't burn your lips.

A 12-by-12-inch piece of 1/4- or 1/2-inch plywood will insulate your stove from surface cold and prevent a lit stove from melting into the snow. A wind-screen designed specifically for your stove will concentrate heat. Cover pots with lids to speed up cooking.

Pack along a small whisk broom to sweep snow off your clothing and out of your tent.

Avoiding Cold-Weather Emergencies

Prepare well and keep your wits about you, and you should seldom encounter cold emergencies. Increase your comfort and safety by wearing layers of clothing to stay warm and dry. Eat plenty of food and drink lots of fluids. If bad weather catches you, make camp and crawl into your sleeping bag.

Visit the outdoors in small groups—*never alone.* Use the buddy system, pairing up so that all group members are watching out for one another. Stay alert for symptoms of hypothermia, frostbite, and dehydration—the medical emergencies most often associated with cold weather. The intensity of reflected sunlight can make sunscreen and a broad-brimmed hat vital protection when you are traveling and camping on snowfields. Protect your eyes with sunglasses and your lips with zinc oxide or a lip balm with an SPF of at least 15.

For more on hypothermia, frostbite, avalanches, and other cold-weather hazards, see the chapter titled "Managing Risk."

Travel into areas prone to avalanches is beyond the scope of the *Fieldbook.* If your interests lead you in that direction, prepare by taking winter backcountry travel courses and learning how to use avalanche beacons, probes, and snow shovels.

Leave No Trace While Cold-Weather Camping

Winter conditions provide unique challenges and opportunities for travelers to leave no sign of their passing except for prints in the snow.

Plan Ahead and Prepare

Learn about the area where you are going and know what to expect. Check weather reports before setting out, and prepare for the worst conditions that might occur.

If visibility on your return trip might be a concern, be ready to mark your route with flagging tape or pin flags. (Both are available at hardware stores. Or you can make flagging with strips of brightly colored cloth.) Remove all flags and flagging on your way home.

Travel and Camp on Durable Surfaces

Stay on deep snow whenever you can. Walk in the middle of muddy pathways to avoid damaging trailside plants. Choose campsites on snow, rock, or mineral soil well away from avalanche paths, cornices (overhangs), and steep snow slopes. Take care not to trample tundra vegetation.

Dispose of Waste Properly

Frozen ground, snow cover, and frigid conditions can make disposal of human waste an interesting endeavor. Plan ahead by asking land managers of the area you intend to visit for guidelines on what to do about waste. *Pack-it-out kits* might be a workable solution, as can using snow for toilet paper. A small dispenser of waterless hand cleanser rounds out your ability to make outdoor hygiene simple and convenient.

For information on making and using pack-it-out kits, see the chapter titled "Hygiene and Waste Disposal."

13

Leave What You Find

Leave dead branches on trees—breaking them off for firewood leaves sharp, ugly protruding ends.

Minimize Campfire Impacts

The ease of using lightweight stoves makes them a natural choice for cold-weather camping and travel. Factor in additional fuel if you expect to melt snow for water. Where fires are appropriate, gather wood from the base of trees, where doing so will have no lasting impact on the appearance or health of the environment. Where the ground is bare, follow the Leave No Trace fire-building principles. When the earth is covered with snow, you can use a fire pan to contain a blaze and prevent it from extinguishing itself by sinking into the snow.

For more information, see the chapter titled "Using Stoves and Campfires."

Respect Wildlife

Winter can be an especially vulnerable time for animals. Low temperatures, scarcity of food, and greater danger from predators can place a great deal of stress on them. Observe wildlife from a distance.

Be Considerate of Other Visitors

Share winter trails with other users. Don't hike or snowshoe on ski tracks. While traveling on skis, yield to downhill traffic and those catching up with you from behind, and be especially diligent as you approach blind corners. When you stop to rest, move off the trail.

"Take long walks in stormy weather or through deep snow in the fields and woods, if you would keep your spirits up. Deal with brute nature."

—Henry David Thoreau (1817–1862), American author, philosopher, and naturalist

CHAPTER
14

Hot-Weather Travel and Camping

"The weather was hardly the best for walking. Across the first two States it was oppressively hot, and then I had several days of trudging in a pouring rain. However, it did not drench the spirits within, and it was welcome as an experience."

—Charles F. Lummis (long-distance hiker, journalist, archaeologist, and adviser to President Theodore Roosevelt), *A Tramp Across the Continent,* 1892

The ability to travel and camp in hot weather can expand the range of your adventures to include magnificent portions of North America throughout the year. Go to the desert and find yourself surrounded by space and sagebrush, shimmering clarity and quiet. Discover a fragile environment of arid lands, wildlife, and vegetation shaped by water, and by its absence. Go to the tropics and find yourself deep in complicated ecosystems millions of years in the making.

Explore the magnificent wetlands and tangled forests of the Southern states, delighting in terrain you might have thought you already knew. Set off in rafts, canoes, and kayaks to paddle the rivers of summer, drifting through the timbered territory of the Southeast and Midwest and between the sheer canyon walls of the Southwest. Make your way to the sparkling coastlines of bays, gulfs, and oceans where you can camp just above the high-tide mark and then snorkel, swim, and hike as you enjoy the rich ecology where the land meets the sea.

Why go in hot weather? You'll find your own reasons when you get there; environments baked by the sun can stir your soul like no other landscapes on Earth.

14

Staying Cool in Hot Weather

Coping with heat is the flip side of camping
and traveling in cold weather. Just as winter
adventurers must plan ahead, choose your
hot-weather equipment and food with care,
and then use lots of common sense. In frigid
conditions, the focus is on staying warm
and well-hydrated. When the thermometer
soars, the most important factors are keeping
yourself hydrated and cool and matching your
activities to the conditions.

　　　Understanding how your body reacts
to high temperatures can help you plan your
clothing, gear, and provisions for the trek. It
also can guide you in deciding *when* to carry
out activities during a trip. The big issues to
cope with are *heat, humidity,* and *hydration.*

Heat

Your body operates best
with a core temperature
of about 98 degrees,
shedding excess warmth
primarily by means of
radiation and *evaporation.*
Radiation takes place
when body heat dissipates
into cooler surrounding air.
That ceases to be effective
as the outside temperature
rises. *Evaporation* is your
body's other mechanism
for staying cool, occurring
when you perspire. As
moisture on the skin
evaporates, it carries heat
away with it.

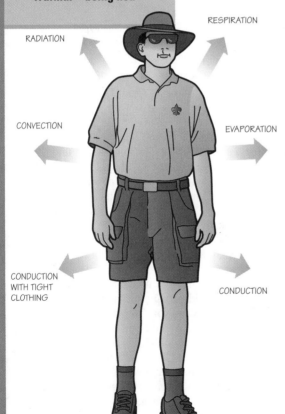

RADIATION

RESPIRATION

CONVECTION

EVAPORATION

CONDUCTION
WITH TIGHT
CLOTHING

CONDUCTION

Types of body heat loss

Humidity

Dry climates are ideal for evaporation to occur. However, air saturated with humidity can't absorb much additional moisture from evaporation. People sweating heavily on a hot, humid day might not be losing much heat at all.

Hydration

Perspiration draws a great deal of fluid from the body, depleting it of water and essential electrolytes. Water requirements vary among people, based on their size, physical makeup, activity levels, and general health, as well as environmental factors.

Drink, Drink, Drink

Thirst is not always the best indicator of your body's need for water. Instead, drink often enough for your urine to remain light-colored or clear.

- In hot weather, refresh your water containers at every opportunity. Drink your fill, then refill your container before leaving a water source.

- Keep water readily available and drink small amounts frequently.

- Don't ration water. If you are thirsty, you need to drink.

- Avoid consuming a lot of caffeinated drinks, which can act as *diuretics*—agents that purge fluids from the body.

- Don't underestimate your need for water. During strenuous activities in hot weather, your body might require two to three gallons of water per day.

14

Planning Hot-Weather Trips

In some ways, planning adventures for hot weather is not much different from getting ready in any season of the year. Your group will need food and gear, a route to travel, and a way to get to and from the trailhead. You will check with the land managers of the area you wish to visit for current information on conditions, for permits you might need, and for guidelines on the best ways to use Leave No Trace principles as you travel and camp. Permits for popular stretches of rivers, canyons, and other public lands might be in great demand and could take weeks or months to acquire.

Preparing for hot-weather journeys also demands a few special considerations not common for trips into more hospitable climes. The following are among the most important:

- Water weighs about 8 pounds a gallon. You can carry only so much. Determine where you will be able to refill your water bottles—desert route selection might be a matter of stringing together a series of reliable water sources. For longer trips with critical water needs, have backup plans—points where you can change your route and get to certain water in a reasonable amount of time.

- Once in the field, travel early in the morning and in the evening rather than in the midday heat.

- Be aware of seasonal trends. Some years are drier than others, and that could have an impact on your ability to find water in the region you intend to visit.

- Packing lightly lessens the effort it takes to hike. That, in turn, reduces the exertion that generates body heat.

- If you know that the area where you are going is remote with few visitors, then be prepared to camp in pristine areas and practice stringent Leave No Trace techniques. In areas popular with the public, expect to see more people and plan on camping in existing campsites. Check with land managers for camping regulations, permit information, and suggestions about your route.

Hot-Weather Nutrition

14

Hot weather can cause you to feel less hungry than you might in more temperate conditions. Even so, a nourishing diet is important to maintaining your health and keeping up the energy you need to make the most of outdoor activities. A balanced menu with a higher percentage of carbohydrates will serve you well. Some people prefer eating snacks and light meals throughout the day rather than having a large lunch and supper.

When planning provisions, shy away from fresh meat, eggs, dairy products, and other protein-rich foods that can spoil in the heat; grains, dehydrated foods, and trail mix are durable and lend themselves to a diet more appropriate for hot weather. Groups planning canoe journeys without long portages can take along heavier provisions than groups toting everything on their shoulders. Rafts, sailboats, and other watercraft might be equipped with ice chests capable of keeping almost any foodstuffs fresh for several days or more. The larger the raft or boat, the less the concern over the weight and bulk of provisions.

For more on selecting food for a trek, see the chapter titled "Outdoor Menus."

Finding Water in Arid Regions

To be certain of your water supply in dry environments, bring plenty of fluids with you. Embarking on any trip beyond a day hike, though, will probably require you to refresh your water containers along the way and to treat any water you intend to drink.

Up-to-date information provided by land managers and other travelers can be your best guide to the locations of backcountry water. Check your map for springs, wells, stock watering tanks, and windmills. Look for bright green vegetation that might indicate a seep or spring. Clusters of cottonwoods,  sycamores, and willows are indicators that water might be close at hand. Damp sand or earth might yield seepage if you dig far enough, and in canyon country, water sometimes collects in shaded depressions in the rock. Assume that potential water sources could be dry when you reach them, though, and carry enough water to enable you to reach second and third sources of water.

Hot-Weather Clothing and Body Protection

Selecting the right clothing will go a long way toward keeping you happy and healthy in hot weather. As with any form of adventure travel and camping, use the layering system to ensure the greatest versatility in the clothing that you carry and wear. Keep these basics in mind:

- Nylon shorts and shirts are the favorites of many hot-weather travelers. The fabric is cool, durable, and quick to dry. Shirts might be most comfortable when made of a nylon-cotton blend.

- Cotton can be a good choice for warm days. It absorbs sweat and ventilates well. However, it will prove useless if it becomes wet in chilly weather.

- Polyester is a good insulator, does not hold water, and dries easily.

- Pick light-colored fabrics not as likely to absorb heat, and stay dressed. Going without a hat or a shirt can lead to an increase in water loss and much greater potential for sunburn and overheating.

- Temperatures at night can be chilly or even cold. Plan your clothing and sleeping gear accordingly.

- In insect-infested areas, you might want a head net, long-sleeved shirt, long pants, and lightweight gloves.

Hot, wet climate

RN# 61661
CA# 30516
V0104004

SHELL/EXTERIEUR:
100% NYLON
LINING/DOUBLURE:
100% POLYESTER

MENS/HOMMES

M/M

MADE IN CHINA
FABRIQUE EN CHINE

100% COTTON

MACHINE WASH WARM
INSIDE OUT
TUMBLE DRY MEDIUM
DO NOT BLEACH
DO NOT DRY CLEAN
DO NOT IRON EMBLEM

Made in the U.S.A.
Overland Park, KS
RN # 90142

Hot, dry climate

14

Beyond Clothing

Use sunscreen to protect exposed skin, giving special attention to your face, ears, nose, and neck. Although skin appears to recover from sunburn, damage to the cellular structure accumulates and can, in later years, lead to skin cancer. (To be effective, sunscreen should have an SPF of at least 15. SPF numbers greater than 30, however, add little extra protection.) Sunlight reflected off open water can intensify the negative impact of solar radiation, and a wet T-shirt offers little defense against the sun. Wear sunglasses to prevent eyestrain, and shield your lips against chapping and sun damage by applying a lip balm with an SPF of 15 or higher.

Insect repellents containing the chemical DEET (N, N-diethyl-meta-toluamide) are effective but, to avoid the possibility of negative side effects, closely follow the manufacturer's recommendations for use. Hot-weather travelers in wooded regions might successfully ward off ticks, chiggers, and other insects by lightly spraying their clothing with repellent containing permethrin.

Hot-Weather Gear

Your pack for hot-weather camping can be much lighter than the one you carry in the winter. You'll need less in the way of clothing, and you won't require nearly as much in the way of a shelter and a sleeping bag. Because you won't be melting snow for water, you can get away with less fuel. Regions experiencing high humidity might be subjected to frequent showers and occasional storms, so pack your rain gear. Layers of warmer clothing will see you through a chilly night.

Shelters for Hot-Weather Camping

For hot, dry weather, a lightweight sleeping bag spread out under the stars is ideal. A ground cloth will keep it clean, and a sleeping pad will provide plenty of cushioning and insulation. If you need more shelter, choose from among bivouac bags, tarps, lightweight tents, and hammocks.

Tarp

A nylon tarp or a 4-mil sheet of plastic, offering maximum ventilation with minimum weight, often are just right for hot environments, especially if there aren't many insects.

Leave No Trace in Hot-Weather Environments

For traveling and camping in deserts, see the chapter titled "Traveling and Camping in Special Environments."

In addition, the *Fieldbook* Web site can lead you to plenty of online resources for techniques, gear, training opportunities, and destinations for hot-weather adventure. 🔍

Hot-Weather Tent

A tent might be the most practical shelter in humid climates and where insects and crawling creatures are an issue. A tent with large mosquito-netting panels can be used without the rain fly unless the skies threaten.

Four-season tents, single-wall tents, and other shelters that don't allow much ventilation can be stuffy, damp, and uncomfortable.

Hammock

A hammock designed for tropical camping is essentially a small shelter complete with mosquito netting and a pitched nylon roof to shed the rain.

"If you cannot endure a certain amount of thirst, heat, fatigue, and hunger without getting cross with Nature, it is best to stay home."

—William T. Hornaday (author, wildlife advocate, and founder of the National Zoo in Washington, D.C.), *Campfires on Desert and Lava*, 1913

CHAPTER 15

Backpacking

"We are born wanderers, followers of obscure trails, or blazers of new ones. The mind, too, is a natural wanderer, ever seeking, and occasionally discovering, new ideas, fresh insights."

—Royal Robbins, U.S. mountaineer and climber whose interest in the outdoors was stimulated by Scouting

Nothing promises adventure so clearly as a pack loaded and ready for the trail. Add to it a group of like-minded friends and a well-considered plan, and you are almost certain to discover much more in the out-of-doors, and in yourself, than you had ever hoped to find. With a pack on your shoulders, you can go wherever your legs will take you. Use your navigation skills to find your way, and rely on your knowledge and experience to make the right decisions as your route leads you far from any road. Live simply and well with only the gear and provisions you've chosen to carry, and take pride in knowing how to keep yourself comfortable and well-fed. In the freedom of backpacking you will find yourself closer to the land, closer to your companions, and closer to the core of life itself.

What You Carry in Your Head

Backpacking well requires a good grasp of many outdoor skills. The gear and provisions you take along can make your travels easier. More important, though, is the knowledge you have in your head to keep yourself and those with you safe and to appreciate and protect the country through which you travel.

Every outdoor experience you have will add to your storehouse of backpacking know-how. Information found throughout the *Fieldbook* and on the *Fieldbook* Web site can guide you in preparing for your journeys and in making the most of your time on the trail.

What You Carry on Your Back

In 1913 a man named Joseph Knowles went sans clothing into the New England woods where he claimed he was able to build a campfire, live on berries, kill a partridge and a bear, and use charcoal on birch bark to write accounts of his adventures. Perhaps somewhat fanciful, Knowles' experience does point out the fact that much of what backpackers carry today could just as well be left at home. The chapter titled "Gearing Up" will help you decide what you need for backpacking and what you don't. One item you are almost certain to require is, of course, a backpack.

Backpack

A good backpack will ride easily on your shoulders, sit comfortably on your hips, protect your gear from the weather, and provide easy access to things you need along the way. Nearly all modern backpacks have weight-bearing hip belts that allow backpackers to shift the weight of pack loads from their shoulders to the bone structure and strong muscles of their hips and legs. Beyond that, backpackers can choose between internal-frame packs and those with external frames.

ADJUSTABLE STRAP

LOW PRESSURE ON SHOULDER

BELT ON HIP REST

PAD EXTENDS JUST BELOW CHEST

15

Invention of the Modern Backpack

An American inventor named Merriam patented the load-bearing hip belt in 1886. However, the widespread use of belts to transfer the weight of a pack load had to wait until after World War II, when aircraft riveters and welders turned their skills from building fighter planes and bombers to manufacturing aluminum canoes and pack frames. Before long, lightweight frames outfitted with hip belts and nylon packs had transformed backpacking into an activity accessible to almost anyone eager to lace up a pair of hiking boots and set off on a trail.

Internal-Frame Pack

Stiff metal or plastic *stays* positioned inside a pack act as its frame, providing structural rigidity for transferring the weight of the pack load to the hip belt. With their compact shapes and snug fit, internal-frame packs are ideal for travel through heavy brush, in steep terrain, and while snowshoeing or cross-country skiing. They also are comfortable on open trails. Some are outfitted with removable top flaps or rear compartments that can be converted into day packs for hikes from a base camp.

External-Frame Pack

The weight distribution principles of an external-frame pack are essentially the same as for a pack with an internal frame, but because the frame is on the outside of the bag it can be larger and more rigid, and can efficiently transfer the weight from the shoulder straps to the hip belt. Most external frames also provide room for lashing on a sleeping bag or tent.

Internal-frame pack

External-frame pack

Pack Weight

How much your pack weighs depends on the length of the adventure you've planned, the amount of food and equipment you must carry, and your personal preferences. Traveling with a troop or crew lets you divide up tents, food packages, cooking equipment, and other group gear. For comfort on the trail, a pack containing everything you need for a safe trek should tip the scales at no more than 25 percent of your body's weight. If your pack weighs less, so much the better.

Pack Capacity

The capacity of packs is often noted in cubic inches:

- **2,500 to 3,000 cubic inches. Good as a large day pack or for overnight trips in warm weather when you need only a lightweight sleeping bag and a minimum of other gear.**

- **3,000 to 4,500 cubic inches. With space for camp essentials, extra food, and additional layers of clothing, a pack of this size works well for two- or three-day trips in the spring, summer, and autumn.**

- **4,500 to 6,000 cubic inches. The majority of standard backpacks are of this dimension. Intended for trips of several days or more, they have the room to haul all the food and equipment you need, as well as a few extras.**

Choosing a Backpack

Look for a backpack that best matches the kinds of adventures for which you'll use it most. The pack might be a little large for one-night campouts, but just right for treks of several days. Put some weight in a pack you like and wear it around the store to see how it feels. Will it ride close to your back? Does the weight rest on your hips rather than on your shoulders or waist? Could you carry it all day? Many packs have adjustment features to fine-tune the fit. Knowledgeable backpackers and salespeople can help you find a pack that will seem tailored just for you.

Loading a Pack

Once you've determined what to carry, the next step in preparing for a backpacking trip is to pack everything for the trail. Frequently used items can go in the pockets of your clothing or pockets on the outside of your pack—your pocketknife, compass, map, water bottle, sunscreen, insect repellent, personal first-aid kit, and perhaps a notebook and pencil. Stow your tarp or tent where you can reach it without digging through everything else; on a stormy day, you might want to get a shelter up quickly.

Equipment you won't need until you have made camp can go deeper in your pack, but rain gear, a fleece or wool sweater, clean socks, and food for the trail should ride where you can easily reach them. Reserve at least one pack pocket for your fuel containers so that they will be isolated from the rest of your supplies.

Anything you carry on the outside of the pack—cup, water bottle, cook pot, etc.—should be securely tied, strapped, or clipped in place so that nothing can swing or fall off.

If you will be hiking on open trails, arrange the contents of your pack so that its center of gravity is high and close to your back. For cross-country hiking, skiing, or snowshoeing, trade a little comfort for a lot of stability by placing heavier gear in the bottom of the pack and thus lowering the center of gravity. In either case, pad the front of the pack's interior with a layer of clothing to provide extra cushioning against your back.

Most backpacks will shield your gear from light showers, but heavy rains might seep through the pack fabric. Carry a waterproof nylon rain

Prepack your clothing and food in stuff sacks to protect them from the elements and to organize your pack. A few nylon sacks with drawstrings and a handful of self-sealing plastic bags will do the trick.

15

cover sized to the shape of your pack, and slip it on when the weather turns bad. It's a good idea to put the cover in place when you leave your pack outside during the night, too. If you're caught on the trail without a rain cover, you can use one of the large plastic trash bags you have along for stashing litter. Cut a slit in one side of the bag, then cover the pack and tuck the loose ends of the bag beneath the straps or under the frame in a way that leaves the shoulder straps free. Some outdoor travelers make their packs completely watertight by lining the compartments with trash bags and sealing their food and gear inside.

Hoisting and Carrying a Pack

An effective way to get a pack on your shoulders is to enlist the aid of a partner who can lift the load while you slip your arms through the shoulder straps. Return the favor by hoisting your buddy's pack.

To get into a pack on your own, loosen the shoulder straps, then grasp them and lift the pack waist high. Rest the bottom of the pack on your thigh and slip an arm through the appropriate shoulder strap. As you do so, smoothly swing the pack onto your back and slip your other arm through the remaining strap. Lean a little forward at the waist to hoist your pack into position, buckle and tighten the hip belt, and adjust the shoulder straps so that when you stand upright most of the pack's weight rides on your hips.

Many packs have additional straps to stabilize the load or compress it closer to your back. Play around with these straps to see if they improve the way the pack feels.

Hitting the Trail

Hiking with a backpack can be much different from walking without one. A pack on your shoulders alters your sense of balance. Its weight puts extra strain on your feet, ankles, and knees, especially when you're pounding downhill. Begin each day's journey by stretching to warm up and loosen your muscles, then hike slowly at first to allow your pack to settle into place. Match clothing layers to changing weather conditions, check your feet for hot spots, drink plenty of water, and adjust the way your pack is riding on your hips and shoulders. When taking breaks, do so on durable surfaces off the trail—rocks, sandy areas, dry grasses—rather than on vegetation that could suffer from being trampled.

Over the course of a long hike, the straps and belt on your pack might make your shoulders and hips sore, especially if you're lean and don't have a great deal of natural padding on your bones. Ease any discomfort by occasionally adjusting the pack straps to shift the weight of the load. You also can use a couple of socks for padding by folding them over the hip belt or tucking them under your shoulder straps.

Setting a reasonable pace will enable everyone to enjoy a trek. Position slower hikers near the front where they can more easily maintain a steady stride. Stronger backpackers can carry a greater proportion of group gear, though no one should be made to feel inferior for toting a light load, or superior for enduring a heavier pack.

Hiking Sticks and Trekking Poles

The hiking stick has long been a symbol of the traveler. It swings comfortably in your hand, giving balance and rhythm to your pace. Use it to push back branches or brush. A hiking stick can be especially useful when you are wading a stream; added to your own two legs, a stick will give you the stability of a tripod. (For more on stream crossings, see the chapter titled "Mountain Travel.")

Some backpackers like to use a pair of trekking poles for balance and to reduce weight on their knees, much as a skier uses ski poles. Telescoping poles can be adjusted in length or collapsed and strapped out of the way on your pack. Be kind to the environment by using blunt, rubber-tipped poles that minimize impact on trail margins.

> If you have a history of blisters forming at particular locations on your foot, try reinforcing the areas with moleskin or gel pads before you start hiking.

Preventing Blisters

Blisters develop when skin is irritated, usually by friction or heat. For outdoor travelers, blisters on the feet are the most common. Prevent them by wearing boots or hiking shoes that fit well, by breaking in your footwear before a trek, and by changing into dry socks whenever your feet become damp. Many hikers find success in deterring blisters by wearing two pairs of socks—a thin liner sock of a synthetic material (not cotton), and a thick wool hiking sock.

Treating Blisters

A *hot spot* is a warning that a blister might be forming. Treat a hot spot or blister as soon as you notice it. Gel pads can be taped directly over a hot spot or blister to reduce friction and speed healing. Follow the instructions on the package. To treat a hot spot or blister with moleskin, cut the moleskin into the shape of a doughnut and fit it around the injury to shield it from further rubbing. Used together, a gel pad and a moleskin doughnut can provide maximum relief for hot spots and blisters. Change bandages every day to keep wounds clean and to avoid infection.

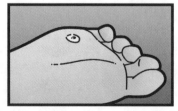 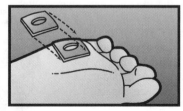

A hot spot is a warning that a blister might be forming. As soon as you notice it, treat a hot spot or blister with a "doughnut bandage" to relieve the pressure on your skin.

Leave No Trace Backpacking

Just as carrying a lightweight pack can make your outdoor adventures easier and leave you with more time and energy for enjoying your surroundings, following the principles of Leave No Trace can ensure that your impact on the land is as insignificant as possible.

For more on backpacking responsibly, see the "Leaving No Trace" section of this book.

Extended Backpacking Treks

Have you ever reached the end of a weekend camping trip and wished you didn't have to go home? Have you ever looked out over ranges of mountains that seemed to invite you to hike all the way to the horizon and beyond? Ever wanted a challenge that would put your backcountry skills to a real test? If your answer to these questions is yes, you and your group might be ready for an extended backpacking trek.

Terrific challenges await long-distance backpackers on famous foot-paths including the Appalachian Trail, Pacific Crest Trail, and Continental Divide Trail. Of course, you can plot an extended trek anywhere in the country by studying maps, finding interesting hiking trails, and figuring out ways to link them into a continuous route.

The Rhythm of a Long Hike

The first days of a long backpacking trip are a time of adjustment as you and your companions get used to carrying your packs, the hours of walking, and the rigors of spending all of your time outdoors. Along with the excitement of the adventure, you might even have some doubts about the wisdom of so distant a goal.

However, changes will begin to occur as soon as you take your first step. As the miles roll beneath your boots, calluses will form to protect your once-tender feet. You will gradually become accustomed to the weight on your shoulders. The routines of camp chores will become quick and efficient. Your legs and heart will strengthen, and before long you will find yourselves settling into the rhythm of motion of long-distance hikers.

Food for Extended Treks

Just as your mind and muscles become attuned to long stretches of trail, your digestive tract will become streamlined and more efficient. The food you carry on an extended trek will differ little from what you take on any backpacking trek, though you might find yourself hungry for greater volumes of food in the later stages of a journey. Scrutinize your food lists with weight of ingredients in mind, and make sure that nothing in your pack will spoil before you can use it.

For more on selecting and preparing food for backpacking trips, see the chapter titled "Outdoor Menus."

Resupplying

When a trek will keep you on the trail more than a week, it's unlikely you will be able to carry all the provisions and fuel you will need. Some routes come close enough to towns for you to shop at a grocery store for the menu items you need. If that isn't possible, two other ways to resupply are *trailhead rendezvous* and *mail drops.*

15

Whichever of these two methods you choose, gather and pack supplies for the entire trek before you leave home. Use sturdy cardboard boxes reinforced with strong tape. Line the interior of each box with a large plastic trash bag and stow your provisions inside. Don't seal the box until absolutely necessary. That way you or your support crew can add last-minute items.

Trailhead Rendezvous

Unless your trek takes you into the heart of a huge wilderness area, you probably will cross roads now and then where you can arrange to meet up with leaders of your Scout unit or other reliable adults. They can bring the food and stove fuel you need for the next leg of your journey.

Mail Drop

Mail drops are particularly effective when you hike a long trail far from home. Research the route ahead of time and find post offices to which you can send parcels to yourself. (Ask a postmaster to explain the packing and mailing regulations you should follow.) You also can contact park and forest rangers who might know of addresses within parks to which you can mail your provisions.

Time the shipment of mail drops so that your boxes will have plenty of time to arrive, then schedule your pickups for hours you are certain the post offices will be open. Keep in mind that most are closed on Saturday afternoons, Sundays, and holidays, and those in remote areas also might have limited hours during the week. When you're hungry, tired, and eager to get into your next box of food, there's nothing more frustrating than reaching a post office just after it has closed for the weekend.

A Final Word on Backpacking

Regardless of your destination, the real joy of any adventure is the journey itself. Allow yourself plenty of time to delight in every aspect of a trip. Don't be in such a hurry that you can't stop to watch the wildlife, study the flowers, and take in the beauty of the landscape through which you are passing.

"What do you suppose will satisfy the soul, except to walk free and own no superior?"

—Walt Whitman (1819–1892),
American author and poet

Few adventures can compare to the experience of Philmont Scout Ranch in northern New Mexico. Older Scouts and Venturers can backpack or ride horses over Philmont's 137,000 acres of rugged, mountainous terrain and enjoy a variety of exciting programs in backcountry camps.

CHAPTER 16

Watercraft Adventure Safety

"Boat smart from the start. Wear your life jacket."

—North American Safe Boating Campaign slogan

Rivers and their environments are always changing. Water levels, current speeds, temperatures, and the presence or absence of obstacles can vary from one hour to the next. The same is true of open water where, in a matter of minutes, wind can transform mirror-smooth lakes and salt water into maelstroms. That tremendous variety brings with it magnificent opportunities for setting out in human-powered watercraft to enjoy streams, rivers, lakes, and the sea. With those opportunities comes the responsibility to do all you can to maximize your safety and that of the people around you.

Some concerns are easy to address. You're likely to get wet. You will often be out in the sun. You might get thirsty and hungry. Having the Outdoor Essentials with you (and knowing how to use them) will allow you to deal with those situations in the same ways on water as you would on land. (For more on the Outdoor Essentials, see the chapter titled "Gearing Up.")

Water also carries with it the potential of more serious danger. Conditions ideal for hypothermia lurk in the chill of rivers, lakes, and oceans. Possibilities of impact injuries hide against boulders in a rapids and at the foot of cliffs pounded by the surf. Every year, several hundred Americans drown, many while taking part in watercraft activities. From the quietest pond to the roughest sea, managing risks begins by following the guidelines of the Boy Scouts of America's Safe Swim Defense plan and those of Safety Afloat.

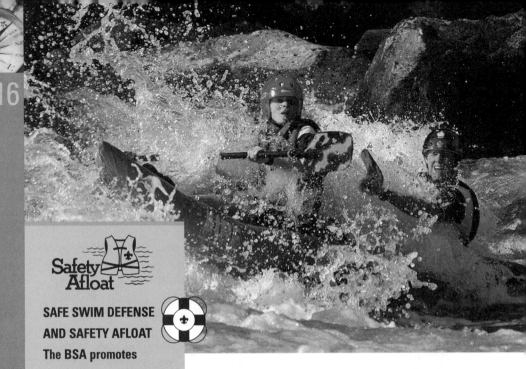

Watercraft Adventure Safety Equipment

Personal Flotation Device

People participating in watercraft adventures will, from time to time, find themselves in the water. If that happens to you, a personal flotation device (PFD) will keep you afloat.

Properly fitted U.S. Coast Guard–approved PFDs must be worn by all persons engaged in activity on the open water (rowing, canoeing, sailing, boardsailing, motorboating, waterskiing, rafting, tubing, and kayaking). Type II and Type III PFDs are recommended; Type III PFDs can be more comfortable for persons involved in strenuous watercraft activities.

Wear a PFD *all the time* while in watercraft, and while scouting rapids, loading gear, or lining a watercraft from shore (holding ropes attached to a watercraft that is allowed to float).

A personal flotation device is lifesaving equipment deserving of good treatment. Never sit on a PFD or leave it lying around in camp. Secure it when you have come ashore so that wind cannot carry it into the water. At the end of a trip, allow each PFD to dry, and hang it in a sheltered storage area.

16

Emergency Whistle and Rescue Knife

Since you will be wearing your PFD at all times, emergency items attached to it will be close at hand if you need them:

- Clipped to a loop on the PFD, a loud, sturdy whistle can be used if you must signal your position. (Don't attach the whistle to a PFD's zipper; currents pulling on a whistle might loosen the zipper and cause you to lose your PFD.)

- Advanced watercraft adventurers often attach a sheathed rescue knife to their PFDs. The knife must be sharp and used only for emergencies— cutting free a tangle of lines, for example.

Testing the Fit of a PFD

Never set out on a watercraft unless you are wearing a personal flotation device that fits well. To see if a PFD fits well enough to use, put it on and cinch any adjustments until it is tight but comfortable. Kneel down and stretch your arms overhead. Have a buddy grasp the PFD at the shoulders or by the shoulder straps and try to tug it up over your head. If the PFD slips upward very far, it is poorly fitted or simply too large for you. A PFD that can be pulled out of position while you are on dry land will slip even more readily if you are being tossed about by currents, white water, or waves.

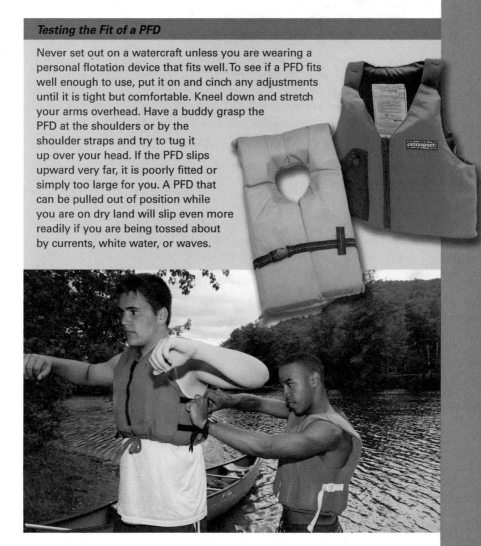

16

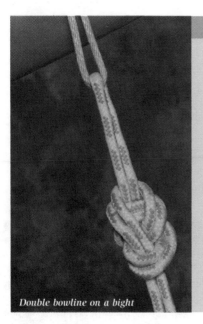

Double bowline on a bight

Boats and Ropes

Ropes are a necessity around watercraft, but every line on a canoe, raft, kayak, or sailboat must be there for a reason. It should be of the correct length and must be stowed so that it is readily available but will not become an entrapment hazard if the boat capsizes. The ideal choice for line used with boats is floating polypropylene rope, soft laid, in diameters of 3/8 inch, 5/16 inch, or 7/16 inch.

For more on stowing ropes, see the chapters titled "Canoeing," "Kayaking and Rafting," and "Sailing."

Clothing for Canoeing, Kayaking, Rafting, and Sailing

The clothing you choose for watercraft adventures should be quick-drying and should help you stay warm even when the fabric is wet (and it *will* become wet)—in other words, layers of nylon, fleece, and wool. Choose clothing based on the temperature of the water rather than the temperature of the air, keeping in mind that bodies of water often are much colder than the air above them. Cotton clothing should be avoided altogether because it provides no insulation when it is wet, even in midsummer heat. Hypothermia can be a serious danger, and wet cotton is no defense.

Rain gear and spare clothes are a must, even on short watercraft trips. Stow extra clothing in a waterproof bag or a watertight compartment so that it will stay dry even if your boat capsizes.

For more on selecting outdoor clothing, see the chapter titled "Gearing Up."

Watercraft Footwear

The shoes you wear while boating should provide traction and comfort, especially while you are moving about on shore, along portage trails, and on the sometimes-slippery decks of sailboats, or when you are wading as you load and launch canoes, kayaks, and rafts. Shoes also should protect your feet from the sun and from insect bites as well as from glass, thorns, fishhooks, sharp stones, and other unpleasantries underfoot. A pair of old tennis shoes or running shoes can be just right.

Shorty wet suit

Dry suit

Wet Suits and Dry Suits

Cold water poses a real danger for kayakers, rafters, and canoeists, especially when they are likely to capsize or to be soaked by waves, rapids, and spray. Wet suits and dry suits provide maximum protection and make possible watercraft adventures in conditions conducive to hypothermia.

- A *wet suit* traps a layer of water next to the skin where it can be warmed by body heat. Among the most popular styles is the sleeveless "Farmer John" two-piece wet suit with overalls and a jacket.

- A *dry suit* serves as a barrier that keeps water away from the skin. It does not insulate; a boater wears fleece insulating layers under a dry suit. Dry suits must be protected from abrasion and tears that could cause leakage.

- Neoprene booties and paddling gloves can extend the coverage of wet suits and dry suits to include boaters' feet and hands.

Neoprene booties and paddling gloves

Characteristics of Rivers

The power of a river can be astounding, especially if the current is squeezed between narrow banks. An obstacle such as a boulder will force the water to go around and sometimes over it, causing turbulence downstream where the river becomes whole once more. A series of obstructions can create the standing waves, eddies, and holes that are the sources of delight and of potential danger for whitewater enthusiasts. The key to kayaking, rafting, and canoeing these waters safely lies in understanding the dynamics involved as a river tumbles along, and then managing a boat so that it works with the stream rather than fighting against it.

When in Doubt, Scout

Before running a section of white water, a blind corner, or a potential drop of any sort, land your boat and scout ahead along the shore to ensure that there are no upcoming obstacles that might be beyond your ability to navigate. As a rule of thumb, don't try running any stretch of water that you wouldn't feel confident about swimming.

Scouting ahead also will allow you to pick a route through rough water. Begin by identifying the end of the run, then work your way back upstream. (There's a hole to avoid on the left, for example, and above that is an eddy that will slow the boat and give you a chance to rest, and above that are three rocks to skirt on the right, and to make that happen you'll need to enter the rapids just off the right shoreline.) In this way, a section of river that at first appeared to be an imposing plunge of foam and spray can be broken down into a series of controlled maneuvers.

If you can, walk the shore next to a section of white water so that you can see how it appears up close. Identify alternative routes to use in case the chaos of the rapids overwhelms your route planning midway through a run. Careful inspection of the river also could reveal features and obstacles that you otherwise might not have noticed. In addition to the standing waves that give white water much of its drama, watch for eddies, strainers, heavy hydraulics, and drops.

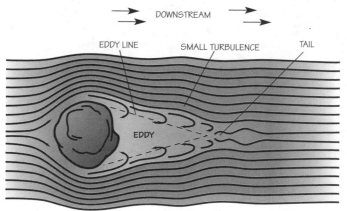

An eddy *can form on the downstream side of a boulder.*

Eddies

A boulder in the water or a stream bank jutting out will absorb the brunt of the river's force on its upstream side. Just downstream, the water swirls back toward the obstruction, forming a quiet pool called an *eddy.* Proficient boaters can slip into eddies to take momentary refuge from the full impact of the current, and they sometimes run a rapids by moving from eddy to eddy rather than racing the full length of the wild water in a single dash.

Strainers

Strainers are among the most hazardous river obstacles. A *strainer* is created when a tree leans over the water with its trunk or some of its branches submerged, or when the current flows through a fence, logjam, junked automobile, industrial debris, or other obstacles in the stream. Water can flow under, around, and through a strainer, but it will snare and trap

A strainer can be caused by low-hanging tree branches.

anything or anyone the current draws in. Cracks in rocks also can act as strainers, allowing water to pass but trapping unwary paddlers.

When you see a strainer up ahead, plot a route that will keep you far away, a maneuver that might involve leaving the stream's main current. If that's not possible, paddle ashore and carry your boat, or *portage*, around to safer water farther downstream.

Heavy Hydraulics

The standing waves, whirlpools, and holes that make up the *heavy hydraulics* of white water can be a paradise for rafters, kayakers, and canoeists playing out the best of their sport. The key to enjoying hydraulics is to take on stretches of water that are within your level of skill and your degree of preparation.

Currents moving over and around boulders form the heavy hydraulics typical of white water.

16

Drops

The *drops* that occur when a stream goes over a ledge or a dam might seem like obvious dangers, but even experienced boaters can be surprised by them if they haven't scouted their routes. As with strainers, changing water levels might expose drops that were not present even a few hours before.

Drops no more than a few feet high can force a river into a spinning reversal of current that could be all but inescapable for boaters who wander into it. An unbroken horizontal line on the water (an almost certain sign of an upcoming drop) should be a shrill warning to get ashore, scout ahead, discover its cause, and plan the portage around it.

A horizontal line on the water is a warning of a dangerous drop ahead.

Broaching and Wrapping

Broaching happens when a strong current traps a raft, kayak, or canoe against the upstream side of a boulder or other river obstacle. If a broached boat capsizes, tons of pressure from the river's current can literally *wrap* it around an obstacle.

Make every effort to keep your craft far from anything upon which it could broach. If despite your best efforts you cannot avoid crashing into a boulder, logjam, strainer, or other obstruction, lean into the obstacle to help prevent your craft from being flipped over. Try to get past the barrier by pushing the boat around one side or the other. Failing that, climb as high as you can and await the assistance of rescuers using throw ropes. Never lean upstream—that can cause the boat to tip far enough into the current to be flooded and wrapped.

Rating the Difficulty of Rivers

The International Scale of River Difficulty provides a standard classification system for rating the difficulty and gauging the risks of running rapids. The scale is at best a rough estimate; it will vary depending on who does the evaluation, when the rating applies (during spring runoff, summer low water, etc.), and the condition of the stream. Bank erosion, fallen trees, flooding, and other factors can significantly affect the difficulty of a particular stretch of river. (Increase each rating by one class if the temperature of the water or the air is below 50 degrees Fahrenheit, or if your trip is an extended trek in a wilderness area.)

Use the scale to help decide whether to embark on a section of a river. Remember, though, that the scale is useful only if you understand your own capabilities and limitations, and those of others who will participate in a watercraft outing. The most important rating still will be the one you base on your firsthand observations.

International Scale of River Difficulty

The International Scale of River Difficulty distinguishes six classes of difficulty:

Class I. Moving water with a few riffles and small waves. Few or no obstructions.

Class II. Easy rapids with waves up to 3 feet, and wide, clear channels that are obvious without scouting from shore. Some maneuvering required.

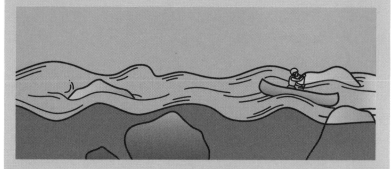

Class III. Rapids with high, irregular waves capable of swamping an open canoe. Narrow passages that often require complex maneuvering. Might require scouting from shore.

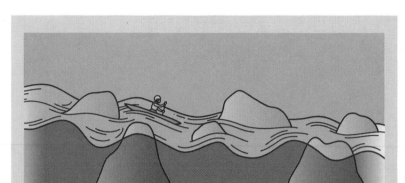

Class IV. Long, difficult rapids with constricted passages that often require precise maneuvering in very turbulent waters. Scouting from shore is often necessary, and rescue could be difficult. Generally not possible for open canoes. Boaters in covered canoes and kayaks should know how to Eskimo-roll.

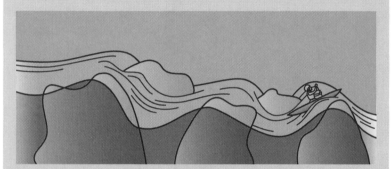

Class V. Extremely difficult, long, and very violent rapids with highly congested routes that nearly always must be scouted from shore. Rescue conditions are difficult, and there is significant hazard to life in the event of a mishap. The ability to Eskimo-roll kayaks is essential.

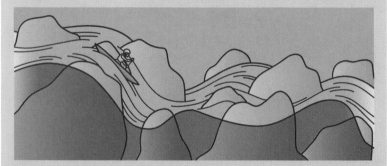

Class VI. Difficulties of Class V carried to the extreme of navigability. Nearly impossible to negotiate and very dangerous. For teams of experts only, after close study and with every precaution taken.

River Runner Signals

River runners scouting a river downstream from their fellow boaters or going first on a stretch of water can use signals to let those behind them know important information about what awaits them. Before beginning a day on a river, a group should agree upon the signals they will use and then practice them so that there will be no confusion later on.

• Come Ahead/All Clear

• Stop

• Go This Way

• Gaining Attention (Problem or Emergency Ahead)

16

Ferrying

Much of the maneuvering employed by river canoeists, kayakers, and rafters involves *ferrying*—moving a boat laterally as those at the paddles or oars seek out optimum routes. Here's how ferrying works:

A craft going straight down a river generally will hold that course. If you turn the boat at an angle to the current and paddle against the flow, however, the boat will begin to move across the current. Boaters can row or paddle to maintain the correct ferrying angle and to move more quickly toward different portions of the stream. Ferrying can be used to position a boat to miss an upcoming obstacle, to tuck into an inviting eddy, or to catch a tongue of smooth water for a fast, easy ride through the rapids. There are many fine points to the art of ferrying, some applying to all kinds of boats, others specific only to kayaks or canoes or rafts.

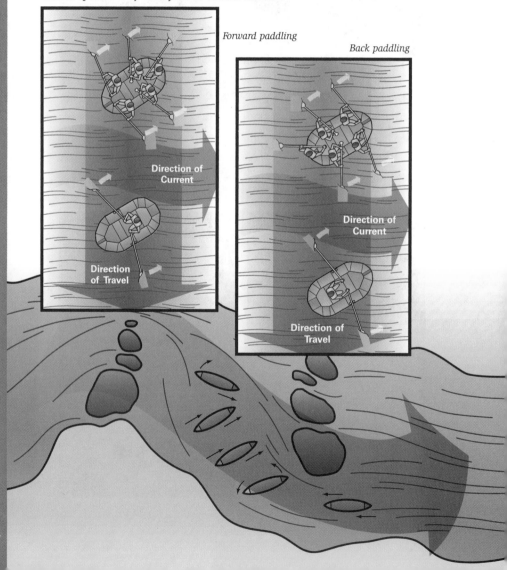

Forward paddling

Back paddling

Direction of Current

Direction of Current

Direction of Travel

Direction of Travel

Watercraft Emergency Procedures

Every kayaker, rafter, and canoeist capsizes now and then. Whenever that happens, the safety of people comes first. You can always retrieve watercraft and equipment after everyone has been brought ashore. Arranging for competent leaders trained in coping with watercraft emergencies is an important preparation for groups setting out on trips into challenging waters.

(Dinghies and other sailboats also can capsize. For additional guidelines on what to do when that happens, see the chapter titled "Sailing.")

THINGS CAN BE REPLACED; YOU CAN'T

Life is more valuable than gear. Regardless of what happens to boats and equipment, always focus your efforts on ensuring the safety of yourself and everyone else.

When You Capsize

When you do capsize, follow these steps:

1 If you can, stay in your righted boat even though it is flooded. The hull of the craft can protect you from banging into obstacles, and you might be able to paddle to shallow water. (Experienced kayakers often right their craft using an Eskimo roll.) Whitewater canoeists may be able to right the canoe in less turbulent water.

2 If you have been tossed into the water, hang onto your boat. It will stay afloat, and it will be easy for rescuers to spot. Quickly work your way to the upstream end of the craft to shield yourself from being slammed or pinned against upcoming obstacles.

3 In the following situations, swim aggressively for shore:

a. You have been thrown clear of your boat.

b. The water is very cold.

c. You are approaching worsening rapids.

d. No rescue is imminent.

4 If you must ride out a rapids before swimming to safety or catching a rescue line, go downstream feetfirst with your legs acting as shock absorbers to fend off rocks. Use a backstroke to maneuver past obstacles, and watch for eddies that might protect you.

5 Do not stand up in swift-moving water. You risk foot entrapment in the rocks on the river bottom, which could pull you under.

6 When rescuers are trying to assist you, do all you can to help them help you.

16

Using a Throw Rope

A rescue line, or *throw rope*, is floating rope 60 to 70 feet in length. When stuffed into a *throw bag*, the rope will pay out neatly when the bag is tossed. Whether in a throw bag or coiled, a throw rope should be secured to the floor of your canoe, kayak, or raft in such a way that in case of an upset it cannot ensnare people in the water or snag on obstacles and trap the boat.

In rapids where upsets are likely, station people with throw ropes on shore or in boats at the end of the section of rough water. If a boat capsizes, follow these steps:

❶ Get the attention of people in the water by yelling or blowing your emergency whistle.

❷ Grasp the free end of the throw rope and toss the throw bag or the coiled rope directly at the boater in the water. If you miss, coil the rope and try another throw.

❸ Pull in the line to bring the person to safety, but take great care not to be pulled into the water or otherwise get yourself into a situation where you must be rescued, too. Walking along the shore as you haul in line might help the person you are rescuing cope with the current.

Advanced techniques of watercraft rescue require practice and qualified instruction. Find out about good training courses by checking with your BSA local council service center and with organizations such as the American Red Cross, American Whitewater Association, and American Canoe Association. (Links to boating organizations and to other information about rescue on the water can be found on the *Fieldbook* Web site.) ⬕

Characteristics of Open Water

Boaters on large lakes and salt water will encounter many of the same safety challenges as do kayakers, rafters, and canoeists on rivers. Additional concerns include navigating, encountering marine traffic, and changes in the weather while a group is afloat.

Sea kayakers who have spray skirts to keep rain out of their boats and rain gear to keep themselves dry might not be discouraged by wet weather as long as the water remains calm and the visibility good. Making headway into the wind can be difficult, however, rain or shine. Wind also can pile up waves, increasing the challenge of getting anywhere. Kayakers and open-water canoeists might find that their best course of action in foul weather is to get ashore and wait until the wind dies down or changes direction.

Tides can be the friend or foe of sea kayakers, sailors, and canoeists. In regions such as Puget Sound or the coast of Maine with many small islands and inlets, an incoming tide creates strong currents through channels and passes. Six hours later, the outgoing tide forms currents of equal power running in the opposite direction. Boaters can time their saltwater travels to use those currents, knowing full well it can be all but fruitless to paddle against the tide.

Local forecasts often are available from commercial radio and television stations. Weather information also is provided by the National Oceanic and Atmospheric Administration over AM/FM radios with a weather frequency, and via VHF marine weather and distress radios.

For more on weather, see the chapter titled "Monitoring Weather." For more on open-water concerns, see the chapters titled "Canoeing," "Kayaking and Rafting," and "Sailing."

> *"Swift or smooth, broad as the Hudson or narrow enough to scrape your gunwales, every river is a world of its own, unique in pattern and personality. Each mile on a river will take you further from home than a hundred miles on a road."*
>
> —Bob Marshall, wilderness advocate, mountain traveler, and principal founder of the Wilderness Society

Canoeing

"The movement of a canoe is like a reed in the wind. Silence is part of it, and the sounds of lapping water, bird songs, and wind in the trees. It is part of the medium through which it floats, the sky, the water, the shores . . . ."

—Sigurd Olsen, *The Singing Wilderness,* 1956 (A naturalist, backcountry traveler, and one of the founding fathers of the Boundary Waters Canoe Area, Olsen received the 1974 John Burroughs Medal, the highest honor in nature writing.)

Perhaps it would be best to discourage you from paddling away in a canoe. Maybe you should be warned not to stow your camping gear beneath its gunwales and aim its bow toward territory you've never seen before. It might be a good idea to discourage you from ever taking a whitewater canoe into the rapids of a wild river. If you don't want to become hooked, stay away from canoes, because once you dip a paddle in the water, your life will change.

Canoeing has been part of the Scouting experience since the earliest days of the Boy Scouts of America. Materials used to build canoes have changed, and so has the world in which people paddle them. The basic skills of canoeing are the same as they have always been, though, and the joy of canoeing is as strong today as ever.

So turn your bow toward open territory. Push off from shore and you could be setting out on a lifelong journey of canoeing adventures that will take you farther, show you more, and bring you a greater abundance of joy than almost any other means of outdoor travel.

A fine canoe is never the result of chance.

—J. Henry Rushton, 19th-century canoe builder

SAFETY ESSENTIALS FOR CANOEING

For a discussion of safety issues that apply to canoeists, see the chapter titled "Watercraft Adventure Safety."

Canoes

The classic birch-bark canoe is one of our continent's great technological and artistic achievements. American Indians of the northeastern woodlands long ago perfected the art of using split roots to stitch birch bark over wooden frames, then sealing the stitch holes and seams with tree pitch. The results were swift, elegant watercraft ideal for maneuvering on rivers and lakes and for hauling heavy loads. If bark canoes were damaged by rocks or snags, paddlers could find repair materials as close as the next birch tree on shore.

Modern canoes bear a striking resemblance to the design of their birch-bark ancestors, although the materials from which they are made have changed dramatically. By the late 1800s birch-bark canoes were being replaced by canoes made of thin strips of wood carefully fitted together, or of canvas laid over wooden frames and stiffened with lacquer. Aluminum canoes appeared in large numbers after World War II when several aircraft manufacturers retrofitted their production lines to build canoes from metal. Today aluminum is giving way to specialized fabrics, epoxy, vinyl, and resin forming solo and tandem canoes designed for activities ranging from quiet journeys on gentle waters to long-distance wilderness expeditions and runs through the rapids of whitewater rivers.

The canoes you learn to paddle are likely to be whatever boats are handy—the aluminum fleet at a camp or high-adventure base, the canoes of a local watercraft organization, boats available to your family or neighbors. As you move beyond the basics, you might want to find a canoe of a size, material, and design that better matches your activities on the water. Solo canoes, tandems, and canoes outfitted for white water are just a few of the options from which to choose. Don't let a lack of options hold you back, though. Every canoe floats, and any adventure on the water is better than not going at all. Settle into the best boat you can find, and the rest of the journey will fall into place.

Types of Canoes

Aluminum canoes are durable and relatively inexpensive, factors that make them common at many summer camps. They can be noisy on the water, are often less sophisticated in shape and design than canoes made of other materials, and can get hung up on rocks in shallow passages, but they withstand hard use and are the only canoes that can be stored outdoors for long periods without suffering damage from weather or ultraviolet light.

Fiberglass canoes also are sturdy, but vary widely in weight, quality, and price. Fiberglass can be molded into hull shapes that make good flatwater canoes.

Royalex® canoes are made of *acrylonitrile butadiene styrene,* a material with a strength and flexibility beyond that of aluminum, fiberglass, or polyethylene. These canoes are the choice of many experienced paddlers for running rapids and embarking on extended expeditions. A Royalex® canoe will slide over rocks just beneath the surface of the water without damaging the hull of the canoe.

Polyethylene canoes are tough, economical, and reliable. They are similar in design to Royalex® canoes, but they are heavier and more difficult to repair.

Kevlar® canoes are constructed with layers of Kevlar®, a material also used to make bulletproof vests. Light and expensive, Kevlar® canoes often are finished with a fiberglass skin that is easy to maintain.

Folding canoes can be disassembled and compressed to a size that will fit in the trunk of a car or the cargo hold of a bush plane. Composed of metal or plastic frames covered with sturdy vinyl fabric, folding canoes can be a good solution when reaching the put-in point is as challenging as the journey itself. Well-built folding canoes are surprisingly sturdy and have considerable grace and maneuverability on the water.

Wood-strip canoes and canvas canoes employing construction methods more than a century old still hold a place in canoeing. Canoes fashioned from strips of cedar sandwiched with fiberglass can be beautiful and capable of high performance. Lacquered canvas over wooden ribs and planks can be challenging for avid watercraft crews to construct and maintain, and a delight to use on the water.

Whitewater Canoes

Long the domain of kayaks and rafts, an increasing number of paddlers are taking on rapids in whitewater canoes built to turn quickly and provide stability through heavy hydraulics. Many whitewater canoes carry flotation bags and have decks—features also found in kayaks. While whitewater canoe designs might vary, the basics of watercraft safety remain the same for any boaters setting out for adventure on rivers and open water.

For more on whitewater considerations, see the chapter titled "Kayaking and Rafting."

Parts of a Canoe

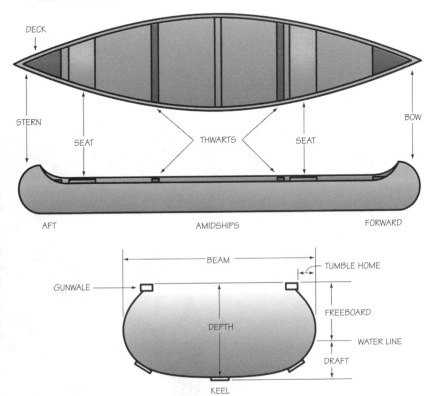

Outfitting Your Canoe

Whether you're setting out for an hour of paddling on a lake, a day of playing in whitewater rapids, or a month of wilderness exploration, your canoe must be outfitted with essentials to propel it and to protect its passengers.

Personal Flotation Device

A personal flotation device (PFD) for each person is as important as any piece of gear you have on the water, perhaps even more vital than the canoe itself. PFDs work only if they are worn and if they fit well. For guidelines on selecting, fitting, and caring for PFDs, see the chapter titled "Watercraft Adventure Safety."

Lines

Any lines on a canoe must float and should be securely stowed when not in use. Those used for tethering gear must be as short as possible so that they cannot become entanglement hazards if the canoe capsizes. *Painters*—lines attached to the bow and stern of a canoe—are helpful for maneuvering the craft through shallow waters and for tying up ashore. Each painter should be half again as long as the canoe to which it is attached.

Bailer and Sponge

Canoes are bound to take on some water no matter how calm a lake or stream. A large sponge secured to a thwart with a very short bungee cord is handy for sopping up puddles. You can make a bailer for emptying greater volumes of water from your canoe by cutting a section out of a 1-gallon plastic jug. An ideal way to secure a bailer to a boat is with a plastic buckle. Secure one portion of the buckle to a D-ring cemented to the floor of the boat. Attach the other part of the buckle to the handle of the bailer with no more than an inch or two of slack in the buckle webbing. Clipping the buckle will hold the bailer in the boat when you don't need it, but will keep it readily available for use when you do.

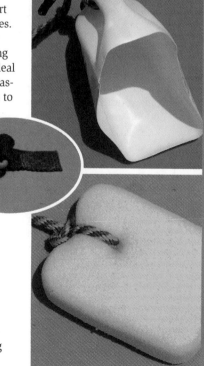

By all means, avoid tying a bailer to your canoe with a long length of cord. A five-cent bailer that snags on submerged rocks can trash a capsized thousand-dollar canoe by anchoring it in a bad spot in the river. Secure bailers—and all other gear—to your canoe with short pieces of line, leaving minimum slack.

Yoke

Whether on a long wilderness portage or a short trip down a trail from a road to the edge of a lake, there are going to be times when you carry your canoe. A yoke makes it possible for one person to do that. Some yokes are built into canoes as a center thwart while others can be temporarily clamped to the gunwales. Using a yoke is discussed later in this chapter.

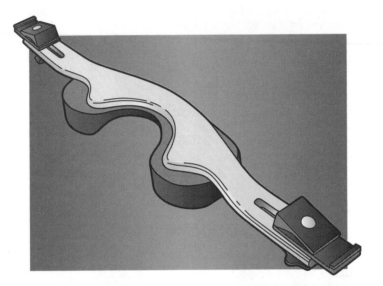

Knee Pads

Knee pads glued into a canoe with contact cement can provide essential comfort during long days of paddling and for strenuous workouts in white water. Pads are commercially available, or can be cut from closed-cell foam sleeping pads.

Duct Tape

Duct tape is handy for everything from repairing torn canoes and splintered paddles to plugging boat leaks and patching the seat of your pants. Stow a roll in your repair kit, or wind some tape around a canoe thwart where it will be handy when you need it. Be sure that the duct tape you carry is waterproof and sturdy enough for watercraft repair.

Paddles

On even the shortest canoe journey, you'll lift your paddle thousands of times, making a lightweight paddle worth plenty. Paddle shape is important, too. Some paddles are noisy in the water, splashing canoeists and providing little propulsion for the effort. Avoid heavy, all-plastic paddles that flex. Other paddles, though, are hydrodynamically gifted, moving through the water as if by magic and giving pleasure with each stroke.

Canoe paddles are made of wood, aluminum, plastic, or combinations of all three. Wooden paddles have a classic look and feel. Shorter blades are best for shallow rivers, while blades that are long and narrow can be quieter and easier to manage, and are ideal for canoeing on lakes. A blade width of seven to eight inches is good for beginners.

The blade of a paddle might be in line with its loom or it might be bent at an angle of up to 15 degrees. Because the paddle remains at a right angle to the surface of the water through most of a forward stroke, a *bent-loom paddle* allows a canoeist to maximize the power of each stroke. Canoeists playing in white water often choose straight-loom paddles for better control.

GRIP

LOOM

THROAT

BLADE

GALYAN'S

TIP

17

Sizing a Canoe Paddle

The length of paddle you need depends in large part on the kind of canoeing you will be doing (a solo canoeist might prefer a longer paddle for flat water and a shorter paddle for white water), whether you will be sitting or kneeling in your canoe, and whether the paddle is straight or bent (many bent-loom paddles are sized a little shorter than paddles with straight looms).

To get a general idea of the paddle length that's right for you, take your normal paddling position sitting or kneeling in a floating canoe, then have someone measure the vertical distance from your nose to the surface of the water. That's about the length of the *loom* of your first paddle. Add to that the length of the *blade*—usually another 20 to 25 inches. Lighter paddles are better than heavier ones, if all else is equal. As you gain experience, you will be able to fine-tune paddle size and design to match your needs on the water.

Loading, Launching, and Landing a Canoe

Canoes are creatures of the water. Get them on land or in the transition zone between land and water, and they can be awkward to handle and prone to damage. Before loading and launching a canoe, put on your PFD and shoes that you won't mind getting wet. Team up with another person to lift the canoe by the bow and stern thwarts or decks, then carry it into water deep enough for it to float. Never *bridge* a canoe by resting it on a small section of its bottom or side, and never leave the bow on a dock or the shoreline while the stern is afloat.

A canoe should be in calf-deep water, parallel to the shore as you load it and get aboard. Stow packs, duffels, and dry bags low and close to the middle of the canoe, packing them in tightly and tying them down with short lines so that they will stay in place if the canoe overturns. Hold the craft steady while your partner gets aboard and settled, then place your hands on the gunwales and keep your weight centered and low as you step into the canoe and take your position. Push off and you're on your way.

Land a canoe by reversing the steps of launching. Bring the canoe parallel to the shore and step out of the craft while it is still fully afloat. Stabilize the canoe while your partner disembarks, then remove the paddles and gear before carrying the canoe onto land. Never run the bow of a canoe onto the shore—that's a sure way to cause damage.

17

Paddling a Canoe

Good position and body mechanics lead to effective paddling. Whether you canoe with a partner or alone, either kneel in the canoe with your weight against a thwart or the front edge of a seat and your knees wedged against the sides of the craft, or sit solidly on a seat and brace your knees against the gunwales. Think of yourself as a part of the canoe, locked in place. Maintain a smooth rhythm with your paddle, keeping your strokes steady and light. Use your arms to guide your paddle, but power the strokes with the larger muscle groups of your abdomen, shoulders, and back. To maintain a steady pace over long distances, practice the *forward stroke, J-stroke, solo-C stroke,* and *hit-and-switch (Minnesota switch)*. To maneuver through currents, eddies, and white water, become familiar with the *backstroke, drawstroke,* and *pry.*

Forward Stroke and Backstroke

Bow paddlers, stern paddlers, and solo canoeists all can use the *forward stroke.* Hold the paddle by the grip and loom, your hands about shoulder-width apart, and twist your torso to move the paddle forward. Keeping your grip hand over the gunwale and lower than the top of your head, submerge the paddle blade, then use the muscles of your abdomen and back to pull the canoe ahead of the paddle. The sensation should be that the paddle remains stationary in the water while the canoe moves to it and then beyond. As it comes out of the water, flip the blade sideways, or *feather* it, so that it will cut through the wind as you swing the paddle ahead to begin the next stroke. Tandem paddlers can synchronize their strokes on opposite sides to keep a canoe running true.

Stop a canoe's forward progress and move it backward by using the *backstroke.* Place the paddle blade in the water near your hip at a right angle to the water. Push forward until paddle comes out of the water. Feather it back to the starting point and repeat the stroke.

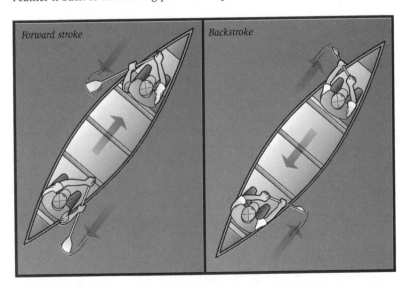

Forward stroke

Backstroke

J-Stroke

The forward strokes of a paddler in the stern of a canoe will have more effect on the direction a canoe travels than will those of a paddler in the bow, causing the craft to turn away from the strokes of the stern paddler. One way to counteract that mechanical advantage is for the paddler in the stern to use a *J-stroke*.

Begin this stroke as you would a forward stroke. When you have pulled the paddle past your hip, rotate your grip hand so that your thumb rolls down and the paddle blade is vertical. Push the paddle *away from the canoe*. Seen from above, the stroke forms the shape of the letter **J**, the hook in the **J** forming as you push the paddle away from the canoe to correct its course.

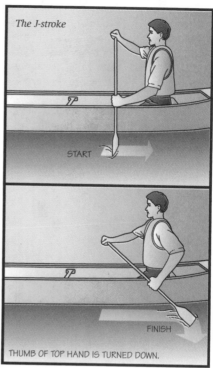

The J-stroke

START

FINISH

THUMB OF TOP HAND IS TURNED DOWN.

Solo-C Stroke

A solo paddler kneeling in the center of a canoe can steer by using the *solo-C stroke*. Begin by placing the paddle in the water ahead and away from the canoe. Draw the blade in toward your knee. In a smooth motion, continue pulling the paddle alongside the canoe and then sweep it outward, turning your thumb down as you do so. The forces created as the paddle cuts a **C** shape in the water will counteract the turning power of the forward stroke and keep the craft in line.

Hit-and-Switch (Minnesota Switch)

An effective means of maintaining a canoe's bearing is by using a forward stroke and switching your paddle from one side of the craft to the other after every few strokes. In a tandem canoe, the stern paddler calls out, "Hut!" to let the paddler in the bow know they will make the switch before the next stroke so that they always have one paddle on each side of their boat, a technique known as the *hit-and-switch* or *Minnesota switch*. A solo paddler can make the switch whenever the canoe's heading begins to drift. Unlike other forward strokes, paddles are not feathered during these switches.

This means of paddling works well on flat water and when traveling into the wind. Accomplished canoe racers can hit and switch without missing a beat, maintaining a paddling rate of 60 to 70 strokes a minute. The hit-and-switch is not appropriate for white water, though, since during changeovers it leaves canoeists without the stability of paddles in the water serving as braces.

Drawstroke

A *drawstroke* will move your canoe sideways toward the paddle. Keeping the paddle loom vertical and the blade facing the canoe, place the blade into the water. (Keep your center of balance over the center line of your boat; leaning out can capsize the canoe.) Feel the blade stick in the water and draw the canoe toward the paddle using the muscles of your torso. Slip the blade out of the water sideways just before it touches the canoe.

Pry

The *pry* will move your canoe away from the paddling side. Holding the paddle as you would for a drawstroke, slip the blade into the water next to the canoe and pry it away. Though it can be hard on the paddle loom, you can brace the loom against the canoe, using the gunwale as a fulcrum for leveraging the stern away from the blade of the paddle.

Draw and Pry Combinations

When paddling tandem, draws and prys can be used to move the canoe sideways or spin it in place. If the bow paddler does a draw while the stern paddler does a pry, the canoe will move sideways toward the side of the bow paddle. To move in the opposite direction, reverse the strokes—a pry in the bow and a draw in the stern. To change direction from a stop, you can pivot or spin the canoe in place by both paddlers doing a draw at the same time. To spin in the other direction, both do a pry.

Portaging

Canoes are best carried over long distances by one person, though hoisting overhead for a carry is often better done by a team of two.

Two-Person Portage Lift

Position yourself near the bow of the canoe, your partner near the stern. Reach across the canoe and grasp the gunwales, then in unison lift the canoe and flip it over your heads, turning yourselves forward as you do. As your partner stabilizes the canoe, walk your hands backward along the gunwales until you can tuck your shoulders against the yoke. Your partner is free to duck out from under the canoe, and you are ready to begin a portage. Your partner leads the way as you walk, alerting you to obstacles or turns in the trail. If you tire before the end of the portage, lean the bow of the canoe into the crotch of a tree and rest the stern on the ground.

One-Person Portage Lift

With practice, one canoeist can lift a canoe for portaging. To begin, stand at one side of the upright canoe, near the stern and facing the bow. Grasp the gunwales, one in each hand, a few feet from the stern. Turn the canoe over and lift it over your head, allowing the bow to remain on the ground. Holding the gunwales, begin "walking" toward the bow. As you reach the center of the canoe, its weight will balance over your shoulders and the bow will lift off the ground. Ease the yoke onto your shoulders to carry the canoe.

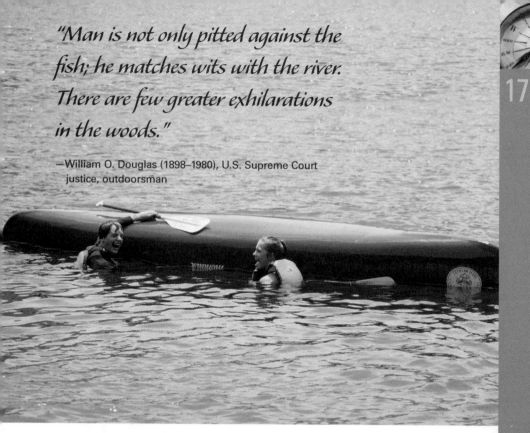

> *"Man is not only pitted against the fish; he matches wits with the river. There are few greater exhilarations in the woods."*
>
> —William O. Douglas (1898–1980), U.S. Supreme Court justice, outdoorsman

Canoe Safety and Rescue

Safety is the most important word in canoeing. Every water sport has its hazards, but if you are aware of the dangers and are prepared to manage common risks, you can enjoy a lifetime of canoeing adventures without serious mishap.

For starters, you should be a good swimmer. Training in lifesaving will give you added confidence. While you are on the water, wear a PFD. Stay within shouting distance of other canoes in your party, and be aware of weather and water conditions. When paddling on lakes, keeping near a shoreline will allow you to get ashore quickly if a storm is brewing or if the wind whips up waves that make you uneasy.

On rivers, tie up your canoe and scout ahead on foot if the water downstream is rough or you have any suspicion that there might be snags, rapids, or drops. Before running a rapids, gather all the canoes in your group and plan not only how to navigate the stretch of white water, but also how to support one another should a canoe overturn. Precautions might include stationing people with throw ropes at the end of a rapids. If in doubt about the wisdom of paddling through any stretch of water, portage around it.

For more on canoeing safely and using throw ropes, see the chapter titled "Watercraft Adventure Safety." The BSA's Safe Swim Defense plan and Safety Afloat provide guidelines for appropriate ways to conduct activities in and on the water. For the full text of these publications, see the *Fieldbook* Web site.

Rescues

A canoe will stay afloat even if it is full of water. Usually your best bet after capsizing, especially on a quiet lake or stream, is to stay with the canoe. Rocking it back and forth might slosh much of the water from your craft. Climb back in, sit on the bottom, and use your hands or a paddle to propel yourself to shore.

If there are other paddlers nearby, they can bring their canoes alongside the swamped craft, assist wet canoeists, retrieve floating gear, and help get the waterlogged canoe to shallow water where it can be righted and repacked. (Never tie a line from a capsized canoe to yourself or your watercraft. A swamped canoe is heavy; if the current carries it off, you don't want to be dragged along with it.)

Every canoeist manages now and then to swamp a canoe. Intentionally capsize your craft in calm water and practice various kinds of rescues and recoveries until they become automatic. That way you'll know what to do when you upset accidentally.

Canoe-Over-Canoe Recovery

If paddlers capsize far from shore in a calm lake, a canoe-over-canoe procedure might be in order to empty a swamped canoe.

❶ Come alongside the capsized canoe on the side away from people in the water.

❷ Hold the capsized canoe and direct canoeists in the water to hang onto your canoe near the ends on the side opposite the swamped canoe.

17

③ Swing the capsized canoe at a right angle to yours. As you raise the bow, tilt the canoe to let the water drain out. Then lift the canoe and set it on your gunwale.

④ Ease the canoe across the gunwales of your canoe, scooting it along until it is balanced.

⑤ Roll the capsized canoe upright on your canoe's gunwales, then slide it back onto the water.

⑥ Hold the emptied canoe alongside yours and stabilize it as its crew climbs back aboard.

Packing for a Canoe Trip

For canoe trips involving overnight camps, you'll need all the gear a backpacker would use. Even though the capacity of a canoe allows you to carry plenty of cargo, pack light and tight. That will make it easier for you to complete portages and can increase the ease of traveling and camping without leaving a trace. Pack as if you are certain your canoe will be capsized, too, even though you hope it won't.

There are many watertight containers on the market for canoeists, rafters, and kayakers, or you can pack all your items into heavy-duty plastic bags. Close each bag with a *gooseneck* by twisting the top and then bending it over and wrapping it with a strong rubber band. Put the bags into packs or duffels lined with larger plastic bags such as trash-can liners and gooseneck those, as well. Stow cameras, binoculars, maps, compasses, lunches, and other items you'll want during the day in neoprene or nylon dry bags that can be rolled closed to keep out moisture. Double-bag anything that must be kept absolutely dry.

Secure each pack, duffel, and bag tightly in your canoe so that nothing can come out if the craft overturns. Put the heaviest gear on the floor of the canoe and lash everything to D-rings cemented to the floor or under the inside of the gunwales. Use short pieces of floating rope for tying in gear and leave no more than a couple of inches of loose ends beyond the knots. If your canoe does flip over, you want everything in it to stay positioned deep inside the canoe where it will add flotation. Tethered bags that float out of the canoe will, at best, make righting the boat more difficult, and at worst can snag on obstructions in a river or entangle swimming paddlers in tether lines.

Canoe Storage and Care

Caring for a canoe between trips will ensure that it will be in top condition when you are ready to put it back on the water.

- Wash a canoe inside and out with fresh water. Check bolts, rivets, and other fasteners, and survey joints for cracks. Repair any damage.

- Regularly treat wood trim with a good marine finish. Several times during the canoeing season, apply an ultraviolet barrier to plastic trim and plastic boats. Follow manufacturers' instructions.

- Store the canoe upside down on a canoe rack or sawhorses.

"The canoe is the simplest, most functional yet aesthetically pleasing object ever created."

—Bill Mason (Canadian author, filmmaker, and canoe enthusiast), *Path of the Paddle,* 1984

CHAPTER

18

Kayaking and Rafting

"It is calm, the smooth sea heaves in a long swell towards the rocky islets that fringe the shore, a light haze still lies over the sounds between them, and the seabirds floating on the surface seem double their natural size. The kayaks cut their way forward, side by side, making only a silent ripple."

—Fridtjof Nansen, *Eskimo Life*, 1894

Tumbling down mountain valleys, foaming through sandstone canyons, heaving, boiling, and swirling between the walls of narrow gorges, wild rivers were once the bane of travelers. They were to be avoided rather than relished, gone around rather than down. Today, all of that has changed. Kayakers and rafters are discovering that rivers can be fluid pathways into some of the finest unspoiled country anywhere. Many offer the bonus of rapids challenging river runners of every skill level. Sea kayaks are expanding the range of possibilities beyond streams, too, as paddlers explore shorelines, coves, and bays, and set out on extended journeys across open water.

Terrific adventures await you just beyond the bows of kayaks and rafts. With some essential preparation and basic training, you'll soon be taking a paddle in hand or grasping a pair of oars and launching out on your own great watercraft trips.

Kayaks

Natives of the far northern latitudes have been building kayaks for thousands of years, stretching sealskins over sturdy frames fashioned from driftwood to make light, streamlined boats. Modern sport kayaks, while similar in appearance to their sealskin ancestors, are constructed of some of the same durable materials as modern canoes. The most obvious distinctions can be seen in the differences between kayaks built for white water and those intended for the sea.

Touring Kayaks

Touring kayaks are shaped to maintain a course over long distances rather than to make rapid changes in direction. Touring kayaks also are known as sea kayaks, although many never touch salt water, instead leaving their wakes on quiet rivers, lakes, and inland waterways. They are quite a bit longer and flatter than whitewater kayaks, and some have a movable rudder or a stationary fin, called a *skeg*, to help them track a true line—a useful feature when paddlers must contend with winds, tides, and currents.

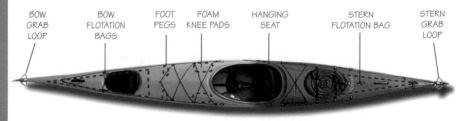

BOW GRAB LOOP   BOW FLOTATION BAGS   FOOT PEGS   FOAM KNEE PADS   HANGING SEAT   STERN FLOTATION BAG   STERN GRAB LOOP

Touring kayak

Storage compartments and roomy interiors allow kayakers to carry provisions and gear for camping trips of several days or more. Some touring kayaks feature two cockpits so that partners can paddle in tandem.

Folding and Inflatable Kayaks

Kayaks that can be dismantled for packing and transport make it possible for boaters to reach put-in points on rivers and lakes that might be inaccessible for more conventional boats. Inflatable kayaks offer terrific portability and ease of storage, and they are less expensive than many rigid kayaks, though inflatables don't have decks or cockpits, and thus no way to seal out water.

Hybrid Kayaks

Thanks to its rounded hull and pronounced bottom curve, or *rocker,* a hybrid kayak can manage the quick maneuvers needed for running rapids. The compact interiors of whitewater kayaks offer little room for storing gear.

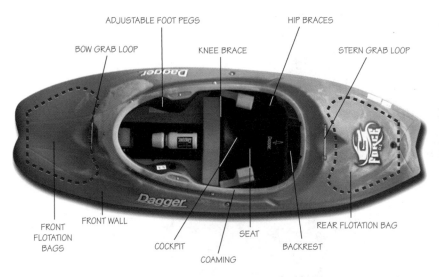

ADJUSTABLE FOOT PEGS · HIP BRACES · BOW GRAB LOOP · KNEE BRACE · STERN GRAB LOOP · FRONT FLOTATION BAGS · FRONT WALL · COCKPIT · SEAT · COAMING · BACKREST · REAR FLOTATION BAG

Hybrid kayak—squirt or stunt boat

Kayak Materials

Anyone familiar with canoe construction will recognize that many of the same materials are used to build kayaks. The *polyethylene* found in most molded whitewater kayaks is tough and relatively inexpensive. *Fiberglass* kayaks are durable and lightweight. They can be more easily damaged than boats made of other materials, but they are easy to repair. A kayak that includes layers of *Kevlar®* fabric can be strong, light, and pricey.

Outfitting Your Kayak

There is more to a kayak than simply the boat. As with canoeing, rafting, sailing, and any other activities involving watercraft, you'll need a personal flotation device (PFD), clothing appropriate for the conditions, and protection from the sun. Kayakers and canoeists venturing into white water also must wear helmets. Sea kayakers might require navigational aids and additional items of emergency gear. A spray skirt, paddle, flotation bags, and bilge pump round out the basic kayaking equipment. (For more on preparing for watercraft activities, see the chapter titled "Watercraft Adventure Safety.")

Spray Skirt

A spray skirt made of neoprene or coated nylon fits tightly around your waist and, when you are seated in a kayak, attaches to the rim of the cockpit. The skirt will prevent water from flooding the craft while you negotiate rapids, are hit by spray and waves, or roll upside down. A release loop at the front of the skirt allows you to detach it quickly if you must bail out of the boat.

SAFETY ESSENTIALS FOR KAYAKING AND RAFTING

For a discussion of safety issues that apply to kayakers and rafters, see the chapter titled "Watercraft Adventure Safety." For the text of the BSA's Safe Swim Defense and Safety Afloat, see the *Fieldbook* Web site.

Paddles

Kayak paddles are made of fiberglass, plastic, wood, aluminum, or combinations of materials, and feature double blades that are either *feathered* or *unfeathered*. Seasoned kayakers argue both sides of the paddle angle issue, revealing the advantages of each:

- *Feathered paddles.* The blades are offset from one another, or *feathered*, most commonly at an angle of about 45 degrees. As one blade pulls against the water, the other blade is positioned to cut through the wind. With a twist of the wrist, a kayaker rotates the paddle shaft to position the blades for each stroke. The shafts of most paddles are oval rather than round, enabling paddlers to sense by feel the pitch of the blades.

- *Unfeathered paddles.* The blades share the same alignment. Unfeathered paddles require no wrist adjustment between strokes, and can be easier for beginning kayakers to manage. However, as each blade is lifted above the water, it can catch the brunt of the wind and reduce forward momentum.

Breakdown paddles are two-piece paddles with a joint in the center of the shaft; this allows them to be stowed in smaller spaces than required for one-piece paddles, which makes them excellent spares. Breakdown paddles often are the choice of boaters using inflatable or folding kayaks. They can be feathered or unfeathered, depending on how they are assembled. *One-piece paddles* have no joints, and thus little can go wrong with them.

18

Sizing a Kayak Paddle

Hold a kayak paddle over your head with your elbows bent at a 90-degree angle. For a whitewater paddle, there should be about 6 inches of shaft between your hand and the paddle blade. For a touring paddle, that distance should be at least 12 inches. In general, a paddle that is too short is better than one that is too long, and narrow blades will be easier to manage than wide ones.

Flotation Bags

The watertight storage compartments of most sea kayaks double as flotation chambers. A whitewater kayak, however, might not possess enough buoyancy by itself to stay afloat when filled with water. *Flotation bags* inserted in the bow and stern prevent water from completely filling a capsized craft, and will keep it from sinking. Vertical walls under the bow and stern decks strengthen the kayak and help prevent it from collapsing when the boat is under the extreme pressure of rough water.

"The best bilge pump is a scared man with a bucket."

—Traditional maritime lore

Bilge Pump

A spray skirt will keep most of the water out of a kayak, but during a long paddle on open seas or on an outing when a spray skirt isn't essential, some water is bound to get into your boat. A handheld pump can be the answer for getting rid of it while you are afloat. When not in use, the pump can ride under elastic cords on the deck. (Some boats are equipped with built-in pumps that can be operated by a kayaker without removing the spray skirt. Sponges and bailers, common in canoes, also are efficient means for rafters and kayakers to remove water from their boats.)

Carrying a Kayak

Many kayaks have toggles installed at the bow and stern, positioned for two people to lift and carry a craft. For a solo carry, reach across the cockpit, lift the kayak, and flip it onto your shoulder. (If the kayak is heavy, allow the stern to stay on the ground as you lift and position it.) Shift the cockpit on your shoulder to reach the kayak's balance point, and you should be ready for a relatively easy tote to your destination.

Getting Into a Kayak

A kayak is an extension of your body, responding not only to the thrust of the paddle, but also to the motion of your torso, legs, and hips. You won't sit in a kayak so much as wear it, the tight fit helping you move the kayak with you as you maneuver.

Put the spray skirt around your waist. Provide stability to the floating kayak by placing one paddle blade across the back of the cockpit and resting the other blade on the shore or dock. Grasp the center of the paddle and the back edge of the cockpit with one hand, then ease yourself into the boat. Attach the spray skirt to the cockpit rim and you're ready to paddle off.

18

Paddle strokes used to move a kayak forward employ the *power face* of a paddle blade. Strokes for moving backward use the *back face*.

Propelling a Kayak

With a few basic strokes, you can make a kayak dance. The best place to learn is in quiet water, practicing until the strokes are automatic.

Forward Stroke

Use the *forward stroke* to move a kayak forward: Extend the right paddle blade as far toward the bow of the boat as you can, rotating your body to increase your reach, but not leaning forward. Extending your right arm, place the blade in the water close to the bow. Power comes primarily from the strong muscles of your torso as you pull your right arm back and push your left arm forward to move the kayak past the blade. When your shoulders are fully rotated to the right, knife the paddle out of the water, drop your right wrist to turn the left blade into proper position, and begin a forward stroke on the left side of the kayak.

Reverse Stroke

Use the *reverse stroke* to slow a moving kayak or move it backward. Perform this stroke by reversing the steps of the forward stroke. Begin by twisting to the right and placing the right paddle blade in the water behind you and close to the boat. Push forward by rotating your torso to the left. As the right blade slips out of the water at the end of the stroke, drop your right wrist to position the left blade, and begin a reverse stroke on the opposite side of the kayak.

Sweep Stroke

A *sweep stroke* on the right side of a kayak turns the bow to the left as it pushes the boat forward, while a sweep on the left side turns the bow the other way. A sweep is useful for moving around obstacles, though it will also slow your boat considerably. Begin a sweep by holding the paddle horizontally over the boat. Extend one arm and rotate your shoulders, then insert a blade into the water as far forward as possible, the power face turned away from the kayak's bow. Pull the paddle in a wide arc that continues all the way to the stern, powering the stroke with the twist of your shoulders and torso.

Reverse Sweep

A *reverse sweep* slows the forward motion of a kayak and turns the boat toward the side on which the stroke is performed. Use it when you need a quick, forceful course change. Holding the paddle horizontally, twist sideways and insert the blade into the water behind the cockpit. Sweep the paddle toward the bow, rotating your shoulders as you do. For best results, sweep wide.

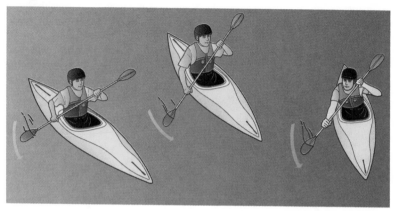

Drawstroke

Executing a *drawstroke* with the paddle aligned with your seat (a *midship draw)* will move a kayak sideways; a draw with the paddle closer to the bow will turn the boat to the stroke side, making the *bow draw* a good turning stroke.

To perform a midship draw, hold the paddle nearly vertical, your upper hand reaching out across the boat. With the power face turned toward the kayak, place the blade in the water and pull it toward the center of the boat. Before the paddle touches your craft, rotate your wrist and knife the blade under water to the starting point of the stroke.

For a bow draw, reach out and place the blade at an angle in the water, then move it toward the boat.

Bow draw

Midship draw

18

Braces

You can use your paddle to balance a kayak in much the same way outriggers give stability to Pacific island canoes. If you hold a paddle blade against the water with its leading edge tilted up slightly and sweep it back and forth, the force of the blade on the water will lift the paddle and, by extension, the boat.

Apply this principle to kayaking by trying a *low brace*. It is similar to a short sweep, but with the paddle blade nearly horizontal rather than vertical. Lean hard on the shaft during the brace; as long as the paddle is moving relative to the water, the back face of the blade will support your weight. If your kayak does begin to tip away from the sweep, roll your hips to right the boat.

Low brace

High brace

A *high brace* can save you from capsizing in rough water and larger waves. The paddle shaft is held at eye level to better position the power face, rather than the back face, of the blade against higher water. Tilt the leading edge of the blade against the push of the current to create a virtual three-point stance. Protect your upper body from injury by keeping your hands in front of your shoulders.

Kayakers can position themselves below rapids to assist boaters who might capsize.

Capsizing and Righting a Kayak

Capsizing is a part of kayaking. It might be a rare event for a sea kayaker, but in white water it can happen frequently. Practice capsizing in warm, gentle waters—a swimming pool is ideal—so that you will know what to do in a river or on open water. (Wearing a diving mask can make your experience more pleasant and enable you to study the physics of upsetting from a capsizer's point of view.) Become accustomed to making a *wet exit* from a capsized kayak by first pulling the skirt's release loop. Then lean forward to pull your legs from the boat by pushing it forward, with your hands grasping the back edges of the cockpit coaming.

Sea kayakers can use the help of other boaters to get back into their craft, or can do it alone with the aid of a *paddle float.* Both whitewater and sea kayakers can use the *Eskimo roll,* a way of righting themselves without exiting their kayaks.

Assistance From Other Boaters

Fellow kayakers can corral your capsized boat and lift one end to let water dump out of the cockpit. They also can stabilize your kayak by grasping the cockpit from one side while you scramble back in from the other side.

Hang onto your capsized kayak. It will help keep you afloat, shield you from river obstacles, and enable others to find you more easily as they come to your assistance. Keeping the boat upside down will trap air inside and cause it to float higher in the water.

Paddle Float

A *paddle float* is an inflatable bag that is carried under the bungee cord on the deck of a sea kayak. When an upset occurs, you can fit the bag over the blade of a paddle and inflate it with your breath. Then, place the opposite paddle blade across the stern deck of the swamped kayak, and scramble aboard using the floating paddle as a brace. Once you are in the cockpit, empty the boat with the bilge pump, reattach the spray skirt, and continue on your way.

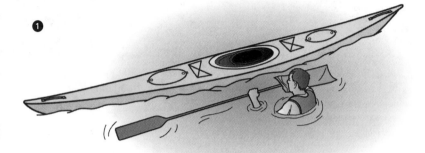

3

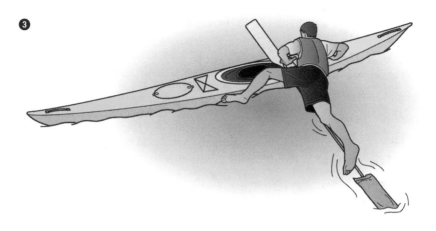

4

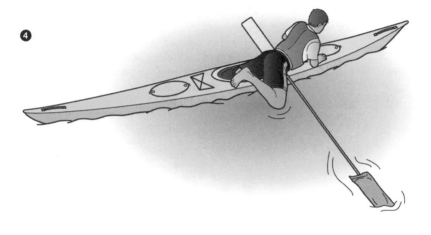

5

18

Whenever a kayak capsizes, other boaters must focus their attention on that situation until the paddler is back in the boat or has reached shore. Everyone must stand ready to help a swimming person, right a capsized craft, gather up floating gear and paddles, and render any other assistance that might be called for at the moment.

Eskimo Roll

An *Eskimo roll* allows you to recover from capsizing without having to get out of your kayak, a real advantage when you are running a rapids or in a sea kayak far from shore. Before practicing an Eskimo roll, it is crucial to know how to exit an overturned kayak. As with other responses to upsets, the Eskimo roll should be learned in quiet water. You almost certainly will need the assistance of a capable instructor to guide you through the steps.

Here's how the Eskimo roll works. As your kayak goes over, lean forward against the deck. Extend so that your face is down and one arm is across the deck. Position the paddle with the front blade's power face up and the shaft parallel to the boat. Use your shoulders, arms, and torso to move the blade in a strong sweep stroke to the kayak stern (keep the front blade on top of the water as it sweeps out from the boat). Wrap your back arm over the hull to give yourself a fulcrum for a powerful stroke. As the force of the stroke rolls you toward the surface of the water, snap the boat upright with your hips.

❶ *Position the paddle parallel and alongside the kayak.*

❷ *Lean toward the deck.*

3 As you sweep, you will roll toward the surface.

4 Keep the paddle entirely above water and bend forward over the deck.

5 Snap your hips to set the boat upright.

6 Recover the boat's balance with a high brace.

Sea Kayaking Considerations

Getting lost is an unlikely possibility for whitewater paddlers. Open water, though, especially that of large lakes, oceans, or straits and sounds dotted with islands, brings with it conditions much different from those facing river runners. Sea kayakers must develop an understanding of tides, waves, currents, and nautical navigation, and keep their skill levels ahead of the adventures on which they embark.

Essentials carried by a sea kayaker should include a personal flotation device, a spare paddle, a compass, a whistle or similar audible signal for attracting the attention of other boaters, a paddle float, and a bilge pump. The whistle can be attached to a short loop on your PFD (not the zipper pull). The compass also can be clipped to your PFD or secured to the deck where it can be seen from the kayak cockpit. More ambitious sea kayaking trips might require charts, tide tables, a marine VHF two-way radio, a GPS (global positioning system) receiver, emergency shelter and rations, a parasail, and rigging for one sea kayak to tow another.

As with many outdoor activities, sea kayaking is a social sport. Going with others allows you to enjoy an experience with your friends and, through sheer numbers of people and boats, adds considerably to everyone's margin of safety.

For more on the challenges of open water, see the chapter titled "Watercraft Adventure Safety."

Leave No Trace Kayaking

The shallow drafts and extensive range of sea kayaks allow paddlers to venture into salt marshes and mangroves, and along rocky coastlines that are largely inaccessible to other boaters or visitors on foot. Among the most pristine places on Earth, these areas serve as refuges for a tremendous range of wildlife. Enter and treat these environments with the greatest care.

For more on responsible kayaking, see the "Leaving No Trace" section of this book.

Whitewater Kayaking Considerations

A whitewater kayaking trip might be an hour or two of playing in the rapids on a short section of river, or it could be a multiday wilderness adventure with camping gear carried on a support raft. Whatever the case, stay within your abilities. Scout rapids from shore to get a good read on the river ahead so that you will know what you are getting into and how to get back out again. If an upcoming stretch of river appears to be beyond your skill level or if there are strainers, drops, or other water hazards that concern you, make a portage and rejoin the river downstream from the obstacles. There is never

any shame in carrying your boat around a rapid you aren't convinced you should run.

For more on sizing up river conditions, see the chapter titled "Watercraft Adventure Safety."

Kayak Storage

When not in use, store a kayak in a dry place sheltered from the sun. Allow it to rest upright, fully supported by its keel, or suspended on edge by three or more wide slings.

A wooden boat (Grand Canyon style)

Rafts

Many early explorers making their way down the great rivers of the American West rowed wooden boats large enough to carry their gear and rugged enough (they hoped) to withstand raging rapids. While wooden boats are still used by some traditional river runners, the sport of whitewater rafting was born shortly after World War II when adventurers began using large Army surplus rafts to challenge the enormous hydraulics of the Colorado River in the heart of the Grand Canyon.

The rafts navigating wild rivers today are direct descendants of those military rafts, but are now made of neoprene or rubberized materials resistant to abrasion and puncture. They are constructed with several inflatable chambers, each capable of keeping a raft afloat even if all the others are damaged. Many modern rafts are *self-bailing*—water they take on drains out through grommet holes surrounding an inflatable floor. Depending upon their configuration, human-powered rafts can be propelled either with paddles or with oars.

Paddle Rafts

Paddling a raft is a group activity requiring the cooperation of everyone on board. Facing forward, several river runners sit on each side of the boat and use canoe paddles to guide their raft. A group leader calls out commands, instructing the team how to stroke in order to maneuver the boat. The leader might be one of the paddlers, or might sit in the stern and use a paddle as a rudder. Paddle rafts have a distinct advantage in rock-strewn rivers with channels too tight for oar-maneuvered craft. They also allow everyone on board to take an active role in the progress of the trip.

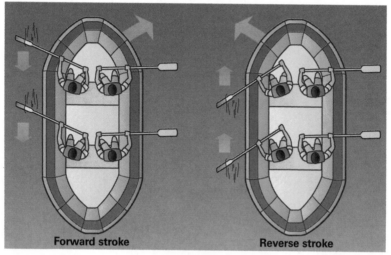

Forward stroke   **Reverse stroke**

Paddlers using a forward stroke on one side of their raft will cause it to turn away from the paddling side. A reverse stroke will pull the bow toward the paddling side.

Oar Rafts

A raft equipped with oars can best be steered by a single experienced person. Perched atop a platform in the middle of the raft, he or she has a commanding view of the river and can control the motion of the raft by pulling on oars secured to the boat's rigid frame.

Pin and clip

Oarlock

Pins and clips securing oars to a raft set the blades of the oars at the best angle to the water and make it difficult for a big wave to jerk the oars out of a rafter's hands. Oars set in oarlocks can be drawn into the boat when rafters are negotiating swift, narrow passages.

Since a raft with oars needs only one seasoned boater on board, passengers can sometimes run a river even if they don't have much white-water experience. Of course, they'll need to know how to swim, must wear personal flotation devices, and might need helmets. As the raft splashes and churns downstream, they can learn some of the basics of handling a raft in rough water by watching the person at the oars.

Steering an Oar Raft

On moving water, a rafter faces downstream and rows against the current, moving the raft laterally as the boater ferries left and right across the river for the best line through the obstacles ahead.

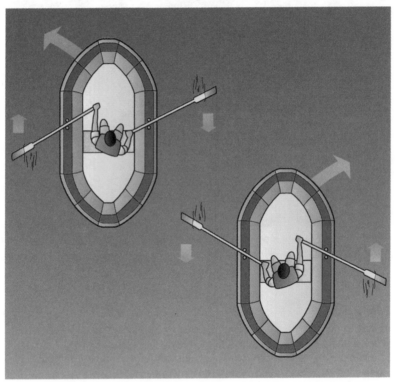

A pull stroke on one side of the raft will cause the boat to turn in that direction. A push stroke on one side will turn the boat away from the oar. Combine a pull stroke with one oar and a push stroke with the other to make a quick double oar turn, or pivot.

For more on managing river hazards and maneuvering rafts by ferrying, see the chapter titled "Watercraft Adventure Safety."

Rafts and River Journeys

While running rapids is often the high-light of a river trip, floating through a linear wilderness can open opportunities for ecology studies, fishing, camping, navigation, and many other outdoor activities. The carrying capacity of rafts makes them ideal for river trips of several days or more. A raft might be the watercraft of choice for everyone on a journey, or it might serve as the supply vehicle for a fleet that includes several kayaks or canoes.

The ability of rafters to haul lots of cargo and large numbers of people into remote areas brings with it a tremendous responsibility to understand and use the principles of Leave No Trace. That begins during the planning stages of a trip. Contact the agencies managing the river system you wish to visit and learn about any permits or restrictions that apply to you and your group. Of great importance will be methods of waste disposal (perhaps involving bringing along portable toilets called *rocket boxes* for carrying human waste to the end of your journey), fire management (using camp stoves or fire pans), and food handling (leaving shorelines and camp-sites as clean as you found them).

For more on kayaking and rafting responsibly, see the "Leaving No Trace" section of this book.

Sailing

"Your reason and your passion are the rudder and sails of your seafaring soul. If either your sails or your rudder be broken, you can but toss and drift, or else be held at a standstill in midseas."

—Kahlil Gibran (1883–1931), Lebanese novelist, poet, philosopher, and artist

A boat, the wind, open water. Nothing could be simpler, and yet no other three factors, when mixed in proper proportion, possess so much potential for adventure and delight. Cast off from a dock, hoist a sail, grasp the tiller or wheel, and you are embarking into a realm of motion, of closeness with nature, and of the pleasure of nonmotorized travel for which there simply is no comparison.

As a sailor, you can go where the wind lets you go, traveling on the wind's schedule rather than your own. While you can't force a boat to move, you can enjoy the constant adjustments of sails and rigging to take advantage of invisible vectors of sky and sea as you will your boat to cruise along a course you have plotted. With your weight to the windward, you can feel the sail pulling your boat through the water, the hull heeling to one side, water humming past the keel, the breeze a steady force in the rigging.

Sailing is one of humankind's oldest modes of travel, steeped in tradition and lore. The wisdom of sailing comes to modern sailors through thousands of years of experimentation, experience, and simple human intuition. While sailing might seem complicated to someone just starting out, it is, at its heart, the union of wind, water, and craft in constantly changing variations. You can learn the basics in an afternoon. You can spend the rest of your life striving to master them.

First Things First

Whether you are sailing for the first time or are one with the wind and confident in your abilities to navigate open seas, safety always must be your highest priority. Knowing the safety rules, knowing your boat, knowing the weather and the body of water are all essential ingredients to a safe and rewarding sail. (Novices should sail only in the company of those whose experience is more than a match for the conditions and situation.)

In addition to ensuring that the boat is in top condition, look after your own comfort and safety by having the following items with you:

- U.S. Coast Guard–approved personal flotation device (PFD)
- Rubber-soled, nonskid shoes you won't mind getting wet
- Drinking water
- Food
- Sun protection and sunglasses
- Extra clothing
- Emergency communication and signaling equipment (radio, flares, etc.)

You also might want to wear sailing gloves to protect your hands and improve your grip as you handle lines aboard a boat. Stow anything you want to keep dry in dry bags or sealed inside plastic bags. Stash the bags below decks or in some other boat storage compartment.

For more on issues of concern for sailors, see the chapters titled "Managing Risk" and "Watercraft Adventure Safety."

Sailboats

Boats designed for sailing feature either a *centerboard* or a *keel*. A centerboard is a movable plate of wood, metal, or fiberglass that can be raised and lowered through the bottom of the boat. (Variations of the centerboard are the *daggerboard* that can be removed from the hull, and the *leeboard* that pivots on a dinghy's gunwale.) A keel, on the other hand, typically is a portion of the hull and does not move. It extends beneath the boat in much the same manner as a centerboard and serves the same purposes of providing stability and lateral resistance. Keels (found on *keelboats*) are weighted with enough ballast to keep the boat upright despite the forces of water and wind.

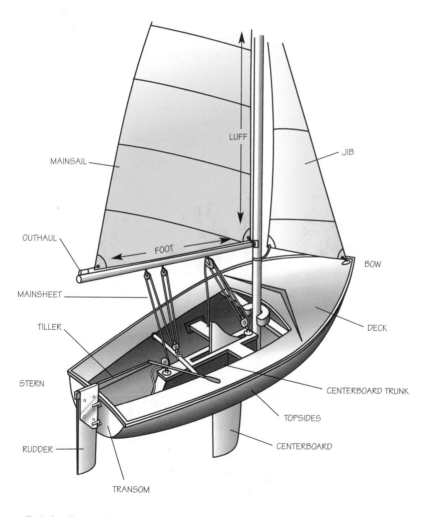

Typical sailboat with a centerboard

Beyond their classification based on keels or centerboards, boats come by their names based in part on the number and orientation of their masts and sails: One-masted boats include *sloops, cutters,* and *catboats.* Two-masted boats include *ketches, yawls,* and *schooners.*

There also are boats with more than one hull. *Catamarans* feature two hulls, and *trimarans* have three.

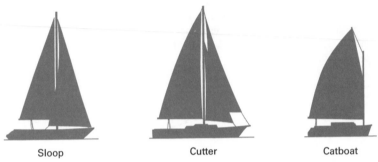

One-masted boats include the sloop, the cutter, and the catboat.

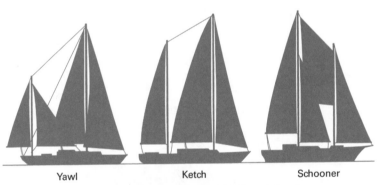

Two-masted boats include the yawl, the ketch, and the schooner.

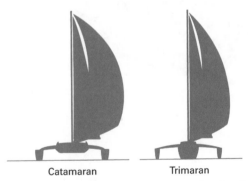

A two-hulled boat is a catamaran. A trimaran has three hulls.

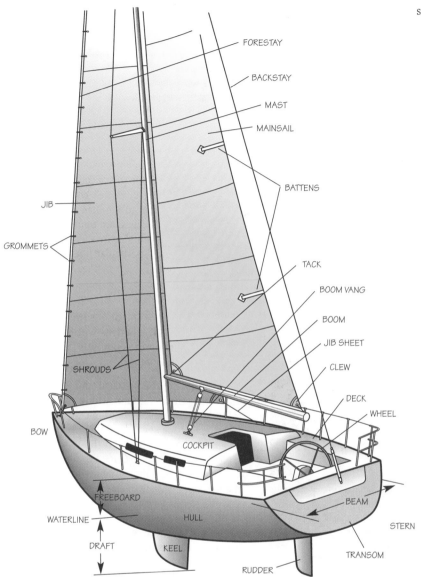

FORESTAY

BACKSTAY

MAST

MAINSAIL

BATTENS

JIB

GROMMETS

TACK

BOOM VANG

BOOM

JIB SHEET

CLEW

SHROUDS

DECK

WHEEL

BOW

COCKPIT

FREEBOARD

BEAM

WATERLINE

HULL

DRAFT

KEEL

STERN

TRANSOM

RUDDER

Typical sailboat with a keel

The Vocabulary of Sailing

Sailing has a vocabulary all its own. The words *starboard* (the right side of the boat as you face forward), *port* (the left side), *windward* (toward the wind), and *leeward* (away from the wind) give sailors clear spatial orientation as their boats move across the water. Speed across the water is measured in *knots,* each knot being *one nautical mile per hour.* A nautical mile is ¹/₆₀ degree (1 minute) of latitude, or 6,076 feet, whereas a *statute mile* used to measure distance on land is 5,280 feet. A boat traveling at 10 knots is moving at about 11.5 miles per hour.

For more on latitude, see the chapter titled "Navigation."

Getting Aboard

The smaller the boat, the more care you'll need while boarding, since your weight can upset a small craft. Hold the mast or the rigging securing the mast, then step into the center of the boat. Larger boats often can be boarded by stepping from the dock to the deck, again grasping lines for balance.

Rigging the Boat

Preparing small boats for sailing can include raising, or *stepping*, the mast and securing the standing rigging that holds it in place. For almost all boats, it will require getting sails out of storage and attaching them to the mast so that they are in position to be hoisted. There are many variations on the ways in which sails are matched to boats. Your best bet in learning to rig a particular boat is to work alongside sailors experienced with that craft. With their guidance, you can complete some or all of the following steps:

COILING LINES

Keeping lines coiled and neatly stowed are matters both of sailing safety and of pride in seamanship.

❶ Slide fiberglass or wooden *battens* into pockets on the trailing edge of the mainsail. The battens will stiffen the sail and help it maintain the optimum shape for taking advantage of the wind.

❷ Slide the foot of the mainsail into the *boom*—the horizontal arm of the mast. Attachments made of plastic or metal, or a rope sewn onto the sail's lower edge, are designed to slip into a groove in the boom. Once the foot is in place, secure the corners with the *tack*—a fitting near the mast—and the *clew*—a fitting at the far end of the boom. The final corner of the sail is attached to the *halyard*—the line used to hoist the sail.

❸ Rig the *jib*—the sail ahead of the mast—if the boat has one. Jib design varies every bit as much as does that of mainsails; follow the lead of those who have rigged the boat before.

Rigging a boat also involves checking all the lines to ensure they are correctly positioned and ready for use. If the boat is equipped with a centerboard, it must be lowered and locked into position. Any loose objects should be stowed away. Everyone going on the trip must be on board, wearing a PFD, and ready to carry out any responsibilities he or she will have while the boat is under way.

Raising the Sails

Before raising the sails, turn the bow of the boat into the wind. That way you can get the sails fully hoisted before the wind begins to fill them.

Sails are raised by hauling the *halyard*—a line running through a block at the top of the mast and fastened at one end to the sail's upper corner. The halyard can be hauled by hand or, on larger boats, by winding it on a winch. The leading edge of the mainsail might have a rope sewn into it that must be fed into a groove in the mast as the sail is being raised.

Securing a Line to a Cleat

Lines that control sails must be secured in such a way that they will hold under great tension, but can be released quickly. The simplest means of achieving that goal is to use a cleat. Bring the line around the horns of the cleat, then wrap it several times in a figure-eight fashion. 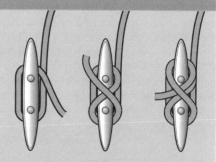 The turns of the line against itself will create enough friction to prevent the line from loosening. A final half hitch thrown around one of the horns will secure the running end of the line. Loosening the line is simply a matter of undoing the half hitch and releasing only enough of the loops to allow the line to run out in a controlled manner.

Some boats also have *jammers* or *rope clutches* to secure lines, particularly if the sails are large and the rigging is complicated.

How a Boat Sails

If there is no wind, you aren't sailing—you're just floating. Sailing is much more fun than floating, especially when you understand the physics of how moving air affects the sails. Whether that motion is graceful, awkward, or counterproductive often depends upon sailors' understanding of the forces coming to bear on a boat, and a crew's ability to adjust to changing circumstances.

A sail mounted on a mast can catch breezes and move a boat in the same direction the wind is blowing. However, when the sail curves into the shape of an airfoil similar to the profile of an aircraft wing, wind flowing

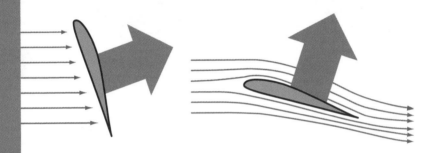

past creates an area of low pressure in front of the fabric and an area of high pressure behind it. The sail is pushed from high pressure toward low pressure, carrying the boat with it. That allows the boat to move with greater efficiency at angles to the wind than otherwise possible with a flat sail.

A *rudder* at or near the stern of a boat sets the direction the craft will go. A keel or a centerboard extending downward from the center of the hull serves as an underwater wing preventing the boat from being blown sideways by the wind. The rudders of smaller boats are controlled with a *tiller*—a lever providing direct response to the rudder. Larger boats have rudders managed by wheels; sailors make directional changes as they would with the steering wheel of an automobile.

Two Kinds of Wind

True wind—the wind you experience while standing still and having your hair blown by a breeze.

Apparent wind—air motion you experience while moving forward, even on a windless day. If you are riding a bicycle, for example, the movement of the bike causes your hair to blow with the oncoming breeze. This wind created by the bicycle's motion, along with any true wind, is known as *apparent wind*.

Sailing Maneuvers

Manage a sailboat well and you can travel in any direction you wish—your *points of sail*—with one exception. You cannot sail directly into the wind. Turning the bow of the boat into this *no-sail zone* is a no-go proposition. The wind will work contrary to your wishes, causing the sails to flutter uselessly, or *luff*, and gradually pushing the boat backward.

While sailing directly into the no-sail zone is impossible, sailing at an angle to the wind can be extremely fast. You can make headway by setting the sails in various ways. Adjusting the rudder and, on smaller boats, the positioning of the weight of the crew will further influence the heading and speed of a boat.

Depending on the course you wish to travel in relation to the wind, the basic maneuvers of sailing are *running*, *reaching*, and *beating*. The primary means of changing directions are *tacking* (coming about) and *jibing*.

Practice your sailing skills in the clear, aquamarine waters of the Florida Keys at the Florida National High Adventure Sea Base. Located in Islamorada, Florida, the BSA's high-adventure facility offers a variety of aquatics programs for older Boy Scouts, Varsity Scouts, Sea Scouts, and Venturers.

Running

Sailing a boat downwind, or *running*, requires close attention, but setting the sails is easy. Simply let out the sails so that they gather in the wind and carry the boat forward. Since the wind is coming over the stern of the boat rather than over a side, the boat will stay level rather than heel over.

19

Reaching

As the bow of a boat begins turning away from a run and toward the wind, the sails no longer will be positioned to act simply as wind collectors. You can take advantage of the fact that the sails now form airfoils that help pull the boat forward. Sailing at an intermediate angle to the wind is called *reaching*.

Reaching can occur whenever a boat is on points of sail between running and beating—from about 7:00 to 10:00 on the *starboard* (right) side, and 2:00 to 5:00 on the *port* (left) side. A boat on a beam reach travels faster than it can with sails set for any other bearings.

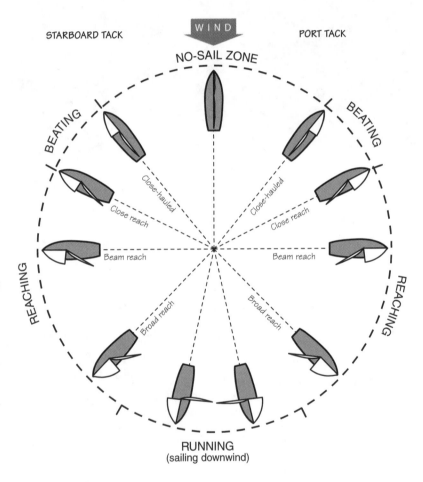

STARBOARD TACK

WIND

PORT TACK

NO-SAIL ZONE

BEATING

BEATING

Close-hauled

Close-hauled

Close reach

Close reach

REACHING

Beam reach

Beam reach

REACHING

Broad reach

Broad reach

RUNNING
(sailing downwind)

Beating

Beating makes it possible for a boat to sail as close as possible to the no-sail zone—points of sail with bearings at about 10:30 starboard and 1:30 port. If the sails begin to lose their airfoil shape even though they are trimmed as much as possible, the boat must turn a little more away from the direction of the wind in order for the sails to fill.

Trimming the Sails

Adjusting the sails, known as *trimming*, will position them for maximum efficiency for the bearing you are following. Sails that are too loose will flutter, or *luff*, along the leading edge. Pull in the lines controlling the set of the sails until the luff disappears and the sails are taut and full.

Overtrimming the sails by setting them too tightly also can diminish their airfoil effect and rob the boat of speed. To determine if that is the case, let out on the lines until the sails begin to luff, then haul them in just until the luffing disappears. That should be the perfect amount of trim for your current heading.

Of course, wind direction will continually change and your heading might not long remain the same. Trimming the sails will be an ongoing part of sailing, requiring your focused attention throughout a journey under sail.

Tacking (Coming About)

A boat cannot sail directly into the wind. However, you can make headway toward the wind by *tacking*—beating in one direction, then turning the bow through the no-sail zone and beating in another direction. The boat can zigzag to a destination upwind either by using one tack with legs long enough to make the distance, or by making a series of short tacks that gradually work the boat close to its goal.

Tacking requires cooperation of everyone on a boat's crew, both to reset the sails for the new bearing and to be alert as the boom swings over the deck. On smaller boats, crew members also might need to shift their weight to the windward side of the craft to help prevent it from capsizing.

If you are the boat's captain, the steps involved in tacking are these:

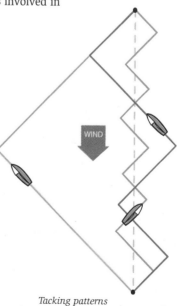

❶ Announce "Ready about!" and then give your crew the time they need to position themselves for the maneuver.

❷ When you are certain all is in readiness, shout "Tacking!"

❸ If the boat has a jib, release tension on the lines controlling it.

❹ Instruct crew members to switch sides on the boat.

❺ Move the tiller or turn the wheel *toward* the boom to turn the bow of the boat through the no-sail zone. Crew members must be alert to avoid the boom as it swings over the cockpit.

❻ Trim the sails and set out on the new heading.

Tacking patterns

19

> ### Caught in Irons
>
> A boat beating too close to the no-sail zone, or one moving too slowly through that zone while tacking, might stall as the wind comes directly over the bow and renders the sails useless for making forward progress. This situation, known by the traditional sailing term *caught in irons*, can be frustrating, to say the least.
>
> To get out of irons, loosen the mainsail and, if you have one, extend the jib to one side or the other. The wind will push the bow toward the side on which the jib is set. Once the bow clears the no-sail zone, trim the mainsail and continue on your way. If the boat has no jib, loosen the mainsail, then move the tiller or turn the wheel hard to one side and wait for the wind to push the bow out of the no-sail zone.

Jibing

Tacking involves turning *into* the wind. *Jibing* is a maneuver that changes the boat's heading from starboard to port as the boat is running (sailing downwind). The boom will be extended far out from the boat, and can swing back and across the deck with a suddenness that sailors must anticipate in order to keep themselves out of harm's way.

❶ If not already on a run, gradually adjust the bearing of the boat until the wind is almost directly behind it.

❷ Shout the command "Prepare to jibe!" Anticipate the maneuver so that your crew will have time to get themselves ready to do whatever needs to be done.

❸ Shout "Jibing!" and move the tiller or turn the wheel *away* from the boom to turn the boat toward the new bearing.

❹ Shorten the line attached to the boom to move it toward the deck as wind pressure on the sail lessens, then ease the line out as the boom swings over the cockpit and the sail begins to refill.

❺ Trim the sails for the new bearing. In smaller boats, crew members should move to the other side to improve the balance of the craft.

Righting a Small Sailboat

Many sailboats are small enough and light enough to capsize on occasion, especially as you are learning sailing maneuvers. Be prepared for this by practicing the following steps:

1 Loosen the sheet to free the mainsail, then climb or swim around the hull so that you can put your weight on the centerboard.

2 As you grasp lines or the edge of the deck, gently push down on the centerboard with your feet.

3 Pull the boat upright.

4 Get yourself and everyone else back on board before turning your attention to bailing out the boat and resetting the sail.

Leadership and Sailing

A crew on a sailboat must carry out many tasks that require cooperative effort. The responsibilities of each crew member often are obvious, though at times someone must call for quick action. The most experienced sailor often serves as a boat's captain, exercising authority when decisions must be made. In some cases, though, a person with outstanding leadership skills may guide the crew with the support and advice from crew members with more seamanship experience. Likewise, a crew member learning to sail might serve as a boat's captain, mentored by an experienced sailor prepared to step in and take command if situations arise that are beyond the skill of the novice.

Human waste and litter should be properly disposed of at the next port in facilities designed for that purpose, never tossed overboard. Leave No Trace applies to sailing similarly to other outdoor activities.

Even when a crew is composed of no more than two or three people, leadership can become a critical issue. A chain of command should be worked out before a crew leaves dry land.

For more on responsibilities of crew members and leaders, see the chapters titled "Organizing for Adventures" and "Outdoor Leadership."

Several knots familiar to Scouting take their name from sailing terms, such as the *bowline*, which is named after the front end *(bow)* of the boat, and the *sheet bend,* which comes to us from both the bend formed in one of the ropes and from *sheet,* a nautical term for a line used to haul a sail.

Setting a Lifelong Course

The way to become proficient at sailing is to go sailing. Have fun, learn from your mistakes, and seek out opportunities to learn from others.

Sea Scout units provide terrific opportunities for mastering the basics of sailing and enjoying plenty of time on the water. (See the *Sea Scout Manual.*) Many Venturing crews also specialize in sailing as one of their primary activities. Sailing clubs, community colleges, and universities around the country offer courses in sailing and opportunities for young people to join sailing crews.

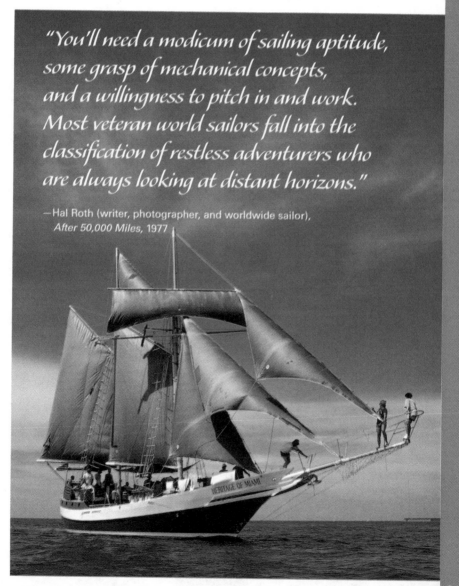

"You'll need a modicum of sailing aptitude, some grasp of mechanical concepts, and a willingness to pitch in and work. Most veteran world sailors fall into the classification of restless adventurers who are always looking at distant horizons."

—Hal Roth (writer, photographer, and worldwide sailor),
After 50,000 Miles, 1977

CHAPTER
20

Be Prepared

Always wear a helmet.
Bring water, food, an
extra tube, pump, and
patch kit & know how
to use them.

Bicycle Touring and Mountain Biking

"The flying abandon of a bicycle, legs pumping, body and wheels skimming above the land, cycling for the sake of cycling, because it felt good in my body, because the drip of salty sweat, the deep, rhythmic breathing, the stretching, pushing muscles were pure and cleansing and glorious."

—Erika Warmbrunn, *Where the Pavement Ends*, 2001 (An actor, writer, and Russian translator, she pedaled solo across Mongolia, China, and Vietnam.)

Bicycling is human-powered adventure at its best. The whir of spoked wheels and the click of a chain are sounds of independence, of possibility, and of the potential of the open road. On bike tours of a few days, weeks, or even months, you and your group can pedal anywhere from the Pacific to the Atlantic, and from the Florida Keys to the northernmost point in Alaska. Mountain bikes also offer the means for you to journey away from well-traveled routes. With a clear understanding of Leave No Trace principles, you can find hours of challenge and fun on quiet backroads and on durable trails designated for cycling.

Bicycle touring is an act of chasing the horizon. The goal is to move forward, feeling the Earth roll beneath your wheels as the landscape flows past on either side. *Mountain biking*, on the other hand, is a vertical pursuit highlighted by demanding climbs and steep downhill runs. At times, riders might even become airborne to clear an obstacle, or just for the sheer delight of two-wheeled flight.

This chapter takes a look at the basics of bicycle touring and the essentials of mountain biking, providing guidelines for you to make the most of cycling opportunities in ways that are safe, fun, satisfying, and environmentally responsible.

Fitting a Bike

Like hiking boots, bicycles for touring or mountain riding must fit well if you are to get the best use out of them. An experienced bicycle salesperson can help you select a bike matched to the size of your body. With your feet flat on the ground, you'll want to be able to straddle the top tube of the bike frame with a couple of inches to spare, and you'll need to be able to reach the handlebars comfortably when you are seated in the saddle. Adjust the height of the saddle so that your leg will be slightly flexed at the low point of each pedal rotation.

Another way to find a bicycle that fits is to measure the inside of your leg from your inseam to the floor and subtract 10 inches. The figure you get is the approximate frame size of the bike you should have. Don't confuse frame size with the diameter of the wheel; most bikes have 27-inch wheels regardless of the size of the frame.

Bicycle Helmets

Put on a bicycle helmet every time you step into the pedals. Your helmet must be designed specifically for cycling; have ANSI, SNELL, or ASTM certification; and fit well. With the strap secured, you shouldn't be able to push your helmet very far forward, backward, or sideways.

Bicycle Touring

Plan a bicycle tour and you'll find yourself and a group of your friends setting out to discover the world one turn of the pedals at a time. Your two-wheeled adventures can start right outside your door and might lead to the far reaches of the continent.

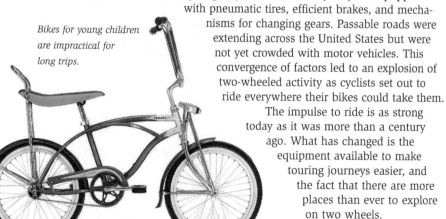

Boneshaker, a nineteenth-century ancestor of today's efficient bikes

Along the way, you are sure to be traveling in the tracks of many who pedaled before you, as long-distance cycling has a long tradition in the story of adventure travel.

Bicycle touring in America dates back to the 1890s, a golden age of cycling. "Boneshaker" bikes with steel wheels and the "regular" bikes with a huge front wheel were giving way to modern safety bicycles equipped with pneumatic tires, efficient brakes, and mechanisms for changing gears. Passable roads were extending across the United States but were not yet crowded with motor vehicles. This convergence of factors led to an explosion of two-wheeled activity as cyclists set out to ride everywhere their bikes could take them.

Bikes for young children are impractical for long trips.

The impulse to ride is as strong today as it was more than a century ago. What has changed is the equipment available to make touring journeys easier, and the fact that there are more places than ever to explore on two wheels.

Touring Bikes

Almost any bicycle will get you a few miles down the road on a sunny day. When you begin setting your sights on more distant destinations, though, a touring bike of the right size can maximize your pedaling efficiency and riding comfort.

Touring Bike Frame

Bicycles devoted to touring are built with stiff, lightweight frames that allow an effective transfer of power from the pedals to the wheels.

Drop Handlebars

The drop handlebars on touring bikes offer riders a variety of hand placements, allowing them to lean over the frame in the most efficient position for pedaling.

Pedals

Clipless pedals and pedals with toe clips position a rider's feet for optimum pedaling power. A *toe clip* is a metal or plastic cage set atop a pedal. Slip the toe of your shoe into the toe clip and tighten the strap over the arch of your foot. Rather than a cage, a *clipless pedal* relies on a shoe-sole cleat matched to a spring-loaded pedal fitting. Click the cleat into the pedal and you're on your way. To release the clip, turn your heel sharply outward and the cleat should snap free.

Pedals with toe clips

Clipless pedals

Ankling

With your shoes secured by toe clips or clipless pedals, you can push down on a pedal, then pull it back, up, and over. Known as *ankling*, the maneuver allows you to apply power throughout the full rotation of the chainwheel.

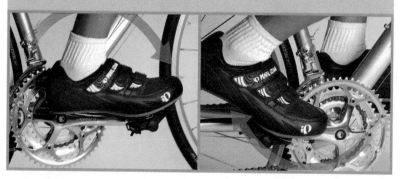

Derailleurs

Most touring bikes feature *derailleur gears* controlled by levers on the handlebars or on the bike frames. The rear hub of a typical touring bike has five gearwheels. Shifting the rear derailleur moves the chain from one toothed wheel to another, offering a rider five gear options. The larger the gearwheel, the farther the chain must go on each revolution, resulting in easier pedaling at the cost of shorter forward progress.

The front derailleur of a touring bike moves the chain among two or three gearwheels set around the pedal crank. If there are two front gearwheels and each can be used with the five rear gearwheels, the bicycle has a total capacity of 10 gears—thus, a 10-speed bike. Add a third front gearwheel, and it becomes a bicycle with 15 speeds.

Derailleur mechanisms shift gears most efficiently when the pedals are turning and the chain is in motion. Experiment as you ride to find the gear combination that feels right for the moment. Expect to shift often so that you can maintain a steady, sustainable pedaling cadence even as terrain, wind, and your energy level alter. Anticipate changes and shift to a new gear before you need to apply full pressure to the pedals.

Brakes

On most touring bikes, *caliper brakes* slow momentum by squeezing the wheel rims with brake pads. Brakes in good working order can stop a bike very quickly. Use the front and rear brakes at the same time, gradually increasing the pressure on the levers to slow the bike smoothly. Stopping with only the rear brake might be less effective than you want, while using the front brake by itself might cause the wheel to seize and send you flying over the handlebars.

Packing a Touring Bike

A small pack attached to the back of the seat, or a fanny pack around your waist, may offer enough capacity for you to carry your lunch, some extra clothing, and a bicycle repair kit. One or more water bottles in cages attached to the frame will round out your basic outfit for day rides. Many touring bicycles have mounting points for attaching racks for *panniers*—packs for bikes—to stow camping gear for more extended travels. Panniers should fit securely with no chance of swinging loose as you pedal. They should be set low on the bicycle so that their weight will not upset your balance.

Just as backpackers shed all the weight they can from their packs, bicycle tourists will want to carry only what they need. A lightweight tent and sleeping bag, a backpacking stove, rain gear, and adequate clothing that can be layered for warmth will form the heart of your long-distance touring outfit. Conduct a shakedown before each trip to help you eliminate unnecessary items. Unlike wilderness journeys, you often can buy food each day along the route of a bicycle tour. That can simplify menu planning and offer the option of preparing meals with plenty of fresh, nutritious ingredients.

Rather than stowing your tent inside a pannier, you can strap it on top of your bicycle's rear fender. Your sleeping bag can go on the fender, too, but protect your sleeping gear from rain by lining its stuff sack with a plastic trash bag. A handlebar pannier will give you quick access to items you will want during the day, and it might have a clear, waterproof pocket built into the top flap for holding maps. If that's not the case, slip your map into a self-sealing plastic bag and carry it where you can get it out without leaving the saddle.

For more on deciding what to carry while bicycle touring, see the chapter titled "Gearing Up."

Touring Bike Techniques

A fully loaded touring bicycle handles differently from one without the weight of provisions and gear. Get used to controlling your bike by riding it in a parking lot or other area free of traffic. Notice, too, if anything is loose. Your touring bike and all your gear should be a tight unit with nothing shifting around except the derailleurs, and those only when you are changing gears.

Once you and your group are on the road, settle into a pedaling rhythm that you can maintain over the miles. In most cases, you will want to ride single file on the far right side of the road. Tucking in just behind the rider in front of you, a technique called *drafting,* will draw you along in the windbreak formed by the first rider's bike and body. Riders can take turns in the lead position, especially when riding into a headwind.

Keep an eye on the weather. Rain, fog, and mist can make roads slippery. They also can impair the vision of the motorists with whom you share the road. If conditions are not conducive to riding safely, seek shelter and wait out the storm.

Hills shouldn't discourage you too much if you gear down, stay in the saddle, and keep your pedaling cadence steady. Control your speed on descents by braking occasionally, applying pressure evenly to both brake levers. A headwind can be as demoralizing as a tailwind is refreshing. Shift into a low gear when the wind is in your face, keep up your cadence, and be patient. In both wet weather and dry, approach railroad tracks, bridge joints, and other potentially slippery road obstacles at a perpendicular angle, slowing to make a controlled crossing.

Hand Signals

Right turn   *Stopping*   *Left turn*

Bicycling Road Rules

Consider yourself to be a part of the traffic. Obey all regulations that apply to motorists, and do everything you can to make it easy for drivers to see you and to pass safely. Learn and follow these common sense safety and courtesy guidelines:

1. Stay close to the right side of the road.

2. When riding abreast, be ready at all times to merge back into single file.

3. Don't delay traffic.

4. Plan routes that avoid busy roads.

5. Ride defensively. Be visible and anticipate the actions of motorists, pedestrians, and other cyclists.

Seeing and Being Seen

Make yourself clearly visible with brightly colored clothing. An orange fluorescent construction-worker vest, reflectors, and lights are a good idea, too.

A mirror attached to your handlebars or helmet can give you a sense of what's happening behind you. Even more important, though, are listening carefully for approaching traffic and glancing over your shoulder now and then to see what traffic might be overtaking your group.

Mountain Biking

Mountain biking can take you along back-country roads and designated trails into the rugged terrain beyond the pavement. Today's riders are fully embracing the responsibilities that come with the opportunity to pedal away from highways and other paved routes. They are riding only on trails and backroads where cycling is appropriate, and are sharing those pathways with hikers, horseback riders, and other outdoors enthusiasts in ways that present mountain biking in a positive light. Most importantly, these riders are protecting the environment by making good decisions about where, when, and how they ride.

INTERNATIONAL MOUNTAIN BICYCLING ASSOCIATION RULES OF THE TRAIL

1. **Ride on open trails only.**
2. **Leave no trace.**
3. **Control your bicycle!**
4. **Yield to other trekkers.**
5. **Never scare animals.**
6. **Plan ahead.**

Used wisely, a mountain bike can be a wonderful vehicle for exploring rural roads and designated trails. Ridden thoughtlessly, though, a mountain bike has the potential to cause serious environmental damage and to spoil the experiences of other backcountry users. Making the right choices about where, when, and how to ride will help ensure that roads and designated trails will stay open for you and other riders to enjoy in the future.

Where and When to Ride a Mountain Bike

Two words are at the heart of mountain bike routes—*designated* and *durable*.

Designated routes are those that land management agencies have deemed appropriate for mountain bikers to use. Find out which trails are designated by checking at agency offices or Web sites, or by asking at local bicycle shops. Agencies often provide maps with mountain bike routes highlighted. Signs at trailheads also can give clear indications of the trails that you can ride.

Even more important than finding designated routes is learning which trails are off-limits to bike riders, and then avoiding them. Trails might be closed to bicycles for any number of reasons: fragile surfaces, heavy use by other outdoor enthusiasts, wet weather, wildlife issues. Respect all trail closures by staying off trails not specifically designated for mountain biking.

Durable mountain bike routes are trail surfaces that are hard, dry, and able to withstand the impact of many bicycles passing over them. When you set out on a designated mountain bike trail, your responsibilities to protect the environment still rest on the decisions you make with each turn of the pedals.

Leave No Trace Mountain Biking

Avoid muddy trails. The tread of mountain bike tires can churn up wet earth, gouging out tracks that can lead to erosion and trail degradation. Leave your mountain bike at home when the weather is wet. If an otherwise dry ride brings you to a muddy stretch of trail, it might be best to dismount and walk your bike through it. Don't detour by riding on the edges of the trail, though—that can break down the soil and vegetation, causing unnecessary widening of the trail.

Stay on the trail. Resist the temptation to take shortcuts down hillsides. That's a sure invitation to erosion and to the closing of areas to future mountain biking. Go all the way around trail switchbacks, making your turns in a controlled manner that prevents the wheels from skidding and causing damage to tread surfaces.

Mountain Bikes

Mountain bikes first appeared in California in the 1970s and early 1980s. Early mountain bikes were simply regular bicycles that riders wheeled up and down steep trails. Over time, the bikes have become sturdier and more fun to ride, evolving into machines that are distinctly different from the bikes used for touring or for riding around town.

Mountain Bike Frame

In order to absorb the impact of rough roads and trails, the frames of mountain bikes are not as stiff as those used for touring. Advanced mountain bikes are equipped with suspension springs and flexible joints for diffusing the force of hard riding on rugged terrain.

Straight Handlebars

Straight handlebars will help you maintain the most effective body positions for climbing, descending, and negotiating obstacles.

Knobby Tires

Mountain bikers often choose tires with knobby tread patterns because they are ideal for gaining traction without spinning out and are just right for creating maximum braking power.

Pedals

The clipless pedals of many mountain bikes will keep your feet positioned even when the going gets crazy. Harder to tighten and to release, toe-clip pedals are less popular among riders.

Brakes

The brakes of most mountain bikes are caliper brakes similar to those found on touring bicycles. Use both brakes to slow your bike, but rely more on the rear brake during descents. Clamping down hard on the front brake alone might cause you to overturn.

STRAIGHT HANDLEBARS

FRAME

BRAKE

BRAKE

KNOBBY TIRES

PEDAL

Mountain Bike Techniques

Body Position

Mountain bikes are built to withstand tough territory, but the real suspension system of mountain biking is a rider's body. Stay relaxed and ride with your knees and elbows flexed to dissipate jolts from the bike. By moving forward or backward over the seat, you also can shift your weight from one wheel to the other. This ability to *weight* and *unweight* the wheels plays a major role in handling a mountain bike as you climb and descend trails and negotiate tight turns.

Climbing

Mountain bike gearwheels offer a high ratio of power to distance, allowing you to crank steadily up slopes even when your speed is very slow. Lean into the handlebars as a route steepens, and keep your weight hovering above the seat. If the rear wheel begins to lose traction, move your body back to put more weight over that wheel. Stalling out during a climb means you might need to twist a foot out of a pedal, so anticipate the gears you will need and shift the derailleurs while you are on the move.

Descending

Controlled descents on a mountain bike involve more than simply pointing the front wheel down a road or trail and letting go of the brakes. Shift your body position so that your weight is over the back wheel—the steeper the route, the farther back your weight should be. That will provide the most stability as you ride and can maximize the stopping power of your brakes. Scan the route ahead, envisioning where you want to go rather than locking your eyes onto obstacles that you want to avoid. Ride no faster than the route, your level of skill, and the presence of other trail users will allow.

20

Rollovers

Mountain bikers often get past logs, water bars, and other low obstacles simply by rolling over them. Keep up your speed as you approach an obstacle and shift your position to weight the rear wheel. As the bike rolls over the obstruction, don't touch the front brake—that could send you hurtling over the handlebars. Grip the handlebars so that they can't twist out of your grasp when the front wheel reaches the obstacle.

Bunny Hops

To overcome an obstacle too high to roll over, try going airborne with a bunny hop. Flex the frame as you approach by pushing down on the handlebars, then spring the bike upward, lifting the front wheel with the handlebars and the back wheel with your body. Keep your weight shifted toward the rear, and don't touch the front brake as you come down. Land on the back wheel first.

Trackstand

Now and then you will want to stop your bike for a moment to size up the route ahead. Performing a *trackstand* allows you to do that without taking your feet off the pedals. Learn to do a trackstand by aiming your bike up a slight slope. Rotate the pedals until they are level, and turn the front wheel a little to one side of the bike. Standing in the pedals, hold the bike in position with enough weight on the forward pedal to prevent the bike from rolling backward, but not so much pressure that the bike moves forward.

20

Upsets

Occasional extremes of mountain biking make tumbles a possibility. Minimize that risk by riding in a controlled manner with your full attention on the route ahead. A helmet is essential for every mountain biker, and cycling gloves will help protect your hands. If you do go down, tuck your body and roll to absorb the impact of your fall rather than trying to catch your weight with straight arms. Stay with the bike if you can—it might absorb some of the impact to your body.

Bicycle Care and Repair

20

Among the great pleasures of bicycling is learning to maintain and repair your own machine. Local cycling clubs often offer opportunities for learning bicycle mechanics, and some cycling stores present classes in tuning up bikes, trueing wheels, and making other adjustments. Experienced riders in your group also can be storehouses of information as you master the art of bicycle repair.

Whether you do your pedaling on mountain trails or open roads, keeping your bike in top mechanical condition will add to the joy of every journey. A well-tuned machine also is much less likely to break down when you are miles into a ride. The maintenance concerns are the same for both mountain bikes and touring bicycles, and many of the mechanical difficulties you encounter in the field can be resolved, at least long enough for you to get home, by using a bicycle pump and the contents of a repair kit carried in your panniers, a fanny pack, or a small pack attached to the saddle.

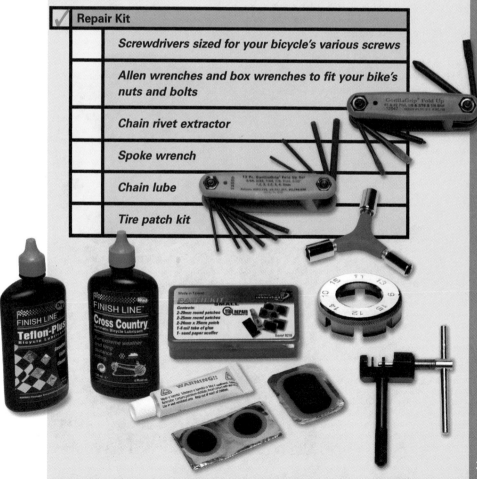

✓	Repair Kit
	Screwdrivers sized for your bicycle's various screws
	Allen wrenches and box wrenches to fit your bike's nuts and bolts
	Chain rivet extractor
	Spoke wrench
	Chain lube
	Tire patch kit

20

Pre-Ride Mechanical Check

Look over your bike before a ride to be sure everything is in order. Some of the items you will want to check follow:

Brakes

Squeeze the brake levers to ensure that the brake pads will securely grip the wheel rims. Brake pads should be clean and not badly worn. The cables controlling the brakes should not be frayed or damaged.

Chain

The chain should be clean and properly lubricated to prevent squeaking and excessive wear. Apply a good lubricant to the moving chain as you turn the pedals backward, then wipe off any excess with a rag.

Gears and Derailleurs

Derailleurs and the cables controlling them must be free of road grit. Run through the gears as you begin pedaling to be sure that you can click smoothly into all combinations of front and rear gearwheels.

Wheels

Feel for loose spokes, then spin each wheel and watch the rim to see that it spins true. Any wobble needs to be corrected in the shop.

Tires

Press down on each tire with your hand to get a general idea of whether or not there is sufficient air pressure for a ride. Better yet, use a pressure gauge. Keep tires inflated to the pressure noted on their sidewalls.

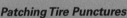

Patching Tire Punctures

An absolute truth of bicycling is that flat tires happen. Carry a patch kit and perhaps even a spare tube, and you'll be ready to repair most tire damage and quickly get back in the saddle.

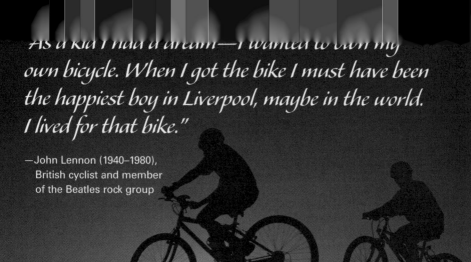

As a kid I had a dream—I wanted to own my own bicycle. When I got the bike I must have been the happiest boy in Liverpool, maybe in the world. I lived for that bike."

—John Lennon (1940–1980),
   British cyclist and member
   of the Beatles rock group

Post-Ride Bicycle Care

The end of a ride might be the best time of all to attend to the mechanical needs of your bicycle. Checking and tuning up your bike right away means it will be ready to go the next time you want to hit the road or the trail. You also can deal with any time-consuming mechanical problems that you discover.

Clean mud and grit from your bicycle and, if necessary, lubricate the chain. Test bolts, screws, and fittings to see that everything is secure. In addition to examining derailleurs and brakes, pull sideways on the wheels and the pedal crank to ensure that there is no play in the hubs and bearings.

Lastly, store your bike in a safe, out-of-the-way place, but don't expect it to stay there very long. The whir of wheels against the highway and the thrill of pedaling hard up a mountain trail are temptations you won't be able to ignore for long.

Riding and Packing

"The surest thing there is is we are riders,
And though none too successful at it, guiders,
Through everything presented, land and tide
And now the very air, of what we ride."

—Robert Frost (1874—1963), American poet

Explorers, mountain travelers, American Indians, miners, cowboys, soldiers, and settlers all have used horses and pack animals, and for good reason. The animals increase by many miles the distances that travelers can cover, and allow them to haul heavy loads over rough terrain. Today, you can swing into the saddle, touch your heels to a horse's sides, and know the pleasure of riding. You can feel the confidence that comes with knowing how to groom a horse, saddle it, and care for it in the stable and on the trail. You can learn to manage mules and burros, too, getting to know their habits as they carry your provisions and gear on extended treks.

Much of the American outdoors can be enjoyed on horseback and with pack animals. A successful trip requires sound planning, dependable livestock, and a commitment to using the principles of Leave No Trace. Veteran horse handlers can give you guidance as you learn the ways of saddle and pack stock, and to get you equipped.

Members of a Philmont Cavalcade ride horseback over some of Philmont's most scenic trails. Designed for chartered troops or Venturing crews, Cavalcade participants acquire riding and packing skills long in use in the American West. The final day of the eight-day Cavalcade is spent in competition at an equestrian gymkhana.

Horses

For much of human history, horses provided the fastest means by which anyone could travel. Horses were introduced to North America by Spanish explorers, rapidly becoming an indispensable means of transportation for many American Indians, explorers, settlers, and wilderness wanderers. The traditions and techniques of those riders have been passed down through the centuries, forming the basis of the ways in which humans and horses still relate to each other.

A calm, reassuring voice can be one of your best tools for dealing with horses and pack animals. So can an understanding of the ways in which horses perceive the world. Each horse has its own set of preferences and habits. Perhaps it is shy about gates, doesn't want to be approached from a certain direction, or likes to have its nose rubbed. Moving objects might alarm a horse until it is able to identify them, usually with its keen senses of hearing and smell. When horses feel threatened, their first instincts are to run or to fight. On the other hand, horses will respond well to your confidence, kindness, and quiet authority and, over time, likely will come to trust you and be willing to work easily with you.

Quick-Release Hitch

Use a quick-release hitch when tying the lead rope of a saddle horse or pack animal. The hitch will hold even if the animal pulls against it, but unties easily when you tug the end of the rope.

Bridling and Saddling

Getting a horse ready for the trail will become second nature after you've done it several times, especially if you've mastered that skill with the help of experienced wranglers. Begin by catching your mount, slipping the halter over its nose, and leading it to a hitch rail near the tack room or saddle shed. Tie the lead rope to the rail with a quick-release hitch, then use a curry comb and brush to groom the horse's back, sides, and belly. Remove any dirt, sweat, and matted hair by combing in the direction that the hair naturally lies. Lift and inspect the hooves, cleaning them if necessary with a hoof pick, and check for loose shoes.

Saddle

The Western stock saddle is the most versatile saddle for trail riding. Rugged enough to take a hard pounding, the saddle has a shape that helps a rider stay seated on steep climbs and descents. Sturdy blankets or pads placed beneath the saddle help to cushion and protect the horse's back.

> **TACK**
>
> **The gear used for preparing a horse to ride is called *tack* and includes a saddle, bridle, and halter.**

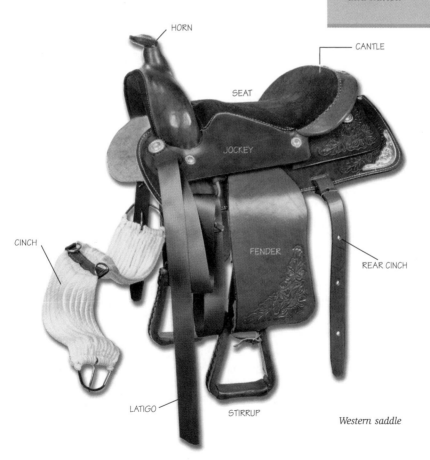

HORN

CANTLE

SEAT

JOCKEY

CINCH

FENDER

REAR CINCH

LATIGO

STIRRUP

Western saddle

21

21

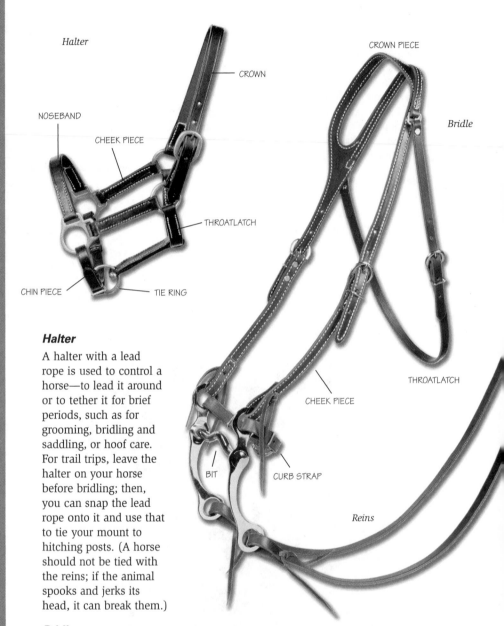

Halter

CROWN

CROWN PIECE

NOSEBAND

Bridle

CHEEK PIECE

THROATLATCH

CHIN PIECE

TIE RING

CHEEK PIECE

THROATLATCH

BIT

CURB STRAP

Reins

Halter

A halter with a lead rope is used to control a horse—to lead it around or to tether it for brief periods, such as for grooming, bridling and saddling, or hoof care. For trail trips, leave the halter on your horse before bridling; then, you can snap the lead rope onto it and use that to tie your mount to hitching posts. (A horse should not be tied with the reins; if the animal spooks and jerks its head, it can break them.)

Bridle

A bridle consists of a headstall, bit, and reins, and is used to control and guide a horse from its back. Bits come in various shapes and sizes to match the age, experience level, preference, and training of different animals.

Bridling a Horse

❶ Working from the left side of the horse, put the reins around the horse's neck. Hold the top of the bridle in your right hand and the bit in your left.

❷ Without bumping the teeth, ease the bit into the horse's mouth and pull the headstall over its head. Be gentle with the horse's ears.

❸ Pull out the forelock, straighten the brow band, and buckle the throatlatch.

Saddling a Horse

1. Use a curry comb and brush to remove dirt, sweat, and matted hair from the horse's back, sides, and belly.

2. Position the saddle blankets or pads well forward on the horse's back. The hair beneath must lie flat.

3. Lift the saddle onto the blankets or pads and shake it into position. Straighten the cinches on the far (right) side of the horse.

4. On the near (left) side, place the stirrup over the saddle seat and reach under the horse for the front cinch ring. (Note: Another option is to hook the stirrup over the saddle horn to prevent it from slipping.) Thread the latigo twice through the cinch ring and rigging ring, then pull it snug and secure it.

5. Buckle the rear cinch just tightly enough to be snug against the horse's belly.

6. Buckle the breast collar onto a near-side rigging ring, snap the lower strap into the center ring of the cinch (6a), then buckle the other end of the breast collar onto a far-side rigging ring.

Mounting a Horse

First, check the front cinch and retighten it if necessary. Then, standing on the horse's left side, grasp the reins around the animal's neck in front of the saddle horn, holding them short enough in your left hand so that you can control the horse if it should move while you are mounting. With the same hand, grab some of the horse's mane. Use your free hand to position the left stirrup and guide your left foot into it, then grasp the saddle horn and step up in the stirrup. Swing your right leg over the horse and ease yourself into the saddle. The balls of your feet should rest in the stirrups with your heels slightly lower. You might need to dismount and adjust the length of the stirrups if they are too long or too short.

RIDING HELMET

Riding helmets are growing in popularity, and are strongly recommended to help protect horseback riders from head injury. A helmet must be correctly sized, adjusted, and always worn with the chin strap secured.

Riding

Holding the reins with one between your thumb and index finger and the second between the index and middle fingers of the same hand, squeeze the horse with your legs or tap with your heels, and the animal should move out. Many horses are trained to *neck-rein*, responding to the pressure of reins against their necks. To turn left, move the reins to the left and touch the horse's neck with the right rein. For a right turn, move the reins the other way. To stop, pull back lightly on the reins and then release the pressure. The bit serves only to cue the animal; too much force on the reins can cause pain and perhaps injury.

Match the speed at which you ride with the terrain you are covering. Allow your horse to walk when the grade is steep or rocky, and whenever you are leading pack animals. To ride up a steep grade, stay seated in the saddle but shift your weight forward so that the horse bears more of your weight with its shoulders and front legs. When riding downhill, lean back in the saddle. You can let the horse lope across level ground where the footing is sure. On a long day's ride, get off your horse and walk now and then to give the animal a breather.

"The country has gone sane and got back to horses."

—Will Rogers (1879–1935),
American cowboy humorist

Pack Animals

No history of the American West is complete without the image of prospectors making their way through the mountains, their pack animals loaded with shovels, hardtack, beans, and maybe even a poke of gold. Mules, burros, and pack horses provided the power to move settlers across the continent, pull the plows of farmers, and transport the supplies of soldiers and trappers as well as prospectors.

You'll probably get your first taste of working with pack animals under the watchful eyes of veteran packers. They might begin by explaining that a burro is a species that can reproduce its own kind, while a mule is a sterile cross between a male burro and a female horse.

Equipment

Pack animals need saddles if they are to carry heavy loads. The most common pack saddle is the *sawbuck,* named for its resemblance in appearance to the wooden stand used to hold logs for sawing. Each saddle is shaped to fit a particular size of animal. The saddle will be rigged with a double cinch to keep it and its load on the animal, and a breast strap and back breeching to prevent the saddle from sliding backward or forward.

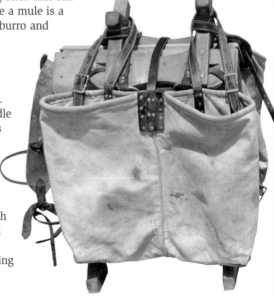

Sawbuck saddle with panniers

A pack animal is groomed and saddled in much the same way as a saddle horse, the sawbuck resting on two or three saddle pads and the cinch pulled tight. The breast strap and breeching should be snug, but not so tight that they hamper the animal's movement. A pack animal doesn't wear a bridle; a hiker or horseback rider can control it with a halter and a lead rope.

Llama Packing

Wooly haired natives of South America, llamas are being used with increasing frequency as pack animals on North American trails. They are easy to handle and train, and they travel at a pace comfortable for most hikers. Even though their foot pads cause less environmental impact than do the hooves of horses and mules, llamas must be managed according to the same principles of Leave No Trace.

Packing Up

Pack horses and mules can carry up to 180 pounds each, a llama can carry 90 pounds, and a burro can haul about 60 pounds. Even though pack animals might be able to bear much more weight than you can, keep their loads light. There's no reason for them to haul equipment you don't really need. A smaller load makes it safer for the animals to travel rugged trails, and will ease your challenge of following the principles of Leave No Trace.

Provisions and gear are commonly stowed in *panniers*—wooden or plastic boxes, or large leather or canvas bags designed to hang by loops from a sawbuck. Use a scale hung from a tree branch or fence rail to check pannier weight. Each pannier in a pair should weigh the same, since an unbalanced load can cause the sawbuck to slip or rub sores into an animal's back. Pack provisions and gear in such a way that nothing will rattle. Strange noises coming from a pannier can spook even the steadiest trail animal.

Clothing

The traditional clothing of the American cowboy evolved over many years to serve the needs of horseback riders. A long-sleeved shirt and long denim pants will guard you against the sun and dust. The wide brim of a cowboy hat will shade your face and keep rain from running down your collar. A bandanna around your neck can be pulled over your mouth and nose when the trail becomes dusty. The pointed toes and slick soles of traditional Western boots evolved to slide easily into and out of saddle stirrups. Avoid riding while wearing boots with big soles that could get caught in the stirrups.

Loading Panniers on a Pack Animal

❶ Set a balanced pair of panniers on a sawbuck so that they hang evenly. Place tightly rolled tents, sleeping bags in stuff sacks, and other soft baggage on top of the saddle.

❷ Position a tarp over the load and tuck the ends under the panniers.

❸ Toss a lash cinch over the load and pull the end under the animal's belly. Keeping the rope taut, secure the load with a diamond hitch.

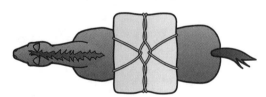

Diamond hitch

Twist doubled rope.

Pull loop through opening in twisted rope.

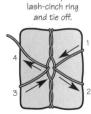
Return rope to lash-cinch ring and tie off.

Pull tight 1, 2, 3, 4.

21

Mantie Loads

Another traditional means of packing grub and gear is to form *mantie loads*. Mantie loads offer greater flexibility than panniers for securing odd-sized equipment, and are ideal for food supplies packed inside square plastic buckets with snap-on lids. Items are placed on a tarp, then folded into a tight bundle and tied with a mantie rope.

On the Trail With Pack Animals

If you will be riding, you might find it most convenient to mount your horse and then have a partner hand you the lead rope of your pack animal. Hold the rope in your hand as you travel, or give it one loose wrap around the saddle horn, but *never* tie it to any part of the saddle or wrap it around your hand in such a way that it will not easily come loose.

When leading several pack animals, tie the lead rope of one animal to the pack saddle of the animal in front of it. Keep each lead rope short enough so that the animals cannot step over it, but not so short that they impede one another's motion. Ideally, a second rider following the pack string stays alert for signs of shifting loads, loose saddles, or fatigue or lameness in the animals. Correct problems as soon as you notice them so that they don't become serious.

Leave No Trace Riding and Packing

Lightweight gear and well-planned menus will allow you to minimize the number of animals required to support a trek. Choose animals that are fit, calm, and accustomed to rugged travel. Take care to prevent hoof damage to stream banks, wetlands, tundra, and other sensitive areas. Well in advance of a journey, contact the management agencies of the area you wish to visit and learn about any permits you will need and restrictions affecting the use of livestock. Land managers also can provide information about trailhead access, designated sites for horse camps, and trail conditions. Check for updates a few days before departure; there could be trail closures or other developing situations that would make it necessary for you to alter your plans.

Selecting Campsites

Use sites designated for horse groups whenever possible. Most will have hitch rails or corrals to accommodate livestock. Allow animals to graze only if there is enough feed for them *and* for native wildlife—livestock overgrazing an area could be removing food needed by deer, elk, and other wild animals during winter months. Avoid soft meadows and fragile shorelines that could be torn up by hooves. Water the stock by leading them to stream banks that can withstand hard use.

Horses, mules, and burros, generating pressure of up to 1,500 pounds per square foot with each hoof, have great potential for causing wear and tear on the land. Horseshoes intensify the shearing force of hooves on soils and vegetation. Pack animals and riding stock that graze can compete with wildlife for available feed. Responsible riders and packers can lessen these concerns by following Leave No Trace principles as they plan and take part in trips with livestock.

Confining Stock in Camp

Take care of your animals as soon as you reach your destination. They've worked hard for you and have earned their rest. Get the weight off your pack animals before you unsaddle your riding horse. Loosen the sawbucks, then fold the cinches, breast straps, and breechings over the top. Place the saddles on a log or pole, lay the pads on top (wet side up), and cover everything with tarps. Then do the same for the riding horses.

After the animals have been cooled, brushed, fed, watered, and checked for saddle sores and foot damage, you may be able to set them out to graze. Allow them freedom to wander, and thus reduce their impact on the land, by using as little restraint as possible. *Hobbles*—leather or nylon straps buckled onto the lower front legs of animals—permit livestock a degree of freedom without straying too far. If livestock must be tied to stakes, picket pins, or high lines, keep an eye on your animals and move them before signs of trampling become evident.

Taking along supplemental feed for livestock can help prevent over-grazing around camp. In areas where grazing is not permitted, you will need to bring enough feed and hay for the entire trip. Land management regulations might require the use of certified feed and hay that prevents the spread of noxious plants.

Breaking Camp

Scatter manure to aid in its decomposition, to discourage concentrations of flies, and as a courtesy to other travelers. Fill areas dug up by animal hooves. Remove excess hay or other feed, and pack it with you. When all is in order, swing back into the saddle, tap your horse with your heels, and set off to see where the trail will take you next.

"When you are on a great horse, you have the best seat you will ever have."

—Sir Winston Churchill (1874—1965), British statesman, prime minister, and author

CHAPTER
22

Ski Touring and Snowshoeing

*"In the end, to ski is to travel fast and free—
free over untouched snow country . . . to follow
the lure of peaks which tempt on the horizon
and to be alone for a few days or even hours
in clear, mysterious surroundings."*

—Hans Gmoser, Canadian mountain guide and a founder of heli-skiing

The tracks of snowshoes and skis can be traced over the snows of thousands of years of human history. Modern skis and snowshoes are durable and easy to use, and the challenge of getting outdoors in winter is every bit as inviting. Combining vigorous exercise with agility and endurance, cross-country skiing and snowshoeing can be ideal additions to your physical fitness routine. Once you have mastered the basics, skis and snowshoes might become an essential part of your cold-weather camping gear, launching you into some of the best winter treks of your life.

Cross-Country Skiing

Cross-country skiing is a magnificent means of winter travel. In recent years, skis for traveling cross-country have evolved dramatically. Many are intended for specific conditions of snow and terrain—groomed tracks, for example, or deep powder. Variations in length, width, shape, base, edge, and flexibility can make ski selection bewildering for a beginner. Fortunately, just about every ski shop will have people who can help you find the right skis in the correct size to match your activities and level of expertise.

You can learn a great deal about what you need by renting cross-country skis, poles, and footwear. It won't take very many trips for you to discover the advantages of various styles of gear, and to narrow down your choices to the equipment that is just right for you.

Boots

Boots for cross-country skiing must be matched to the bindings with which they will be used. Beyond that, your choices depend on the weight and warmth you want in your footwear. For most recreational skiing, lighter boots are just the thing, while treks into rugged mountain country demand the security of sturdy, insulated boots. Check the fit of ski boots as you would hiking boots. Break them in on short trips before attempting any extensive touring, and wear gaiters to keep out the snow.

Bindings

Despite their differences, something that all skis have in common is a
binding to hold a ski boot in place.

Three-Pin Binding

This traditional cross-country ski binding consists of a movable bail and
three pins protruding upward from a metal plate attached to the ski. Holes
in the sole of a boot made to fit the binding slip over the pins, and the bail
snaps down to hold the boot toe against the ski. The heel of the boot is free
to move up and down as the skier kicks and glides across the snow.

Nordic Binding

The Nordic binding features a horizontal bar rather
than pins. A fitting molded into the toe of a
Nordic boot clips around the bar. As with
three-pin bindings, boot heels are free to
rise and fall with the skier's movements.

Nordic binding

Cable Binding

A cable binding holds the toe of a
skier's boot with a three-pin or Nordic
binding, and includes a cable tensioned
around the heel of the boot. The cable
increases a skier's lateral stability for
making turns on downhill runs.

Cable binding

Alpine Touring Binding

An alpine touring binding employs
a rigid, hinged plate designed to
accommodate a stiff leather or plastic
mountaineering boot. The heel is free
to rise and fall while a skier is on flat
terrain or going uphill, and many are fitted
with *heel lifts*—braces that can be positioned to
allow better foot position and more comfort on
steep ascents. Alpine bindings also can be locked
to the skis so that touring skiers can use the same
descent techniques as downhill skiers.

Alpine touring binding

Berwin Binding

The Berwin binding will accommodate mukluks,
shoepacs, and just about any other sort of
winter footwear. Toe cups and straps position
the skis and hold boots in place. Berwin
bindings are a good choice for travelers
crossing gentle terrain, especially if they
are pulling sleds loaded with gear.

Berwin binding

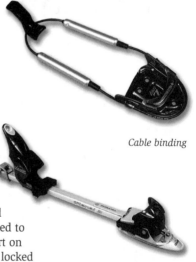

22

How Cross-Country Skis Work

Perhaps you've seen a good cross-country skier
skimming over the snow. The traveler kicks
forward on one ski, glides on it a moment, then
kicks the other ski ahead. One motion flows into
the next, and soon the skier is out of sight.

How can a ski that slides forward
also provide the traction a skier needs to
kick along a track? The problem has two
solutions—*waxless* and *waxable* skis.

Waxless Skis

Look at the underside, or *base,* of a waxless
ski and you probably will discover that the
middle third of the length has a molded
pattern that resembles overlapping fish
scales, diamonds, half-moons, or ripples.
Notice that the raised edges of the pattern
face the tail of the ski. It is much easier to
run your hand over the ski base from tip
to tail than it is to go the other way.

Now place the ski flat on the
floor and look at it from the side.
It's slightly bent, a characteristic
known as *camber.* With no weight
on the ski, the patterned portion
of the base doesn't touch the floor.
However, when someone stands
squarely in the binding, the ski
flattens until nearly all the pattern
is in contact with the floor. On snow,
the weight of a skier pushing off on a
ski flattens it, pressing the pattern down
where it can grip the snow. When the
skier glides, there is less pressure on the
ski, allowing it to flex upward and lift the
pattern clear of the snow. The ski coasts
forward on the smooth areas of the base.

Waxless skis can be noisy on downhill
runs and a bit slow, but they are great for
beginners, for skiing in variable temperatures
and snow conditions, and for any skier who
doesn't want to deal with waxes.

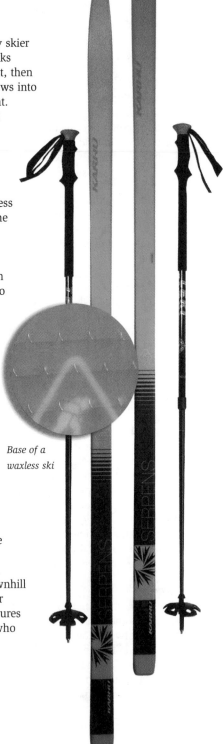

*Base of a
waxless ski*

22

Waxable Skis

The base of a waxable ski has no molded pattern. Instead, a skier applies a thin layer of special wax to the middle third of the base. As the skier's weight presses the ski down, microscopic crystals of snow dig into the wax and hold the ski steady. As the skier's weight shifts to the other ski, the waxed portion of the base rises a little above the snow, allowing the tip and tail of the ski to glide.

Waxable skis can be swifter and quieter than waxless models, but using wax effectively takes experience. Different snow conditions require different waxes for maximum efficiency, and you'll need to know the approximate temperature of the snow in order to choose the right wax. Packed in tubes or sticks marked with effective temperature ranges, waxes can be rubbed directly onto the base and then smoothed with a block of cork.

Typical Ski Waxes and Temperature Ranges	
WAX	**TEMPERATURES**
Universal	*Variable wet snow conditions*
Yellow	*34 to 39 degrees Fahrenheit*
Red	*32 to 36 degrees Fahrenheit*
Purple	*32 degrees Fahrenheit*
Orange	*21 to 31 degrees Fahrenheit*
Blue	*14 to 23 degrees Fahrenheit*
Green	*–22 to 14 degrees Fahrenheit*

The Kanik snow camping program offered by Philmont Scout Ranch is a premier cold-weather camping experience featuring ski touring, snow shelter building, snow camping, and winter ecology. Philmont awards a distinctive patch to each youth and adult participant who successfully completes the Kanik program. *Kanik* (pronounced *CAN-ick*) is from the Eskimo word for "snowflake."

22

Track Skiing

A good way to learn to ski is to follow the tracks of other skiers over rolling terrain. The tracks will help guide your skis while you practice the skills you'll use later for backcountry treks. Low hills will give you a chance to try gradual ascents, easy downhill runs, and plenty of kicking and gliding.

Getting Started

Begin by striding forward, putting your weight on your left ski while you slide the right one out in front. Shift your weight to your right foot as if you were taking a step and, as the right ski grips the snow, slide the left ski ahead of it. Repeat the sequence in steady rhythm—kick and glide, kick and glide—using your skis as platforms from which you propel yourself along.

Improve your balance and control by leaning forward as you ski. Check the way you use your poles; rather than gripping the handles, let your wrists press against the straps. As the left ski moves forward, plant the right pole ahead of yourself and push off with it. Do the same with the left pole as the right ski glides ahead. The motion of your arms will be much the same as when you swing them while walking, though a bit more exaggerated. The power of your arm and shoulder muscles will enhance your speed, and the smooth use of the poles will help you perfect the forward motion of cross-country skiing.

The right length of skis depends on the skier's weight, the width of the skis, and the ways in which the skis will be used. Poles for cross-country skiing should extend to a skier's chest.

Double Poling

Another way to make headway on flat routes is *double poling*—that is, using both poles in unison to push yourself along. Leaning forward at the waist with your knees flexed and feet together, plant your poles a little ahead of your boots. With a light grasp on the handles, push against the wrist straps and let your skis slide forward. Recover the poles by swinging your arms like pendulums, and plant the poles again, repeating the sequence with a relaxed, steady rhythm.

Turning

If you are skiing in a track, the track itself usually will guide the ski through gradual turns. Step out of the tracks, though, or set out across pristine snow, and turning is up to you. Several techniques can be used to change direction.

Step Turn

Make small route changes while you are in motion with the *step turn*.
Lift one ski and turn the tip in the direction you wish to travel. As you
put your weight onto that ski, lift and turn the other ski. For larger
changes in direction, you might need to make a series of step turns.

Kick Turn

Reverse your direction while standing still by using the *kick turn*. Lift one
ski above the snow, raise its tip, and carefully rotate your leg until you can
put the tip down beside the tail of your other ski. Shift your weight off that
ski, then lift it and twist around to place it in the normal position alongside
the first ski.

22

Snowplow Turn

Influence the direction and speed of your descents with *snowplow turns*. Position the skis in the shape of a V—the snowplow—and lean on the skis' inside edges. More pressure on the right ski will cause you to turn left, while pressure on the left ski will take you to the right. Equal pressure on the skis can slow your progress or bring you to a full stop.

Telemark Turn

As your skiing skills increase, you might want to learn to *telemark*. It will give you more versatility and control while you make your descents. The best way to learn is by having an experienced telemarker coach you, though you might be able to ease into the telemark turn from a snowplow turn. The primary difference between the two turns is one of position. In a snowplow turn, the skis form a V shape; in a telemark, the skis are parallel and one is a bit ahead of the other.

As you make a series of turns, gradually adjust the position of your skis from the V of the snowplow to the single line of the telemark. Put your weight on the forward ski, twist it to the outside with your ankle to begin the turn, and as the forward ski carves an arc in the snow, shift your weight to the back ski. To turn the other direction, slide the back ski forward, twist

it with your ankle, and let the inside edge of the ski lead you where you want to go.

You'll find you can balance best if you keep your hips turned downhill. That means you'll twist your torso to the right as you turn left, and to the left as you turn right. Lean downhill, too; leaning backward might cause your skis to slide out from under you.

Sidestep

Climbing

The pattern or wax on the base of your skis should grip the snow well enough for you to kick and glide up gradual slopes. For moderate slopes, switch to the *herringbone step*. Spread the tips of your skis until they form a 90-degree angle, plant your poles behind the skis with each step, and walk up the snow.

On ascents too steep to herringbone, turn your skis sideways to the hill and either *zigzag* (making switchbacks as you go) or *sidestep* (stepping up with the uphill ski, then bringing the downhill ski close to it). If a climb will be long, you might want to attach *climbing skins* to your skis.

Herringbone step

Climbing Skins

As a winter route becomes steeper, waxes and molded bases lose their ability to give a skier enough traction to proceed. One answer is to attach a *climbing skin* to each ski. Once made of animal hides, the best modern climbing skins feature mohair or nylon fibers secured to a tough, narrow strap about as long as a ski. A loop on one end slips over the ski tip, and a sticky adhesive holds the skin on the base of the ski. The fibers are angled toward the tail of the ski, providing a maximum of traction on kicks while still allowing a skier a bit of forward glide. Remove the skins before a descent, roll up each one with the sticky surface adhering to itself, pack them up, and head down the slope.

A more economical option is the *snakeskin*, a flexible plastic skin that can be strapped to a ski. The snakeskin works very well for climbing; it allows no forward glide, effectively turning a ski into a very long snowshoe.

Falling and Getting Up From a Fall

Every skier falls, and beginning skiers fall often. It's important to know how to fall without injury and, when you do go down, how to untangle yourself from your skis and get back on your feet.

First of all, don't fall if you can avoid it. Size up the terrain ahead. Is there room for you to make your way? Are there trees or drop-offs to avoid? Rocks or logs you would rather not hit? Is the snow soft and forgiving, or will an icy surface make turns difficult and stopping all but impossible? Where falling is likely, consider changing your route.

Rest a moment after a tumble to gather your wits. Slip out of your pack and, if there is a chance the pack might slide, anchor it to the slope with a ski pole. Twist around until your skis are on your downhill side and sideways to the hill. Plant your poles next to your hip and pull yourself onto your knees, then brace yourself by pushing downward on the poles as you regain your feet. Brush yourself off, swing your pack onto your shoulders, and you'll be ready to go.

Breaking Trail

When the snow is relatively settled, kicking and gliding, double poling, and downhill running will get you where you want to go. However, when you sink into fresh powder with every step, the track in the snow made by the first skier can be used by those who follow. Breaking trail can be exhausting, so group members will want to take turns; the lead skier simply steps to the side of the track, waits for the line to go by, then falls in at the rear. Rotate every few minutes to give each skier opportunities to lead and to rest.

Skiing With a Pack

On day trips, a small pack on your shoulders or a fanny pack strapped around your waist can hold the food, water, and extra clothing you'll need, but it shouldn't interfere with your skiing. You might need a backpack for overnight trips. For skiing, those with internal frames are easier to manage than ones with frames on the outside. Load the pack so that the center of gravity is a little lower than usual and adjust the straps so that the pack fits securely against your back and can't sway from side to side.

Skiing With a Sled

Pulling your gear in a sled takes less effort than supporting the same weight in a pack on your back. You might want to carry a small pack with water, food, and other items you will need during the day, then stash the rest of your load in the sled.

Caring for Ski Gear

If something goes wrong with your skis miles from civilization, you could be in for a long, weary trudge home. Avoid that possibility by carrying an emergency kit containing a pair of pliers, a small roll of duct tape, a screwdriver that will fit the screws on your bindings, an emergency ski tip that can be slipped over the end of a broken ski, and any other items that could come in handy for making repairs.

Pay attention to the surfaces over which you ski. Beware of rocks and sticks poking through the snow; they can gouge the bases of your skis and cause them to become sluggish. Keep your speed under control, especially as you ski through forests. Go around ditches, drops, and other sharp depressions that could excessively bend your skis.

Store your skis upright in camp by leaning them against a tree or by sticking the tails into the snow, so they will not be covered by falling or drifting snow. Face the bases east before you bed down; the morning sun might warm them and make waxing easier.

When you get home, let your gear dry at room temperature and use a metal scraper and/or a wax remover to clean the bases of waxable skis. Recondition ski boots as you would any outdoor footwear, and stow your equipment where you can get at it quickly. It won't be long before you glance out the window on a cold day and give in to the joy of clipping into your skis and pushing off for another winter adventure.

"*There is only one way to learn to walk on snowshoes, and that is to put them on and try.*"

—Daniel Carter Beard, 1925 (Beard served as the first national Scout commissioner.)

Snowshoeing

Snowshoes might well have been around every bit as long as skis. By the time European settlers arrived in North America, American Indians of the northern woodlands had developed snowshoe making into a high art, shaping wood and rawhide into snowshoes that were as beautiful as they were efficient. Since then, wanderers of the winter wilderness have found snowshoes to be an invaluable part of their gear, allowing them to move over snow that otherwise would be impassable. With a little practice, you, too, can enjoy the quiet, rhythmic stride of snowshoeing.

How Snowshoes Work

When you hike in snow with only boots on your feet, all of your weight presses down on a relatively small surface area, causing your feet to punch into the drifts. Snowshoes put a larger platform beneath your soles, spreading your weight over a much greater surface area. If they are the right size for the snow conditions and the amount of weight put on them, your snowshoes will float near the top of the snow, and you will be able to travel about with ease.

Kinds of Snowshoes

The gorgeous wood and rawhide snowshoes of generations past have almost all been replaced by snowshoes featuring lightweight metal frames and flotation decks made of plastic, neoprene, rubberized fabric, and other durable materials. Today's snowshoes are specialized for certain kinds of adventures, too. Those used for short jaunts near a cabin or by fitness runners can be very light and just slightly longer and wider than running shoes. At the other end of the scale are expedition snowshoes—up to 4 feet long—that provide enough flotation to support a wilderness traveler carrying a backpack loaded with camping gear. Some snowshoes have traction bars secured to their bases and crampons built into their bindings to give snowshoers a secure grip on steep slopes, while snowshoes with smooth bases can be used to slide down hillsides.

Local experts might be able to provide the best guidance for choosing the right snowshoes in the correct size. Check with outing clubs in your area and with winter sports equipment stores for advice. If you can, rent snowshoes before you buy and see what you think of them in the field.

From expedition snowshoes to those used for fast dashes over the drifts, modern snowshoes are tough, lightweight, and easy to use.

Bindings

Bindings do just what the word implies—they bind your footgear to your snowshoes. All bindings are similar in that they can be used with almost any boots, mukluks, or other winter wear. They allow the easy up-and-down motion of your heels, and are balanced so that the toe of each snowshoe rises and the tail drags on the snow.

Ski Poles and Ice-Ax Baskets

Many snowshoers use one or two ski poles to help them maintain their balance. You'll find that poles can be especially helpful as you make turns and get up from falls.

Some mountain travelers attach a special basket to the end of an ice ax and use it for balance in much the same manner as they would a ski pole. The ax can be a lifesaver in stopping a fall on a steep slope.

Using Snowshoes

"If you can walk, you can snowshoe." That bit of traditional advice for beginning snowshoers is most of what you need to know to get started. Put on your snowshoes, head out across snowy terrain, and your body mechanics will do the rest.

As you step forward, let the inside edge of the snowshoe in motion pass over the inside edge of the stationary snowshoe. Swing your foot just far enough forward so that the snowshoes don't touch when you step down. Firmly plant the leading snowshoe to create a stable platform on which to place your weight, and pause an instant after each step. That will allow the snow to consolidate beneath the snowshoe and will give you a momentary rest. Lift each shoe just high enough to make forward progress, allowing the snowshoe tail to drag on the snow.

The BSA's Northern Tier National High Adventure Program offers the perfect setting for cold-weather camping, cross-country skiing, and snowshoeing. Visitors to the Charles L. Sommers High Adventure Base in Ely, Minnesota, are treated to a winter wonderland and allowed a chance to hone winter camping and sports skills with such activities as dog sledding, ice fishing, and shelter building.

Turning

The easiest way to change your direction of travel is by using the *arc turn*. Simply turn your snowshoes a little with each step, gradually curving around until you're lined up on your new course.

A *step turn* alters your direction more quickly. While standing in one spot, lift and turn your snowshoes one after the other, repeating the motion until the toes are facing the direction you want to go. Your movements should be smooth and precise, with your legs spread apart far enough to prevent the tail of one snowshoe from being pinned beneath the edge of the other.

For a fast 180-degree reversal, use the *kick turn*. Leaning on a ski pole for balance, lift one snowshoe, twist around until you are facing the opposite direction, and plant the shoe firmly beside the stationary one. Lift the second snowshoe, rotate around, and then plant it beside the first.

Traveling Uphill

Many snowshoes are equipped with traction bars or with crampons on their bindings that allow snowshoers to make their way directly up steep hills. When the snow is soft, travel technique is much the same as on flat ground. On harder snow, kick the toes of your boots into the slope, forcing the crampon teeth to grip the crust. Lean forward a bit and take shorter steps.

Traveling Downhill

Downhill travel can be surprisingly difficult on snowshoes. Bindings must be snug to handle the increased pressure on your feet, and you'll need to alter your stride to keep your snowshoes flat on the snow. You can do that on gradual grades by leaning back enough to put extra weight on the tails of your snowshoes. On steeper slopes, tie a cord to the tip of each snowshoe; pulling up on the cords as you plant your snowshoes can keep them ideally positioned.

Breaking Trail

As you snowshoe you'll soon discover what cross-country skiers know—travel is much easier if you have a track to follow. The tracks of other snowshoers will pack down the snow ahead, allowing you to make good time.

Break your own trail where there are no tracks, shortening your steps and keeping the tips of your snowshoes high to prevent them from becoming loaded with snow. Trail breaking can be tiring work, especially in deep snow, so organize your group to allow lead changes every few minutes.

Ski and Snowshoe Within Your Level of Skill

In flat or gently rolling regions of the country, skis and snowshoes can allow you to explore wintry landscapes that would prove difficult or impossible to reach on foot. Snowshoes and skis also are terrific for travel in steeper terrain. Stay within your skill level as you plan journeys into snowy areas. If avalanches are a possibility, go somewhere else until you have gained the training and experience you need to size up avalanche potential and to carry out rescues if avalanches do occur.

For more on winter safety, equipment, and concerns, see the chapters titled "Managing Risk," "Gearing Up," "Cold-Weather Travel and Camping," and "Mountain Travel."

22

Snowshoe Care and Storage

Inspect snowshoes after every outing for signs of wear. Frames might become dented or bent, and the webbing can be nicked or cut. Repair minor damage before it can become severe, and your snowshoes will be in top condition whenever you're ready to head for the hills.

> *"The goal of all blind skiers is more freedom. You don't have to see where you are going, as long as you go. In skiing, you ski with your legs and not with your eyes. In life, you experience things with your mind and your body. And if you're lacking one of the five senses, you adapt."*
>
> —Lorita Bertraun, blind American skier

Mountain Travel

"Double happy . . . is the man to whom lofty mountaintops are within reach, for the lights that shine there illumine all that lies below."

—John Muir (1838–1914), 19th-century naturalist, mountain traveler, and a founder of the Sierra Club

Climb far above the meadows and valleys into a lofty world of summits, ridges, boulder fields, and snow. There you'll find a remarkable ecology thriving in harsh alpine conditions. In yourself, you can find a keen sense of confidence in your ability to travel safely and well through even the wildest territory. Reaching the high country often involves cross-country travel over tough terrain. That's where a knowledge of mountain travel pays off. It can take over where the trail ends, lift you far above the lowlands, and help you explore the great, solitary realm where the summits meet the sky.

Mountain travel can be done as day hikes from trailheads or base camps, or might include nights of camping at high elevations. It is an advanced form of adventure that draws on a mastery of backpacking, wilderness navigation, and risk management. Most of all, it demands maturity and judgment.

23

Climb On Safely

The skills of mountain travel bridge the gap between trail hiking and *technical mountaineering* (mountain travel that involves the use of ropes, anchors, and other technical expertise). Unlike rock climbers who seek out steep, difficult routes, mountain travelers strive to reach their destinations with a minimum of exposure to potential danger. The techniques described in this chapter are intended to alert you to important considerations for planning and enjoying treks in mountainous terrain.

Leaders of Scout units interested in rock climbing or any forms of technical mountaineering must follow the points of Climb On Safely—the Boy Scouts of America's recommended procedure for organizing climbing and rappelling activities at a natural site or a specifically designed facility such as a climbing wall or tower— to provide qualified instruction and adult supervision, and to conduct these activities in a manner that conforms with the policies and guidelines of the BSA.

For the full text of the BSA's Climb On Safely, see the *Fieldbook* Web site.

Deciding Where to Go

Perhaps you have heard of a lake high in a mountain valley that you would like to visit, or a mountain you want to climb, or an alpine pass that can lead you to a faraway destination. On visits to parks, forests, and high-adventure bases you might have seen inviting summits and decided you would someday make your way to the top. Choosing a destination for your mountain travel is often a matter of narrowing down a wealth of opportunities.

Nearly every mountain of any size is featured in local guidebooks that include descriptions of routes, degrees of difficulty, permits required, group size limitations, and hazards to avoid. Land management personnel might also provide information that will help you determine whether destinations are within your skill levels and, if so, how best to reach them.

Planning a Mountain Travel Journey

The challenges raised by mountain travel often are matters of distance and remoteness. You and your group will require appropriate gear and provisions, just as for any trek adventure, but you also might need to prepare to be more self-reliant than when you are close to a trailhead. Risk management, first-aid training, and reliable means of emergency communication must be carefully considered in the planning stages of a trip. So should writing down a detailed trip plan and leaving it with responsible adults.

Monitor weather forecasts in the days leading up to your departure and check with land management personnel for the latest reports. Use your best weather sense while you are in the field, too. If stormy conditions turn you back, remember that the mountains will still be there the next time you want to head for the high country.

For more on preparing for a mountaineering adventure, see the chapter titled "Planning a Trek."

Leave No Trace Mountain Travel

Alpine environments can be especially sensitive to human impact. The principles discussed in the chapter titled "Implementing Leave No Trace" are excellent guidelines for conducting mountain travel adventures in ways that are enjoyable and environmentally sound. Respect limitations on group size, stay on trails whenever you can, and use designated campsites. Otherwise, hike and camp on rock, gravel, dry grasses, or snow, and minimize your impact as much as possible.

For more on responsible mountain travel, see the "Leaving No Trace" section of this book.

Mountain Travel Teams

Team development and leadership issues that are important during any outdoor activity are vital for the success of a mountain trip. For safety, a team should be made up of at least four people. Everyone needs to understand the challenges ahead and prepare for them both physically and mentally. Group members who have succeeded together during Project COPE (Challenging Outdoor Personal Experience) or other trek adventures should be well on their way to developing the trust and teamwork that will see them through journeys involving mountain travel.

For more on the dynamics of travel teams, see the "Leadership and Trek Preparation" section of this book.

Mountain Travel Route Finding

Researching a trip before leaving home can give you a general sense of the lay of the land. You might be able to figure out the hiking trails that will lead you to your destination, and designated sites where you can camp. Once you are on your way, though, you might need to adjust your route in response to local conditions. With the landscape in front of you, study your topographic map. Identify landmarks and consider the shape of the terrain. The map will provide clues to the twists and turns of water courses, the shapes of ridges, any obstacles that might lie between you and your objective, and the possibilities of practical ways to get there.

Studying the territory ahead also will reveal what maps and guidebooks cannot—the conditions of the moment. Snow levels, vegetation, and weather conditions can have dramatic effects on potential routes. Experience

and common sense come into play, too, as you evaluate what you see and determine how you will proceed. A skyline ridge might be the best way to go. A boulder slope might offer a virtual highway to the top. A snowfield could be the easiest means of negotiating a climb. Heavy brush, a swollen stream, or a change in the appearance of the clouds all can influence your on-site route-finding decisions, or perhaps convince you that going farther would not be wise until conditions improve, that you should change your intended route, or that you should go home.

The most important steps you can take to make your way off a mountain happen on the way up. Pay close attention to the route behind you, looking back often to see how it will appear when you are coming down. Take note of landmarks that will help you find your way—a boulder where you need to turn, for example, or a large tree near your camp. A group equipped with a global positioning system (GPS) receiver can program in waypoints while they climb, then use the instrument as a backup navigational tool while retracing their steps later in the day.

Summit Packs

Summit packs—day packs used on the day of a climb to the top of a mountain—will allow you to leave large backpacks at your base camp. Include in your summit pack the outdoor essentials and any other gear you might need. A sleeping bag and bivouac bag or tarp will come in handy if you are overtaken by darkness or if a member of your group suffers an injury or illness and must be treated far from camp.

For more on the outdoor essentials, see the chapter titled "Gearing Up."

Rain, snow, fog, and darkness can obscure your ability to see very far, compounding the difficulties of finding routes. Awakening to the sound of wind blowing rain or snow against your tent might be a strong indication that it would be better to stay in camp and read a good book. There's not much point in climbing high if you can't make out which way to go.

When weather is more inviting, accurate compass bearings taken on your way up can be invaluable during your descent, especially if landmarks are few and far between. As you cross large snowfields, you might want to mark your route with *wands.* Usually made of bamboo and topped with strips of brightly colored flagging, wands will show you the way home even in deteriorating weather. Retrieve them as you descend.

If you become disoriented, stop where you are. Gather whatever information you can from what you are able to see. Are there footprints in the snow? Breaks in the clouds that allow you to glimpse your route, or at

least a few recognizable landmarks? Get out your map and compass, talk with others in your group, and figure out where to go next. Whatever you do, don't wander blindly. It is far better to settle in where you are and wait until you can see where you are going, even if that means a night bivouacked on the mountain.

For more on finding your way and staying found, see the chapter titled "Navigation."

Time Management

Start early on the day of an ascent, perhaps even before dawn. That will give you the greatest number of daylight hours for traveling—an important factor if the climb is more strenuous than you had anticipated or if an emergency arises—and allow you to return from exposed heights before unstable afternoon weather moves in.

Enthusiasm to reach a summit or other remote destination can sometimes cloud the judgment of mountain travelers. A late departure from camp, changing weather conditions, and unexpected delays can slow a group's progress. Even though a destination might seem within reach, the lateness of the day could make the return trip difficult and even risky as fatigue and darkness set in.

Before leaving home, decide on an appropriate turnaround time to use on the day of a summit attempt. When that moment comes on the mountain—2 o'clock in the afternoon, for example—all members of your group will begin descending even if they have not reached the summit. The turnaround time should allow you to reach your camp or the trailhead with plenty of daylight to spare.

For more on preventing accidents by planning well and using good judgment, see the chapters titled "Planning a Trek" and "Managing Risk."

Reaching a summit
can be the high point
of a mountain travel
trip, both literally
and emotionally.
The real goal,
though, is getting
down safely.

Descending

The focus on reaching a mountaintop can energize
travelers and push them to remarkable achievements.
More accidents occur on the descent to camp than
on an ascent. People often are weary from the
ascent. Hunger and thirst can dull their senses,
impair their judgment, and take the edge off their
physical abilities. Impatience to get back to the
comforts of camp will cause teamwork to suffer
if some group members hurry ahead of others.

Travelers retreating down a mountainside might be
further tested by deteriorating weather, evening cold, and the dark of night.

Throughout a descent, refer to the compass bearings you took and
the mental pictures you made of how the route looked behind you during
your ascent. If your group is using a GPS receiver, refer to the waypoints
you recorded. It also is important to keep the big picture in mind. The
heights can afford you a bird's-eye view of the terrain below and, when
coupled with a close look at a topographic map, a good understanding of
your primary route and any feasible alternatives. Small changes in direction
high up can lead to dramatically different destinations. From a ridge top,
for example, it might be easy to start down any of several valleys or to turn
your footsteps down either side of a wide snowfield. Consider where you
will end up with each of the options presented to you, then choose the one
that holds the most promise. Keep your group together, traveling at a pace
that can be managed by the slowest member of the team.

Challenges of Mountain Travel

Surrounded by heavy brush, deep forests, rushing streams, rocky slopes, and snowfields, many mountains seem to defy hikers' attempts to climb them. However, overcoming the difficulties of an ascent can make the view from the top all the sweeter. Here are some pointers on dealing with common mountain challenges:

Brush

Brush can be the bane of cross-country travel. Brambles and briars sometimes choke hillsides and streambeds. Mountains scarred by fire or logging operations can be covered with thick, low, second-growth timber. Avalanches can scour steep slopes, leaving them inhabitable only by dense thickets of low-growing vegetation.

The best way to negotiate brush might be simply to avoid it. Look for a clear route around overgrowth, perhaps by running the crest of a ridge or by ascending the side of a valley until you can pass above the heaviest of the vegetation. When you must wade into the brush, wear clothing that will protect you from snags and scratches. If you will be in the tall tangles for a while, follow a compass bearing so that you can come out where you want on the other side of the thicket.

Before crossing any stream, unbuckle the waist belt of your backpack and loosen the shoulder straps so that you can quickly escape from the load if you fall into the water.

Streams

Crossing streams is always serious business. Twisting your foot on a mossy rock, soaking a sleeping bag in the current, or falling into the water on a chilly day can quickly complicate the best travel plans. Unless it is a brook you can step over or a stream with a bridge you can use, take plenty of time before crossing to size up the situation.

Water more than knee-deep can make you buoyant; add a swift current, and you might have difficulty keeping your footing. Your best crossing places often will be where the stream is widest and the water is calm. Next, look downstream. If you should fall, is there a chance you could be swept into a rapids, against rocks, or over a falls? Don't tempt fate by challenging a stream that might not give you a second chance.

In mountainous country where snowfields blanket the peaks, snow melting on warm spring and summer afternoons can cause streams to rise. A raging torrent at midday might, after a cool night, be tame enough at dawn to negotiate with ease. When you come upon such a stream, make camp and wait until morning when the crossing can be made safely.

Stepping Stones

Decide which rocks you can use as a route across a stream, and in what order. Plant your feet squarely in the center of large stones, moving smoothly from one to the next. Are the rocks wet or mossy? Expect them to be slippery. A walking stick will help you maintain your balance.

Fallen Logs

While it's usually not too difficult to walk the backs of large, stable logs close to the surface of the water, a more secure (though less graceful) means of crossing is to straddle the log and scoot your way to the far bank. Beware of loose bark and bare wood slick with sap, spray, or rain.

Wading

Wearing shoes while you wade streams will give you better footing on wet rocks and protect your feet from cuts and bruises. If you're carrying running shoes to wear in camp, you can put them on for stream crossings and keep your boots dry. If not, wear your boots without socks. Station one person downstream with a rescue line in case someone loses his or her footing. When you reach the far side, dry your feet before you put your socks and boots back on.

Members of a group usually can wade shallow streams one at a time, but if the water is deep or the stream is wide, they might do better crossing in pairs or groups of three.

Scree, Talus, and Boulder Fields

As mountains break down over the centuries, cliffs fracture, fall, and cover slopes with broken rock. The largest of these stones are *boulders* heavy enough to wedge together. Smaller rocks prone to moving under a traveler's weight are known as *talus*. If the material resembles gravel, it's called *scree*.

Climbing on scree is similar to walking on snow. You sometimes can make headway by kicking toeholds or by pointing your toes out and herringboning up an incline like a cross-country skier. Think of snow as you descend, too, leaning well forward to keep your weight over your feet.

Many rocks on a talus slope are large enough to hold the soles of your boots, but due to their modest size, they can be easily tilted or dislodged. Place your weight in the center of each rock rather than near the edge, and be ready for a seemingly stable stone to move underfoot. Members of a group traversing a scree or talus slope should stay on the same horizontal plane so that rocks loosened by one of them will not endanger others.

Negotiate boulder fields by stepping lightly from one rock to the next. When possible, step to the center of large, dry boulders that are likely to be more stable. Be ready to catch yourself if your feet slip or a boulder tips and upsets your balance. Point out loose boulders to those following you so that they can avoid them or prepare for unstable footing.

23

The Rest Step

During long climbs, the *rest step* can give your body a moment to recover after every stride. Move your right foot ahead and place the sole of your boot flat on the ground. Swing forward and lock your knee for a moment or two; the bones of your leg and pelvis will support your weight, allowing your thigh and calf muscles a momentary rest. Swing your left foot forward and repeat the sequence. Even though you might be moving slowly, a rhythmic pace will lift you steadily up a mountainside.

Snowfields

In the winter and at higher altitudes during much of the summer, snowfields can be inviting routes for cross-country travel and for reaching summits. Snow on flat terrain and gentle slopes can be traversed with few concerns for hazards. Snowshoes or cross-country skis can add speed and range to your travels, and might be essential if snow is deep and too soft to sustain the weight of your footsteps.

Before venturing onto steeper mountain snow, however, you must understand the danger of avalanches and avoid those areas where avalanches are possible. You also must know how to stop yourself if you lose your footing and begin to slide. For that, you need an ice ax and plenty of practice using it.

For more on avalanches, see the chapter titled "Managing Risk."

Ice Axes and Self-Arrest

An ice ax can greatly enhance your security as you travel on snowy slopes. Have an experienced snow hiker demonstrate proper ice-ax technique, and master it before you need it.

Ice ax for mountain travel

The head of an ice ax features a *pick* for self-arrests and a short, wide blade called an *adz* for chopping steps in hard snow. Some mountain travelers choose axes with shafts long enough to reach from their palms to the ground so that they can use the axes as walking sticks between snowfields. Mountaineers usually select shorter axes, finding them easier to manage on steep slopes. On the trail, carry an ice ax as you would a cane, or slip it through a loop on your pack and lash the shaft to the pack itself.

The primary reason to have an ice ax is for *self-arrest*—stopping yourself if you fall on a steep snow slope. As you begin to slide, grip the head of your ice ax with one hand (the point of the pick turned away from you) and hold the shaft with the other. Roll *toward* the head of the ax until you are on your belly. The pick will embed itself in the snow and stop you in a surprisingly short distance. If a fall turns into a headfirst tumble, roll toward the pick and, as it bites into the snow and begins to slow your descent, swing your feet around until they are below you.

Self-arresting is a technique that requires expert instruction and plenty of drill. Practice by purposely sliding on a slope with a safe runout (that is, it flattens gradually). Slide in every imaginable position, even headfirst on your back. When you can automatically make the right moves to arrest your fall, you will have mastered one of mountain travel's most effective safety skills.

Snowfield Travel

The consistency of the snow will affect the speed with which you can travel on a snowfield. Deep, powdery snow can engulf your feet and make you feel as though you are wading, while hard, windblown slabs can be slippery. When a snowy slope is not too steep, you can zigzag your way up. On more severe inclines, you also might need to kick steps with the toes or edges of your boots. Holding your ice ax in your uphill hand, drive the shaft into the slope and use the momentum of your strides to kick steps. Settle into your new stance, then move the ax forward and plant it again. Having made the ax a solid anchor before you move your feet, you'll have something sturdy to grip if you lose your footing.

Descending Snowfields

Where a snowfield is free of rocks, trees, and other obstacles, you might be able to descend by *glissading.* Holding your ice ax in the ready position, aim your toes down the slope and ski on the soles of your boots. Keep your knees bent and lean forward. When leaning forward over your boots, you are less likely to slip or fall. Carve small turns by angling your feet and digging the sides of your boot soles into the snow in much the same manner as if you were on skis.

The *plunge step* is another effective descent technique. Lean forward ("nose over toes"), kick out with your foot, lock your knee, and goose-step down the snowfield. The farther forward you lean, the more stable your footing will be.

Crampons

Climbers in the early years of mountain travel wore hobnailed boots for traction and used their ice axes to chop steps in difficult, frozen pitches. Today's mountain travelers can put crampons on their boots and make good progress across slippery and steep snow slopes. They nearly always have ice axes at the ready to self-arrest if they do begin to slide.

Crampons must be matched to the boots on which they will be used. More traditional models are hinged, can be strapped in place, and can be used with some hiking boots. The latest crampons are designed to snap in place on plastic mountaineering boots.

Glacier Travel

Mountain travel, as it is described in this book, does not include the skills required to travel on glaciers.

Glaciers occur when snowfall does not completely melt each year, compressing into slowly moving rivers of ice. The primary hazards awaiting glacier travelers are *crevasses*—cracks in a glacier that can be extremely deep and quite wide. The opening of a crevasse can be hidden by a roof of snow.

Glacier travel demands training in specific mountaineering techniques, and should be done only by teams of experienced mountaineers roped together, ready to stop a climber's fall into a crevasse, and able to conduct a crevasse rescue.

Acute Mountain Sickness

The human body requires a week or more to adjust to higher elevations, compensating for the thin air by producing additional red blood cells to carry oxygen to the cells. Ascending no more than a thousand feet of elevation during each day helps avoid acute mountain sickness. It is not unusual for people traveling into the mountains to feel more fatigued than usual and perhaps to experience mild headaches. Ward off the effects of altitude by drinking plenty of liquids, getting enough rest, and spending one or more layover days partway up an ascent.

At elevations above 8,000 feet, some people may suffer *acute mountain sickness* (also known as *AMS* or *altitude sickness*). In its severe forms, fluid passes through membranes of the brain *(cerebral edema)* or of the lungs *(pulmonary edema)*. A victim might become confused, lethargic, nauseated, and incapacitated. If any of these symptoms appear, escort the ill person to lower elevations as quickly as possible. The person should consult a physician upon returning home. Also, prior to high-elevation travel, consult a physician about medication to help avoid AMS.

A Final Word on Mountain Travel

Mastering the fine points of mountain travel will prepare you to meet the challenges of the most rugged terrain. You also can apply many of these skills to your adventures in less demanding regions. The joy of traveling with confidence, with good judgment, and with an openness for discovery is there for you in any direction you go.

"The mountains can be reached in all seasons. They offer a fighting challenge to heart, soul, and mind, both in summer and winter. If throughout time the youth of the nation accept the challenge the mountains offer, they will keep alive in our people the spirit of adventure."

—William O. Douglas (20th-century conservationist and U.S. Supreme Court justice)

Caving

"Mystery, adventure, discovery, beauty, conservation, danger. To many who are avid cavers and speleologists, caves are all of these things and many more, too."

—David R. McClurg (caver, subterranean photographer, caving skills instructor, and longtime member of the National Speleological Society), *The Amateur's Guide to Caves and Caving,* 1973

Beneath the Earth's surface lies a magnificent realm darker than a moonless night. No rain falls. No storms rage. The seasons never change. Other than the ripple of hidden streams and the occasional splash of dripping water, this underground world is silent, yet it is not without life. Bats fly with sure reckoning through mazes of tunnels, and eyeless creatures scurry about. Transparent fish stir the waters of underground streams, and the darkness is home to tiny organisms seldom seen in broad daylight.

This is the world of the cave, as beautiful, alien, and remote as the glaciated crests of lofty mountains. Just as climbers are tempted by summits that rise far above familiar ground, cavers are drawn into a subterranean wilderness every bit as exciting and remarkable as any place warmed by the rays of the sun.

Water is the most common force involved in the creation of caves. As it seeps through the earth, moisture can dissolve limestone, gypsum, and other sedimentary rock. Surf pounding rocky cliffs can, over the centuries, carve out sea caves of spectacular shape and dimension. The surface of lava flowing from a volcanic eruption can cool and harden while molten rock runs out below it, leaving behind lava tubes. Streams running under glaciers can melt caves in the ice that stay around for a season or two, or a century or two.

Boulders tumbling down a mountainside sometimes come to rest against one another in ways that form passageways.

Many caves are so small that people can barely enter, while others extend for miles and include rooms of tremendous dimensions. Features come in all sizes, too, from soaring rock columns to tiny needles of stone. While most caves are stable enough to survive earthquakes, the contents of caves are often extremely fragile.

The forces shaping caves and their features work with exceeding patience. Centuries may pass before groundwater widens a chamber or lengthens a passage by even an inch. A drop of water hanging from the point of a *stalactite* leaves behind a trace of mineral residue when it finally falls, lengthening the stalactite ever so slightly, then splashing on a *stalagmite* rising from the cave floor and depositing a hint of minerals there, too.

Massive and delicate, living and stony, a cave is almost timeless, little touched by the world above. We have the power to explore and enjoy the underground world of caves, but we must always do so in ways that protect these pristine environments.

WHAT IS A CAVE?

A *cave* is a naturally formed void located beneath the surface of the Earth. By definition, it must have passages or rooms large enough to admit a human, and by popular definition, must be long enough so that a caver can get out of the twilight to enter a zone of total darkness.

The Importance of Caves

Cave environments are tightly entwined with the world above. Caves often play a role in rapidly transporting water and providing means for recharging aquifers. Bats, snakes, frogs, insects, and other cave visitors, all known as *trogloxenes,* form webs of interdependency near cave entrances. Permanent underground dwellers such as blind crayfish, blind Texas salamanders, blind shrimp, and the endangered tooth cave spider—the *troglobites*—can live nowhere but in caves. They are parts of fragile ecosystems unique on the planet.

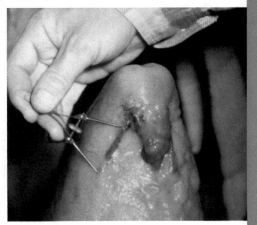

Caves can provide a window into the past for *archaeologists* (those studying past human life), *biologists* (those studying animals), and *paleontologists* (scientists studying fossilized remains to better understand earlier geological periods). For many people, caves are places of breathtaking beauty, challenging adventure, and the promise of the unknown.

Cavers find many strange sights underground, such as the remains of a bat encased in a stalagmite.

Leave No Trace Caving

Caves and the formations within them evolve with such exceeding slowness that underground environments have little capacity for recovering on their own from the negative impact of human visitors. A broken stalactite or stalagmite may grow back, but only after thousands of years. Marks left on stone will be visible for centuries to come. Discarded batteries, orange peels, and other bits of litter will stay exactly where they are until someone carries them away.

Only by protecting caves can today's subterranean travelers ensure that future cavers will have a chance to enjoy their own underground discoveries and adventures. If you aren't willing to protect fully the condition of the caves you want to visit, stay aboveground and find some other way to spend your time.

In addition to following the general Leave No Trace principles, following the guidelines below will ensure that you are caving responsibly:

- Go to the bathroom before entering a cave and/or carry out human waste in containers designed for that purpose.

- In well-traveled caves, stay on established trails. In caves without pathways, choose routes that will have the least impact on the subterranean environment.

- Watch for roosting bats and other cave dwellers, and try not to disturb them. Keep noise down to respect wildlife and other visitors.

24

- Enjoy viewing and photographing cave formations, but don't touch them. Oils and dirt from your hands can impede their growth. Leave cave formations, rocks, and artifacts for others to see.

- Nutrients foreign to a cave ecosystem can be harmful to microbes and may attract mice and other nonnative creatures underground. Before eating in a cave, spread a plastic trash bag on the floor to catch crumbs and other bits of food, then carry them home with you.

- Human waste is disastrous to cave environments. Every caver should consider carrying a *pack-it-out kit* for solid waste removal, and a designated bottle for carrying out urine.

- Wear only boots or shoes with nonmarking soles. Boots with blonde soles or gum rubber soles are acceptable; black-soled hiking boots are not.

Leave interesting cave finds like this calcium formation for future cavers to enjoy.

For details on making and using pack-it-out kits for human waste, see the chapter titled "Hygiene and Waste Disposal."

Caving Organizations and Land Management Agencies

Dedicated to promoting responsible caving, local chapters (or *grottos*) of the National Speleological Society can be very helpful to Scout groups. Two other organizations are the American Cave Conservation Association and the Cave Research Foundation. Public agencies overseeing certain caves are essential resources for cavers of any age and experience level. Among them are the National Park Service, USDA Forest Service, and Bureau of Land Management.

Caving organizations and public agencies might also be able to provide guidance to Scout groups interested in assisting with the restoration of damaged caves. No projects should be undertaken without the permission of the agency or landowners in charge of a cave, and all work should be supervised by people with a knowledge of cave restoration and repair.

For links to these organizations and agencies, see the *Fieldbook* Web site.

"Caving is dangerous, make no mistake about that. But it is also true that caving is only as dangerous as a caver makes it."

—David R. McClurg, *The Amateur's Guide to Caves and Caving,* 1973

Caving Safety

The hazards of caving probably are no greater than those encountered by mountain travelers. However, rescues can be more complicated when a person is injured underground in the remote interior of a cave. Thorough planning and preparation can help you minimize caving's inherent risks. Underground hazards can include flooding, falling, equipment failure, disorientation, hypothermia, heat exhaustion, and exposure to histoplasmosis (a bronchial disease caused by a fungus), rabies, and other biological concerns.

Prepare for safe caving through careful planning, proper leadership and training, carrying the right equipment, and exercising good judgment. Keep the following guidelines in mind when planning for and participating in caving:

- Never cave alone. A group entering a cave should consist of a minimum of four people, at least one of them an experienced caver. If there is an emergency, one person can stay with an injured person while the other two go for help.

- Before you embark, always file a detailed trip plan with a responsible adult. Write down the exact location of the cave entrance, where you intend to go while you are underground, and when you expect to come out. Then stick to your itinerary. If you have not returned by the time noted on your trip plan, the person expecting you must assume you have encountered difficulties and should notify authorities to begin search-and-rescue operations. (For more on trip plans, see the chapter titled "Planning a Trek.")

- Each person should carry at least three reliable sources of light—ideally, good flashlights with fresh batteries. A headlamp will allow you to use both hands while crawling and climbing.

- Don't exceed your capabilities. Caving is a learned skill. Begin with short, easily manageable trips underground. As your understanding of caving grows, you can gradually extend the time and distance of your subterranean journeys.

- Stay out of mines. Caves have endured eons of motion by the earth and can generally be assumed to be relatively stable. The same cannot be said of mines and other excavations created by humans, which are much more prone to rockfall and collapse.

- Be aware of the potential for flooding. It might seem odd that weather can have an impact on the conditions of a cave, but it can. Rainwater seeping underground can have dramatic effects on the levels of subterranean pools and streams long after a storm. As a rule of thumb, enter caves only after several days of fair weather.

- Never use ropes, ladders, anchor points, or other installations in caves unless absolutely assured of their security by group leaders who had a hand in the initial selection and placement of the components and who have made a thorough evaluation of the current status of each item. Mountaineers don't trust ropes or hardware they did not themselves bring on a climb; the same holds true for cavers.

- Caving involves a set of skills that should be learned under the supervision of qualified instructors who have mastered their craft through many caving experiences. Seek out good teachers and group leaders, and study the skills of caving from the ground down.

Lost in a Cave

Do all you can to keep track of your location as you move about underground. Sticking to established routes, traveling in the company of cavers familiar with particular underground passages, and following published maps can all be means of staying found. Turn frequently and study the way you have come, the better to recognize the appearance of your return route.

If you do become confused about where you are while caving, stop immediately and stay as calm as you can. Switch off your headlamp to conserve its power. Have a bite to eat and a sip of water, pull on some extra clothing to help you stay warm, then wait to be found. Give a shout every minute or two and listen for an answer, but don't wander about aimlessly searching for a way out. It might take time, but if you left your trip plan information with a responsible person, someone will come for you.

Caving Equipment and Supplies

Even though you will always travel in caves with several companions, equip yourself to function independently. Carry a day pack or fanny pack that contains the outdoor essentials with a few variations. You won't need rain gear or sun protection, but a pocketknife and a first-aid kit could come in handy underground. A map of the cave and a compass also could prove useful.

For more on the outdoor essentials, see the chapter titled "Gearing Up."

Clothing

Old, rugged clothing or coveralls are a must underground. A caver walks, crawls, climbs, and squirms through passages that may be sloppy with mud, water, and bat guano. Some caves are chilly and damp, conditions conducive to hypothermia, so you might need to pull on layers of wool or fleece to stay warm. Pads for your knees and elbows will provide protection if you will do extensive crawling, and so will gloves. Leave a set of clean clothes outside the cave for the trip home, and a plastic trash bag for stowing your muddy clothing and shoes.

24

Light

The only illumination in a cave is what you take in, so you must carry dependable sources of light that will last as long as you are underground. Nothing is more vital to your safety; a caver stranded without a light has no choice but to sit still in the darkness and wait to be rescued. To be sure that won't happen to you, have at least three independent, reliable sources of light. Even if two of them fail, you can still see to find your way to the cave's entrance. The best caving lights are electric headlamps (with fresh batteries) that can be attached to caving helmets.

Battery-Powered Headlamps vs. Carbide Lamps

Battery-powered headlamps are powerful, reliable, and inexpensive, and have all but replaced the carbide lamps that were the choice of earlier generations of cavers. Carbide lamps do generate bright light, but they also produce undesirable by-products in the forms of acetylene gas and spent fuel residue. Agencies managing many caves have discouraged or banned the use of carbide. You can help ensure the health of other cavers and of the caves you visit by choosing battery-powered lights for all your underground journeys.

Helmet

Think of low, dimly lit cave ceilings, and you'll realize the importance of always wearing protective headgear. Helmets made especially for caving are the best choice, though rock-climbing helmets also are well-suited for cavers. Secure the chin strap to prevent your helmet from slipping off. (Construction hard hats are not suitable for cavers.)

Food and Water

Carry drinking water and enough high-energy food to see you through a caving trip even if you are underground longer than you had planned.

Caving Techniques

The goal of every caving expedition
is to get in and out of the cave
safely, to enjoy yourself while you
are underground, and to leave no
trace of your passing. That requires
planning, beginning by contacting
the agency responsible for managing that area. There might be
limitations on the size of groups
going into a cave, and permits
might be required. Agency officials
might be able to provide you with
maps and suggestions for ways to
enhance your experience.

Move slowly and deliberately in a cave. Avoid jumping and be
especially cautious if you cross ledges or work your way over loose rocks
and alongside streams. The most experienced cavers go first and last. Should
the party become scattered, the skilled caver can bring the stragglers along.

Horizontal Caving

Moving horizontally in a cave can involve a variety of movement methods including bearwalking, crawling, crouching, and duckwalking.

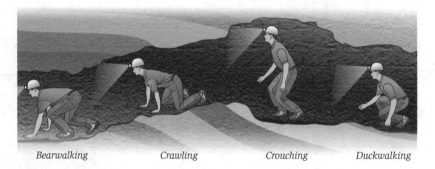

Bearwalking   *Crawling*   *Crouching*   *Duckwalking*

"*The memory of a cave I used to know at home was always in my mind, with its lofty passages, its silence and solitude, its shrouding gloom, its sepulchral echos, its flitting lights, and more than all, its sudden revelation of branching crevices and corridors where we least expected them.*"

—Mark Twain (Mississippi River steamboat pilot, journalist, and acclaimed author of books including *The Adventures of Tom Sawyer* and *Huckleberry Finn)*, *Innocents Abroad,* 1869

Vertical Caving

Many caves include cliffs and pits that rival those encountered by rock climbers aboveground. Descending and ascending these obstacles—*vertical caving*—can require ropes, harnesses, and hardware, and should not be attempted without extensive training and supervision by qualified caving instructors. The BSA's climbing/ rappelling guidelines require that any climber or rappeller more than shoulder height above the ground must be protected by a belayer. Vertical caving is beyond the scope of this book.

For more on the BSA's guidelines for climbing and rappelling, see the *Fieldbook* Web site, and BSA publications Climb On Safely and *Topping Out.*

Speleology

Speleology is the study of caves; a *speleologist* is one who does that studying. Your own explorations and studies of caves can encompass a wide variety of activities, from photographing subterranean features to examining subterranean geology and finding evidence of the creative forces at work. Perhaps you can discover some of the habits of tiny inhabitants of the darkness.

The more caves you visit, the more time you'll want to spend underground. One day you will come to the surface tired and covered with mud, but there will be a smile on your face and you'll know you have become a caver. You will have realized that a caver's happiest moments come when you can visit a cave and then leave it exactly as you found it.

Cave Map Symbols

Surveyed passage		Passage ceiling height	
Underlying (dotted) passage		Large breakdown	
Vertical drop in passage with depth		Small Breakdown	
Sketched passage		Clay	
Sloping passage		Sand	
Stream and pool		Bedrock pillar in passage	
Flowstone		Survey station	
Rimstone dam		Cross section	

Underground experts mapping caves use special symbols to indicate subterranean features.

Fishing

"Ours is the grandest sport. It is an intriguing battle of wits between an angler and a trout; and in addition to appreciating the tradition and grace of the game, we play it in the magnificent out-of-doors."

—Ernest G. Schwiebert Jr. (American author, architect, and lifelong fisherman), *Matching the Hatch*, 1955

When it comes to fishing, it's good to accept the fact that fish are a lot smarter than you are, at least when it comes to being fish. To become fish of much size, they have learned to find enough to eat. They also have figured out how to avoid predators, including the likes of you. If catching fish were easy, you would quickly tire of it. As it is, though, the challenge of matching your wits with those smarter-than-you fish can last a lifetime.

Fishing is many things to many people. It can fill a quiet hour on a summer afternoon. It can be the reason for a week-long backpacking trip to reach remote mountain trout streams. It can be enjoyed with any tackle, from a simple pole with a line, hook, and worm to a fly-casting outfit with homemade lures keyed to the season, the weather, the water, and the species of fish. The larger experience of fishing—enjoying the scenery, appreciating natural surroundings, finding an escape from otherwise busy lifestyles—is heightened when your fishing takes you far from the beaten path.

Every angler has opinions about the best ways to fish, advice on the most effective lures, and sweet memories of favorite fishing holes. And everyone who fishes has a few fish tales. You will, too. As for the size of your fish tales, that's up to you.

Catch-and-release fishing allows you to enjoy the experience of fishing without depleting the species population. Follow the principles of Leave No Trace while you are fishing, and you can be sure that you are reducing your impact on the environment, too.

For more, see the "Leaving No Trace" section of this book.

First Things First

Lakes and streams far from roads often are prime fishing spots that are far less crowded than bodies of water accessible by motor vehicle. Wherever you intend to fish, take care of a few preliminary responsibilities before you bait your hook.

Licenses and Permits

Check with your state's fish and game department to find out if you need a fishing license. If most of your fishing will be near your home, you probably can get an annual license to cover all of your trips. Before traveling to other waters to fish, especially in other states, inquire about any legalities you must follow. A search of Internet Web sites should turn up the licensing requirements for an area, as well as lead you to lots of local information about fishing spots, lures, and seasons.

Keeping or Releasing?

Decide ahead of time whether you will be keeping the fish you catch or releasing them. Many parks and forests permit only catch-and-release fishing, thus making the choice for you. Consider using barbless hooks on your lures to reduce the chances of injuring the fish you will release. (You can permanently disarm a barbed hook by flattening the barb against the hook with a pair of needle-nose pliers.)

Another factor in your decision to release or keep fish may be the presence of bears in the area where you intend to camp. Bears are attracted to aromas, and if there is anything standard about fish, especially those being cooked, it's the fact that they smell. Check with the local land manager, or toss fish remains and entrails in flowing water or carry them out. When bedding down at night, wear clean clothing that is free from any fish smell. If that will be a difficult challenge, you would be wise to practice catch-and-release fishing, or to save your fishing for trips in places where you are not competing with bears.

Finding Fish

Fish like to dwell where there is an abundance of food and an absence of danger. That often means water with a current that will keep a fresh supply of potential food flowing past. Fish also want shelter of some sort—an eddy, the quiet water behind a big rock in a stream, the darkness below a submerged log, or a bed of underwater grasses.

It's highly unlikely that the fish you want to catch will come looking for you. To find them, you'll need to figure out what a fish needs.

A fish is equipped with a sensory organ running the length of its body, called the *lateral line,* that picks up vibrations from its surroundings. That can be good for an angler using lures that give off vibrations resembling those of an injured minnow or some other enticing morsel. It can be bad, though, when the vibrations come from footsteps, unintended splashes in the water, and other noises that fish perceive as threatening rather than inviting. Fish are wary of predators on land and in the air as well as in the water, and will dart away from shadows suddenly cast on a pond or stream.

Mastering Fishing Skills

Fishing involves these steps:

❶ *Choose a lure or bait that will attract fish.*

❷ *Cast effectively and persuade a fish to strike.*

❸ *Set the hook and play the fish close enough to land it.*

❹ *Gently release the fish, or clean and cook it.*

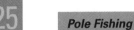

Pole Fishing

One of the simplest ways to catch fish requires little more than some tackle and a lightweight pole—a cane pole is ideal, though fish won't mind if you use a straight stick. Tie one end of a fishing line to the pole; to the other end of the line attach a bobber, a sinker, and a hook baited with a worm, grasshopper, grub, or other natural food of the fish you're after. You might be able to gather the bait you need from grass and bushes along the shore. Toss your line into the water, make yourself comfortable, and wait for the bobber to jiggle.

Casting Systems

Fishing with a pole and bobber consists of brief moments of excitement interrupted by long periods of patient waiting, appreciating the scenery, and napping in the shade. Anglers eager for a more active role in the outcome of their efforts can graduate to one of several casting systems, using rods and reels to cast and retrieve lures that simulate the shape and motion of a fish's natural food. Fishing becomes a game of wits as anglers try to guess which lures to use, where to cast them to attract fish, and how to retrieve them to entice a fish to strike.

A casting system, or *tackle*, is made up of a rod, a reel, some line, and a lure or bait. Figure on several lures, since you might occasionally lose one. When your fishing adventures will take you far from the trailhead, your choices of tackle will depend in part on how you plan to travel. The rod will be the most critical; it's an awkward item to carry in any case, and particularly so as you make your way through brush or along a trail.

A collapsible rod can be dismantled, stored in a lightweight plastic tube, and strapped to the outside of a backpack. Rods of modest length that don't come apart can be lashed under the gunwales of canoes and along the decks of kayaks. Reels can be removed from rods for ease of packing. A small lure box will round out your carrying gear by providing a secure place to stow lures and prevent the hooks from finding their way into your other gear or into you.

Whatever tackle you choose, casting is simply a means of getting a lure or bait onto or into the water where fish are likely to strike it. Each of the four types of casting systems—*spin-casting, spinning, bait-casting,* and *fly-casting*—is suited to particular kinds of lures, baits, and methods of fooling fish.

25

Spin-Casting

The easiest casting system to master is the closed-faced *spin-casting* rig. The equipment you'll need includes a rod (often made of fiberglass) and a reel with the line spool enclosed in a cone-shaped housing. The line comes out of a hole in the point of the cone, and its release is controlled by a push button mounted on the back of the reel. Because the spool is enclosed, the system is difficult to tangle—a great advantage for beginning anglers.

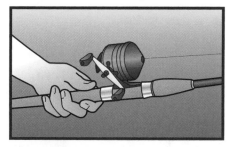

To cast with spin-casting gear, thread the line from the reel through the line guides of the rod and tie on a lure or a hook with bait. (For practice on dry land, use a hookless rubber casting weight instead and a bucket or a circle drawn on the ground as a target.)

Hold the rod in front of you with the reel up, the tip of the rod pointed toward the target. Reel the lure or bait to about 6 inches from the rod tip and depress the button beneath the thumb of your rod hand. While holding the button in, swing the rod back and up until it is nearly vertical, then smoothly snap it forward. When the tip of the rod is about halfway back to its starting position, lift your thumb from the button to release the line and send the lure or bait flying. If it goes too high, your release was early; if it goes low, the release was late. It will take you a few casts to get a feel for the instant to release the line and for the right amount of power needed to arc the lure or bait into the center of your target.

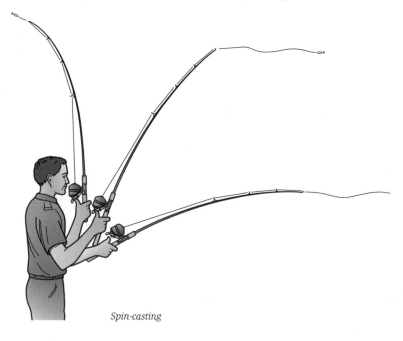

Spin-casting

Spinning

An open-faced *spinning* reel has no cone covering the spool, relying instead on a wire bail to control the line. The reel hangs below the rod handle, and the line feeds out through guides on the underside of the rod.

Reel the lure or bait to about 6 inches from the tip of the rod. Use the index finger of your rod hand to press the line against the rod handle, then move the bail to the open position. Make a cast by moving the rod as you would with a spin-casting outfit, 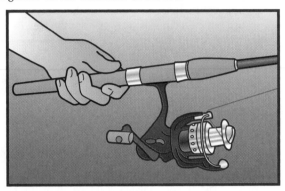 moving your index finger to release the line and send the lure or bait on its way. As the lure or bait approaches its target, you can bring your finger close to the rod handle so that the moving line brushes against it and slows (called *feathering*), causing the lure or bait to drop gently into the water. Turning the reel crank after each cast will return the bail to its closed position and allow you to wind the line back onto the spool.

Bait-Casting

In spin-casting and in spinning, the line peels over the rim of the reel spool but the spool itself does not turn. In *bait-casting*, the spool rotates during the cast, allowing the line to unwind. Anglers often choose bait-casting for fishing with live baits such as minnows, as well as with artificial lures.

To use bait-casting gear, wind the lure or bait to within a few inches of the rod tip. Most bait-casting reels have a button that disengages the crank and allows the spool to turn freely, or *freespool*. Grasp the rod and place your thumb against the back of the spool to secure the line. Depress the freespool button and you're ready to cast.

The casting motion is basically the same as with spin-casting and spinning rigs. Let the line go by lifting your thumb just enough to reduce tension on the spool, keeping your thumb in light contact with the spool to control the distance of the cast and to prevent the tangling overrun, or *backlash*, that can occur if the reel releases line faster than the lure or bait can pull it away.

Fly-Casting

The fourth casting system is the oldest and, with good equipment and instruction, not very difficult to use. While other systems rely on the weight of the lure or bait to pull line from the reel, fly-casters use nearly weightless lures made of bits of feather, fur, hair, and thread. The line itself provides the weight that carries a lure through the air.

Fly rods are long—6 to 10 feet. The reel, located below the rod, is a simple winch to wind line in and out. The line is relatively thick and is made especially for fly-fishing. Some lines will float when they reach the water, while others are designed to sink. Several feet of thin, transparent *leader* is attached to the end of the line, and the lure, usually in the form of an artificial *fly*, is tied to the end of the leader.

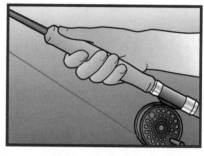

Fly-casting is a skill you can learn in a few minutes, then spend the rest of your life trying to perfect. Slowly arc the rod back and forth over your head, each time feeling the loading energy being transferred from the line to the rod and back to the line again. Control the line with your free hand as you feed out line from the reel. When you've got enough line looping through the air, swing the tip of the rod toward your target. Let the line curl out over the water and lightly place the fly just where you want it. In still water, drop the fly directly over the fish. If the water is moving, cast upstream and let the lure drift near feeding fish where they lie in wait.

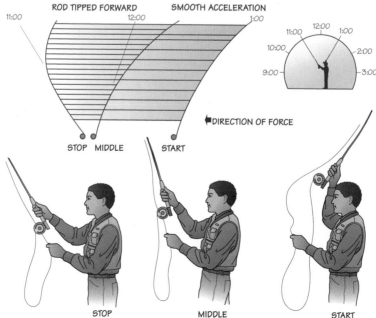

Fly-casting technique

> *"When you catch your fish do as I do—only keep those you specially want for food or as specimens, put back the others the moment you have landed them."*
>
> —Robert S. S. Baden-Powell (1857–1941), founder of the worldwide Scouting movement

Fishing Lures

Knowing how to cast will help make you a good angler. Knowing what lures to use can bring you success, since you will be casting lures that will appeal to fish.

Spinners

Spinners are shiny metal lures that, as their name implies, spin through the water as you reel them in. Steadily retrieve a spinner to make the lure twirl, or reel and stop, reel and stop, allowing the lure to sink a little with each pause.

Spoons

Spoons essentially are spinners that flutter rather than spin. Many are painted red with diagonal white stripes. Spoons with hooks shielded to discourage entanglement in weeds will reach fish that hide in underwater beds of grass and beneath lily pads.

Plugs

Plugs are intended to look like little fish, crawdads, frogs, or other aquatic prey. Some always float; others dive as they are retrieved. Some wobble and gurgle, some make a popping sound, and some wiggle slowly through the water. The goal of using a plug is to manipulate it so that it attracts the attention of hungry fish.

Spinner

Spoon

Plug

Floater/diver

Floater/Diver Lures

Lures that both float and dive typically have the appearance of small fish or frogs. Retrieve them slowly and they'll stay near the surface. Reel them in quickly and they will swim a few feet underwater.

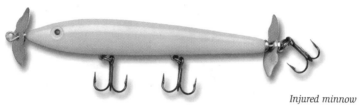

Injured minnow

Injured Minnows

Another effective lure is shaped like a minnow and outfitted with shiny propellers on one or both ends. Retrieve it in fits and starts, causing the lure to struggle along like a hurt minnow trying to escape.

Crank Baits

A *crank bait* dives deeply as you reel it in. It vibrates and rattles to attract fish far below the water's surface.

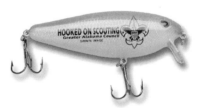

Crank bait

Jigs

A *jig* has a heavy, blunt body embellished with skirts made of hair, feathers, rubber, or plastic. It will sink to the bottom of a stream or lake and bounce as you raise and lower, or *jig,* your rod, reeling in line whenever there is slack. Jig lures come in many sizes and styles, and are effective for catching everything from small panfish to big trout, bass, walleyes, pike, and many saltwater species.

Jig

25

Soft Plastic Lures

While some *soft plastic lures* are molded to mimic insects, grubs, and small aquatic animals, the most popular type looks like an earthworm. Hooks embedded in the worm and attached to a leader provide the bite of the bait, and a small lead sinker provides extra weight to increase casting distance. A good way to fish with a plastic worm is to cast it near a submerged log or stump, or into the shallows close to shore, then jig the rod to drag the worm along.

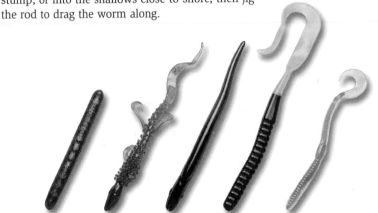

Flies

There was a time when a lure called a *fly* looked much like what its name implied—an insect called a mayfly, one of the primary food sources of trout. Many fishing flies still match the appearance of insects near trout streams, but variations abound. *Dry flies* are designed to float on the surface of the water; *wet flies* and *nymphs* are meant to sink. *Streamers* look like small minnows. Bass and some saltwater fish also can be taken with fly-fishing tackle, often by using flies you have made yourself.

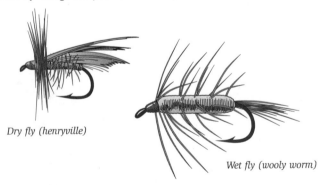

Dry fly (henryville)

Wet fly (wooly worm)

Live Bait

Live bait, including minnows, earthworms, and leeches, should never be released. It can cause undesirable environmental impacts.

Rigging Your Tackle

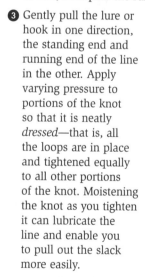

Successful fishing relies on well-tied knots. The most important knots are those used for tying lines to lures, hooks, and leaders.

Improved Clinch Knot

Use the *improved clinch knot* to secure a line directly to a hook or to the eye of a lure:

❶ Pass the end of the line (the *running end*) through the eye of the hook or lure. (Holding the hook with needle-nose pliers will shield your hand from possible injury.) Pull through about 8 inches of line. Bend it back away from the lure or hook, and wind it five or six times around the body of the line (the *standing end*).

❷ Pass the running end through the loop closest to the eye of the hook or lure, then pass the running end through the newly created large loop.

❸ Gently pull the lure or hook in one direction, the standing end and running end of the line in the other. Apply varying pressure to portions of the knot so that it is neatly *dressed*—that is, all the loops are in place and tightened equally to all other portions of the knot. Moistening the knot as you tighten it can lubricate the line and enable you to pull out the slack more easily.

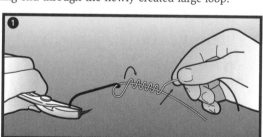

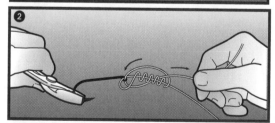

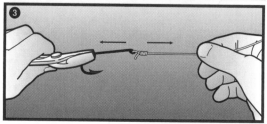

With a knife blade or fingernail clippers, snip off nearly all of the remaining running end.

Improved clinch knot

25

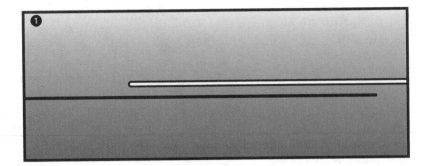

Surgeon's Knot

To join a leader to a line, rely on the *surgeon's knot:*

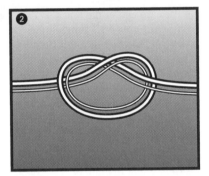

❶ Lay the line and leader side by side, overlapping the ends 6 to 8 inches.

❷ Lift the line and leader together, form a loop, and tie a loose overhand knot by passing the entire leader and the end of the line through the loop.

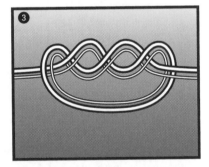

❸ Pass the leader and end of the line through the loop a second time.

❹ Tighten the knot by gradually pulling slack out of the leader and line. Snip off excess ends of the line and leader.

Surgeon's knot

Playing a Fish

You've picked the right lure, cast it in a promising location, and felt the line suddenly jump as a fish strikes. The game of playing a fish has just begun.

A strong fish can snap a light line with a twist of its body. It can dive beneath sunken logs, or tangle your tackle in a bed of weeds. To prevent that from happening, draw the tip of the rod upward and then reel in line as you dip the rod back toward the water. Do what you can with the line to steer the fish away from underwater obstructions, and keep pressure on the line. Don't waste time. The longer it fights, the greater the chance a fish will free itself from the hook, break your line, or become ensnared in obstructions.

A speedy retrieval is especially important when you intend to release a fish. Its chances of recovery will be higher than if it had been played to the point of exhaustion.

Releasing a Fish

Try to leave a fish in the water if you are planning to set it loose. You might be able to release it simply by running your hand down the line to the lure and twisting the hook free. If you must lift the fish, wet your hands first to protect the mucus on the fish's skin. Continue to support the fish when you have returned it to the water. Position it with its head upstream so that water will flow through its gills until it seems to have regained its energy and can swim away on its own.

Releasing a Hooked Angler

If you fish long enough, there will come a time when you put a hook in yourself rather than in a fish. Catch-and-release takes on new meaning when it is you (or one of your companions) in need of being released. If possible, let a physician or medic remove the hook from the flesh. On a long fishing trip, you might have to do the job yourself.

When the hook is embedded in flesh where the barb cannot be pushed through, a quick way to extract the hook is to use a length of fishing line.

❶ Tie the ends of a piece of sturdy fishing line together to form a loop.

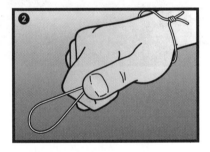

❷ Place the loop around your wrist and grip the line between your thumb and index finger.

❸ Slip the loop over the hook.

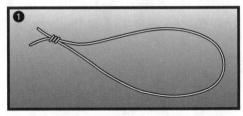

❹ Press the hook's eye against the skin, then remove the hook with a quick jerk of the loop.

Thoroughly wash the wound and treat it with antibiotic ointment. Bandage the wound to help prevent it from getting dirty.

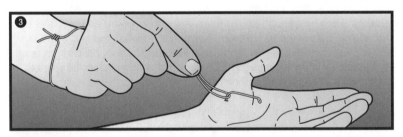

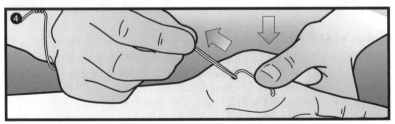

Cleaning Your Catch

Trout and some other species of fish have scales so small they don't need to be removed before cooking; nor do catfish and similar species that can be skinned. For other fish, begin preparing them for the kitchen by scaling.

❶ Remove the scales by scraping the skin from tail to head with a knife blade or fish scaler.

❷ Gut the fish by making a slit from vent to throat. Strip the entrails from the body cavity with your fingers, then thoroughly wash the fish inside and out.

❸ You can fillet a fish by slicing along each side close to the spine. The result should be two boneless pieces of fish.

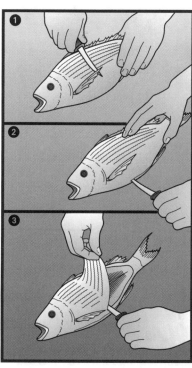

Fishing Tips

Every angler has a creel full of tricks for making fishing easier and more fun. Here are a few:

- Sunglasses with polarized lenses can enable you to see beneath the surface of the water even when the sun is bright.

- Fish swimming in a swift stream usually face into the current. They aren't as likely to see you if you approach from downstream. Cast over them and let your lures drift toward them.

- Reeling in a lure very slowly might bring it through submerged vegetation without snagging.

- Make short casts first, then cast farther out into the water. That way, fish farther away will still be around after you've given those closer in a chance to attach themselves to your lure.

- Fish early in the day and at dusk when fish are more likely to be feeding. Overcast days also can be good.

- For beginning anglers, it's hard to beat worms, grasshoppers, grubs, and other live bait collected near a fishing spot.

The Why of Fishing

This chapter has explored the *how* of fishing—how to prepare a bait or lure, how to rig a rod and reel, how to approach a body of water where fish are likely to lurk. As to the *why* of fishing, well, that's going to be answered every time you take your tackle and make your way to the edge of a pond, a lake, a stream, or the pounding surf. You know that fish are there, and that nothing stands between you and them but your skill, cunning, and luck.

The adventure of fishing is also a terrific way to appreciate the environment. Your awareness of your surroundings is heightened by an eagerness to understand the habits and habitat of the fish you want to catch. You have a wonderful excuse to slow down, to spend plenty of time in one spot, and to notice everything going on around you. If you do catch a fish, that's a bonus to an otherwise fine day, but if not, the experience is never wasted.

Fishing is as varied and interesting an outdoor activity as you can find. Every kind of fish, every body of water, every sort of tackle, and each season of the year brings its own variety and challenge for anglers. Sometimes you'll have terrific luck; other days the fish will win. The bottom line, though, is that any time you spend with a fishing rod in your hand is quality time—time for having fun, time for making memories, and time simply to realize how great it is to be alive.

"God never did make a more calm, quiet, innocent recreation than angling."

—Isaak Walton, *The Compleat Angler*, 1653 (His book on fishing is the third most published work in English, following the Bible and the works of Shakespeare.)

Search and Rescue

"The people who I see performing best in a crisis are people who are honest and forthright. They don't hide their personalities or their weaknesses. They're genuine."

—Sharon Wood, the first North American woman to summit Mount Everest

A mountain climber rushes down a trail to report that a companion on a snowy peak has fallen and broken an ankle. Children wander away from a picnic area and their parents are frantic. A group of hikers is overdue as night settles upon a wet, chilly forest. In each case, search-and-rescue teams are mobilized and, following well-practiced procedures, set out to meet the challenge. Before long the children are reunited with their families. By midnight the overdue hikers have been located, warmed, fed, and brought out of the woods. A rescue team has flown by helicopter to the top of the peak and rappelled down to the fallen climber. They treat his injuries and monitor his condition through the night while more rescuers approach on foot to carry the victim to the trailhead the next morning.

The happy endings to many potential wilderness tragedies are due to the dedication and efforts of search-and-rescue teams. In the frontcountry, people seldom are far from a road. Reacting to a medical emergency is often as simple as summoning assistance and then performing first aid for a few minutes while waiting for an ambulance to arrive. The rules change as you get farther from a road, though—rescuers often have to *find* the person in distress before beginning a treatment plan. Once victims of injury or illness have been located, transporting them immediately might not be practical or even possible. Weather, location, nightfall, and other variables might make it necessary for an aid team to stabilize patients and maintain their safety for a period of hours or even a full day or more until an evacuation can be undertaken.

This chapter is an introduction to some of the main concepts and techniques of search-and-rescue (SAR) teams. It is not intended to teach all you need to know in order to take part in searches, but it might spark your interest in finding a SAR organization that can train you and then draw on your strengths and dedication in emergency situations.

> ### Incident Command System
>
> The *incident command system (ICS)* is a flexible management protocol often mandated by law to be used when conducting search-and-rescue activities. The ICS is particularly effective when two or more agencies involved in an effort (especially those with differing legal, geographic, and functional responsibilities) must coordinate their responses.

Organizational Plan for Search and Rescue

The organizational plan for a search-and-rescue effort depends upon the needs of official state and local agencies, the kinds of operations the unit will be expected to handle, and the existence of other SAR organizations with whom efforts can be coordinated. A typical search-and-rescue organizational chart looks like this:

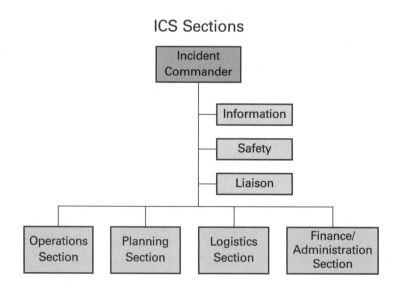

ICS Sections

It might surprise you to learn that a search-and-rescue operation involves the participation of so many people. The expanses of territory to be searched and the effort required to bring injured persons to safety can require a large number of personnel. In addition, teams in the field must be backed by an extensive support staff responsible for everything from supplying warm blankets and dry clothing to organizing transportation home for everyone after a rescue has been completed. If there are enough people, one team member can be assigned to each position; however, each team member might be assigned to handle several jobs on a search-and-rescue organizational chart.

Resources for SAR Operations

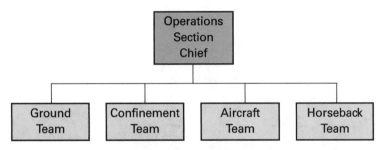

SAR Unit

A *search-and-rescue (SAR) unit* is a highly organized group of people who understand the serious nature of their responsibilities. Long before an emergency arises, leaders of any SAR group must meet with agency officials to clarify the exact nature of their relationship and to sort out lines of authority. Embarking on unauthorized search-and-rescue efforts is poor manners at best, and at worst can create problems. SAR units— aware of the limits within which they must operate—attempt only those rescues that are within the scope of their abilities.

Called out to respond to an incident, members of a SAR unit might be divided up to serve on several teams—as individuals helping with the confinement of an area, for example, or as participants on search teams. Depending on the nature of an evolving event, incident commanders can add teams to address the needs of the search-and-rescue effort.

Teamwork is the glue that holds together every search-and-rescue effort. The food service volunteers making sandwiches and soup at a base of operations are every bit as important as the searchers following footprints in the snow. A search-and-rescue operation is no place for glory seekers unless, of course, they see the glory of serving in quiet roles that are essential to the success of the overall effort.

Personal Equipment

The personal gear that SAR team members carry in the field will vary according to the season of the year and the environment in which they expect to operate. A *24-hour pack* contains everything a searcher will need for a full day in the field—the outdoor essentials plus additional food, water, first-aid supplies, and emergency communications equipment. A *48-hour pack* adds a sleeping bag, shelter, stove, and more provisions. In either case, searchers carry more than they expect to need; they might be out longer than intended, and they might need to share their food and equipment with the subjects of their search.

Call-Out

Officials of each of the 50 states have determined who will be responsible for planning and managing search-and-rescue operations within the boundaries of their state. Those duties often fall within the authority of local sheriffs, state or local emergency management offices, or a state natural resources department. Using this means to coordinate the efforts of search-and-rescue personnel, most search efforts are resolved within 24 hours.

When asked to help by an agency legally authorized to request assistance, a search-and-rescue unit must mobilize quickly. SAR team members often are equipped with pagers that a unit leader can use to alert them to emergency situations. Another option is a telephone tree, with various team members responsible for calling others.

Search Tactics

A SAR team deployed to help find missing persons will have been trained to use a variety of search tactics, each intended to be effective for a wide range of situations. The three search methods that have proven the most successful are *investigation, hasty search,* and *confinement.*

Investigation

Good information is vital to the quick success of a search-and-rescue operation. Team members can be assigned to individually interview people who might have recently seen the subject of the search or who might know about the subject's current appearance, habits, health, or other factors that can help SAR teams narrow the range of their efforts. The team may expand their investigative opportunities by leaving notes on vehicles in the area with the subject's description and contact information to be used by anyone with information that might be of assistance.

Confinement

Confinement is the effort made by a SAR team to prevent lost persons from wandering beyond a search area. Since the unconfined area in which a person could be lost grows in size with each passing moment, confinement must be achieved as quickly and thoroughly as the availability of resources will allow. Methods include assigning team members to monitor trailheads, roads, and other points where a lost person could leave the primary search area. Barriers such as rivers or mountain ridges can aid confinement by acting as natural barricades.

Hasty Search

In the early stages of a search, there often are several areas that team leaders and the incident commander pinpoint as probable locations of the lost person. A child who has wandered away from a campground, for instance, might have gone up a trail, across a meadow, or down to a beach. SAR team members can split up and go immediately to each of those areas to conduct hasty, informal searches.

Critical Separation

Critical separation—the distance maintained between SAR team members as they make their way through a search area—allows the incident commander to balance the need for covering an area quickly with the importance of being thorough. The technique takes into account local terrain, foliage, and weather.

To determine the distance of critical separation for a particular search, SAR team leaders select a location that is typical of the area their team has been assigned to search. They lay a backpack (or something of equal size) on the ground and, if they have it, cover the pack with clothing similar to that last seen on the missing person. Three team members walk away in different directions until each loses sight of the object. Next, they walk directly back to the object, counting their steps as they return. Team leaders average those step counts and double the result to come up with the distance of critical separation—that is, the number of steps from one another that searchers should maintain as they sweep through an area, knowing as they go that they will have a high probability of seeing the subject of their search.

Probability of Area

A means found effective by many teams to limit the initial area of a search draws upon the input of five experienced team members who are knowledgeable of the terrain, studying a map overlaid with a grid. Using all they know about the terrain, climatic conditions, time of day, the subject of the search, and details of the subject's disappearance, each of the team members independently rates the likelihood that the subject will be found in each section of the map grid. When these *probability of area (POA)* predictions are tallied, the team will have a consensus on the order in which areas should be searched to achieve a high possibility of early success.

Seasoned team members might also draw upon their expertise to estimate the *probability of detection (POD)* of clues and search subjects in a particular area. As with POA considerations, they take into account all the variables of a search situation, then predict their expected success rate. For example, if experts predict there are likely to be 10 useful clues in a grid section on the map but time and personnel are limited, the incident commander might order that the segment be searched with sufficient care to locate half the clues—a POD of 50 percent.

Clue Finding

Despite the emphasis on Leave No Trace methods of travel, no one can move about without leaving some signs of passing, especially if the traveler is making no effort to hide. While it takes considerable skill to recognize many of these clues, some signs are obvious even to untrained observers, provided they are looking for them. Footprints on a damp shoreline or in patches of snow are easily seen, and a candy wrapper in the brush had to be left by someone. Finding and evaluating even a few clues can substantially reduce the potential area of search.

Two critical factors in clue finding are preserving the clues and evaluating them effectively. Searchers must take care not to disturb areas where footprints are likely or where other subtle signs might exist. Team members also should document all they can about clues—where they were found, in what condition, etc.—so that SAR leaders and the incident commander can effectively consider and use the information presented to them.

Advanced Search Methods

Some search methods require advanced expertise or equipment. Among them are the following:

Trailing Dogs

Certain breeds of dogs, notably bloodhounds, have such keen senses of smell that after being allowed to smell an article of a lost person's clothing, they can follow the scent trail left by that person. Success is dependent upon many factors including the training of the dogs, air temperature and humidity, and presence or absence of wind.

Air-Scenting Dogs

Unlike trailing dogs, air-scenting dogs will follow to its source any human scent they find in a search area. As a result, they might locate the subject of the search, though they are just as likely to follow the scent of a SAR team member or a passerby. Air-scenting dogs (frequently German shepherds) have the greatest success when there have been few persons in the area they are to search.

Tracking

A trained and talented tracker may be able to follow the trail left by a lost person. It is very important to prevent other people from entering the search area if a tracker is to be successful.

26

Vehicle Search

Using four-wheel-drive vehicles, team members can travel backroads to gather information about the terrain and to set up roadblocks to prevent lost travelers from wandering away from a search area.

Aircraft Search

Searches from the air can be very effective, but they are highly dependent upon weather and the density of ground cover. Most searches from fixed-wing aircraft are conducted by the Civil Air Patrol. Helicopters might be supplied by the military, or by municipalities and corporations. The efforts of airborne searches can be greatly enhanced by SAR incident commanders drawing upon the resources of satellites, emergency location transmitters (ELTs), and the Air Force Rescue Coordination Center (AFRCC).

Airplanes are equipped with emergency location transmitters (ELTs), devices that are activated by significant impact. If an airplane goes down, the ELT on board sends out a signal that can lead rescuers to the crash site.

Tracking Stick

Searchers engaged in tracking can increase the likelihood of success by using a *tracking stick*—a rod about 4 feet long. (A straight branch with notches cut for measurements will work nicely, too.) When trackers find two footprints in a row, they can measure the distance from the heel of one print to the heel of the next and mark that distance on the stick with a rubber band. Then, by measuring the same distance ahead and slightly to the side of the forward print, they'll know approximately where the next track should be. At night, a lantern or flashlight held near the ground will produce shadows that make tracks more visible.

First Aid

Search-and-rescue teams must number among their members persons trained to provide first-aid treatment to victims of accident or illness. The challenges facing first-aiders can be heightened because of weather conditions, location of a victim, distance from a road or aircraft landing zone, and the need to render aid using only the supplies and equipment the team has carried with them. Advanced first-aid training with an emphasis on wilderness emergencies prepares team members with the medical skills they need and a methodology for addressing emergencies in remote settings.

Upon finding an injured or ill person, a SAR team's routine generally will follow the same protocol as for incidents in the frontcountry:

Take Charge

Team members will focus their attention on the job of making people safe. Their training and experience will nearly always infuse their efforts with an air of authority.

Approach With Care

Rescuers must be aware of falling rocks, slippery footing, steep slopes, and other hazards as they come to the aid of ill or injured persons. Becoming injured themselves or causing further injury to the subject can dramatically compound the seriousness of an emergency situation.

Provide Urgent Treatment

The first rescuers on the scene will make a quick assessment of the victim's situation and address any conditions that could be life-threatening; this includes checking and treating for shock if necessary.

26

Conduct a Thorough Examination

Once the victim is out of immediate danger, first-aiders will conduct a systematic and thorough head-to-toe evaluation.

Develop and Carry Out a Plan

At the completion of the full evaluation, team members will determine what to do next, often by including radio consultation with the SAR incident commander and other SAR personnel. In some cases, evacuation to a trailhead can begin immediately. In other instances, an ill or injured person must be cared for over a period of time while awaiting the arrival of additional SAR team members or the preparation of an evacuation plan. In either case, first-aiders will continually monitor the victim's condition and maintain a written record of their findings and any treatment they have given.

First-Aider Notes

First-aiders dealing with persons who have suffered injury or illness record each patient's condition by monitoring vital signs at regular intervals and writing down the data. These written records often include information that is subjective and objective, that makes assessments of the situation based on all available data, and that suggests a plan of action.

First-aider notes are essential for tracking changes in a patient's condition—information that can be critical in determining the nature and degree of an illness or injury and the urgency with which evacuation might be required. The notes also can remind first-aiders to be thorough in their examination, treatment, and monitoring of every person in their care.

Wilderness Incident Note

SCENE		Assessment of Situation and Plan of Treatment	
	Name:	Injury List	Potential Problems
	Location:		
	Other Patients? N / Y How Many?		

OBJECTIVE

Chief Complaint:

(list most important first)   (estimate time course)

Plan of Action

Patient Ambulatory?
Litter carry?
Spinal Immobilization?
Urgency: Critical   Stable   Minor
Plan for each injury:

OBJECTIVE: Patient Physical Exam

Airway:	Abdomen:
Breathing	Back:
Circulation: major bleeding?	Pelvis:
	Extremities:
	RArm: LArm:
	RLeg: LLeg:

Notes

Notes

Evacuation

Once the subject of a search has been found, evaluated, treated, and stabilized, the team must decide on the best way to transport that person to safety. Searchers in radio contact with an incident commander can develop a coordinated effort to bring the victim to the frontcountry.

Foot Power

Evacuees who can walk without further injuring themselves should be encouraged to do so. SAR team members must continue to monitor the person's physical condition and respond to significant changes.

Hand Carry

If the subjects are not seriously incapacitated, they may be carried short distances piggyback or with a two-person carry. Rescuers must use proper technique to protect themselves from injury.

Horseback

Gentle saddle horses or mules can be used to transport victims whose illness or injuries would not be further complicated by the ride. Team members might need to ride double or walk alongside the animals to steady the evacuees.

Vehicle

Where there are convenient roads, four-wheel-drive vehicles generally provide the easiest and most efficient means of evacuating subjects of searches to a rendezvous with an urban ambulance service. In some areas, specially equipped ambulances can bring out ill or injured parties.

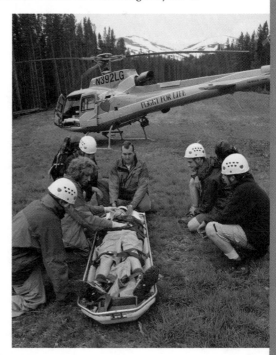

Aircraft

If a rescue helicopter is available, it might be used to evacuate a subject by winch lift from a remote site or it might land at a nearby helispot to pick up the subject. Fixed-wing air ambulances also can be used for evacuations from remote locations if there is a suitable landing strip nearby. Ideally, subjects are flown directly to a medical facility for further evaluation and treatment.

Litter Carry

Carrying an ill or injured person over a long distance can be demanding and difficult. It might require a large, well-drilled team, especially if the terrain is rough or the victim's location is far from a road. Because of the complexity of a litter evacuation, many SAR units have special litter teams to handle the procedure.

The field operations leader is responsible for the evacuation and for the safety of all personnel. The litter boss supervises the carrying of the litter. In matters pertaining to the well-being of the evacuee, the first-aider has the last word. Trail clearers lead the way and prepare the route for the litter bearers until it is their turn to serve as litter bearers. Belayers and rope handlers are required if there might be a need for a technical evacuation.

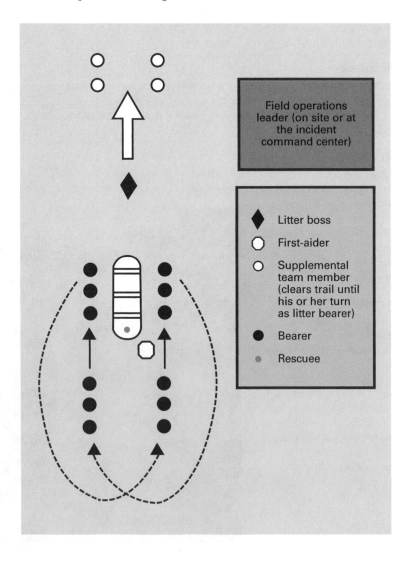

Field operations leader (on site or at the incident command center)

◆ Litter boss

◯ First-aider

○ Supplemental team member (clears trail until his or her turn as litter bearer)

● Bearer

• Rescuee

Litter-Carrying Techniques

Prepare a litter by padding it with foam pads and a sleeping bag. To place an injured person on a litter, six team members kneel next to the subject, three on each side, and work their hands beneath the person. On command, they raise the patient high enough for the litter to be slipped underneath, then lower him or her gently into position. Depending on the weather, more sleeping bags and perhaps a nylon tarp can be used to insulate the patient in a warm, protective cocoon.

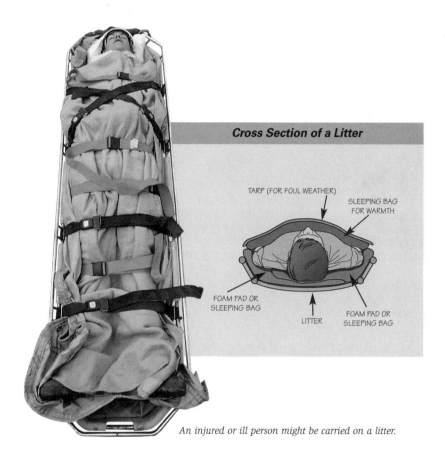

Cross Section of a Litter

TARP (FOR FOUL WEATHER)

SLEEPING BAG
FOR WARMTH

FOAM PAD OR
SLEEPING BAG

LITTER

FOAM PAD OR
SLEEPING BAG

An injured or ill person might be carried on a litter.

Having sent the trail clearers ahead to remove any obstacles, the litter boss in charge of the carry will have bearers of similar height pair off on opposite sides of the litter. The SAR team member with primary responsibility for first aid will take a position near the victim's head, and all other team members will follow behind. The bearers kneel by the litter and, if available, place carrying straps across their backs and over their shoulders. By holding onto a knot in the strap, a bearer can distribute the weight of the load across his or her back and opposite arm, rather than bearing the weight with only one arm.

UNIVERSAL LITTER WHEEL

With a universal litter wheel, a small SAR team can roll a loaded litter over trails, rough roads, and open, low-angle terrain.

On command from the litter boss, the bearers lift the litter and move forward, walking out of step to avoid swinging the victim. Litter bearers change positions every few minutes. A fresh pair of bearers grasp the foot of the litter while the pair of bearers at the head of the litter step to the side of the trail. The active bearers adjust their grips to ensure correct spacing on either side of the litter. Using this technique, bearers can keep the litter moving, refreshing the carrying team without setting down the litter.

Communications and Navigation

Reliable communications are essential to the success of an SAR operation and for the safety of everyone involved. For this reason, portable two-way radios are carried by team leaders, litter bosses, field coordinators, and members of the support staff, giving the incident commander control over the entire search and evacuation. (Many SAR teams use ham radio technology, especially the two-meter band and the FCC "technician" license, to facilitate communications. During operations involving large numbers of searchers and rescuers, coordinators sometimes rely on Family Radio Service radios for inter-team communications.)

Search-and-rescue teams can use global positioning systems (GPS) for finding their way, plotting the parameters of search areas, and generating records of locations pinpointed during their activities. Transmitters can relay information about a team's position back to a search base where the data can be downloaded into laptop computers and incorporated with topographic mapping software to give the incident commander real-time awareness of the progression and status of every team in the field.

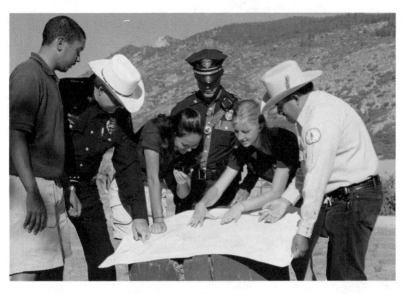

Evaluation and Training

At the conclusion of every SAR mission, unit members review and evaluate everything that happened. This is not a faultfinding session, but rather an objective attempt to uncover weaknesses in a team's performance and to determine ways to rectify them. Good SAR units improve their operations with each mission; with honest evaluations and effective training, they seldom repeat a mistake.

SAR training must include instruction and practice in search methods, evacuation, wilderness navigation, first aid, and the maintenance of personal and team equipment. Field exercises and simulated searches and rescues should be conducted on various types of terrain in all weather conditions. SAR missions might be risky for both subjects and rescuers. Training and preparation of rescuers maximizes the chances for success and minimizes the chances for further injuries.

"SAR providers conduct ground search-and-rescue incidents to safely locate, access, stabilize, and transport the subject in the shortest possible time frame with the most efficient type and number of resources while following any applicable laws, rules, regulations, and policies."

—Robert Koester, *Field Operations Guide for Search and Rescue*, 1996

Appreciating
Our
Environment

"... Therefore am I still

A lover of the meadows

and the woods,

And mountains; and

of all that we behold

From this green earth;

of all the mighty

world ..."

—William Wordsworth (1770–1850), English poet

CHAPTER 27

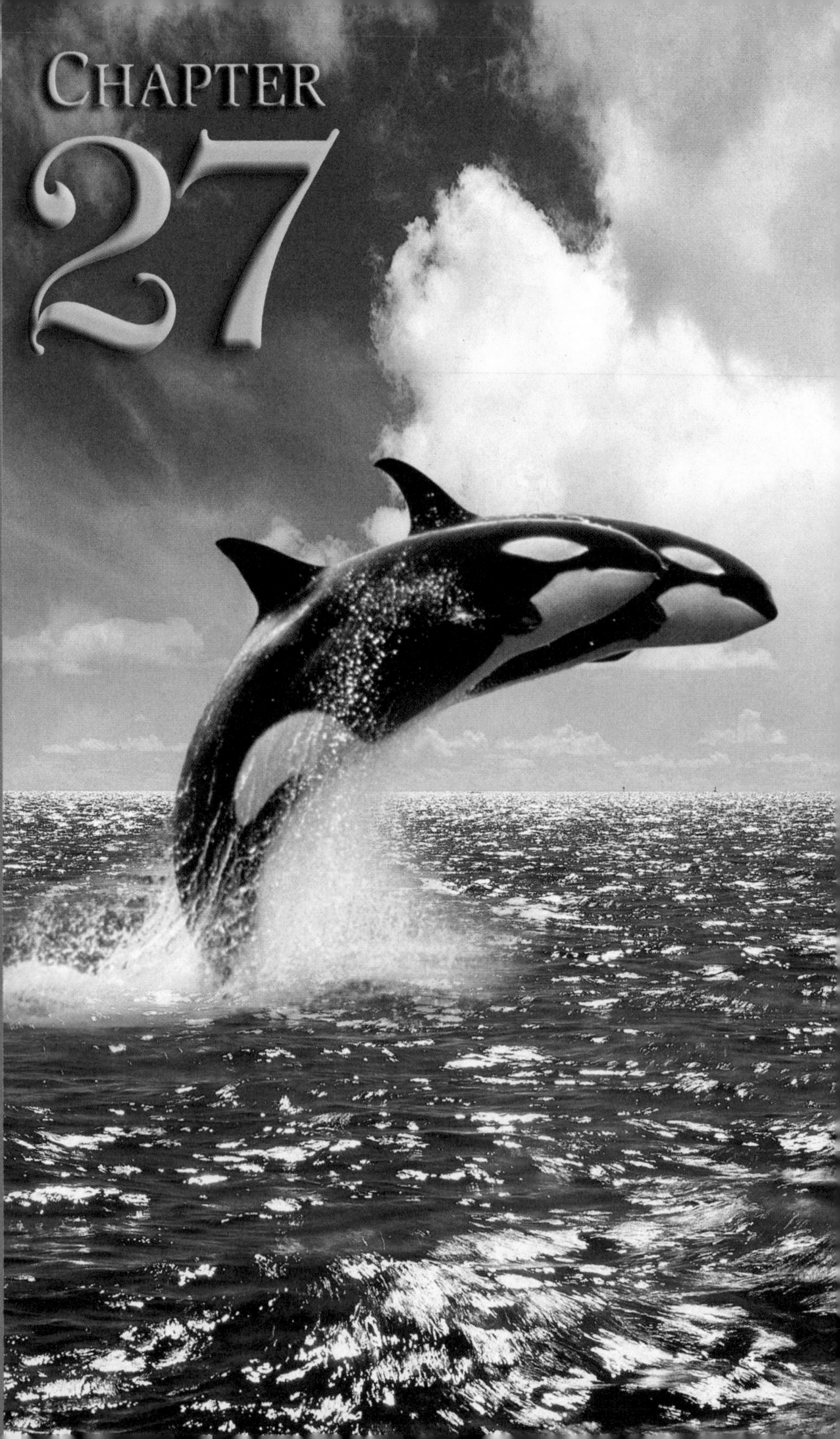

Understanding Nature

"When we try to pick out anything by itself, we find it hitched to everything else in the Universe."

—John Muir (naturalist, wanderer, and a founder of the Sierra Club),
  My First Summer in the Sierra, 1911

Turning in the rising air, a hawk drifts above a mountain forest. A lizard stands motionless in the shade of a desert cactus. Fireflies in the bushes near a prairie stream light up a humid summer evening. Tides beneath your kayak rise and fall. Geese, whales, salmon, and butterflies follow the calls of distant migrations, while an earthworm in the cool soil burrows a few feet in its lifetime. Overhead, a mere hint of universal expanse twinkles in the past light of galaxies and stars.

The natural world around us is spectacular beyond our wildest imagination. It can be gigantic—towering redwoods, rivers coursing for a thousand miles or more, great herds of animals nearly covering a grassy plain. Nature is tiny, too— the eye of an insect, the veins of a leaf, the microscopic structures of cells, the ecosystems of your neighborhood.

In the eruption of a volcano, the jolt of an earthquake, the roar of a forest fire, and the howl of a storm, nature makes itself known with explosive power. Natural phenomena also can move so slowly that we might notice no change in our lifetimes. Continents drift about the globe at mere inches a year. Through many generations, animals evolve, adapt, and sometimes disappear.

The more we learn about nature, the more we realize how interconnected are its parts. The relationships among plants, animals, and their surroundings are so intricate we can unravel only the most obvious mysteries. Even so, doing our

27

best to understand our world is essential to the planet's well-being and, ultimately, to our own. It is vital that we make good choices in how we treat nature.

Learning about nature is as easy as getting out into the middle of it with our senses wide open. We can step outside our homes and, wherever we are, nature is all around. Hiking can give us a sense of the shape of the terrain as it rolls beneath our feet. We can discover the folds of valleys, the heights of mountains, the breadth of deserts and prairies. Being outdoors allows us to appreciate heat, cold, wind, and precipitation firsthand. We can hear birds, the rush of water, the songs of frogs, and the drumming of grouse, or perhaps delight in the silence of a moment. Touch, smell, and taste come into play as well, as we feel the textures of stones, note the aromas of flowers in bloom, and savor the sweetness of a mountain huckleberry.

Every outdoor adventure is a doorway opening into understandings of the environment that can be as satisfying and challenging as any other aspect of a journey. In its complexity and simplicity, nature presents us with an overwhelming certainty that we are sharing Earth with other members of a worldwide community, and that their fates—and ours—are intertwined.

The World Around Us

Gaining an understanding of nature begins with paying attention. Look around. Ask why things are as they are. Start anywhere—watching wildlife near your camp, wondering why the leaves on trees near your school change color in the autumn, poking around a beach at low tide to see what the receding waters have revealed. Enjoy the puzzles and the wonder of the planet we call home. The more you see, the more you will be aware of what there is to notice. Nature will pull you in, presenting you with some answers and posing more questions. The mysteries are endless, and so is the delight.

You don't have to be a scientist or a scholar to enjoy nature—just interested and willing to ask questions. And you don't need to know scientific names of plants and animals, rock formations, or types of clouds to appreciate what you observe, at least not at first. It helps, though, and over time you will want to read and learn more.

One way to increase your understanding of nature is to look for the larger ways in which nature is organized—the systems, cycles, and chains providing the frameworks of existence.

Learning about nature can be as simple as a walk through a park or as involved as a lifetime career. There are many vocational possibilities in the study and management of natural resources, including fish and wildlife management, forestry, and soil and water conservation. Understanding nature is carried on in a variety of academic fields such as the following:

- **Astronomy**—the study of the heavens and celestial phenomena

- **Biology**—the study of living organisms

- **Botany**—the study of plant life

- **Geology**—the study of minerals, formations, and occurrences in the Earth

- **Meteorology**—the study of weather and atmospheric patterns

- **Paleontology**—the study of life forms and systems through fossil evidence

- **Zoology**—the study of animals

Ecosystems

A *population* is a group of the same animal or plant species living together. A *community* is all the populations of plants and animals in an area. An *ecosystem* is made up of those communities plus their physical surroundings—the land, weather, water, amount of sunlight, and everything else coming together to form the web of life.

No two ecosystems are alike. Many, however, share general similarities based on their locations, elevations, and other factors. Those similarities enable us to compare one area to another, and help us better comprehend what we are seeing.

Examining ecosystems can help us understand why the principles of Leave No Trace are important guidelines to follow during every outdoor adventure. It also can heighten our awareness of the importance of stewardship—giving something back to the environment that provides us not only pleasure and challenge, but also the basic necessities of life for all species.

For more on exploring ecosystems, see the chapter titled "Observing Nature."

ECOLOGY

Studying animals and plants in the context of their surroundings is called *ecology.* The term comes from the Greek words *oikos,* meaning "house," and *logos,* meaning "word" and "reason."

27

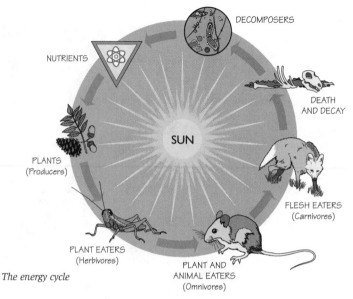

DECOMPOSERS

NUTRIENTS

DEATH
AND DECAY

PLANTS
(Producers)

SUN

FLESH EATERS
(Carnivores)

PLANT EATERS
(Herbivores)

PLANT AND
ANIMAL EATERS
(Omnivores)

The energy cycle

Energy Cycles

Living things must have nourishment in order to exist, to grow, and to reproduce. Calories providing that nourishment move through the environment, changing form as they transfer from one being to another. Solar energy propels the cycle. Combined with water and nutrients from the soil, for example, sunshine provides the means for plants to produce leaves. Insects eat those leaves. Spiders snare the insects in their webs and feast on them; the spiders, in turn, are devoured by field mice. Hawks swoop down and make meals of the mice. As the birds die, their remains decay and become nutrients enriching the soil, cycling back into the growth of new vegetation that insects can eat.

Every living organism, humans included, is part of an energy cycle. While all share a common need for nourishment, species have developed nearly endless variations in the ways they have adapted, both to thrive in the environments in which they find themselves and to give shape to the ecosystems of which they are a part.

For more on the complexities of species, see the chapters titled "Plants" and "Wildlife."

> *"There is value in any experience that reminds us of our dependency on the soil-plant-animal-man food chain, and of the fundamental organization of the biota."*
>
> —Aldo Leopold, *Sand County Almanac,* 1949 (His writings explore the complexity of the environment and the importance of caring for it.)

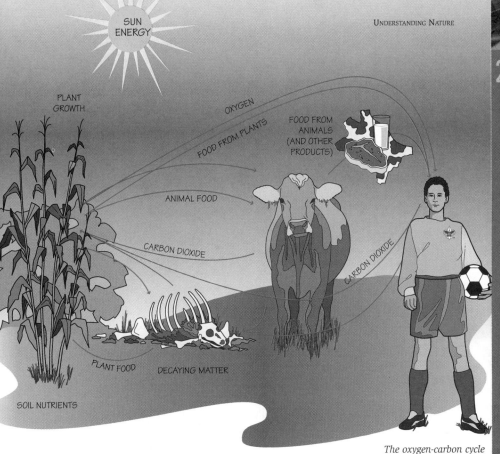

SUN ENERGY

PLANT GROWTH

OXYGEN

FOOD FROM PLANTS

FOOD FROM ANIMALS (AND OTHER PRODUCTS)

ANIMAL FOOD

CARBON DIOXIDE

CARBON DIOXIDE

PLANT FOOD   DECAYING MATTER

SOIL NUTRIENTS

The oxygen-carbon cycle

Oxygen-Carbon Cycle

Animals absorb oxygen, use it in processes that provide energy for their bodies, and exhale carbon dioxide. Carbon dioxide is also produced when plants and animals decay, and when wood, coal, and other carbon-based materials burn.

Plants must absorb carbon dioxide in order to survive. In a chemical reaction powered by sunlight, chlorophyll allows plants to combine water with carbon dioxide to produce the simple sugars that plants use for food. The process is called *photosynthesis*—making something with the aid of light. A by-product of photosynthesis is the oxygen relied upon by animals.

Animals use oxygen and exhale carbon dioxide. Plants absorb carbon dioxide and give off oxygen. Animals and plants are dependent upon one another, interacting in ways that make it possible for many species to thrive. These cooperative arrangements are forms of *symbiosis*—interdependence of species—and are an essential aspect of life on Earth.

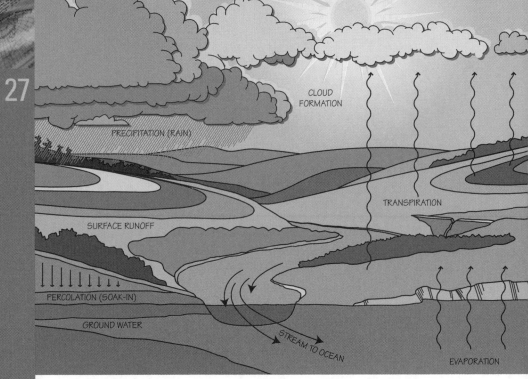

CLOUD
FORMATION

PRECIPITATION (RAIN)

TRANSPIRATION

SURFACE RUNOFF

PERCOLATION (SOAK-IN)

GROUND WATER

STREAM TO OCEAN

EVAPORATION

The water cycle

Water Cycle

From the driest desert cactus to fluid creatures in the ocean's depths, all living things must have water. Water allows nutrients and gases to pass through the cells of plants and the tissues of animals. It washes away wastes and regulates temperatures. It serves as a means of transportation for many species and a lifelong habitat for many others.

Water circulates through the environment in a cycle that, like the energy cycles and oxygen-carbon cycle, is energized by the sun. Heat from the sun evaporates water from oceans, lakes, and streams. The vapors form clouds that can be carried long distances by the wind. When the air cools or becomes loaded with moisture, the vapor can fall as rain, snow, sleet, or hail.

Much of the precipitation percolates into the soil where it can be absorbed by the roots of plants. Some finds its way into underground aquifers and other natural reservoirs, then rises again to flow from springs or wells. Small streams join together to form rivers returning water to lakes and oceans and, through evaporation, once again to the sky.

As with the intricacies and variety of the energy cycles and oxygen-carbon cycle, the Earth's water cycle interacts with all beings in remarkable, far-reaching ways. Marine scientists, for example, are discovering that water in the Earth's oceans circulates in patterns as profound as air masses overhead. Warmer water cools and sinks as it approaches the Arctic Ocean and Antarctica, and cold, dense currents deep beneath the surface can flow for thousands of miles. Water warming and swelling back toward the surface churns nutrients upward where they can be utilized by great varieties of sea life.

Change/Succession

Nature is forever changing. Regions of the planet that once were sea beds now are prairies, deserts, and mountain ranges. Shifts in the climate have sometimes transformed lush jungles and wetlands into snowfields and glaciers, then changed again to create conditions in which animals and vegetation could thrive. Plants and animals must adapt to meet the challenges of their environments. Species unable to change have disappeared forever—traces of them today are found only in fossils unearthed by paleontologists.

Changes in ecosystems can occur in shorter time spans, too. For example, picture a pond near a forest. Over a period of years, soil washing from hillsides into the water slowly collects along the edges of the pond. Grass seeds carried by the wind sprout in that new mud. As the grasses die, they mat down and decay, creating a nutrient-rich bed for larger rushes and cattails. Increasing numbers of fish and amphibians find safety among the roots and stalks, and insects lay their eggs on the leaves.

The remains of those plants and animals also sink into the mud, building more of the fertile soil and slowly raising and drying the edge of the pond. Shrubs and small trees move in, with slower-growing trees establishing themselves in the shade of trees that have grown more quickly. They, too, will live, die, and form more soil. At last, large trees mature into a stand called a *climax forest.*

The pond might have disappeared completely, and the forest might stand for many years. Change will continue to occur, though. Fire might sweep through the trees, or an insect blight might dramatically alter the forest's composition and appearance, and a new phase of the plant succession cycle will begin.

Change and Diversity

From microscopic bacteria to eagles, bears, wolves, and other predators at the top of a food chain, an ecosystem is healthiest when it is rich in the variety and numbers of species thriving within it. The more species in an area, the more flexible the ecosystem is as a whole, and the better able plants and animals will be to adapt to change. A *diversity* of species—that is, many plants and animals that are unlike one another—provides a storehouse of environmental possibilities, the raw material for adaptation and survival.

For instance, when bees harvest nectar from clover blossoms to make honey, pollen sticks to their legs and they carry it from one clover plant to another. It's a symbiotic relationship that benefits both species. The clover provides nourishment for bees, and the bees play a vital role in the pollination of the vegetation. If bee populations don't survive a harsh winter, though, or if they succumb to pesticides sprayed too near their hives, the clover will have lost a reliable means

27

of spreading pollen and might not be able to reproduce. Other species dependent on the clover might also go into decline.

A diverse ecosystem might include hummingbirds, insects, and other animals who carry pollen, too. By helping to fertilize the clover, they will have filled the void created by the absence of the bees. If there are no pollen-carrying alternatives to the bees, the clover may be replaced by plant species that don't rely on insects for pollination. Diversity of this sort cushions the effects that change has upon an area, and that increases the stability and health of an ecosystem.

As individuals and as a society, our treatment of the environment is our legacy to the future. Our legacy is up to us.

Human-Caused Change

Healthy, diverse ecosystems tend to be stable and to evolve slowly. Aside from the effects of storms, droughts, volcanic activity, and fire, the forces of nature in forests, prairies, riparian zones, and other environments often take decades or centuries to create perceivable change.

When humans become involved, however, ecosystem change can happen quickly. We can pave open land for highways, parking lots, and developments; and plow under prairie grasses to make way for crops.

Our vehicles, factories, and power plants can pump exhaust into the atmosphere, and the waste products of modern society often find their way into our landfills and waterways. A dam built across a river will generate electricity for dozens of cities and bring an end to annual floods, but it also will alter fish migrations, shoreline vegetation, and the lives of river species for dozens of miles up and down the stream.

Our ability to cause dramatic change carries with it the responsibility to make wise decisions on issues and actions that can affect the health of the environment. While humans are capable of activities that are destructive to ecosystems, we also can do much to conserve and heal the environment.

Small actions matter, and personal choices are important. As individuals, we can become informed consumers and active recyclers. As groups of people, we can work toward creating sustainable communities that exist in harmony with the environment. As citizens of our states and nation, we can learn about the issues and take part in the political processes that determine the fates of our public lands.

For more on caring for the environment, see the *Fieldbook* Web site and the chapter titled "Being Good Stewards of Our Resources."

Wilderness Recreation

The national park system came into existence to protect America's natural and cultural heritage. The USDA Forest Service, Bureau of Land Management, U.S. Fish and Wildlife Service, Soil Conservation Service, and other federal, state, and local agencies were established with the goal of managing America's natural resources with conservation stewardship that endures long-term sustainability for future generations. Many legislative mandates have attempted to guide our relationship with the environment. Among the most striking is the Wilderness Act, passed by Congress in 1964 to set aside large tracts of unspoiled lands to be protected in their natural states.

"A wilderness, in contrast with those areas where man and his own works dominate the landscape, is hereby recognized as an area where the earth and its community of life are untrammeled by man, where man himself is a visitor who does not remain."

—from the Wilderness Act of 1964, U.S. Congress

As a result of the Wilderness Act of 1964, Congress established
the National Wilderness Preservation System to protect some of America's
remaining wild lands. To be considered wilderness, an area had to be at
least 5,000 acres in size. No public roads could penetrate it, and it could
have no significant ecological disturbances caused by human activity.
The intent of Congress is that people should be able to see and enjoy
environments unchanged by the influence of humans.

Identifying wilderness areas is one way to help preserve environmental
complexity and diversity to the greatest extent possible, and to allow the
processes of nature to run their courses. Wilderness landscapes give us
examples of how the environment functions when we leave it alone, and
that can help us better understand and manage areas that have been developed. Wilderness also serves as an environmental bank account, preserving
a storehouse of species and systems that might otherwise disappear.

"*Nature is rude and incomprehensible at first, Be not discouraged, keep on, there are divine things . . . more beautiful than words can tell.*"

—Walt Whitman (American poet), "Song of the Open Road," 1856

In addition to its infinite scientific value, wilderness can nourish the human spirit and refresh the soul. By bringing us close to nature undisturbed, to these remnants of our once-wild continent, wilderness allows us to recognize and cherish the complexity of ecosystems everywhere and to act with the best interests of the environment foremost in our minds.

For more on understanding nature and discovering hands-on ways to protect and improve the environment, see the other chapters in the "Appreciating Our Environment" section, especially "Examining the Earth."

Observing Nature

*"When we use all of our senses outdoors,
we live fully in the present moment,
and so live more richly and intensely."*

—Joseph Cornell, environmentalist, outdoor educator, and Scouter

Here are some truths about observing nature. There is always something going on. What's going on is always exciting. We often look, but don't see, though we can change that by learning the skills of effective observation. What we see can help us understand that everything is connected. Observing the relationships of organisms to one another helps us expand our vision beyond ourselves, increasing our appreciation for all forms of life.

Every environment has much to teach us. Have you ever snorkeled around a coral reef or gone skin-diving to the ocean floor? At low tide many people wander along beaches searching for signs of marine life that have washed ashore, and during certain seasons some go out in boats and watch pods of migrating whales. The great swamps of the Southern states are full of remarkable plants and animals, and so are the deserts of the Southwest, the prairies of the Midwest, and the forests of the Northeast. So might be a city park, a Scout camp, and a backyard. In fact, nearly every spot on the globe supports natural communities varied and diverse beyond your wildest imagination.

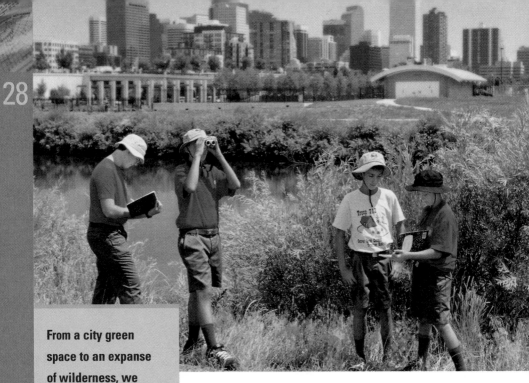

From a city green space to an expanse of wilderness, we go out into the world to see what's there. And what's there—everywhere we look—is evidence of the complexity and wonder of nature.

The Big Picture

Flora is the Latin word for plants. *Fauna* refers to animal life. In their sound and rhythm, they are words that seem to go together. In the environment, what they represent is absolutely inseparable—vegetation and animals interacting in ways that form balanced ecosystems.

Most of us enjoy observing animals in the wild. There can be real pleasure in watching deer and elk grazing, a beaver working on a dam, an eagle on the wing, or perhaps even a bear crossing a distant ridge. Plant life is nearly infinite in its variety, complexity, and mystery, too. Add the geology of an area, the weather patterns, and there is no end to what can be observed, enjoyed, and studied.

Respect What You Observe

One of the principles of Leave No Trace is to respect wildlife. It reminds us to stay far enough from animals not to disturb their natural patterns of behavior, and to be especially thoughtful of their need for space during seasons when they are mating, nesting, raising young, and enduring winter. As observers, we can extend that level of respect to the rest of the environment, too, acting in ways that leave the areas we visit, and their inhabitants, in the same condition when we depart as when we arrived.

Being a Good Observer

28

Drop a pebble into a pool of water and notice how the ripples run out in circles, one outside the next. A skilled observer's line of sight is similar to those rings of ripples. First, scan the area a few feet to the front and sides of you. Sweep your eyes along, taking in the whole scene rather than focusing on just one or two things.

Then sweep your eyes to take in the next line of "ripples"—an arc about 20 feet away. Look out a little farther and do the same thing. With practice, you can scan a wide area quickly. Animals, plants, tracks, and curious geologic phenomena will seem to pop out of the background. You'll also have a sense of the area as a whole, rather than seeing just a few highlights.

Extending Your Range

An eagle can see much better than you can, even if you have 20/20 eyesight. While our senses are not as acute as those of many animals, we do have the power to expand our range with mechanical aids, and to enhance our ability to capture experiences with cameras, pens, brushes, and paper. We also can extend our observational abilities by going out early in the morning and in the evening, on stormy afternoons and moonlit nights—every season and every hour of the day presents different aspects of nature.

Binoculars and Magnifying Glasses

Binoculars allow you to study wildlife without approaching too closely, and to bring into view details too small to be seen by the naked eye. They can be invaluable for watching birds and other animals. A magnifying glass is ideal for examining plants, insects, and the details of soils and stones.

Most binoculars are marked with an equation—7 × 35, for instance. The first number represents the magnifying power of the binoculars; in this case, an object will appear seven times larger than normal. The second number indicates the diameter of a binoculars' larger lenses, measured in millimeters. Binoculars with higher numbers will capture a wider range of vision in more detail, but also might be heavier and more difficult to hold steady. Binoculars also vary greatly in the amount of light they capture, and thus the brightness of the image.

Photography

Photographing flowers, animals, and landscapes provides a memorable means for you to record high points of your adventures and to share your discoveries with others. Any reliable camera can provide the means for you to begin capturing nature on film. As you become adept at the basics, the addition of telephoto and close-up lenses can augment your photographic range. Digital cameras and computerized image-management programs offer a variety of ways to gather and present your images, all without the cost of film.

Drawing

Robert S. S. Baden-Powell, Daniel Carter Beard, and Ernest Thompson Seton—individuals who played key roles in establishing the Scouting movement—shared a common passion for sketching outdoor scenes. Each carried sketchbooks and pencils on adventures and filled page after page with pictures of wild animals, plants, and backcountry life.

You don't have to be a great artist to enjoy drawing what you see. Examining plants, animals, and landscapes with an eye toward capturing them on paper can give you fresh perceptions of nature, and trigger a special relationship with the subjects of your art.

Baden-Powell found great joy in sketching outdoor scenes.

Journals

During their three-year journey across the American West in the early 1800s, the explorers Meriwether Lewis and William Clark wrote daily in their journals. They noted their locations, the vegetation and wildlife they saw, and accounts of their activities and those of others in their expedition.

To this day, their journals are invaluable records of one of the great American adventures.

Try keeping a journal during your own trips, and you might discover the same pleasure and personal value in writing as did Lewis and Clark. A simple notebook is all you need—just write something every day you are in the backcountry. Keep a log of animals and plants you see, make notes about the weather, and write descriptions of other natural phenomena that catch your attention. Your skill as a keeper of journals will grow, and you will have a record that years from now will remind you of some of your favorite journeys.

Tracking Animals

Every animal traveling on land leaves tracks where it passed. Following those tracks can teach you much about what an animal eats, where it sleeps, and its daily habits. With luck, your tracking skill might lead you to the creature itself.

Tracking is detective work, the solving of mysteries. Why is that twig broken? Did an animal rooting for grubs turn over those stones? What made these scratches on the trunk of a tree? One by one, clues can lead you along the route traveled by an animal and deeper into its life. Are you able to guess where it is headed? Can you find a spot where it might have slept? Did it leave any droppings? Is there evidence of what it has been eating?

You have to find some tracks before you can follow them. Winter snows hold a surprising number of tracks. During other seasons, try the soft soil near ponds and streams. In dry country, scan the dust for prints and look for pebbles and rocks that have been disturbed.

Study a Single Track

Closely examine the shape of a track you wish to follow. Measuring and sketching it can help you find it later even if it becomes mixed in with other tracks.

Becoming an expert tracker takes patience and practice. The more time you spend at it, the easier it will be for you to decipher signs left by wildlife, and the more surely you can figure out behavior patterns and activities of animals you are following.

Wolf tracks in sand

457

Track Early or Late

Tracking can be easiest early in the morning and late in the day when shadows cast in the prints make them stand out more than when the sun is directly overhead. Sharply defined tracks probably were left more recently than those with eroded edges.

Look for More Than Just the Prints

Bent or matted grass, broken twigs, stripped bark, and displaced pebbles might help you see an animal's path. Watch for burrows, caves, insect mounds, and nests.

Droppings, known as scat, can give evidence of an animal's diet. Break scat apart with a stick. Hulls of seeds, skins of berries, and bits of leaves suggest the animal is an *herbivore*—an animal that eats only plants. Small bones, fur, and feathers might appear in the scat of *carnivores*— animals that feed on other animals. Mixed scat indicates an *omnivore*—

a species whose diet includes both animal and plant material. Scat tends to dry from the outside in. If it is completely dry, you know the animal passed by some time ago. Moist scat is much fresher; the animal might be near.

Imagine Yourself in the Place of the Animal

Should you lose the line of footprints you are following, ask yourself where you would go if you were the animal, then look in that direction. Mark the last print with a stick and explore all around it until you again pick up the animal's trail.

Notice Landmarks

Tracking can be an absorbing activity, but don't become so interested that you get lost. Be alert to your surroundings, noticing and remembering landmarks that will guide you back to your starting point.

Beaver gnawings on a tree is one obvious sign of an animal habitat.

Collect Tracks

Perhaps you've heard the old saying, "Take only photographs, leave only footprints." By making plaster casts, you can bring home the footprints, too.

When you find a track you want to preserve, mix up some plaster of paris. (Plaster of paris is available at pharmacies. Container labels will have mixing instructions.) Turn a cardboard strip into a collar by notching the ends together. Place the collar around the track and pour in the mix. Let it harden—10 to 15 minutes in warm weather—then lift the cast and brush off the dirt. On the back of the cast, write the date, the location where you found the track, and the identity of the animal that made it.

You can also cast plaster molds of tracks in the snow. In addition to plaster of paris, you'll need a mist bottle such as those used with glass cleaner. Spray the track with a fine mist of water and wait a few moments while it freezes. Mix the plaster using cold water (warm plaster will melt the print). Put a collar around the track and pour in the plaster. Give it plenty of time to harden.

By themselves, casts of prints are fine souvenirs of your adventures. You can also press them into damp sand to recreate the original prints.

Casting a mold is a way to bring home a souvenir of a track you found.

> "Something, I think, also [could] be done toward developing the boy's mind by increasing his powers of observation, and teaching him to notice details."
>
> —Robert S. S. Baden-Powell (1857–1941), founder of the worldwide Scouting movement

Though tracking wildlife requires movement on your part, perhaps the best way to observe animals is not to travel at all. You are likely to see more in an hour of sitting quietly than during a full day of hiking.

Observing Wildlife

Humans traveling in the backcountry usually create enough disturbance to send wildlife scurrying for cover, but if you are motionless and silent, many animals will have difficulty detecting your presence. Use this to your advantage by finding a place to sit comfortably. Hide in the brush, or climb into a tree and wait to see what animals pass nearby. Crouch behind a snowdrift, at the edge of a meadow, or beside a game trail. Position yourself downwind from the likely locations of wildlife so that your scent doesn't give you away. Before long, animals will resume their normal activities and come into your field of view.

Sunrise and dusk often are the best times to observe animals, when they can be more active than during the middle of the day. A great many animals are active at night. Under a full or partial moon, you are likely to discover lots of wildlife activity, though your observations might lean more toward sounds than sights.

Attracting Animals

Blow on a duck call and you might bring a circling flock of birds near your hiding place. Make a kissing sound against the back of your hand and deer might come to investigate. Whistle softly and a running rabbit might stop in its tracks, while a shrill whistle in high mountain country can bring marmots out of their burrows to see what's going on.

Stalking Wildlife

Stalking wild animals is a skill as old as humankind. For eons, it was a means of getting close enough to animals to increase hunting success. Today, stalking can be a way to observe their habits and to take photographs and make sketches. Stalking also can be a demanding discipline that depends on your ability to use all of your senses, on your understanding of the animals you are observing, and on your willingness to practice patience.

You might, for example, see a deer grazing in a meadow. Although the deer is busy eating, it raises its head now and then to sniff the air, listen, and glance around for signs of danger.

Study the landscape and decide how you might slip closer to the animal. Are there folds in the terrain where you can hide, or trees and brush that will conceal your presence as you ease toward the meadow? What is the wind direction? If a breeze is blowing toward the deer, it can pick up your scent long before it sees you. Is the ground covered with dry leaves that will crunch beneath your footsteps, or with soft grass that will muffle the sound of your approach? Is the deer standing still or in motion? Will mist or fog help conceal your presence and dampen noises? Are there other animals or people in the vicinity that might startle the deer before you get close?

The mark of an expert stalker is the ability to reach a point where animals can be observed, and then to leave so quietly that the animals are never aware you were there.

As you stalk toward the deer, remember that while its senses are keen, it has trouble seeing things that don't move. Freeze whenever the deer lifts its head, and hold still until it looks away. Stay in shadows as much as you can. When you reach an observation spot with a clear view of the animal, enjoy watching for as long as you want, then withdraw as quietly and invisibly as you approached. Always keep enough distance between yourself and wildlife so that you aren't disturbing their activities, causing them anxiety, or blocking their access to sources of food, water, or critical habitat.

Watching Birds

As you observe birds, the six S's—size, shape, shadings, song, sweep, and surroundings—offer a means for you to gather clues that can lead to a bird's identification. Even if you aren't interested in finding out its name, noticing the S's will solve some of the mysteries about a bird.

Size

Hummingbirds are just a few inches long and weigh only ounces. A turkey vulture weighs several pounds and has a wing span of 3 feet or more. Compare the size of a bird you see with the sizes of birds you know. Is the new one larger than a sparrow? About the same size as a robin? Smaller than a crow? A bird's size might affect its methods of gathering food, making its nests, and avoiding predators.

Hummingbird

Shape

Notice the shapes of birds and try to guess how their physical features play into their abilities to adapt to their environments. The great wings and powerful talons of eagles, hawks, and other raptors allow them to drift overhead and then to snag their prey and lift it into the sky. The long, slender legs of herons and many other shorebirds enable them to wade in waters where they can feed on small fish. Beaks are clues to the diets of birds, capable of tasks ranging from cracking small seeds or drilling holes in wood to sipping flower nectar or catching insects on the wing.

Shadings

Bright feathers help many birds attract mates. For others, drab colors act as lifesaving camouflage. The ptarmigan is a good example. Its brown feathers hide it during summers in mountain forests. When winter comes, the ptarmigan's feathers become as white as the snow.

Song

Birds use their songs to warn of danger, mark their territories, and find mates. When you know the songs of birds, you can identify them even without seeing them.

Ptarmigan

Goliath heron

Sweep

"Sweep" refers to the movements a bird makes. Some hop or scurry across the ground. Others flit from tree to tree. Soaring birds can catch updrafts of wind and hover without flapping their wings. Some birds dive into bodies of water in pursuit of prey. Close observation of the sweep of birds can lead to a greater understanding of how each has adapted to its surroundings.

Surroundings

Like all animals, birds have certain habitat needs. They must find food, cover, water, protection from predators, and places to mate and raise their young. The first five S's (size, shape, shadings, song, and sweep) are ways that birds have adapted to their surroundings.

Great blue herons during their courtship ritual

28

Observing Plants

Vegetation is so much a part of our outdoor experiences that we may hardly notice it all around us. Noticing, though, is what observing nature is all about, and when it comes to seeing plants, there is enough of interest to keep a careful observer occupied for a lifetime.

The chapter titled "Plants" will discuss specific means of examining and identifying vegetation. More general observation can help you unravel some of the ways in which plants are intertwined with animals, terrain, and other aspects of an ecosystem.

Notice, for example, the sizes and shapes of the trees, and how close together they are growing. Pick a single tree and examine the color of the leaves or needles. Smell the bark and feel its texture. Have birds built nests in the branches? Has a woodpecker in search of a meal drilled holes in the trunk? Have deer rubbed their antlers against the bark, or have hungry elk standing on drifts of snow nibbled the low-hanging twigs? Is there evidence of fire, disease, or strong winds? Study the network of fine lines crisscrossing the surface of a leaf. Search the ground for fruit, seed pods, or nuts, and break one open. If you have a plant identification book, find a description of the tree and read about its uses, range, longevity, and special characteristics.

Trees, grasses, flowers, and other forms of vegetation serve as living habitats for all kinds of life. The following questions can help you begin your exploration of a plant and the ways in which it is woven into its ecosystem.

---

1. How is it similar to and different from nearby plants?

---

2. How are the leaves or needles shaped?

---

3. Does it bear flowers or fruiting bodies?

---

4. What kind of soil is it growing in? Sandy, wet, dry, gravel, black dirt?

---

5. Who is visiting the plant? Do any creatures use it for food or as a home?

---

6. How is the environment influencing the plant? (For example, is the plant growing in sunshine or shade?)

---

7. How is the plant affecting the environment around it?

Pressing Leaves

When you have leaves you would like to preserve, put each one between two sheets of paper, lay the sheets on a board or other flat surface, then place heavy books or some other flat weight on top. Give the leaves several days to flatten and dry. Mount them in a scrapbook along with the details of where and when you found them, the identity of each plant, and any other information you have learned about each plant's natural history.

Making Leaf Ink Prints

Use a rubber roller to spread a dab of printer's ink on a glass plate. Place a leaf on the glass with the veined side against the ink. Run the roller over the leaf several times, then lay the leaf, inked side down, on a clean sheet of paper.

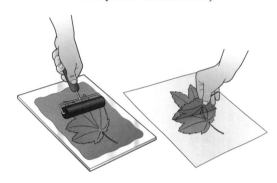

Cover the leaf with a piece of newspaper and run the roller over it to make a print. After the ink dries, arrange the pages in a scrapbook.

Observing the Earth (and Its Neighborhood)

All of nature is interesting, all its parts are connected with all the others, and trying to make sense of it is tremendously important. The following chapters in this book provide guidance to help you explore geology, meteorology, botany, biology, and astronomy. In every case, the key to understanding is simply to begin looking.

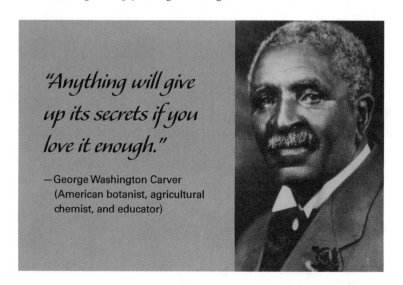

"Anything will give up its secrets if you love it enough."

—George Washington Carver
   (American botanist, agricultural
   chemist, and educator)

CHAPTER

29

Examining the Earth

"These cliff-bound glaciers, seemingly wedged and immovable, are flowing like water and grinding the rocks beneath them. The lakes are lapping their granite shores and wearing them away, and every one of these rills and young rivers is fretting the air into music, and carrying the mountains to the plains."

—John Muir (19th-century naturalist and a founder of the Sierra Club), 1868

Many of us are drawn to the out-of-doors by its timeless tranquility and beauty. We're sure that the mountains we climb this summer will be there next year, too. The tumbling streams that lull us to sleep seem to have flowed forever, and it might be difficult to imagine that the deep valleys and broad plains could ever have been much different from how they are today.

Yet the seeming permanence of terrain is an illusion, as the land is always changing. The quiet, wooded campsites we like so much might once have been at the bottom of an ocean or buried beneath immense expanses of ice. The hills we hike could have been seared by the heat of volcanic blasts or torn apart by earthquakes. Even as we stand on them, granite mountains are slowly rising, or dissolving beneath our feet. Eruption and erosion, creation and decay—the Earth is being continually reshaped, time and again cast anew. It is a relentless, powerful, and fascinating process, and as we explore the world, we are surrounded everywhere by evidence of its complexity and grace.

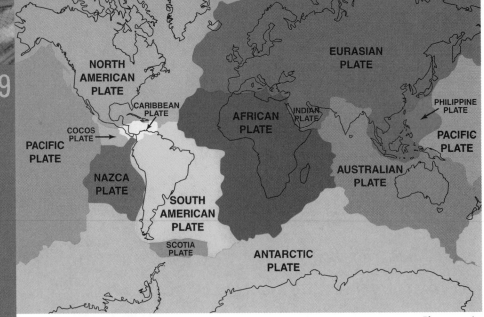

Plate tectonics

Formation of the Earth

Scientists suggest imagining a time-lapse camera photographing the Earth's surface from its beginnings to the present. Even at a rate of one frame exposed every 100 years, the finished film would take weeks to show. Opening scenes of molten rock glowing red gradually give way to those of a globe with its surface dividing into continents and oceans. Mountain ranges heave through the Earth's crust only to diminish. Ice fields flow out from the polar caps, then recede. Seas draw back to reveal vast prairies. Earthquakes and volcanoes abruptly alter the landscape, and the continents drift slowly about the globe. Strange plants and animals flicker into view and then are gone, the dinosaurs perhaps the most recognizable. Humans finally appear on the screen, the history of their civilizations taking only a few seconds at the end of the long film of the Earth's history.

Many geologists studying the development of the planet believe the Earth came into existence as a molten ball composed of various elements. The lighter elements drifted toward the surface of the globe, leaving at the center a dense iron core. A crust formed as the Earth's surface cooled, and even today that crust ranges from about 9 to about 47 miles thick. Temperatures and pressures deep within the Earth are still high enough to keep rock in elastic or plastic form. The great slabs, or *plates,* of the Earth's crust float upon this mantle like so many gigantic islands, drifting, colliding, and overlapping. Known as *plate tectonics,* this slow, remarkable motion can drive mountain ranges skyward.

> ### GEOLOGY
>
> *Geo* means "earth"; the suffix *-logy* indicates "a subject of study." *Geology,* then, is the scientific examination of the formation and development of our planet.

Plate Tectonics

The major plates of the Earth's crust are named for the areas of land and sea under which they lie. The *North American Plate*, for example, is the underpinning of most of North America and a good share of the Atlantic Ocean. Bordering its western edge is the *Pacific Plate* extending beneath the Pacific Ocean. Other prominent plates are the *Australian, African, South American, Eurasian, Philippine*, and *Antarctic*.

The plates might move only inches a year, but even so slow a migration has far-reaching effects. The motion of adjoining plates takes one of four forms—*separating, sliding, undercutting*, and *colliding*. These motions are caused by convection currents as magma slowly churns deep inside the Earth.

Separating

When two plates pull away from one another, they create a *zone of divergence*. The African Great Rift Valley and the Red Sea are good examples. Occurring primarily under the oceans, zones of divergence allow magma to rise and fill the gaps between the plates.

Sliding

Plates moving parallel to one another can cause earthquakes, especially along the *fault zone* at the edges of the plates, such as occurs in California.

Undercutting

When one plate slides under another plate, it can curve downward, creating a *subduction zone* that is a source of volcanoes, earthquakes, and mountain building, as found in the Ring of Fire surrounding the Pacifc Rim.

Colliding

When one plate slams into another, layers of rock thrust upward can form mountain ranges, such as in the Himalayas, where the Indian Plate is smashing into Asia.

Terrain Formation

The center of the North American Plate, near the Appalachian Mountains, is relatively stable. Far from the active edges of the tectonic plates, the prairie states tend to be flat, often layered with the sediment of ancient oceans that once flowed over them. Farther west, stress in the Earth's crust has created mountain ranges in a variety of ways, primarily through *volcanic activity, faults, folds*, and *continental uplifts*.

Volcanic eruptions occurring in California, Oregon, Washington, and Alaska are caused by pressure and instability as tectonic plates sliding under one another sometimes form cracks in the Earth's crust that allow magma to flow to the surface. The colliding edges of the North American and Pacific plates can be traced along the West Coast of the United States, past British Columbia, and through the Aleutian Islands.

Volcanoes

When hot, fluid rock called *magma* finds passage to the surface, it may erupt as a volcano. In some cases an initial eruption can explode with devastating force, as did Mount Saint Helens in the state of Washington, and the flow of magma may continue for a long time, as does that from Mauna Loa on the island of Hawaii. The Cascade Range of the Pacific Northwest is volcanic in origin, and the Hawaiian Islands are the tops of immense volcanoes that, when measured from their bases on the ocean floor, are the tallest mountains on the planet.

Faults

Pressured by plate movement, the Earth's crust may fracture and shift, creating high walls, zones of broken rock, and disrupted streambeds. Additional plate movement can jumble these terrain features and create the angular shapes of mountain ranges that include the Sierra Nevada and the Tetons.

Folds

Instead of fracturing, a plate of soft, sedimentary rocks may fold. Sections of the Appalachian Mountains were formed this way.

Continental Uplifts

Large sections of the Earth's crust are sometimes forced upward by internal pressures created by plate motion. When that happened in western North America, the towering Rocky Mountains came into being.

Mica

Quartz

Gypsum

Calcite

Dolomite

Rocks

The elements that make up the Earth (oxygen, silicon, etc.) bind together to form dozens of *minerals* including mica, quartz, gypsum, calcite, dolomite, and feldspar. These are the building blocks of rocks, combining in myriad ways to create the enormous variety you see in the field. Geologists identify the minerals that compose particular rocks by using measurements including hardness, color, and fracturing qualities as the basis of their classifications. A good rock identification book will give you the information you need to do this, too, and you might find that the delights of being a rock hound are as satisfying as being able to identify trees, animals, and cloud formations.

To simplify matters, geologists have divided all rocks into one of three categories, depending on their origins— *igneous*, *sedimentary*, and *metamorphic*. Every rock bears clues of the process that formed it. By deciphering those signs, you can not only learn how certain rocks came into being, but also perhaps better understand the makeup of entire landscapes.

Feldspar

Igneous Rock

Igneous rock forms from cooling molten rock.
When magma stays beneath the Earth's
surface, it cools slowly, forming crystals.
The slower the cooling process, the larger
the crystals. Magma thrown up by a volcano
is an *extrusive* igneous rock, meaning it cools
on the Earth's surface. Since it cools quickly,
the crystals are very small—you might need
a magnifying glass to see them. Obsidian, for
example, is magma that cooled so rapidly it
became a kind of glass that can be black,
green, gray, or even red in color. Basalt is
another extrusive igneous rock. Granite, on
the other hand, is an *intrusive* igneous rock,
meaning it cooled slowly under the surface
of the Earth. The crystals in granite are large
and very easy to see and identify.

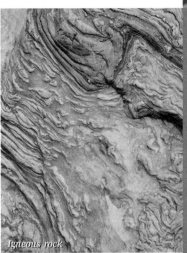

Igneous rock

Sedimentary Rock

Sedimentary rock forms as eroded particles
settle out of the water in which they have
been transported. Layers of sediment piling
on top of one another become compacted,
and moisture percolating through the
sediment may deposit calcium carbonate,
silica, or iron oxide, which binds the
particles. Limestone is among the most
common sedimentary rocks, often composed
of the skeletal remains of ancient plants
and animals. Grains of sand can become
sandstone. Pebbles and larger stones can
become cemented together to form layers
of *conglomerates,* while shale primarily is
composed of silt and clay particles. With a
sharp eye you often can find tiny, beautifully
preserved fossils in sedimentary rock.

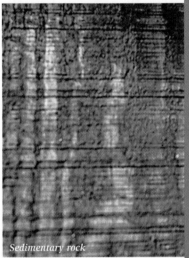

Sedimentary rock

Metamorphic Rock

Igneous and sedimentary rocks are sometimes heated enough or put under enough
pressure for their minerals to take on new
forms. The rocks that result are said to
be *metamorphic.* For instance, shale can
metamorphose into slate, and limestone
into marble. Granite might change into
banded gneiss. Under tremendous pressure,
graphite can be transformed into diamonds.

Metamorphic rock

29

29 Soils

Soil is so familiar to us we seldom give it a second thought. "As common as dirt," goes an old saying, but there is nothing common about soil. It is an ecosystem composed of a complicated combination of mineral matter (a mix of silt, sand, and clay), water, air, and organic material (plant roots, bacteria, fungi, nematodes, protozoa, arthropods, earthworms, etc.).

Decomposing organic matter breaks down into phosphorus, nitrogen, sulfur, and other compounds that vegetation must have in order to thrive. As plants and animals die, their decomposition refreshes the organic material of the soil, making possible one of the environment's most important energy cycles.

Those who study soil classify samples according to a variety of measurements:

- *Composition*—the ratio of sand, silt, and clay

- *Water-holding capacity*— the ability of a soil sample to absorb moisture

- *Biotic contents*—the amount and kind of organic material found in a sample

Another useful measurement for identifying a particular soil is its color, classified by its hue (degrees of red, yellow, green, blue, and purple), darkness or lightness, and strength of color (known as *chroma*). In general, darker soils contain more organic matter, and thus are more fertile, than soils of lighter color. Darker soils also are less likely to erode.

Erosion

Coupled with the creative forces of plate tectonics is the relentless power of erosion. Without erosion, the Earth's mountains would be extremely high. There would be no streambeds, no canyons, and little soil. Without erosion, life as we know it could not exist.

The primary agents of erosion are water, chemicals, ice, gravity, and wind. Moisture seeping into rock fissures expands as it freezes, gradually breaking stone apart. The rocks of talus and scree slopes on mountainsides probably were shattered by frost. Chemicals carried by water can dissolve rock or eat away the crystals that hold it together, allowing it to crumble into particles. Limestone is especially susceptible to chemical weathering, as evidenced by old limestone tombstones whose eroded letters have become almost unreadable, and by the formation of sinkholes and caves.

Rain washes away bits of loosened stone that will act as abrasives as they are carried along. Trickles of water combine to form rivulets, rivulets unite into streams, and streams join into rivers, all patiently cutting channels into the Earth. The steeper the grade of the land, the faster and more erosive

River deltas and weathered rock are both results of erosion.

the movement of the water and the sediment in it. When the grade lessens and streams lose momentum, particles suspended in the water settle to the bottoms of lakes or help create deltas at the mouths of rivers. Floodplains are formed by the deposition of sediment during flooding.

Glaciers are among the most spectacular agents of erosion. A glacier is a long-lasting body of ice formed when yearly accumulations of snow exceed the amounts that melt. The weight of new snow compresses that below it, eventually turning it into ice. As more snow falls on the upper reaches of a glacier, it pushes the ice field downhill in a motion much like that of a very slow river.

Stresses upon glacial ice cause fractures called *crevasses* that can be hundreds of feet deep. When a glacier pushes its way down a steep valley or over a cliff, it creates an *icefall,* a chaotic tangle of frozen walls and pillars known as *seracs* that can topple without warning. If a glacier reaches the ocean, as do many in Alaska and Antarctica, great chunks of ice shear away and drop into the sea. Called *calving,* this glacial activity is a primary source of icebergs.

As a glacier moves across the land, gravel and rocks trapped beneath the weight of the ice scour the surfaces over which they travel. Glaciers can reshape the sharp, V-shaped canyons cut by streams into broad U-shaped valleys. Melting glaciers can leave behind *moraines*—distinctive ridges of rock, boulders, cobbles, and sand they might have pushed along for many miles.

Erratics are boulders carried along by glaciers and deposited in a new location.

Scientists believe that when the climate of the Earth cooled, continental glaciers crept down from the Arctic to cover much of North America. When the weather warmed and the glaciers retreated, they left behind thick deposits of soil and, here and there, solitary boulders known as *glacial erratics*. Much of the rich American prairie was formed by *loess*, windblown soil deposits in glaciated areas. Alpine glaciers continue to cloak the summits and high basins of many mountain ranges in Canada and the United States.

The power of erosion is astonishing. Over the eons it has carved the Grand Canyon, worn down the Appalachian Mountains, and helped shape every landscape you've ever hiked. In fact, you'll find the effects of erosion everywhere you look, but it must be seen in perspective. Erosion plays an essential role in the creation of the soil in which forests, grasslands, and crops can take root, but it has an insatiable appetite. Poor management and abuse of natural resources can allow erosion to take away soil far more quickly than it can be formed.

For more on the effects of erosion and ways to avoid its negative effects, see the section titled "Leaving No Trace." For ways to repair landscapes harmed by erosion, see the chapter titled "Being Good Stewards of Our Resources."

Wisely Using Our Resources

Our Earth has countless resources, including minerals, water, forests, wildlife, oil, and open land, to name a few of them. Minerals are extracted for making metals used in construction, factories, heavy equipment, and automobiles. Water is used for human consumption, crop irrigation, manufacturing, hydroelectric power, and recreation. Oil is used to heat and light our homes and offices, as well as for powering machinery and automobiles. Forest lumber is used to construct buildings, homes, and furniture. Land is used for housing and business development; for raising crops, grazing cattle, building highways, and recreation; and for preserving species of plants and animals.

Human beings have many needs and wants. We are responsible for determining how and for what we will use our resources—decisions that have enormous consequences for our daily lives. We can set aside a river for recreation, or we can build a hydroelectric dam that will generate electricity to light hundreds of thousands of homes—but that same dam also might affect the fish habitat of the river. The consequences of our action or inaction need careful consideration based on all of our needs and wants so that we do not act rashly or do something we might come to regret. Alternative uses of resources need to be carefully researched to achieve a solution that serves the most people and the most significant needs. When you learn about a controversy regarding the environment, take time to educate yourself about each of the alternatives and listen to other people's perspectives before reaching a conclusion. There are no easy answers.

As members of the BSA, we have pledged ourselves to be thrifty. As residents of the planet and consumers of its resources, we must be leaders in doing our part to care for the Earth.

We can pitch in and do plenty of good work repairing environmental damage near our homes, in Scout camps, and in parks and forests we enjoy using. We can recycle. We can be smart about what we purchase and what we consume. We can stay informed and become involved in the political processes that lead to many decisions about how the people of our communities, states, and nation will use and protect natural resources.

Other chapters of the *Fieldbook* have emphasized the importance of practicing Leave No Trace principles during outdoor adventures. The chapter titled "Being Good Stewards of Our Resources" suggests many hands-on projects that can make a real difference in the quality of the environment. With hard work, we can protect the places where we camp and hike. With enthusiasm, patience, and dedication, we can extend our efforts to care for all of the Earth.

"The miracle of soil, alive and giving life, lying thin on the only planet for which there is no spare. We need a renewed stirring of love for the Earth."

—David Brower (1912–2000), American conservationist and first executive director of the Sierra Club

Monitoring Weather

"Joy comes from simple and natural things, mists over meadows, sunlight on leaves, the path of the moon over water. Even rain and wind and stormy clouds may bring joy."

—Sigurd Olson, American nature writer, founding father of the Boundary Waters Canoe Area, and recipient of the 1974 John Burroughs Medal, the highest honor in nature writing

The atmosphere swirls above us like a great, restless sea. Jet streams streak across the sky at hundreds of miles an hour. Polar air masses spill off the ice fields and roll toward warmer climes, while hot tropical air can be so still that a ship's sails can hang limp for days. Chinook winds sweep off the mountains, and thunderheads billow over the prairies, while high peaks seem to produce their own storms.

Thunder and silence, drought and rain, the seemingly random effects of weather are everywhere. Yet weather is not a series of isolated events. It is a constantly changing whole that is as remarkable for its thousand-mile bands of storms and calm as for the narrow paths of tornadoes and lightning bolts. As you travel the outdoors, you'll want to piece together the weather clues you see, hear, and feel so that you can predict the conditions to come in the next few hours and days. To do that, it helps to understand the big picture.

The Atmosphere

Breathing it throughout our lives, feeling it blow against our faces, and watching it move smoke, dust, sailboats, and clouds, we usually take the air around us for granted. The air we call atmosphere, composed primarily of nitrogen (78 percent) and oxygen (21 percent), rises some 60 miles above Earth's

30

surface, thinning until it vanishes into the vacuum of space. The atmosphere presses down on us at sea level with a force of about 14.7 pounds per square inch, but we are so accustomed to feeling that weight we seldom realize it is there unless we are changing elevations. Climb a mountain, though, and you will find the air getting thinner as you go higher. You might feel light-headed and short of breath. When you make an alpine camp, you also might notice that water on your backpacking stove boils at a lower temperature than at sea level.

Water's Boiling Point

ELEVATION	DEGREES FAHRENHEIT
Sea level	212
1,000 feet	210
5,000 feet	202
8,000 feet	196
10,000 feet	192
12,000 feet	188
14,000 feet	184

Atmospheric Strata

The layers, or *strata,* of the atmosphere are the *troposphere, stratosphere, mesosphere,* and *thermosphere.* Nearly all weather occurs in the troposphere, the level closest to Earth's surface. The troposphere varies in depth from 4 miles at the North and South Poles to about 10 miles at the equator.

The boundary between the troposphere and troposphere is the *tropopause,* a lid on the weather-filled troposphere. The stratosphere above it is ideal for jet travel, since aircraft at that altitude are above most atmospheric disturbances.

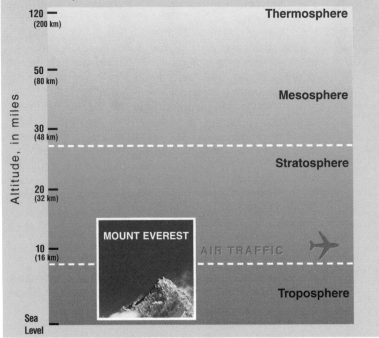

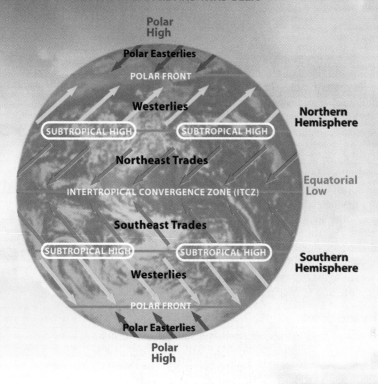

GLOBAL PRESSURE AND WIND BELTS

Polar High

Polar Easterlies

POLAR FRONT

Westerlies

SUBTROPICAL HIGH   SUBTROPICAL HIGH

Northeast Trades

INTERTROPICAL CONVERGENCE ZONE (ITCZ)

Southeast Trades

SUBTROPICAL HIGH   SUBTROPICAL HIGH

Westerlies

POLAR FRONT

Polar Easterlies

Polar High

Northern Hemisphere

Equatorial Low

Southern Hemisphere

Air Pressure and Atmospheric Temperature

The sun is the engine that drives Earth's weather systems. Solar radiation warms Earth, which in turn heats the envelope of air nearest Earth's surface. The sun's rays are more direct, thus more intense, closer to the equator, making the tropical latitudes warmer than the North and South Poles. The temperatures of large bodies of water change more slowly than the temperatures of land masses. The surface of bare soil heats and cools faster than forested regions at similar latitudes and elevations. The seasons affect rates of heating and cooling, too. All these factors result in wide temperature variations around the globe.

As hot tropical air lifts into the sky, cooler air from temperate latitudes is drawn in to fill the void. In turn, that air warms and rises, drawing in even more cooler air. Meanwhile, heated air migrating toward the Poles cools and descends. Warming and rising, cooling and sinking, the cycle goes on and on, producing and affecting patterns of weather all over the planet.

Cold, dense air is associated with higher pressure while lower pressure is the realm of warmer, lighter air. This fact partially explains the presence of semipermanent belts of high and low pressure that power large-scale wind circulations including the westerlies in the midlatitudes carrying storm systems from west to east across the United States.

30

Embedded in the prevailing westerlies are *jet streams*, fast currents in the flowing rivers of air. A few miles wide and some 30,000 feet above Earth, jet streams move along at several hundred miles an hour. Aircraft pilots traveling east across America sometimes seek out these persistent winds to help them speed their planes toward their destinations, though when they are traveling the other way they are careful to avoid the head-on force of a jet stream.

If Earth were smooth and made up of equal areas of land and water, the prevailing winds would blow in predictable patterns. However, the surface of the globe is irregular both in shape and composition. Mountain ranges jut into the sky, while plains and deserts lie flat. Some areas are heavily forested, others bare, some light in color, some dark. As a result of these variations, the atmosphere warms and cools unevenly, and the speeds and directions of the prevailing winds are altered by the drag of friction and by the physical barriers they encounter. Dividing, combining, weakening, and gaining strength, air masses swirl this way and that, responding to local temperature and terrain and to the presence of other air masses.

Highs and Lows

When warm, high-altitude air cools and sinks, it can form an area of high pressure known simply as a *high*. The barometer rises as a high takes shape, indicating an increase in atmospheric pressure. The dense air in a high-pressure region can keep other weather systems at bay, and the skies generally will be clear.

However, there is only so much atmosphere blanketing Earth; if the air is more concentrated in high-pressure areas, other parts of the sky must be areas of low pressure, or *lows*. As indicated by dropping barometric readings, the air in a low is less dense than that in a high, so it tends to draw in winds laden with moisture. As a result, lows are less stable, cloudier, and stormier than highs.

Polar air masses can bring cold, northerly air into the American heartland. When they collide with moist air masses drifting in from the Pacific Ocean and Gulf of Mexico, much of the country can expect rain or snow. Warm air near the equator tends to rise rather than move horizontally, creating great areas of calm called the *equatorial doldrums* and the *horse latitudes*. Sailing ships of old could languish in calm weather for weeks, waiting for a breeze to fill their slack canvas.

Meteorologists chart the sizes and shapes of highs and lows by preparing maps with lines connecting points registering identical pressure readings. While a topographic map shows variations in terrain by using contour lines to connect all points in an area that are the same elevation above sea level, a weather map uses lines called *isobars* to indicate the relationship of locations reporting the same barometric pressure. Just as contour lines ring a mountain, isobars encircle regions of high pressure, decreasing in value as they move away from the center. Likewise, isobars show low-pressure areas as valleys and sinks in the atmosphere in much the same way contour lines indicate valleys and lowlands on maps of dry land.

Weather Maps

You can access weather maps for any area of the globe via the Internet. Maps of your area can be found in daily newspapers and on televised weather reports. Satellite images show cloud movement across the United States and much of Canada.

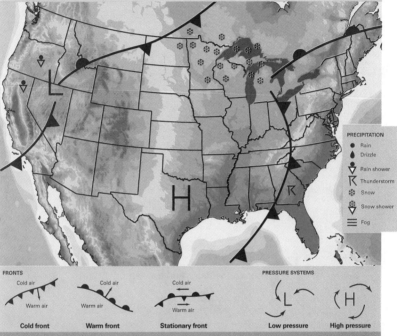

The Coriolis Effect and Prevailing Winds

While Earth's great air masses are flowing from polar regions toward the tropics, the globe is rotating beneath them. As a result, the winds do not appear to travel in straight lines, but rather bend to the right in the northern hemisphere and to the left south of the equator. This phenomenon, named the *Coriolis effect* in honor of its 19th-century French discoverer, causes prevailing weather patterns to curve as they flow across the globe, and at times to overlap, collide, and mesh with one another.

Weather watchers have known about these patterns of air motion for centuries. Sailors since Columbus' time have traveled near the equator to let the trade winds of the tropical Atlantic Ocean push their ships west to America, and then returned to Europe in the westerlies farther north. Today's transcontinental bicyclists know they are more likely to have the wind at their backs when they pedal from the Pacific toward the Atlantic, but if they go the other way, they might fight head-winds much of the time.

30

Beaufort Scale

Developed in the 1800s for the British Royal Navy by Rear Adm. Sir Francis Beaufort, the Beaufort scale is a tool for estimating the force of the wind.

WIND SPEED IN MILES PER HOUR	EFFECTS
Less than 1	Smoke rises straight up; air is calm.
1–3	Smoke drifts.
4–7	Wind is felt on the face; leaves rustle.
8–12	Leaves and twigs constantly rustle; wind extends small flags.
13–18	Dust and small paper are raised; small branches move.
19–24	Crested wavelets form on inland waters; small trees sway.
25–31	Large branches move in trees.
32–38	Large trees sway; must lean to walk.
39–46	Twigs are broken from trees; difficult to walk.
47–54	Limbs break from trees; slight structural damage (chimney posts and shingles are blown off roofs); extremely difficult to walk.
55–63	Trees are uprooted; considerable structural damage occurs.
64–74	Extensive, widespread damage; seldom experienced inland.
75 and up	Hurricane: extreme destruction, severe and extensive damage.

Fronts

Study weather maps for several days in a row, and you'll see that the North American continent can contain a number of air masses, some dominated by high pressure, some by low. Some might be moving very fast, perhaps

pushed along by prevailing winds out of the west. Others might remain stationary for several days. Those pushing in from the Gulf of Mexico or the Pacific Ocean can be loaded with moisture, while cold, high-pressure air masses moving into the prairies between the Appalachians and Rockies are likely to be dry.

As you examine the isobars on a weather map, pay special attention to the areas where different air masses meet. These boundaries are known as *fronts,* and it is along fronts that many changes in weather occur. For instance, a region of cold, dry air overtaking a warm, moist air mass will wedge under the warm air. As the warm air rises, it cools, and the moisture it carries can condense and fall as rain. Observers on the ground probably will notice a shift in the direction of the wind and a variation in temperature as the front moves through and the new air mass establishes itself overhead. They also can watch changes in the shapes of clouds. If they know what to look for, they can predict a change in the weather several hours or even a day before it occurs.

Nimbostratus clouds

Clouds have long fascinated observers, both for the beauty of their shapes and for what they can tell us about changes in the weather.

Clouds

Rising air often lifts moisture into the atmosphere. If it encounters microscopic particles of dust, smoke, or other condensation nuclei, moisture will attach to the particles and form clouds. There are three basic forms of clouds described by their appearance and given their Latin names—*cumulus* (heap), *cirrus* (curl of hair), and *stratus* (layer).

The term *nimbus* (Latin for "violent rain") describes any cloud from which precipitation might fall; thus, a *nimbostratus* is a layer cloud capable of producing rain. The prefix *alto-* indicates that a cloud is in the middle altitudes of the lower atmosphere, between 6,500 and 23,000 feet above Earth's surface. An *altocumulus* is a fluffy heap cloud floating between 1 and 4 miles overhead.

30

The International System of Cloud Classification

Beyond identifying the basic shapes of clouds, meteorologists have devised a system for classifying 10 principal cloud types. Arranged by the clouds that form highest in the atmosphere, they are:

- **Cirrus**—thin, whispy clouds sometimes described as mare's tails or curls of hair
- **Cirrocumulus**—small cloudlets that resemble ripples or grains
- **Cirrostratus**—thin veil of cloud that covers the sky
- **Altocumulus**—globs of clouds in patches or layers
- **Altostratus**—thin cloud sheets or layers that appear bluish or gray

- **Nimbostratus**—dark layers of ragged clouds, usually carrying rain
- **Stratocumulus**—sheets of lumpy clouds, usually with some dark patches
- **Stratus**—uniform, low layers of clouds that cover the entire sky
- **Cumulus**—large, individual puffy clouds that appear in heaps
- **Cumulonimbus**—large, towering clouds associated with thunderstorms

Cumulus

Cirrus

Stratus

Using Clouds to Predict Weather

The movement of a frontal system often is heralded by a procession of different cloud types, each signaling a greater likelihood that local weather conditions are about to change. The first sign of an approaching storm might be the appearance in a clear sky of high, feathery cirrus clouds known as *mare's tails.* Over the course of several hours or days, they will thicken until the sun is hidden behind a thin cirrostratus veil. A gray curtain of altostratus clouds comes next, followed by a moist blanket of dark stratus clouds rolling close to Earth. Finally, nimbostratus clouds, black and threatening, bring the rain.

Of course, not all clouds signal bad weather. Cirrus clouds detached from one another indicate that the weather will stay fair for a while. A mackerel sky formed by cirrocumulus clouds that look like the scales of a fish usually promises fair weather, but it also might bring unsettled conditions with brief showers. Outdoor groups eager for dry trails welcome the sight of cumulus clouds. On hot days, however, travelers are wise to keep an eye on swelling cumulus clouds and take cover if those clouds develop into dark cumulonimbus thunderheads, the breeders of violent storms.

For information on preparing for different kinds of weather in the backcountry, see the chapter titled "Planning a Trek."

Thunderstorms

A thunderstorm bearing lightning, heavy rains, and strong winds can be a menace to anyone in its path. The danger increases if the storm also generates hail or spawns tornadoes.

A thunderstorm begins when cumulus clouds surge into the sky, gaining thousands of feet of elevation in a few minutes. The surge is powered by solar heat churning the atmosphere and by winds converging and forcing moisture-laden air upward. Air will continue to rise, carrying moisture with it, as long as it is warmer than the atmosphere around it. When the moisture begins to cool and condense, cumulus clouds transform into cumulonimbus clouds. These thunderheads can billow to altitudes of 60,000 feet where the boundary of the troposphere prevents further ascent and horizontal winds flatten the tops of the clouds to create the distinctive anvil shapes of fully developed thunderheads.

Eventually the rising air can no longer support all the moisture lifted high into a thunderhead, and the moisture will rush back to Earth as rain and sometimes hail. The descending precipitation drags air with it, and that might create strong winds near the ground. Heavy precipitation also drains the energy from a thunderstorm. Within half an hour of the start of rain, a storm is often over. If it is part of a broader weather front, it might give way to steady rain.

Heat generated as the sun beats down on prairie regions provides the energy driving the formation of thunderstorms. In mountainous zones, warm air rising up alpine slopes can encounter instability in the atmosphere above, generating thunderstorms in the afternoon, even if the morning skies were clear.

Hail

A pellet of ice descending through a thunderhead might grow as it is coated with freezing moisture. Some pellets are caught in a cycle of updrafts and descents, increasing in size as they swirl through the clouds until they become too heavy for the winds to keep aloft.

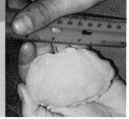

Lightning

Lightning kills about 90 people each year in the United States. Charged with 100 million volts of electricity and traveling at 31,000 miles per second, lightning heats a narrow pathway of air to 45,000 degrees Fahrenheit. The resulting violent expansion and subsequent rapid collapse of the air causes a clap of thunder.

The basic electrical charge of Earth's surface is negative, while that of the upper troposphere is positive. Lightning forms when electricity moves between areas of opposite electrical charge. When the weather is clear, there is nothing between the ground and the sky to conduct electricity, but when a thunderhead forms, positive and negative charges build within its parts, allowing lightning to travel within a cloud, between clouds, or from a cloud to the ground.

The instability of electrical charges within a cloud is heightened by collisions of ice crystals and hail, and by differences in air temperature at different altitudes. When the imbalance becomes great enough between negatively charged and positively charged areas of clouds, or between a cloud and the ground, electrons form a pathway called a leader and flood from one zone to the other. If that connection includes Earth's surface, electrons will take the path of least resistance—through a solitary tree, perhaps, or the summit of a mountain—and a lightning strike occurs.

For information on protecting yourself and others from lightning, see the chapter titled "Managing Risk."

Local Weather

Despite the broad application of basic principles of meteorology, weather conditions in your area might not match the overall patterns of prevailing winds, highs and lows, and fronts. That's because the weather in each part of the country is influenced by local terrain, bodies of water, and a host of other variables. For instance, coastal regions might be cooler and moister than territory a few miles inland. A mountain range might force warm air to rise, wringing out its moisture as snow and rain. Prairies can allow fronts to roll unimpeded for hundreds of miles.

Learning the patterns of weather in your part of the country can be very satisfying and useful. Glance at the sky whenever you are outdoors and notice the kinds of clouds you see, the direction of the wind, and the sort of weather you're having. Gradually you can build up enough observations to realize that winds from a certain direction usually indicate rain, and that clouds of a certain type mean the skies will clear soon.

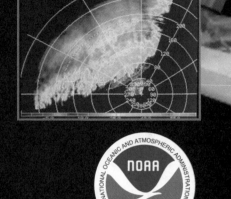

Resources for Forecasting Weather

Radio, television, and newspaper weather reports and forecasts can give you some guidance as you prepare for a trek adventure. So can Internet sites devoted to meteorology. Up-to-the-minute weather information is also available from the National Oceanic and Atmospheric Administration (NOAA). NOAA Weather Radio, operating on high-band FM frequencies, transmits updates that can be received by special receivers and by AM/FM radios equipped with a weather-band feature.

Meteorologists have many tools for gathering information. Among the most effective is Doppler radar, capable of showing squall lines and other weather features moving through an area.

Learn the historical weather extremes for the area you plan to travel, and prepare for somewhat worse conditions than the norms. If extreme weather does occur, you will be able to cope with it.

Traditional Weather Signs

There is plenty of folklore connected with weather. "Red sky at morning, sailor take warning," goes one old saying, often true since the brilliance of a sunrise can be caused by moisture in the air that later in the day turns to rain. As for "Red sky at night, sailor's delight," a brilliant, red sunset usually indicates that there is clear, dry air to the west, the direction from which most storms come.

Animals also play a role in weather lore. Perhaps you've heard old-timers base their predictions of the severity of an upcoming winter upon the woolliness of caterpillars or the thickness of squirrels' coats. Birds, their hollow bones especially sensitive to changes in atmospheric pressure, might alter their flying habits to match certain changes in the weather, and many other animals are thought to become restless and seek shelter long before humans are aware of an approaching storm.

Regardless of whether there is sufficient scientific data to support the claims of folklore adages, old sayings and beliefs provide a fascinating glimpse into the way weather predictions were made before the development of accurate measuring devices. Consider these ages-old indicators of fair weather and foul listed on the following page.

30

Signs of Fair Weather

Expect pleasant weather when you see some of these signs:

- "Red sky at night, sailor's delight." The dust particles in the dry air of tomorrow's weather produce a glowing red sunset.

- "Swallows flying way up high mean there's no rain in the sky." Swallows are birds that catch and eat flying insects. In the high air pressure that comes with fair weather, insects can be carried aloft by air currents.

- "If smoke goes high, no rain comes by." Campfire smoke rises straight up when there is no wind. Still air is generally stable and won't move moisture into an area.

- "When the dew is on the grass, rain will never come to pass." Dew forms when air moisture condenses on cool leaves and grass. That happens especially during the cool, clear nights that come with good weather and high pressure.

Signs of Stormy Weather

The following signs suggest bad weather is on the way:

- "Red sky at morning, sailor take warning." Dry, dusty air is moving away from you toward the east. Clouds and moist air might be coming in from the west.

- "Swallows flying near the ground mean a storm will come around." The low air pressure that pulls in stormy weather causes insects to fly close to the ground on heavy, moist wings. Swallows feeding on them will follow.

- "If smoke hangs low, watch out for a blow." Low air pressure can prevent campfire smoke from rising very high.

- "When grass is dry at morning light, look for rain before the night." On a cloudy night, grass might not cool enough for dew to form.

"The weather is always doing something . . . always getting up new designs and trying them on the people to see how they will go."

—Mark Twain (1835–1910), American author and satirist

CHAPTER
31

Plants

"The earth's vegetation is part of a web of life in which there are intimate and essential relations between plants and the earth, between plants and other plants, between plants and animals."

—Rachel Carson (Her 1962 book *Silent Spring* questioned the use of pesticides and aroused worldwide concern for protecting the environment.)

Shade. Nourishment. Beauty. Breath. Life. The contributions of plants and plant communities are vital to existence. Vegetation is so universal that it is easy for us to overlook what is all around us. When we take notice, though, we can begin to see the astonishing diversity of the plant kingdom. In size, shape, aroma, texture, and means of adapting to their settings, plants are remarkable members of ecosystems, connected with all other species on the planet.

You can find plant life almost anywhere. Deserts, prairies, shorelines, and urban parks abound with a stunning variety of vegetation. Plant communities thrive in the mountains, too, and bring richness and variety to wetlands, woodlands, tundra, and forests.

Plants pump oxygen into the atmosphere and cleanse it of carbon dioxide. They offer shelter and food for wildlife. Vegetation forming ground cover slows the runoff of rain, allowing it to seep into the earth. Roots prevent soil from washing away. Decaying leaves and other plant matter enrich the soil. In their simplicity and grandeur, members of the plant kingdom are key elements in the cycles of nature, and essential components of all ecosystems. Two plant communities of particular interest to outdoor travelers are forests and prairies.

Forests

From the highest branches to the deepest roots, a forest forms a belt of life up to several hundred feet thick composed of thousands of species of plants and animals. Broad-leaved forests dominate the eastern United States, while conifer forests cover much of the West. These great stands of vegetation shield Earth from the forces of wind, rain, and sunlight. They slow erosion, act as watersheds, and provide havens for animals. Photosynthesis—the process by which most plants manufacture their food—produces oxygen and removes carbon dioxide, which continually freshens the air.

A mature forest consists of levels, or *strata*, all of them essential to the health of a forest ecosystem. Typical forest strata are the canopy, understory, shrub layer, herb layer, and litter layer.

Canopy

The branches and leaves forming the highest reaches of a forest—the canopy—capture maximum sunlight. They also provide shelter and shade for the strata below. Formed by the largest and oldest trees, the canopy is home to birds, climbing mammals, and insects.

Understory

Smaller and younger trees thriving in the broken shade beneath the canopy form the understory of the forest. As canopy trees die, some in the understory will grow to take their places.

Shrub Layer

Bushes and thickets of plants with woody stems form the shrub layer, which rises above the ground to about shoulder height. It is this layer that can pose a serious challenge to off-trail travelers when dense vegetation makes hiking difficult.

Herb Layer

A forest's herb layer is composed of the dense ground cover of grasses, flowers, ferns, and other soft-stemmed vegetation.

Litter Layer

This surface layer that botanists call litter is as important to a forest as any of its other layers. Made up of organic material including decomposing leaves, branches, tree trunks, and other parts of dead vegetation, litter is home to beetles, snails, millipedes, and many other animal species. It protects the soil and serves as a moist bed in which new plants can take root. As litter decays, phosphorus, potassium, magnesium, calcium, nitrogen, and other nutrients return to the soil where they can be absorbed by living plants.

Understory layer

Shrub layer

Herb layer

Litter layer

Nurse Logs

Long after their deaths, trees falling to the ground play an important role in the life of a forest. Termites, beetles, worms, and other creatures burrow into the wood, allowing moisture to seep in. Fungi and mosses take hold, softening the wood and creating an inviting germination bed for larger plant species. Covered with young vegetation and slowly decomposing into the forest floor, these old trees act as "nurse logs" that help ensure the health of future generations of vegetation. They also provide important cover for small mammals, reptiles, and amphibians.

Prairies

Grasslands cover nearly a fourth of Earth's land surface, creating ecosystems that rival forests in complexity and importance. The steppes of Asia, the savannas and veldts in Africa, and the pampas of South America all are vast grasslands. In North America, the term for extensive grasslands is prairie.

Just as trees are the most noticeable members of a forest community, prairies are dominated by grasses. Storms batter them, animals trample and graze upon them, droughts dry them out, and fires consume them, but grasses endure, recovering quickly from nearly all abuse to thrive again.

Like a mature forest, a fully formed prairie is made up of distinct layers. Big bluestem and similar grasses tower above other species to form a prairie's tallest stratum. Interspersed among the grasses are wildflowers—pasque-flowers, prairie goldenpea, shooting stars, wild roses, and many others. As prairie grasses and flowers die, they mat down to create a dense, tough ground cover. The roots of plants extend deep below the surface, creating stability and guarding the soil from erosion.

31

Various species of animals thrive upon different levels of the prairie, from antelope, bison, and other mammals grazing on the grasses to earthworms, prairie dogs, and moles finding shelter underground. Many find cover in riparian zones—borders of trees and other woody vegetation growing along the moist banks of prairie streams. By shading the water, the trees of riparian zones can make streams more inviting for fish and other aquatic species. Isolated trees and prairie brush also serve as home for birds and other wildlife.

Old-Growth Forests and Native Prairies

Forests that have never been felled and prairies that have never been plowed are mature ecosystems with finely tuned cycles of growth and decay. Large numbers of plants and animals are interwoven to create a rich diversity that makes these environments very stable. As with wilderness, old-growth forests and native prairies are important for their biological diversity and as reminders of the astonishing ways in which nature functions when left undisturbed by people.

Forest Fires and Prairie Fires

Most fires in forests and prairies are naturally occurring events caused by lightning. Such a fire might burn thousands of acres of timber and sweep across miles of prairie. To those who liked the prairie and the forest as they were, a fire might seem like a great waste. However, the flames that char the trees also consume much of the brush and dead wood choking the understory of the forest, releasing nutrients into the soil and providing a fertile bed for new growth.

Mature trees often can withstand the heat of occasional fires because their bark is dense enough to prevent them from being seriously damaged. The cones of some pines open only after they have felt the heat of a fire, germinating in the ashes and sending up saplings as a new forest begins. Animals can move more freely through land opened by fire, and can browse on the newly sprouted vegetation. Even when large trees are completely burned, the land is left ready for the process of forest succession to begin once more.

Likewise, fire has always been a part of healthy grassland ecosystems. Fire burns away dead prairie vegetation and fire-intolerant invasive plants, releasing nutrients that can be absorbed by the root systems of existing plants and by germinating seeds. The prairie is refreshed and able to thrive again.

Much modern concern about fires results in part from our efforts to manage forests. Forest management practices that seek to eliminate all fires and timbering can allow fuel loads to build up on forest floors, leading to infrequent fires that are hotter and more destructive than might have occurred if the natural cycles of fire and regeneration had been allowed to play themselves out.

For more on ways to help protect the outdoors, see the "Leaving No Trace" section of this book and the chapter titled "Being Good Stewards of Our Resources."

Plant Divisions

31

There are hundreds of thousands of known species of plants. Botanists organizing vegetation into understandable groups have classified all complex plants as members of one of five divisions—mosses, club mosses, horsetails, ferns, and seed plants.

Mosses (Bryophytes)

Mosses are small, nonflowering plants generally not more than a few centimeters tall that grow in rock crevices, on forest floors and tree trunks, and along the banks of streams. Many have a small spore capsule at the end of a stalk that rises above a leafy base. Haircap moss, apple moss, and the closely related liverworts and hornworts typify this group. Most of the mosses and their close relatives live in moist areas on land.

Moss

Club Mosses (Lycopsids)

Despite the name, club mosses differ from true mosses because they are vascular—that is, they have veins. Club mosses play a small role among today's plants. Eons ago though, they included vast forests of trees up to a hundred feet tall, forests that scientists believe were to become many of the coal deposits of Europe and North America.

Ground pine

Horsetails (Equisetophytes)

Horsetails are an ancient group of plants, relatively unchanged for eons. These plants with hollow, jointed, and usually grooved stems reproduce with spores rather than seeds, and thus have no flowers. Strobili, cone-shaped structures atop the horsetail stems, produce the spores. Horsetails have been used for medicinal purposes and as scouring brushes for cleaning pots.

Horsetail

Ferns (Pteridophytes) and Their Allies

Although they share with seed plants the presence of chlorophyll and vascular tissues, ferns reproduce without seeds. Ferns often have lacy leaves called fronds. Uncurling in the spring, the fronds of some ferns resemble the decorative ends of violins, and thus are called fiddleheads. Ferns are most abundant in the shade of moist forests. Fern allies include closely related whisk ferns, horsetails, quillworts, club mosses, and spike mosses.

Fern, showing a fiddlehead

Giant sequoia

Seed Plants (Spermatophytes)

The great majority of Earth's plants are those that produce seeds. Among them are the most ancient living beings on the planet, including 4,000-year-old intermountain bristlecone pines, and the largest, including giant sequoias that can achieve a mass of more than 2,500 metric tons.

Seed plants are divided into two groups: nonflowering plants (gymnosperms), such as conifers, ginkgos, and ephedras; and flowering plants (angiosperms), such as wildflowers, grasses, and flowering trees and shrubs.

Trees

Many thousands of species of trees grow in North America, and thousands more flourish in other parts of the world. Trees are characterized by their size (usually taller than the height of a person) and by the fact that each usually has a single woody stem, or trunk. (Shrubs, on the other hand, have multiple woody stems, and seldom grow much beyond 8 to 10 feet in height.)

Anatomy of a Tree

Roots

Much of a tree is beneath the ground. Tiny root hairs absorb moisture and send it up into the tree. A root system also is the anchor that holds a tree upright, even in high winds. Some trees have taproots that extend deep into the earth. Others, especially those growing in thin or rocky soils, have roots that spread out just below the surface, sometimes achieving a radius as wide as the tree is tall.

Trunk and Bark

Bark is the outer armor of a tree's trunk and branches. Sapwood beneath the bark transports moisture from the roots to the leaves. Between the sapwood and bark is a thin layer of tissue called the *phloem* that channels food produced by the leaves into the trunk and the roots. In the center of the trunk is hardened wood called *heartwood* that gives the tree much of its structural strength. The cambium grows a new layer of sapwood around the trunk each year. Count the rings formed by the layers and you'll know how many years a tree was alive.

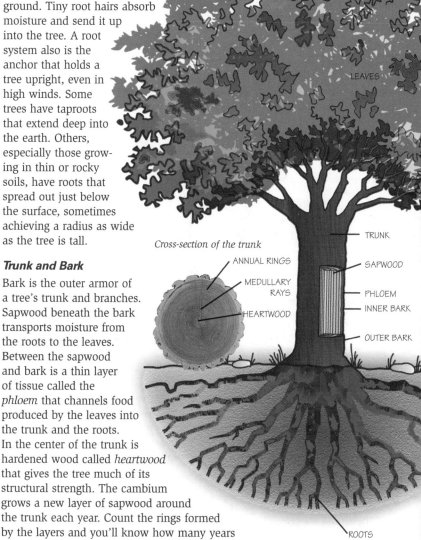

CROWN

LEAVES

TRUNK

Cross-section of the trunk

ANNUAL RINGS

MEDULLARY RAYS

HEARTWOOD

SAPWOOD

PHLOEM

INNER BARK

OUTER BARK

ROOTS

31

Leaves

Chlorophyll, a chemical compound in leaves, draws power from sunlight to convert carbon dioxide and water into plant food. This process, called *photosynthesis*, also returns oxygen to the atmosphere. Green plants produce the oxygen that supports all of Earth's animal life, humans included.

Conifers

Conifers are a type of gymnosperm—plants with naked seeds tucked inside the cones. Exposed to the elements, conifer ovules can be fertilized directly by windblown pollen. Rather than relying on insects to aid in pollenation, conifers release pollen that blows from tree to tree, an ideal transport mechanism in alpine regions and other settings where there are plenty of breezes but perhaps not many bugs. The compact Christmas-tree shape of pines, firs, spruces, and other conifers helps them shed rain, snow, and wind.

Conifers are particularly well-suited to high elevations and northern latitudes where growing seasons are short. The needlelike leaves of most conifers don't fall off, allowing those trees to spur growth as soon as the days begin to warm in the spring. (There are a few deciduous conifers, including cypress, larch, and tamarack, that do lose their leaves.)

PINUS SEED

ROSACEAE FLOWER

Stamen

Petal

Pistil

Ovary

Sepal

Conifers and Broad-Leaved Trees

The two large groups of trees are conifer trees and broad-leaved trees. Broad-leaved trees bear flowers, and most are deciduous—they shed their leaves, typically in autumn, and grow new ones in the spring. Many fruit trees, including the apple, apricot, and plum, are of the rosaceae family. Its flower contains the stamens, pistil, ovary, petals, and sepals, all of which are crucial to reproduction.

Conifers, also known as evergreens, are cone-bearing trees with needlelike or scalelike leaves that stay on many of the trees for several years. The seeds of a pine tree will remain inside the cone for up to two years until the cones open, allowing the seeds to fall out.

Broad-Leaved Trees

Broad-leaved trees are angiosperms—flowering plants with ovules protected inside ovaries. Fertilized ovules develop into seeds. Unlike the cones protecting the seeds of conifers, seeds of broad-leaved trees are enclosed in fruits such as nuts, or some other forms of seed cases.

As their name implies, most of these trees have wide, flat leaves. Many broad-leaved trees have trunks that branch out into round, airy shapes. They do well where conditions during the growing season are not harsh. Everything about them, from leaf shape to the orientation of branches, plays into their survival and their ability to adapt to their environments. Losing their leaves in the autumn, for example, helps protect branches from breaking under the weight of winter snows.

Why Leaves Change Color

Each autumn, the foliage of many broad-leaved trees turns from green to brilliant red, orange, or yellow, and then brown. In fact, those bright hues were in the leaves all summer, hidden beneath the green of the chlorophyll. As the growing season comes to an end, a tree's food production drops and so does the amount of chlorophyll in the leaves. The green fades, allowing the fiery colors to show through.

Another change causes a layer of cells at the base of the leafstalk to cut tissues holding the leaf on the tree. The leaf falls to the ground where it will decompose, returning nutrients to the soil.

Identifying Trees

You don't have to know the names of trees to appreciate them. "The biggest tree in our campsite" might be all the identification you need to share information with friends who have pitched their tents in the same place.

Knowing the name of the tree can open a world of information to you. If you discover that the tree is an ash, you can easily research its geographic range, qualities of the wood, the tree's fruiting bodies, its life span, and ways in which it interacts with other species.

Identifying a tree can be simple. "You can tell a dogwood by its bark," the old-timers say, and they're right. The appearance of the bark is one of several important pieces of evidence that can lead to discovering the name of a tree. Other characteristics to notice are its shape, leaves, and the way it fits into its environment.

Tree Shape

A tree's silhouette can be as distinctive as a fingerprint is for a human. Some trees spread great branches of leaves toward the sky to absorb as much sunlight as possible. Other trees have shorter, tighter shapes that help them endure storms and shed snow. Here are some of the most common tree shapes:

Pyramid	*Column*	*Palm*
Weeping	*Round*	*Cone*
Irregular	*Oval*	*Vase*

Bark

Tree bark is notable for its variations in shape and texture. Some varieties are shown here:

Peeling

Plated

Smooth

Flaked

Furrowed

Leaves

While shape and bark reveal much about a tree, its leaves probably are the most commonly used clues for determining its identity. For starters, leaves of conifer trees are in the shapes of needles or scales. Those of deciduous trees are broad, and might appear singly, in various combinations, or in sets that alternate on a branch or are opposite one another. Basic leaf shapes of broad-leaved trees include the following:

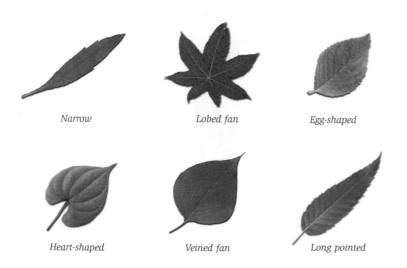

Narrow

Lobed fan

Egg-shaped

Heart-shaped

Veined fan

Long pointed

Nomenclature of Trees and Other Plants

Plant naming can be very specific, using Latin terms to describe each species. This system of using standardized names, or *nomenclature,* allows botanists and others who study plants to share accurate information about particular plant species.

Plant Keys

The most useful tools for studying plants are plant keys, which group plants based on similarities they share. Plant keys are available both as books and as interactive Web sites.

A powerful aspect of a plant key is its ability to guide you step-by-step to the identity of a plant species. Each plant key addresses particular kinds of vegetation (trees, for example, or mushrooms or wildflowers), and may be further focused on a specific region (the trees of North America, for instance, or the mosses and ferns of the Pacific Northwest).

RED OR NORTHERN RED OAK

FAMILY: Fagaceae   SPECIES: *Quercus rubra*

LEAF PERSISTENCE: *Deciduous*

TREE BARK: *Furrowed*

FRUIT: *Acorn*

TREE HEIGHT: *80 feet (25 meters)*

TREE SHAPE: *Broadly spreading*

Using a Plant Key

Plant keys typically are constructed with an either-or format, asking you to answer a series of questions that will steadily narrow your choices until you come upon the specific description of the plant you want to identify. A typical sequence might lead you this way:

❶ Needlelike leaves or broad-leaved? If broad-leaved, then . . .

❷ Compound leaves or simple leaves? If compound, then . . .

❸ Thorns or spines present, or thorns or spines absent? If without thorns or spines, then . . .

❹ Are leaves smooth, toothed, or lobed? If lobed, then . . .

❺ Are leaves arranged opposite each other on the twigs, or do they alternate? If opposite, then . . .

❻ Are leaves heart-shaped or oval? If oval, then . . .

Identification keys are available for trees, shrubs, flowers, and many other plants, as well as for mushrooms and animals.

Once you have identified a plant, the plant key can provide a wealth of information about the species, often including its normal geographic range, its general size and shape, and descriptions of fruiting bodies, leaves, and bark.

Plant identification is most effective when it is done in a plant's natural setting where you have a wide range of clues to help you—appearance, aromas, and evidence of the interaction between a particular plant and other species of plants and animals. You also can observe the full array of leaves and determine whether they are staggered, opposed, or in clusters.

Identifying Dormant Trees

Most conifers look much the same in the winter as they do in the summer; however, dormant broad-leaved trees will have lost their leaves, and also will be missing color, aroma, and other clues useful in determining their identity. You might be able to make an accurate identification using the tree's bark, shape, and orientation of branches and twigs. A leaf picked up from the ground beneath the tree also can be a strong clue, though there's a possibility it is from a different tree, blown there by the wind. Make your best winter guess as to the identity of a tree, then come back in the spring or summer and see if your guess was right.

A Sampling of North American Conifers

Pines

Many species of pine trees thrive in North America, each finding an ecosystem for which it is particularly well-suited.

The white pine, found throughout the Northeast, is recognizable by its smooth, tight bark and leaf clusters of five needles each. It is the tree featured on the state flag of Maine. Other pines common in the Eastern states include the pitch pine with three needles per cluster, and the jack and red pines with two needles. In the Southeast, the longleaf and loblolly pines have three needles to a cluster, while slash and shortleaf pines display two.

The largest pines grow in the mountains of the West. Sugar pines can reach a height of 200 feet. Look for five needles in each of its leaf clusters. The heavy cones of sugar pines can be 18 inches long.

Jeffrey pines have long needles in groups of three. Get close to the bark of a Jeffrey or ponderosa pine and you might smell a pleasant vanillalike aroma. Ponderosa and knobcone are other Western pines with three-needle clusters. Lodgepole pines, named for the straight, clean trunks some American Indian tribes used to set up their tepees and lodges, have clusters of two needles each.

Conifer forests can be found in many parts of the United States.

Lodgepole pine

Ponderosa pine

Red cedar

Redwood

Colorado blue spruce

Many conifers have the Christmas-tree look of an inverted cone.

31

White spruce

Balsam fir

Larch

Tamarack

Eastern hemlock

Douglas fir

Spruces

The needles of spruce trees are four-sided in shape. The Engelmann spruce, found in Southwestern states and in the forests of the Rocky Mountains and the Pacific Coast, has soft needles with a blue-green hue. The blue spruce, growing primarily in New England, the Rockies, and Southwestern states, has needles that are stiff. The tallest American spruce is the Sitka spruce of rain-drenched Pacific Northwest coastal forests.

Firs

Fir needles are flat and flexible, and appear to be arranged in orderly rows along the sides of branches. The needles are dark green on top, while the undersides show two white lines. Fir cones grow upright on the upper branches of the trees. The balsam fir of the East and the white fir of the West are stately, fragrant representatives of these evergreens.

Larches and Tamaracks

The soft needles of the larch grow in tufts out of old-growth bumps on the branches. Unlike those of most other conifers, larch and tamarack leaves fall off in the winter. Larches are tall, slender trees with small cones.

Hemlocks

Hemlocks are large evergreens identified by short, flat needles with dark green tops and silvery undersides. The small cones hang from branches that can droop in the shape of a graceful pyramid.

Douglas Firs

Douglas firs are found primarily in the western United States. Also known as the Douglas spruce, red fir, and Oregon pine, the tree actually is of the pine family, as are spruces, firs, larches, and tamaracks. Its flat needlelike leaves spiral around the branches, giving them the appearance of bottle brushes or squirrels' tails.

Sequoias and Redwoods

The world's largest trees are the redwoods and giant sequoias of California. Redwoods can grow to over 300 feet in height, and sequoias to a diameter of more than 25 feet. Some of these trees reach several thousand years of age.

Cedars, Junipers, and Cypresses

The leaves of cedars are tiny, bright-green scales arranged like small shingles on flattened twigs.

The western red cedar is, in fact, a juniper. Junipers have two kinds of leaves. Some are scaly and flat like a cedar, while others are prickly. Juniper cones look like moldy blueberries.

The bald cypress of the South drops its needles each winter, and some kinds of cypress grow in swamps; portions of their roots exposed above the water are called *knees*.

Bald cypress

Identifying Firs, Spruces, and Pines

As a quick rule of thumb to determine some of the larger groups of conifers, examine their needles and note their shape, then apply these identifications:

Flat needles = fir

Square needles = spruce

Pairs or clusters of needles = pine

Scaly, shingled needles = cedars

Aspen trees

Pussy willows

A Sampling of North American Broad-Leaved Trees

Willows and Aspens

The pussy willow takes its name from its furry flower clusters that resemble tiny kittens clinging to the willow's long, straight branches. The sandbar willow often is one of the first plants to grow on new ground formed by shifting river currents.

Aspens thrive on sunlight. They take root quickly on mountain slopes burned by fire, protecting the soil from erosion and providing browse for deer, elk, moose, and other animals. As slower-growing conifers mature, they tower above the aspens and eventually create so much shade that the aspens must give way.

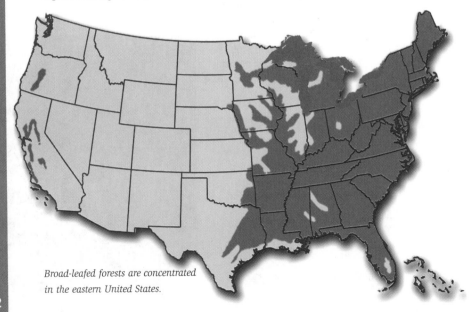

Broad-leafed forests are concentrated in the eastern United States.

Pistache

Western catalpa

American elm

White oak

Paperbark maple

Deciduous trees flourish in the temperate climate of the Northeast.

31

Nut Trees

Walnuts and hickories have compound leaves, each made up of a number of leaflets. A hickory leaf has three to nine leaflets, while the leaf of a walnut tree might have more than a dozen. Walnuts and hickory nuts are the seeds of their trees. Both are good to eat, as are the nuts of pecan trees. Mockernut, bitternut, and pignut trees have small, bitter kernels.

Bitternut hickory

Walnut

The Birch Family

This family of broad-leaved trees includes birches, hornbeams, and alders. The trees are most commonly found in the East and Northeast. Their oval leaves have jagged edges and shiny surfaces.

Birch

American Indians used sheets of white bark from the paper birch to build their canoes. The bark of yellow birch peels away from the trunk in curls. Gray and black birches have much tighter bark.

The wood of the smooth-barked American hornbeam is so tough that the tree is sometimes called ironwood. The trunk resembles a person's muscular arm.

Alders grow in moist ground throughout the country. They have broad leaves, stalked buds, and small, conelike fruits.

Beeches and Chestnuts

American beech

You can identify an American beech tree by its smooth, pale gray bark. Like those of the birches, each beech leaf has a strong midrib and parallel side veins. Its burrlike fruit contains two triangular nuts.

The chestnut was once common in forests of the eastern United States until the appearance of the chestnut blight, a fungal disease that killed so many of the trees you would probably have a hard time locating an American chestnut today.

Oaks

Acorns

Wood from America's oak trees has long been prized by carpenters and cabinetmakers. Oak timbers are slow to rot, even if they are wet. The Revolutionary War ship USS *Constitution* ("Old Ironsides") was made of oak, and hand-hewn oak beams were used in many Colonial homes.

The acorn is the fruit of an oak. Most oaks have notched leaves. The lobes on the leaves of some oaks are rounded, while those of others come to sharp points. One exception is the live oak; its leaves have smooth edges and no lobes at all, but its acorns help you identify it as an oak.

31

Elms

Elms are large, graceful shade trees found at one time in towns and cities throughout the nation. The leaves of American elms and slippery elms are egg-shaped and lopsided with saw-toothed edges. Leaves of American elms are shiny and smooth. Despite the name, the leaves of the slippery elm have dull, rough surfaces. Dutch elm disease, caused by a fungus, has wiped out the elm populations in many parts of the United States.

American elm

Magnolias

Magnolia trees are found in the southeastern United States. Their large, distinctive leaves are shiny dark green on top and pale underneath. One magnolia, the cucumber tree, bears a mass of many small, elongated pods.

Another member of the magnolia family is the tulip tree, a very tall tree named for the tuliplike appearance of its flowers. The tulip tree is one of the few members of the magnolia family that is native to North America. It once flourished throughout the continent, but now grows only in the eastern United States.

Magnolia

Papaws and Sassafras Trees

The common papaw belongs to the custard-apple family. It is found in forests of the East and Midwest. The fruit of the papaw looks and tastes like a chubby, overripe banana.

Tea made from the dried root bark of the sassafras tree is an old household remedy for colds. On the same tree you can find leaves of many shapes—some oval, some like three-fingered mittens.

Papaw

Gums and Sycamores

The sweet gum tree has star-shaped leaves that turn a brilliant red in autumn. Its fruits look like spiny balls.

The fruit of the sycamore has a similar shape, but doesn't have the spines. The bark of a sycamore gives the trunk a distinctive patchwork of large blotches of white, green, and yellow.

American sycamore

Sweet gum

31

Plums and Cherries

A dozen varieties of wild plum trees grow in the eastern United States. Look in the woods for small trees with shiny oval leaves and purple or reddish fruits. The hard pit inside each fruit contains the seed of a new tree.

Wild bird cherry or pin cherry are small trees with tiny red fruits in clusters of two or three. Other wild cherries have fruits arranged in bunches.

Plum

Wild cherry

Maples

The leaves of maples are arranged in pairs opposite each other on the branch. Their main veins come out like fingers from the base of the leaf. Fruits of maple trees, called *samaras,* each have a "wing" attached that causes them to twirl through the air.

Maple

Buckeyes

Inside a tough, spiny burr is the fruit of the buckeye. Its size and shiny brown surface make it look something like the eye of a deer, and thus its name. Leaves of buckeyes have five long leaflets. Ohio, the Buckeye State, takes its nickname from this tree.

Buckeye

Ashes

Many ax handles and baseball bats are made from the hard, smooth wood of the ash tree. Each ash leaf is made up of many leaflets that grow in pairs on either side of the stalk. The leaves are in pairs, too, and so are the branches of the tree.

Flowers

Flowers are the reproductive parts of many plants. The shapes and bright colors of flower petals attract insects and other animals that spread pollen among the plants. The male part of the flower, the *stamen,* produces pollen. The female part of the plant, the *pistil,* receives the pollen. The pistil often is shaped like a stalk with a knob on top. Insects, bats, and birds pollinate many flower species as they move from plant to plant.

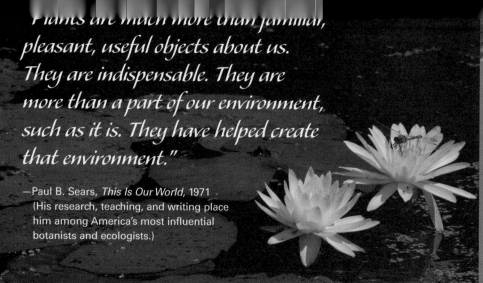

*Plants are much more than familiar,
pleasant, useful objects about us.
They are indispensable. They are
more than a part of our environment,
such as it is. They have helped create
that environment.*"

—Paul B. Sears, *This Is Our World*, 1971
(His research, teaching, and writing place
him among America's most influential
botanists and ecologists.)

Native Plants, Exotics, and Weeds

The role of vegetation in ensuring the diversity of an ecosystem is starkly evident when desirable native plants are pushed out by weeds. The cause of these disruptions often is human activities. Solutions also can rest with our actions.

Native plants are those that are the natural inhabitants of an area. A nonnative plant is one that has been introduced to an area. Whether native or nonnative, plants that spread aggressively and push out species important for a healthy ecosystem often earn the designation of weeds.

A noxious or invasive plant is a weed designated by law as undesirable and requiring control. These plants usually are nonnative and highly invasive; some examples are passion flower, Scotch broom, purple fringe, and spotted knapweed. Weeds crowding out native vegetation can create a monoculture, an area dominated by a single species. When that happens, plant diversity is lost.

Many native plants have fibrous root systems that provide soil cover, stability, and water infiltration while many weeds have narrow taproots that leave bare soil exposed to erosion. Other weeds have roots that penetrate deeper than those of native plants, allowing them to tap more water and thus crowd out native vegetation.

Weed seeds can be spread by wind, water, livestock, wildlife, vehicles, and people. Outdoor users traveling with horses, mules, or other livestock often carry hay that is specially treated to prevent the seeds of weeds it might contain from taking root and competing with native vegetation.

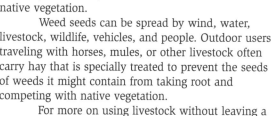

Yellow star thistle

For more on using livestock without leaving a trace, see the chapter titled "Riding and Packing." For more on ways to improve the environment by controlling weeds, see the chapter titled "Being Good Stewards of Our Resources."

Wildlife

"Knowing the names that humans have given to other creatures or things is far from the most important lesson you will teach."

—Rachel Carson (1907–1964), American ecologist and writer

A cocoon warming in the sunlight slowly breaks open, and a majestic butterfly emerges, greatly changed from the caterpillar it once was. A salmon hurls itself against a thundering cascade, fighting upstream to lay its eggs. Bats swirling from the mouth of a cave find their evening meal of flying insects by carefully monitoring the echoes of their high-frequency clicks. A bullfrog watching a newly hatched butterfly dry its wings flicks out its sticky tongue, and the butterfly is no more.

The world's animals are profound in their complexity, astonishing in their variety, and fascinating in their activities and habits. Wildlife thrive almost everywhere—from the depths of the sea to the highest mountain ranges, from the driest deserts to the wettest rain forests, from a city park near your home to the wilderness areas of national forests and parks. By gaining an understanding about animals, you can begin to see how species interact with one another within their ecosystems.

Salmon swimming upstream

No matter what habitat is home—desert, alpine, forest, prairie, aquatic—every animal needs food, water, shelter, and space. Changes in the combination of an ecosystem's basic resources (and changes are constant) affect all species and their abilities to thrive.

"We and the beasts are kin."

—Ernest Thompson Seton,
author, wildlife illustrator,
and the BSA's first Chief Scout

A badger and a mountain lion settle a territory dispute.

Adaptations

Exploring what an animal eats—and what might eat it—is a good starting point for discovering a species' particular traits. An animal's diet and efforts to keep from becoming part of another creature's diet can influence everything from its color and shape to its body covering, ways of perceiving the world, and manner of enduring winter.

Herbivores eat vegetation. Bison and elk are herbivores with mouths adapted for grazing and four stomachs for digesting grasses. Worms, caterpillars, grasshoppers, and thousands of other insects devour the leaves of trees and shrubs. Hummingbirds, nuthatches, and many other birds feed exclusively on plants.

Carnivores eat other animals. They might have talons, claws, or fangs shaped for capturing and tearing apart their prey. Many spiders build elaborate webs to capture insects, and many insects feast on other insects.

Omnivores eat both vegetables and animal matter. For example, grizzly bears dine on berries but also eat grubs, small animals, salmon, and the carcasses of larger beasts. Humans are omnivores, though some people choose to follow a vegetarian diet.

Color and Shape

An animal's adaptation of color or body shape can be surprisingly obvious—once you are aware of it. For example, the walking stick is an insect whose body mimics the surrounding twigs, camouflaging its approach upon tiny insects that become its food. Likewise, the walking stick's natural disguise keeps it hidden from most birds that would feed upon it.

Many fish have dark backs and pale bellies, which naturally blend from above with dark lake or pond waters and from below with the bright sky, so no matter what a predator's position, it will have a tough time seeing the fish in water. A deer's tawny shades allow it to blend into the underbrush, and a fawn's spots enhance its natural camouflage. Some lizards and tree frogs gradually shift color to match their surroundings. The ptarmigan is a grouselike mountain bird whose brown summer plumage begins to turn white with the first snow. Also white in the winter, the snowshoe hare's fur takes on the tundra's earthy hues when summer rolls around.

Snowshoe hare

Not all animals blend with their backgrounds, however. Many birds display brilliant plumage, and some insects are very colorful. The bright red, yellow, and black bands of the poisonous coral snake serve as a warning to the curious.

Body Covering

Some animals' bodies have adapted to physically protect them from predators. A turtle cannot easily flee danger, but it can draw itself into the protection of its shell. A porcupine does not move quickly, but its quills will discourage all but the most persistent predators. An armadillo can curl into a ball, hiding its soft underbelly and presenting an attacker with nothing but bony armor plate.

Cardinal

Body covering also can help protect animals from the elements. Mammals' fur, for example, provides insulation against the cold. Waterfowl are covered with warming layers of down and outer feathers rich with natural oils that shed moisture so the birds stay dry. Scales on snakes' underbellies allow them the traction they need for motion, and the sleek hides of beavers, seals, and other aquatic mammals help them slip smoothly through the water.

To realize the degree to which animals have adapted to their environments, think of an animal outside its natural role. For example, imagine a hummingbird diving out of the sky to snatch a fish in its claws and lift it to a nest on a distant cliff. Now imagine the impossibility of a bald eagle hovering motionless above a field of flowers, sipping nectar from the throat of a blossom.

Perceiving the World

Animals use a variety of strategies to gather information about their surroundings. Humans use combinations of five senses—sight, sound, touch, smell, and taste. Other species use those senses and a range of others not available to humans.

Seeing

Some animals see extremely well, while others are nearly blind. A soaring hawk notices the slight movement of a ground squirrel far below, and a falcon diving on a smaller bird can identify its prey at a glance and gauge its altitude and speed.

Most animals see the world in shades of black rather than in color, which is why game animals like deer and elk do not notice hunters' fluorescent orange hats and vests. Many insects have compound eyes that gather data from a wide arc of vision. Animals with eyes on the sides of their heads can find it difficult to focus both eyes on a single object and might not be able to judge distances well. Moles and bats are blind, at least in the conventional sense of the word, forcing them to rely on organs other than their eyes.

Smelling

Some animals, like wolves, coyotes, bears, sharks, and snakes, have a very keen sense of smell. A faint scent in the breeze or water is all it takes to alert them to danger or lead them to carrion and other food sources.

Sharks' sense of smell does not work like mammals' noses, but they can perceive the presence of blood in the water from great distances. Similarly, many insects can detect odors through specialized organs in their antennae and bodies.

A snake's tongue ranks among the most remarkable sense organs of the animal world. Flicking out in search of predators and prey, a snake's forked tongue delivers particles of air, soil, and water to the roof of its mouth, where a specialized organ called the *Jacobson's organ* interprets the particles much like the human sense of smell.

Hearing

Many animals such as rabbits and owls have ears that are large in proportion to their body size, which can help them pinpoint the sources of faint sounds that give them an early warning of danger or help them locate prey.

Humans can be so accustomed to city noises that the silences of the outdoors can be startling. Listen carefully, though, and you might hear the songs of birds, the splash of water, and the rustle of leaves in the wind. Unique sounds like the snort of a deer, the rhythmic beat of a woodpecker, or the slap of a beaver's tail may help you locate and identify wildlife you might not have noticed otherwise.

Touching

Whiskers, tongues, feelers, antennae, toes—animals rely on all manner of body parts to touch the world around them. Fish have a sensory organ along a lateral line of nerves and pores on their sides that picks up small vibrations in the water and alerts them to changes in their surroundings. When you walk along a stream bank, fish might dart away even if they can't see you; their lateral lines alert them to the weight of your footsteps upon the ground.

Surviving Winter

Perhaps the most profound changes in an ecosystem are driven by Earth's tilt and orbit as it makes its annual trip around the sun. Each season of the year offers wildlife challenges and opportunities, but for many species a central focus of survival is preparing for, and then living through, winter.

Even with its natural camouflage, the hare might soon become dinner for the fox.

Chipmunk

Some animals remain active year-round, foraging and hunting despite cold, snow, and shortages of browse and prey. Bison use their large heads to push away snow to reach frozen grasses. Foxes stalk hares and birds that increase their chances of winter survival by turning white when the first snows cover the ground.

Another strategy for winter survival is stockpiling food. Squirrels spend much of summer and autumn hiding nuts in tree hollows or burying them in the ground in hopes of finding them later. Honeybees build up surpluses of comb honey. Ants gather grass and leaf clippings. Bears and chipmunks preparing to hibernate eat voraciously through the summer to add fat to their bodies before they bed down in their dens and burrows. By the time they awaken in the spring, they might have lost up to a third of their body weight.

Mammals are not the only animals that hibernate. As a pond's water temperature drops in the autumn, frogs burrow into the mud beneath the water. Buried deep enough to be safe from freezing, their bodies undergo complex physiological changes that slow their metabolism, circulation, and other processes until they are expending just enough energy to stay alive. Frogs pass the winter in deep slumber, emerging from the mud only when the temperatures of spring have risen enough for them to again thrive in the water and on land.

Canada geese

Migration routes

Seabirds, gulls, and terns

Shore and wading birds

Waterfowl

Land birds and birds of prey

Migration

An ecosystem is habitable for a species only while conditions remain within certain bounds. In the winter, many animals cannot endure the cold and snow of alpine meadows. However, as the drifts melt and plants make the most of the short growing season, deer, elk, mountain goats, and bighorn sheep in search of good grazing will move up from the shelter of the forests. With them come the predators that feed upon them—mountain lions, cougars, bobcats, and others. Vultures, ravens, magpies, and other scavengers drift higher, too, waiting to pick at the remains of the carnivores' meals.

Some animals migrate tremendous distances. Ducks and geese wing their way from summer breeding grounds in Canada and Alaska to winter havens in the southern United States, Mexico, and South America. Monarch butterflies migrate, too, as do whales, bluefish, and salmon, which swim from the ocean back to the streams where they were hatched to lay and fertilize their own eggs.

Animal Classification

32

Every species has traits that set it apart from all other animals. Each species also shares characteristics in common with certain others. Zoologists and biologists use those similarities and differences to organize animals into a classification system. All creatures, for example, can be divided into one of two large groups—*vertebrates,* which have backbones, and *invertebrates,* which do not. Mammals, birds, reptiles, amphibians, and fish are vertebrates. The other 95 percent of the planet's creatures, including worms, spiders, insects, and crabs, are invertebrates.

As the classification process continues, vertebrates and invertebrates are sorted into increasingly specific groups until only one kind of animal—one *species*—fits a description. The American black bear, for example, is classified this way:

Kingdom—*Animal.* There are five kingdoms: animals, plants, fungi, protists, and monerans.

Phylum—*Chordata,* which includes all animals with backbones

Class—*Mammalia,* which includes all mammals

Order—*Carnivora,* which includes carnivorous mammals

Family—*Ursidae,* which includes all bears

Genus and **Species**—*Ursus americanus,* which includes only American black bears

An animal's genus is always capitalized; the species is not. Together, genus and species are shown in *italics.*

By comparison, grizzly bears share so many similarities with American black bears that they are members of the same kingdom, phylum, class, order, family, and genus. The grizzly bear's classification is *Ursus arctos horribilis,* differentiating it from every other creature on Earth.

Grizzly bear, Ursus arctos horribilis

American black bear, Ursus americanus

Opossum

Elk

Dolphin

A Sampling of North American Animals

Mammals

What do a field mouse and a grizzly bear have in common? For one thing, they are both *mammals*—warm-blooded animals that have backbones, fur or hair, and mammary glands for feeding their young. More than 400 species of mammals are found in North America, many of them sharing the same landscapes where humans hike and camp.

Watch mammals closely to figure out what they are eating, how they find shelter, and the ways they defend themselves. A chipmunk, for instance, scurries among the grasses in search of nuts and seeds. When startled, it relies on speed to carry it to a safe hiding place.

Rabbits also use bursts of speed to escape predators. Powered by muscular hind legs, they scamper from danger in a zigzag course that larger animals cannot easily follow. Rabbits and mice use their smaller front legs to hold the grasses on which they feed.

Squirrels' long tails provide balance as they run along branches, and their claws allow them to grip tree bark. Like chipmunks, they can fill their cheeks with nuts and grains to stash in trees or in the ground, returning to these caches when other sources of food are scarce.

The opossum does not share the rabbit's speed. Instead of fleeing when threatened, it lies limp and still until danger has passed. Close relatives of Australia's kangaroos, opossums are *marsupials*—pouched mammals. A mother opossum carries her newborns in a pouch formed by a fold of skin on her abdomen.

When crowded too closely, the porcupine slaps its tail to drive quills into an attacker's flesh. Skunks can spray an attacker with a chemical that stings the eyes and leaves a foul, long-lasting odor. Omnivorous skunks, close relatives of weasels, feed on insects, reptiles, eggs, and small rodents.

As you hike along a stream, you might notice the stumps of trees cut by beavers. They eat the bark of smaller branches and use some of the wood for constructing and improving their dams. The pond formed behind a dam gives beavers quiet water that is deep enough for swimming and feeding. They build dome-shaped lodges from sticks and mud. Although a beaver's teeth are worn down by chewing through tree trunks, they continue to grow throughout the beaver's life.

Beaver dam

Ponds also are home to muskrats, which use sticks to build lodges just as beavers do. The entrances are beneath the water so that the animals can slip in and out unseen, while the interior room is above water level.

Otters dig burrows in the banks of lakes and streams. Strong, sleek swimmers, they prey on fish. You may come upon an "otter slide" where otters have been tobogganing on their bellies down stream banks and into the water. Otters once were found throughout much of America, but they were hunted and trapped so aggressively for their fur that today they are rarely seen.

Beaver dams often are important to an area's natural succession. Slowed by a beaver's dam, a stream will drop its silt. The beaver pond eventually fills with silt and dries, becoming land where grasses and trees can take root.

32

In the damp soil along a stream, tracks that look like small hands with five long fingers are the marks of a raccoon. Usually traveling at night, raccoons come to the water to feast on frogs and crayfish. Raccoons also are expert climbers, and many live in hollow trees.

Bears have a varied diet that includes berries, grubs, fish, and small animals. Black bears are good tree climbers and can be found in much of North America, weighing as much as 500 pounds. Despite their name, black bears range in color from black to light brown.

Grizzly bears grow to be much larger than black bears and require more territory in which to roam. They once ranged throughout the western United States, but the development of farms, ranches, and cities has led to severe reductions in grizzly bear populations. Most grizzlies now are concentrated in Canada, Alaska, and an ecosystem that stretches from the Grand Tetons north through Yellowstone and Glacier national parks.

Wolves have highly developed social structures and cooperative hunting strategies that can involve up to a dozen members of a pack. Feeding on small animals and on old and sickened deer, elk, and caribou, wolves help keep animal populations in check. Although wolves have been vital members of numerous food chains, they have been driven almost to extinction in much of the nation. Today many land managers are working to return wolf populations to some of our national parks.

Bobcats, mountain lions, and cougars also have suffered from humans' actions. Each must have plenty of open space in which to thrive, and each can be a tempting target for hunters. Their disappearance from America's forests is a reminder that the ways we choose to conduct ourselves in the outdoors can have a dramatic impact upon entire species.

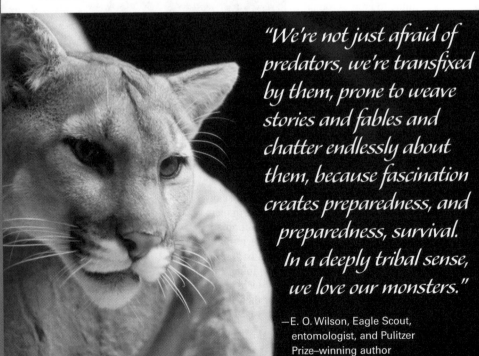

"We're not just afraid of predators, we're transfixed by them, prone to weave stories and fables and chatter endlessly about them, because fascination creates preparedness, and preparedness, survival. In a deeply tribal sense, we love our monsters."

—E. O. Wilson, Eagle Scout, entomologist, and Pulitzer Prize–winning author

Deer live in almost every part of North America. As their names suggest, white-tailed deer can be identified by their distinctive coloration. The larger mule deer, a native of the Rocky Mountain foothills, has a white tail tipped with black and has longer ears.

Moose are the largest members of the deer family. They range through the northern forests of the United States and far into Canada. Like all deer, a moose is a *ruminant*—an animal with four stomachs for digesting grasses, leaves, and twigs.

Wapiti is an Indian name for the American elk, another large deer that makes its home mostly in the western United States. Like other members of the deer family, male elk grow antlers each year, shedding them in the autumn after the mating season.

Caribou, found in Alaska and northern Canada, are unusual deer in that both females and males grow antlers. In herds as large as several thousand, caribou migrate long distances to find food. Caribou calves are able to run soon after they are born, which helps them keep up with the herd and evade predators during migration.

Although deer can kick with their sharp hooves, most flee their enemies rather than trying to fight. Pronghorn antelope are the fastest land animals of North America, able to reach speeds of more than 60 miles an hour.

Mountain goats and bighorn sheep are surefooted enough to scale steep mountain cliffs, while American bison can be seen grazing on the lower grasslands.

Elk

Pronghorn antelope

Moose

Mountain goat

32

Plankton—masses of tiny organisms drifting in the water—serves as food for small sea life and also for some whale species, the largest animals on Earth. Whales strain water through their mouths, trapping food in bristled screens called *baleen.*

Plankton

Captive killer whale giving birth

Although they spend their lives in seawater, whales are mammals, not fish. They are warm-blooded and breathe with lungs rather than through gills, coming to the ocean's surface to inhale fresh air. Instead of laying eggs as fish do, whales bear their young alive and nurse them with milk.

Reptiles

Reptiles such as snakes, lizards, alligators, and turtles have backbones like mammals do, but they are cold-blooded and do not have fur. Their bodies are covered with scales or plates, and they reproduce by laying eggs. More than 300 species of reptiles are found in the United States.

Iguana

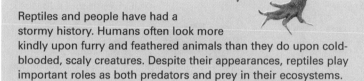

Reptiles and people have had a stormy history. Humans often look more kindly upon furry and feathered animals than they do upon cold-blooded, scaly creatures. Despite their appearances, reptiles play important roles as both predators and prey in their ecosystems.

The secret to a snake's forward motion is *lateral undulation*—the way it makes S-shaped bends with its body and then pushes against the ground. Snakes prefer to use their mobility to get away from a potential threat rather than confront it.

Rattlesnakes, copperheads, and cottonmouths are all pit vipers—snakes that have a distinctive pit beneath each eye that locates prey by detecting small differences in the temperatures of warm-blooded animals and their surroundings.

Perhaps the best known of venomous snakes, the rattlesnake has a tail equipped with dry rattles that sound a warning. Rattlesnakes live throughout much of the continental United States, Mexico, and some parts of Canada.

The copperhead snake can be found in woodlands and rocky outcroppings in the eastern half of the nation. You can recognize it by its copper-brown color with darker, hourglass-shaped cross bands.

Sidewinder

The cottonmouth, also known as the water moccasin, lives in streams and marshes of southern states. A chunky, muddy-brown snake, it sometimes rests in tree branches that hang low over the water. Its name comes from the cotton-white color of the inside of its mouth.

32

The only dangerously venomous American snake that is not a pit viper is the coral snake, found from North Carolina south to Florida, and west into Texas and Arizona. Small and slender, the coral snake has bands of bright yellow scales separating broader bands of black and red. Because it hunts at night, it is seldom seen and rarely a danger to humans.

Many nonvenomous snakes have names that seem to fit their appearance. The worm snake is about the same size, shape, and color as an earthworm. The ring-necked snake is black to steel gray, with a light-colored ring around its neck. The brown snake, red-bellied snake, and green snake take their names from their colors. The hognose snake, or puff adder, is named both for the shape of its head and for its habit of puffing itself up when frightened. Like all snakes, their jaws are hinged so that they can swallow prey larger than their heads.

Coral snake

Among the larger American snakes, the king snake eats rats, mice, and other snakes. The common king snake is black with white or yellow bands, while the bright red, yellow, and black bands of the scarlet king snake make it look much like the venomous coral snake.

The black racer of the eastern states has a smooth, black back. The coach whip snake of the South and the striped whip snake of the West are the racer's close relatives.

Bull snakes are one of the largest nonvenomous snakes in the United States. They are grayish brown with large patches on their backs. An eastern variety is often referred to as the pine snake, and a western form is called the gopher snake.

For guidelines on treating a snakebite, see the chapter titled "Managing Risk."

Lizards share many similarities with snakes, but they differ by having legs, moveable eyelids, and small ear openings on their heads. Many lizards make their homes in arid regions. The thick, rough skin of the horned lizard protects it from its enemies and helps it conserve moisture. Collared lizards and swifts are desert dwellers, whose speed and long, slender tails set them apart from their sluggish neighbor, the Gila monster. Covered with raised round scales that look like beadwork, the Gila monster is America's only venomous lizard.

Gila monster

A turtle's shell, composed of hard scales attached to a cagelike skeleton, encloses the animal's vital organs and protects its head, legs, and tail. Some turtles spend most of their lives on dry land, while others dwell in ponds, streams, and marshes. A few thrive in the open sea.

Turtles have no teeth, but the edges of their jaws are tough enough for them to feed on insects, snails, and small aquatic animals. The snapping turtle settles to the bottom of a pond and lies with its mouth open. A wormlike appendage on the floor of its mouth lures fish close enough for the turtle to catch them.

Amphibians

Frogs, toads, newts, and salamanders are all amphibians, and about 4,000 species of amphibians can be found worldwide. The name *amphibian* comes from two Greek words—*amphi,* meaning "both," and *bios,* meaning "life." After hatching from eggs laid in the water, most amphibians live in the water as *tadpoles,* swimming and eating a vegetarian diet. As they mature, they develop legs and begin spending some of their time on land where they feed on plant and animal matter. Frogs and toads lose their tadpole tails by the time they become adults, while salamanders keep theirs.

Frogs and toads look a lot alike, but frogs' skin is moist and smooth while toads' skin is bumpy and dry. Frogs and toads use their powerful hind legs to propel themselves over the land and through the water.

Frog

Toads are less mobile than frogs because of their shorter legs and heavier bodies, but as a defense, some toads can secrete a poison that irritates their predators' eyes and mouths.

Toad

The croaking you hear near a pond may be a bullfrog, the largest American frog. Seldom away from water, it eats insects, spiders, snails, and crayfish, and is the prey of snakes, birds, and many mammals.

Spring peepers and tree frogs have sticky pads on their toes that allow them to hang onto branches and leaves. Some tropical tree frogs lay their eggs in pockets of water in tree knots, and the tadpoles that hatch then mature high above the ground.

Bullfrog

Adult salamanders live both in and out of water. While the bodies of salamanders and newts resemble that of a lizard, salamanders and newts have smooth, naked skin—not scales.

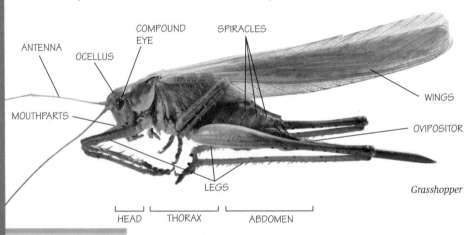

ANTENNA

OCELLUS

COMPOUND EYE

SPIRACLES

MOUTHPARTS

WINGS

OVIPOSITOR

LEGS

Grasshopper

HEAD THORAX ABDOMEN

Spiders are sometimes confused with insects, but they are *arachnids*—animals with eight legs and two body parts.

Insects

In terms of sheer numbers, insects rule the world. Five out of six animals are insects. Some insect species fly, some swim, and some scurry across the ground. They eat everything from leaves and flower nectar to blood, dead animals, and each other. Many display brilliant hues, while others are drab in color and are shaped like dried leaves or twigs. All insects have six legs and a body with three sections—head, abdomen, and thorax.

Tarantula

Butterflies and moths have four broad wings covered with scales so tiny they appear to be fine dust. At rest, butterflies tend to hold their wings upright, while moths keep theirs flat or curled around their bodies. Butterfly antennae are shaped like tiny clubs; those of moths look more like feathers.

Irregular color patterns on moths' and butterflies' wings can play tricks on their predators' eyes, making the insects harder to see. For example, wing spots that look like eyes might cause birds to perceive these insects as much larger animals that should be left alone.

Many species of ants, bees, and wasps live in nests or hives. As a community member, each insect carries out duties that help feed, defend, and maintain its home. Some ants look after tiny insects called *aphids.* When stroked on the back, the aphids produce a sweet liquid that the ants feed to their own larvae. Other ants are farmers, preparing soil in their nests and raising small fungi for food. Some species of wasps feed on insects. Bees collecting nectar for honey aid in plant fertilization by scattering pollen among the flower blossoms.

Polyphemus moth

Forty percent of all insects are beetles. Ranging in size from the 1/4-inch-long snout beetle to the stag beetle which, with its great pincers, can be several inches long, beetles are distinguished from other insects by having two pairs of wings—a back pair used for flying and a protective front pair covering the abdomen.

The ladybug is a very beneficial beetle able to eat many times its own weight in other insects. Many other beetles are scavengers that devour dead plants and animals, helping to continue the energy cycle.

The firefly is one unusual beetle. A chemical reaction in an organ near its tail creates a glowing light, allowing it to flash signals into the darkness as part of the mating ritual.

Flies and mosquitoes each have just two wings. The mosquito has a long *proboscis* that can pierce a mammal's skin and draw blood. The fly's mouthparts are like a sponge made for lapping up liquids. Mosquitoes lay their eggs in still water, while

Stag beetle

32

Grasshopper

flies often leave their eggs in dead and decaying matter. While important to ecosystems, flies and mosquitoes can carry diseases harmful to humans.

Grasshoppers, crickets, and their relatives are among the musicians of the insect world. Grasshoppers click and whir when they fly, and sometimes they make a raspy sound by stroking their wing covers with their hind legs. Male katydids rub their front wings together to produce a rhythmic buzzing. Cicadas do the same by vibrating a timbrel organ in their abdomens.

Cicada nymphs hatch from eggs laid in trees. The young insects burrow into the ground and suck sap from roots, staying buried for up to 17 years. When they do come back out they crawl up trees, shed their old shells, and emerge as full-grown adults ready to lay eggs and keep the cycle going.

Many people call all insects *bugs,* but true bugs form a definite group. Like a beetle, each bug has four wings, the front pair serving as a shell over the abdomen and flight wings. Where a beetle's shell halves form a straight line down its back, though, those of a bug fold into an X shape. All true bugs also have mouthparts made for sucking.

One member of the bug group is the spittlebug, the larvae of which hide in frothy spittle they hang on plant stalks. The water strider is a bug that hurries along the surface of the water, as do the back swimmer and the water boatman.

Elephant beetle

Water strider

Fish

Fossil evidence suggests
that fish were thriving in
Earth's oceans before
animals with backbones
walked on land. Fish have
endured for so many
eons because they are
well-suited to their
environment. With more
than 30,000 kinds of fish

32

alive today, they also are the most numerous vertebrates. You can find them
in nearly every body of water except for very salty, alkaline waters such as
that in Utah's Great Salt Lake, or in water that has become badly polluted.

Rather than lungs, fish have gills through which they absorb oxygen
from the water. Inside the fish is an air-filled organ called a *swim bladder*
that provides buoyancy. Fins help the fish stay upright, move forward, turn,
and stop. The long, sleek shapes of many fish allow them to swim fast
enough to catch their prey and to escape being devoured themselves.

A fish's many sense organs help it find food, escape predators,
and locate mates. Most fish can see, smell, hear, taste, and feel, and they
use sensory organs running the length of their bodies to pick up vibrations
in the water.

Many fish rely on coloration for protection. Perch, bluegills, and
other fish that live among underwater plants sport a camouflage of stripes.
Catfish and other bottom-dwellers might be colored so much like a streambed
that, when lying motionless, they seem almost to disappear.

Catfish

Catfish have mouths designed for vacuuming food from the bottoms
of rivers and lakes, and long, whiskerlike organs on their faces for feeling
their way through murky waters. Thin, sharp, flesh-tearing teeth allow
muskellunge, pike, and barracuda to feed on other fish. Trout, crappie, and
similar fish with a diet of insects can get along with less fearsome teeth.

Frigate birds on Johnson Island in the Pacific Ocean

Birds

Today there are more than 9,000 species of birds spanning nearly the entire globe. Birds are differentiated from other warm-blooded animals by the fact that they have feathers.

Contour feathers make up the visible plumage that gives a bird its shape. Down feathers next to the skin provide insulation to keep a bird warm.

All birds lay eggs, but the different species are as unique as those of any other animal class. Some birds swim, some spend their lives walking on land, and some rarely come down from the sky. Diets, reproductive strategies, and migratory habits also can help define bird species.

Birds that fly have thin, strong, lightweight bones. Their wing shapes help determine how they maneuver in the air. The hummingbird's small, short wings enable it to hover and move both backward and forward. Soaring birds have broader wings to catch updrafts so they can hang in the sky with little motion. With pointed wings, peregrine falcons are able to dive faster than a hundred miles an hour and maneuver quickly to attack airborne prey.

Small birds must eat often. Hummingbirds expend so much energy that they are engaged in feeding activities much of the day and might be so weakened after a night without nourishment that they need the help of the sun to warm them enough to fly. Larger birds can go longer between meals but still are almost constantly in search of food for themselves and their offspring.

Bald eagle

The bills of birds offer clues as to their diets. Woodpeckers have beaks that can be used as chisels. Birds that eat seeds and nuts have short, thick beaks and powerful jaw muscles, while those eating grasses and water plants have wider bills adapted to foliage. Some shorebirds use their long, slender bills to probe the waters for small fish, and other fish-eating birds have sharp, hooked beaks.

Acorn woodpecker

The legs and feet of birds are other indicators of diets and mobility. Waterfowl have webbed feet that are perfect for swimming, and the talons of raptors are just right for grasping prey. Birds that perch tend to have long toes and short legs, while those that walk on the ground have both long legs and toes. Penguins and other cold-water birds have short legs and compact feet that are adapted for keeping them warm and helping to steer.

Mallard drake

Birds are not the first animals to have flown, nor are they the only flying creatures today. Paleontologists have found evidence of *pterosaurs*—prehistoric winged reptiles. The *archaeopteryx* had feathers rather than scales, so it is considered the first true bird.

Wildlife Protection

Ecosystem changes cause animals to adapt to new conditions, migrate to more hospitable locations, or suf-

Oil spills can be disastrous to all kinds of wildlife.

fer reductions in population. Fires moving across woodlands and prairies alter the habitats of many creatures. An early winter storm might catch many animals unprepared for migration or hibernation. Floods can wash away beaver dams and fish spawning grounds. Drought can reduce food for grazing animals and, in turn, for species that depend on those animals for food. While natural changes affect many animals, they often are important to maintaining a healthy balance of wildlife populations. Unfortunately, the same cannot always be said for the disruptions caused by humans.

In the past, overhunting has severely reduced the numbers of many species. The passenger pigeon, a magnificent bird once thriving in the eastern United States, was hunted to extinction, and the bison of the Great Plains almost disappeared from the planet. Laws now protect endangered species, but an even greater threat to the survival of wild animals is the destruction of their habitats. Water pollution upsets entire ecosystems and lessens the carrying capacity of lakes and streams. Industrial and power plant smokestack emissions can cause rain to become acidic enough to harm vegetation and pollute water even miles away. Crop pesticides kill beneficial insects as well as those considered pests. Chemicals introduced into the environment cause some birds' eggs to become so thin that they break before the chicks are ready to hatch.

Humans' economic interests often are based on expansion and development. We transform native prairie into cropland. Our cities push into undeveloped areas, covering them with pavement and seeded lawns. Forests fall to the logger's saw. Dams and irrigation projects flood areas that once were arid and dry out those that were wet. All of these changes present wildlife with increasingly difficult challenges to their continued existence.

Fortunately, generations of Americans have had the wisdom to protect vast tracts of unspoiled land in parks, wilderness areas, forests, and wildlife habitats. As individuals come to realize the effects human actions can have on the environment, many people have adjusted their lifestyles to improve waste disposal processes, city maintenance, and land management.

Humans must adapt to change just as other animals do, including seeing with new wisdom the importance of wildlife, and then deciding to live in harmony with the environment and its animals.

For more on the role of change in ecosystems, see the chapter titled "Understanding Nature." For more on improving wildlife habitat, see the chapter titled "Being Good Stewards of Our Resources."

"The wild things of this earth are not ours to do with as we please. They have been given to us in trust, and we must account for them to the generations which will come after us and audit our accounts."

—William T. Hornaday, author, wildlife advocate, and founder of the National Zoo in Washington, D.C.

CHAPTER 33

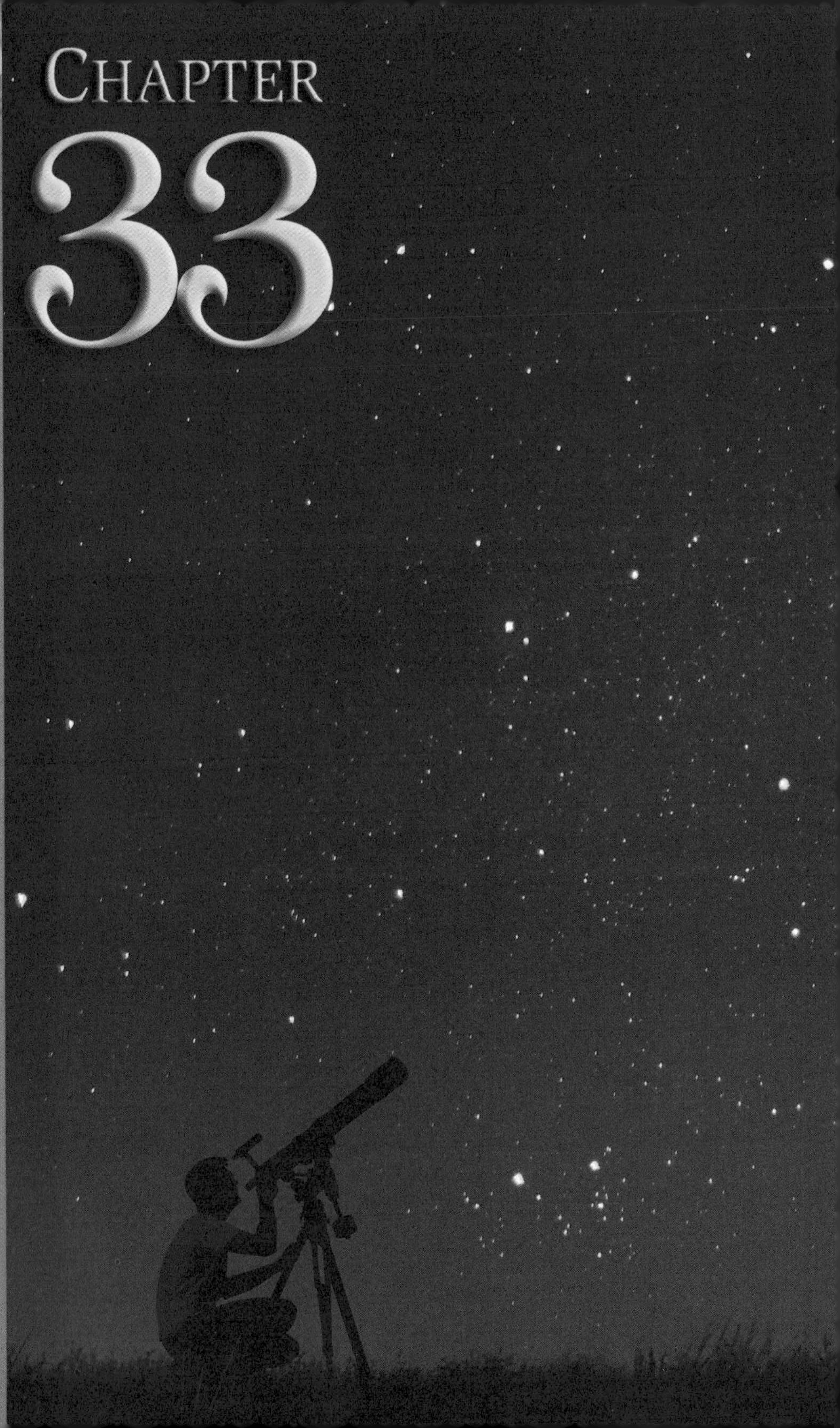

Watching the Night Sky

"Many people tend to postpone their enjoyment of the stars because they are constantly with us, but . . . once you come to know [the stars], they never lose their appeal."

—Helen Hogg (A distinguished 20th-century Canadian astronomer, she helped popularize star study for young people.)

One of the great pleasures of camping out and hiking at night is looking into the heavens. Undimmed by the lights of cities, the sky blazes with stars. Constellations parade overhead and the Milky Way forms a shimmering ribbon against the darkness. Travelers in northern latitudes sometimes watch the aurora borealis draping the sky with shadowy, luminous curtains. Watch for a while and you might see a meteor streaking through the darkness.

At first glance the night sky might seem to hold a random scattering of brilliant points of light. Look more carefully, though, and you will notice that some stars are brighter than others. Night after night, they appear in almost the same places. There is order to their locations, and by learning about that order, you will have an effective method for finding directions after sunset. You also can more fully appreciate the legacy of star study that has come down to us through the ages, for the night sky has been a subject of curiosity and fascination since the beginning of time.

The view of space from planet Earth is an endlessly intriguing panorama of darkness and light, a vision shared through the ages with all of humanity.

33

Observing the Night

Make the most of watching the night sky by choosing good times and places. Of course, you won't be able to view the stars when they are obscured by clouds, fog, or mist. The brilliance of a full moon washes light across the sky. Lunar craters are most visible during lunar eclipses, which limit the intensity of light. Star fields over urban areas can be dimmed by light pollution—the glow created by streetlights, illuminated parking lots, and other sources of artificial lighting. At best, you will be lucky to make out a couple of hundred stars. Get away from cities, though, and the number of visible stars crowding the heavens can rise into the thousands.

Human vision can adapt well to darkness, but it might require up to 30 minutes to adjust fully. Your pupils will expand to capture more light, and the amount of light-sensitive pigment in your retinas will increase, allowing you to observe much more in the night sky. Your eyes can quickly lose their adaptation if they are exposed to bright white light such as that from a lantern or flashlight. If you want to illuminate a star map or find your way through the darkness, cover the lens of your flashlight with red cellophane held in place with a rubber band.

Good binoculars can take you much deeper into the universe than with eyes unassisted, revealing wonders ranging from moon craters to the colors of planets and shapes of nebulae. Telescopes, too, can increase your understanding and enjoyment of nights spent studying the heavens.

For more on binoculars, see the chapter titled "Observing Nature."

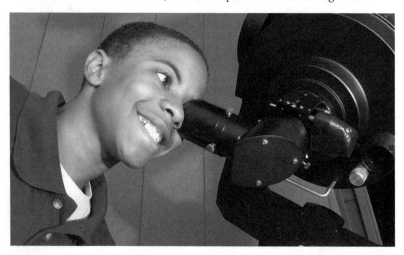

Fascinating shapes in space, such as the Eagle Nebula depicted here, can be an artist's inspiration.

What's Out There

The universe teems with nebulae, stars, galaxies, planets, moons, meteors, novas, pulsars, quasars, black holes, and many forms of matter and energy we are just beginning to understand. From space stations and communications satellites to bits of metal debris, objects created by humans also are visible as they orbit through the night. Among the most interesting of the natural phenomena are nebulae, the birthplaces of stars.

Nebulae

The largest known objects in the skies are great swirls of dust and gas called *nebulae,* taking their name from the Latin word for mist or cloud. As materials composing a nebula compress, stars are born. Many nebulae emit no light of their own, but starlight sometimes illuminates them. Others shine on their own as they condense and become superheated. From the Earth, nebulae visible to the naked eye have an appearance similar to that of stars. With binoculars or a telescope, however, they can emerge from the background of space in spectacular displays of color and shape.

Stars

Stars are gigantic thermonuclear reactors adrift in the heavens. Most are much larger than our sun, the star we know the best. Beyond the sun, even the closest stars are many light-years away. (A light-year is the distance that light will travel in a calendar year. At 186,000 miles a second, that's 5,865,696,000,000 miles a year—almost six trillion miles.)

Stars are ranked according to *magnitude*—their brightness relative to one another. The North Star, for example, is the 46th brightest star in the sky, outshone by Sirius, a first-magnitude blue giant and the brightest star visible from Earth. The color of stars indicates their temperatures, with blue burning hottest, followed by white, yellow, orange, and red. Other than the moon, the brightest nonstellar objects in the night sky are the planets Mars, Venus, Jupiter, and Saturn. Between 200 and 300 stars visible on a dark night have names. The names of most stars can be traced to antiquity, coming from Latin, Greek, and Arab language roots. Polaris, for example, the true name of the North Star, is a Latin term for "pole star." Sirius is a Greek word that means "scorching."

Scintillate, Scintillate, Little Star . . .

Rather than shining with a steady glow, stars appear to twinkle. That's because the light coming from them is distorted by turbulence in the Earth's atmosphere. Dust, heat, smoke, and smog all play roles in causing starlight to scintillate—another word for twinkle.

The Hubble Space Telescope's orbit high above the Earth removes it from atmospheric disturbances and allows it to produce crisp, twinkle-free images from the depths of space.

Galaxies

Many points of light we see in the sky are galaxies, great collections of stars and nebulae. Evidence from the Hubble Space Telescope suggests there might be at least 50 billion galaxies. Some are elliptical galaxies without defined shape. Others are spirals. Our solar system is part of a spiral-shaped galaxy called the Milky Way, which is composed of several hundred billion stars. It is gorgeous to the naked eye, especially on summer evenings. Seen through binoculars, it explodes with stars, nebulae, and, beyond the Milky Way, countless other galaxies. Train your binoculars on the area of sky just above the spout of the teapot-shaped constellation Sagittarius, and you will be looking into the radiant heart of our galaxy.

"What is inconceivable about the universe is that it should be at all conceivable."

—Albert Einstein, Nobel Prize–winning physicist

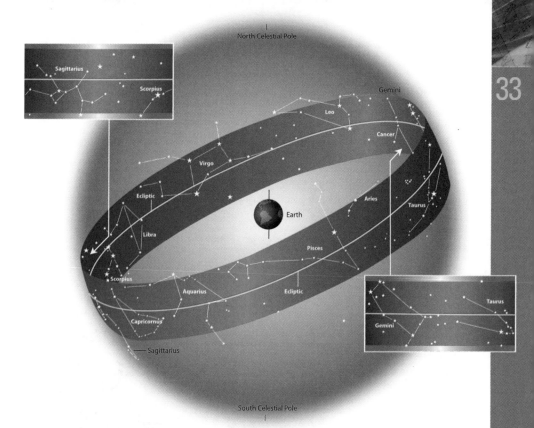

The Constellations

For thousands of years, people gazing at the stars have imagined them forming the shapes of people, animals, and items important to their cultures. Many of the names they gave these connect-the-dot shapes, or constellations, are with us today. Just as the starlight we see coming from stars is an echo of the stellar past, our understanding of constellations represents some of our oldest continuous knowledge, a mix of human history, lore, and belief reaching deep into the mists of time.

The word constellation comes from *con,* meaning "together," and *stella,* meaning "star." The constellations we most often identify today were formally acknowledged in 1929 by the International Astronomical Union (IAU) as a step in standardizing the mapping of the night sky. In all, 88 recognized constellations cover the heavens, with no star appearing in more than one constellation. There are 48 constellations in the southern sky and 28 in the northern sky. Another dozen constellations can be found along or near the ecliptic—the celestial pathway apparently taken across the sky by the sun, the moon, and the planets. (In fact, it is the rotation of the Earth that causes heavenly bodies to appear to move.) The 12 constellations found along the ecliptic are also known as the signs of the zodiac.

The celestial locations of constellations are determined by the time of the year and by an observer's position on the globe. Eighteen of the 88 recognized constellations cannot be viewed from the continental United States. Someone in South America, however, could see those constellations, but might not be able to view the Big Dipper or the North Star.

33

Navigating the Heavens

When giving someone directions for traveling overland to a certain location, you might use landmarks as references. "Go two miles down the Wabash Trace to the Nishnabotna River," you might say. "Waubonsie campsite is a half mile farther by the big oak tree on the left side of the trail."

You can navigate your way around the heavens that way, too, but instead of rivers, trails, and trees for landmarks, use a few easy-to-find constellations as skymarks to guide your eye to destinations overhead. Two of the most recognizable and useful constellations are the Big Dipper and Orion.

The 10-Degree Fist

Astronomers map the heavens with a grid of coordinates much like terrestrial measurements of latitude and longitude. An arc drawn across the sky from the eastern horizon to the western (or from the southern to the northern)
encompasses 180 degrees—half of a complete circle. The measurement of that arc from the horizon to a point directly overhead is 90 degrees. The highest point directly overhead is known as the *zenith*.

A convenient way to measure celestial distances in degrees is to extend your arm and then sight over 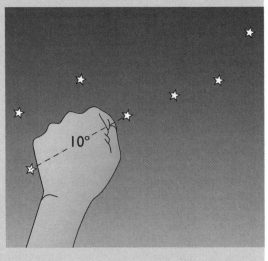 your hand. Viewed against the sky, your little finger represents a width of about 1 degree. Three fingers held up as if in a Scout sign are about 5 degrees in width, and your fist has a relative width of about 10 degrees. Measure 15 degrees in the sky by spreading apart your index and little fingers, and 25 degrees with the span from the tip of your little finger to the tip of your thumb.

Try a few measurements to get the idea. For example, the stars forming the rim of the Big Dipper's cup are 10 degrees apart. Viewed at arm's length, your fist should just fit between them. The width of the Big Dipper is 25 degrees; that's about two and a half fist widths, or about as wide as the span from the tip of your little finger to the tip of your thumb. The 90-degree arc from the horizon to the zenith (the point directly above an observer) can be measured with nine fist widths stacked one atop the next.

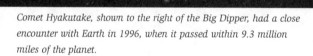

Comet Hyakutake, shown to the right of the Big Dipper, had a close encounter with Earth in 1996, when it passed within 9.3 million miles of the planet.

Look closely and you might see that the middle star of the Big Dipper's handle actually is two stars. Ancient Arab astronomers called them Mizar and Alcor. Some American Indians thought of the larger star as a horse, the smaller as its rider.

The Big Dipper

Perhaps the most familiar of all star patterns seen from North America is Ursa Major, which contains the Big Dipper. On spring and summer evenings it seems to fill the northern sky. Depending on your latitude, it might maintain its dominance in the winter heavens, too, or might disappear in part or in whole beyond the northern horizon.

Legend holds that Ursa Major, the mythical big bear, is guarding the northern territories. The state flag of Alaska features the Big Dipper, showing it along with the North Star.

A skill practiced by generations of Scouts is the ability to use the Big Dipper to find the North Star:

To find the North Star, train your eyes on the pointer stars of the Big Dipper—the two stars farthest from the handle. Imagine a line connecting them and extending upward to a point about five times the span between the two pointers. You should see the North Star at that point. The Earth's North Pole lies directly under the North Star.

— *The Boy Scout Handbook,* 11th edition, Boy Scouts of America, 1999

Caph

CASSIOPEIA

Vega

URSA MINOR

Polaris

Capella

Dubhe

BOÖTES

Merak

URSA MAJOR
(The Big Dipper)

Castor

Pollux

Arcturus

LEO

Regulus

VIRGO

Spica

Northern sky

Like the sun and moon, most stars seem to move from east to west across the sky, an illusion caused by the fact that the Earth is rotating in the opposite direction beneath them. Because it is aligned with the Earth's axis, the North Star does not appear to move at all. Watch through the night and you will see Cassiopeia and the Big Dipper rotating around the northern sky with the North Star apparently motionless between them.

In astronomical measurements, the North Star can be found 28 degrees from the closest star of the Big Dipper. Use your hand at arm's length to estimate that distance across the sky. (Not only is it the North Star, it also is the last star in the handle of the Little Dipper, a portion of the constellation Ursa Minor, or the Little Bear. The cup of the Little Dipper appears to be pouring into the Big Dipper's bowl.)

With the Big Dipper as a primary skymark, similar degree measurements can lead you to other stars and constellations spangled across the northern skies:

❶ Follow the arc of the Big Dipper's handle 30 degrees across the sky to the first-magnitude star Arcturus in the constellation Boötes (the bear driver).

❷ Continue along the same arc another 30 degrees to Spica, a star almost as bright as Arcturus and a primary feature in the zodiac constellation Virgo (the virgin).

❸ Return to the Big Dipper and trace the line through its pointer stars to the North Star. Extend the line almost the same distance again to reach Cassiopeia (named for an ancient Ethiopian queen), a constellation shaped like the letter W with its top opening toward Polaris and the Dippers.

❹ Punch a hole in the ladle of the Big Dipper and go straight down to Regulus, which is also Leo the Lion's front paw.

Orion and the Southern Skies

A winter constellation south of the ecliptic is Orion, known in Greek mythology as the Great Hunter. Two bright stars mark his shoulders. Three small ones form his head and two more his legs. There are three stars in Orion's belt; the three stars hanging from the belt are his sword.

Orion is a constellation composed of wonders. Betelgeuse (pronounced *beetle-juice*), a first-magnitude red giant star emitting 60,000 times more light than our sun, forms the hunter's upper shoulder. Rigel, burning with white light and the brightest of Orion's stars, marks one of the feet. At the middle of the sword is the Orion Nebula—stellar dust and gasses compressing to form new stars. With a pair of binoculars you can begin to unlock the nebula's secrets.

As a skymark, Orion is unparalleled for locating constellations and stars in the winter. Facing south, extend a line to your left through Orion's belt, and at a distance of 20 degrees you will come to Sirius situated in the head of the constellation Canis Major, the Great Dog. Follow the line from the belt 20 degrees to the right of Orion to the first-magnitude red giant star Aldebaran, the eye in the V-shaped head of the constellation Taurus, the Bull. Stay the course for another 15 degrees past Taurus to a tight, faint

Southern sky

cluster of stars called the Pleiades, or Seven Sisters. With good eyesight you might make out six of them. Through binoculars, you might discover that the Pleiades actually are several hundred stars.

With the Big Dipper and Orion as your initial skymarks, you will be well on your way to becoming familiar with many of the features of the night sky. In seasons when those constellations are not visible or are partially obscured by the horizon, use other constellations as skymarks, especially Cassiopeia in the northern heavens and Scorpius in the southern. The star maps in this chapter can help you determine directions and distances in degrees for identifying constellations and stars relative to skymarks you already know.

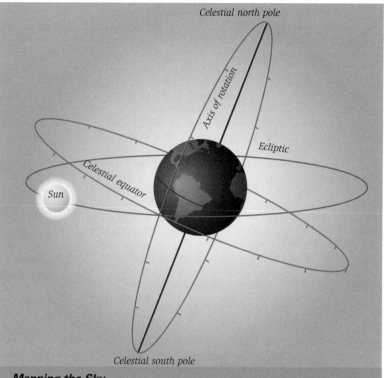

Celestial north pole

Axis of rotation

Ecliptic

Celestial equator

Sun

Celestial south pole

Mapping the Sky

Just as every spot on Earth can be mapped with degrees, minutes, and seconds that form a global grid of longitude and latitude, celestial coordinates are a means astronomers use to pinpoint the locations of objects in the sky.

Imagine yourself in the center of a round birdcage. The bars of the cage encircle you in the same manner that the lines of a sky map encircle you as you look up toward the heavens. The key terms of a sky map include these:

- Right ascension is similar to longitude on a map of the Earth. As with longitude, measurements of right ascension can be noted in degrees. Right ascension also can be measured in hours, minutes, and seconds, based on the fact that every 60 minutes the stars appear to move across an arc of about 15 degrees.

- Declination is similar to latitude on a ground map. Just as latitude measures the distance north or south of the Earth's equator to a point on the ground, declination measures the distance north or south of the celestial equator to a point in the sky.

- The celestial equator, located directly above the Earth's equator, bisects star maps and separates constellations into those of the northern sky and those of the southern.

- The *ecliptic* is the apparent path taken across the sky by the sun, the moon, the planets, and the 12 constellations of the zodiac.

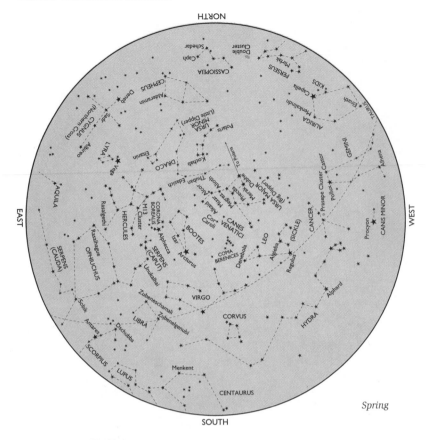

Spring

Star Maps

The rotation of the Earth creates the illusion that the stars we are seeing wheel across the night sky. Likewise, the annual progression of the Earth around the sun affects which stars we can observe on a given night, for we are always looking out from the dark side of the Earth—the side away from the sun. That puts us in position to view the heavens in one direction on summer nights and in the opposite direction on a winter's evening. Some constellations can't be seen at all during certain seasons, as they rise at midday and their light is obscured by sunlight. Orion is one that dominates the sky in the winter but is invisible throughout the summer.

> The angle of the Earth's axis in relation to its orbit around the sun creates the seasons, extends the hours of summer daylight, and shortens our winter days.

To accommodate these variations in location and time, constellation maps give the dates and hours when they best represent what you will see in the sky. The maps in the *Fieldbook* assume a viewer is in the Northern Hemisphere and is viewing the heavens between 9 P.M. and midnight.

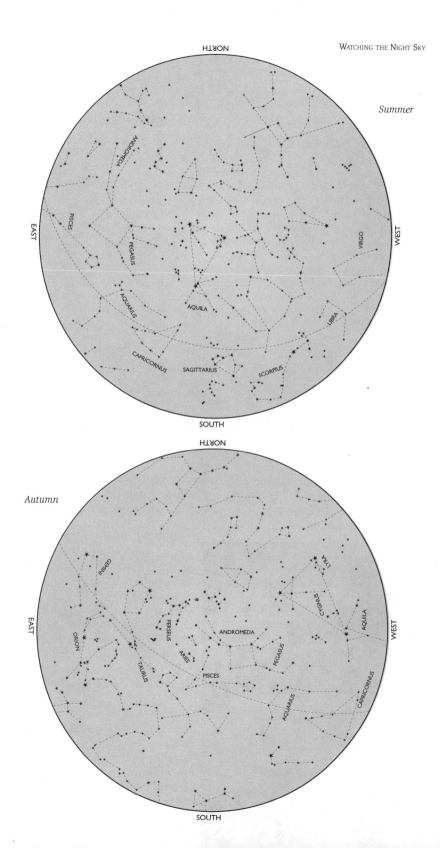

Summer

Autumn

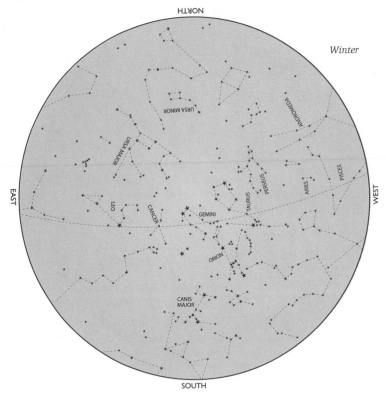

The Planets

From earliest times, star watchers have noticed that five particular points of light did not behave like all the others. Rather than holding their positions in constellations, these five moved about among the stars. The ancient Greeks called them wanderers.

Today we know that these wanderers are planets that, like the Earth, revolve around the sun. Those visible with the naked eye are Mercury, Venus, Mars, Jupiter, and Saturn. All look like bright stars except Mercury, which, as the closest to the sun, makes faint appearances near the western horizon just after sunset. The remaining planets—Uranus, Neptune, and Pluto—can be seen only with the aid of a telescope. A small telescope enables you to view Saturn's rings, Jupiter's red spot (a giant storm), and the moons of other planets.

The Moon

Other than the sun, no heavenly body has more impact on Scout outings than the moon. Revolving around the Earth once in about 28 days, the moon waxes as more of its surface is lit by the sun, and wanes as less of its surface is lit by the sun. (If the right side of the moon, as you face it, is reflecting light, the moon is waxing. When the right side is dark, the moon is waning.)

A moonlit night can be bright enough for you to observe wildlife and to move about in camp without a flashlight. A mountain travel team might schedule a trip so that they will have a full moon to illuminate their route on a summit attempt that begins long before sunrise. Sailors and sea kayakers know that the ebb and flow of tides is caused by the pull of the moon's gravity upon the Earth's oceans.

With the help of binoculars or a telescope, you can make out craters on the moon created by the impact of meteorites. A map of the moon can guide you from one terrain feature to another, and to the locations of lunar landing zones—as yet the only places beyond the Earth where human footprints can be found.

"The surface of the Earth is the shore of the cosmic ocean. From it we have learned most of what we know. Recently, we have waded a little out to sea, enough to dampen our toes or, at most, wet our ankles. The water seems inviting. The ocean calls."

—Carl Sagan, *Cosmos*, 1977 (An astronomer and teacher, he stimulated public interest in science and space through his books and television series.)

CHAPTER
34

Being Good Stewards
of Our Resources

"Never doubt that a small group of thoughtful, committed citizens can change the world. Indeed, it is the only thing that ever has."

—Margaret Mead, American anthropologist and author

Caring for the land is as basic to Scouting as bringing along food for the trail, and as constant as knowing which way we are going and when we will return. Much of this book has discussed terrific outdoor activities and the means to enjoy them in harmony with the outdoors. The principles of Leave No Trace are guidelines for making that happen. When we give careful thought to using a stove or a fire, to choosing appropriate campsites and travel routes, and to other means of minimizing our impact on the land, we are preventing environmental harm.

We can take our responsibilities a step further by rolling up our sleeves and pitching in to help preserve natural resources and restore damaged ecosystems. We have the power to make a difference for the Earth, and there is plenty we can do. Many projects involve stream cleanup, meadow revegetation, erosion control, and habitat improvement. Others address the needs of forests, marshes, lakeshores, campgrounds, beaches, recreational facilities, and trails.

Taking on worthwhile tasks in the field makes the importance of stewardship clear and immediate. That, in turn, helps us understand that we can be good stewards in the daily choices we make as consumers, as users of resources, and as active participants in deciding how to protect the environment.

For more on enjoying the outdoors responsibly, see the "Leaving No Trace" section of this book.

34

The Meaning of Stewardship

Historically, a *steward* is a person who cares for the property of others, striving to return it in comparable or better shape than when it was received. Each of us is a steward of the Earth, entrusted with the planet's care for the years we are here. The condition in which we leave it is our legacy to our children, our grandchildren, and all the generations that follow.

Stewardship is important for many reasons. It allows us to give back something important in return for what we gain from the outdoors. It makes us much more aware of the intricacies of the natural world and the ways in which our actions affect it when we see the environment in terms of maintaining healthy ecosystems rather than simply as consumable resources. It meshes with Leave No Trace ethics by providing the means to erase those traces of human activities that, over time, have injured the environment. As a means of practicing thrift and service, stewardship is an extension of the foundations of Scouting expressed in the Scout Oath and Law, the Outdoor Code, and the Venturing Oath.

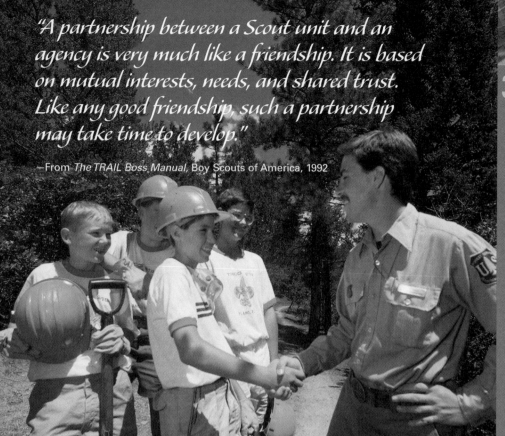

"A partnership between a Scout unit and an agency is very much like a friendship. It is based on mutual interests, needs, and shared trust. Like any good friendship, such a partnership may take time to develop."

—From *The TRAIL Boss Manual,* Boy Scouts of America, 1992

Active Stewardship

The trails we hike and the campsites where we pitch our tents probably fall under the jurisdictions of land management agencies, conservation organizations, or the Boy Scouts of America. By becoming involved in environmental protection, maintenance, and improvement, we can enrich our outdoor experience by serving as active stewards of the places we use and enjoy. Of course, conservation projects must be done correctly or the effort will be wasted. For guidance, groups often can draw on the knowledge and support of BSA camp staffs and of land management personnel overseeing America's public and private lands.

Land managers associated with local agencies such as community parks departments might care for only a few acres. Those involved with large agencies, including the USDA Forest Service, National Park Service, Bureau of Land Management, U.S. Army Corps of Engineers, and U.S. Fish and Wildlife Service, administer tens of thousands of square miles of the American landscape.

BSA local councils and district offices might be able to refer you to agency professionals, Scout camp personnel, or other Scout groups experienced in volunteer stewardship projects on public or BSA property. Many land management agencies and organizations have designated coordinators who are experienced with stewardship volunteers, but some agency personnel might not know what to expect or what is expected of them. That's all right;

34

developing a conservation project partnership includes the time it takes for agencies and volunteer groups to get to know each other.

For more on land management agencies, see the chapter titled "Planning a Trek." For more on organizations involved with stewardship, see the *Fieldbook* Web site. ➤

Involving volunteers in active stewardship is not appropriate for every local land management office or for every group of backcountry users. Some agency personnel simply do not have the time, the resources, or the need. Some groups are not sufficiently committed to the responsibilities involved in developing long-term conservation partnerships. When everyone is willing to explore the potential, though, the possibilities are remarkable.

Planning Stewardship Projects

Volunteers who take on conservation efforts are contributing their time and energy for the good of the environment and should feel pride in their important accomplishments. The following guidelines will help groups and land managers plan projects that serve the needs of the environment and ensure that those involved are using their time well.

Use Good Leadership

Venturers, Boy Scouts, and members of other groups succeed best when they are led well. Leaders can share their responsibilities by involving other members of the group in planning and then providing them with the materials, tools, and skills they require to successfully complete the project.

For more on leadership, see the chapter titled "Outdoor Leadership."

Work Closely With Land Managers

First projects with a particular agency often are as much about getting acquainted with land managers as they are about helping the land. The project should be limited in scope, lasting perhaps a few hours or an afternoon, so that participants can sample hands-on stewardship, and land managers can get a sense of a group's ability and commitment. As volunteers gain experience and confidence, projects can become more lengthy and complex. Each project must have prior approval from the land management agency or the landowner. Once a project is planned, following it through to proper completion is appreciated by land managers.

Consider Skill Levels

A demanding goal can set people up to fail and cause them to lose interest. On the other hand, the best opportunities challenge people to push a little beyond their current abilities and to master new skills. Choose a project with a level of challenge that best fits the group's skills.

Make a Difference

Effective projects allow participants to see that their efforts have meaning. They will be eager to return for future projects if they have gained a sense of pride in doing their best for the land.

Adopt-a-Site

Adopt-a-site partnerships allow Venturing crews, Scout troops, and other groups to pledge themselves to providing long-term care of a campsite or trail, and to see how their efforts protect and improve the area over the months and years.

Preproject Visit

Visiting the project site a week or two before the effort begins allows land managers and group leaders to clarify expectations and to draw up lists of tools, materials, and logistical tasks. Among the questions to be answered during a preproject visit are the following.

- Where is the project located, and how will everyone reach the site?

- What is the project's goal, and who should be included in the planning process?

- What portion of the project can the group reasonably expect to finish?

- What are the steps for completing the project?

- Is the project site safe? If not, assist the agency in eliminating any safety concerns, or move the project to another site.

- Does the group have the skills needed? If not, who can provide the information and/or training they need and help oversee the project?

- What tools and materials are required, and how will they be provided? Will there be enough tools to keep each participant busy, productive, and safe?

- Is the extent of the project comparable to the size of the group? Is leadership adequate?

- Will volunteers need special clothing or personal gear? If they might get wet or muddy, should they bring a change of clothing for the trip home?

- What activities, such as cleaning up the project site, completing evaluations, and returning tools, will effectively conclude the project?

34

Emergency Response Plan

As with any outdoor activity, a troop, crew, or other group planning a stewardship project should put together an emergency response plan that includes emergency contacts in case of injury or illness, the location of the closest medical facilities, and the means of transporting people to and from the project site. Make sure a first-aid kit is available and that there will be people at the project site who know how to use it.

For more on emergency response plans, see the chapter titled "Planning a Trek."

Risk Management

Address safety right from the start of project planning. Agencies often have their own safety standards and will expect volunteers to follow their guidelines. Group leaders and land management personnel should identify any hazards to be avoided and incorporate any methods to enhance safety.

A tailgate safety talk can be a standard project feature. Before the project begins, gather all participants to discuss project goals and safety concerns. In addition to the usual safety issues of being outdoors (weather, insects, sun exposure, etc.), conservation projects have some specific safety considerations:

- **Clothing and equipment.** Depending on the project, sturdy boots, hard hats, gloves, and eye protection might be needed.

- **Safe spacing.** Anyone swinging a tool should be at least two tool-lengths away from every other person.

- **Body mechanics.** Conservation projects provide great opportunities for participants to learn the right ways to lift objects, handle tools, and pace themselves through a day of outdoor activity.

34

Documentation

Keep a written evaluation of each project for your group's records, and provide a copy to the land managers with whom your group is cooperating. Including before-and-after photographs can provide clear evidence of the value of the volunteers' efforts. A typical evaluation answers the following questions:

- How many people were involved in the project, and how many hours did they dedicate? (To figure person-hours, multiply the number of participants by the number of hours it took to complete the project. For example, over an eight-hour day, a group of 10 volunteers has contributed 80 person-hours of effort.)

- What was accomplished? (Detail numbers and/or amounts—feet of trail cleared, number of trees planted, length of shoreline protected, percentage of a campsite repaired, etc.)

- Are there tools or skills that could improve the volunteers' efficiency? Could group leaders or land management personnel provide additional support? Add any comments and recommendations that might help everyone do a better job next time.

Recognition

The BSA honors the importance of stewardship in a variety of ways, including with patches, awards, and advancement. Agency personnel assisting volunteers in the completion of stewardship projects also deserve recognition, and they might be eligible for certain Scouting awards. A letter to an agency supervisor thanking someone for his or her help is always appreciated. Perhaps the most meaningful recognition is sincere thanks and handshakes from volunteers in the field.

The William T. Hornaday Award was established in 1914 by Dr. Hornaday, then director of the New York Zoological Park. The award recognizes BSA members and units for service to conservation and environmental quality. Other BSA awards relating to stewardship are the Conservation Good Turn Award, World Conservation Award, and the Keep America Beautiful Award.

For more on conservation awards, see the *Fieldbook* Web site.

Sample Stewardship Projects

The following is an overview of a few stewardship efforts that volunteers can carry out effectively.

Trail Maintenance

Trails are at the mercy of erosion, encroaching vegetation, and user impact. Water from rain, springs, and snowmelt gouges gullies in trails and narrows the tread with silt deposits. Brush and tree branches can make trail corridors almost impassable. Misuse by hikers, bicyclists, horseback riders, and others creates damaging shortcuts and unnecessary tread widening. Bridges, water bars, and other wooden trail structures eventually will rot away and require replacement. Steps, retaining walls, and other stone fixtures also demand occasional attention.

Nearly every kind of trail damage can be fixed. All it takes is time, skill, and enthusiasm.

"Our ideals, laws, and customs should be based on the proposition that each generation, in turn, becomes the custodian rather than the absolute owner of our resources and each generation has the obligation to pass this inheritance on to the future."

—Charles Lindbergh, 1971 (Celebrated for his 1927 solo flight across the Atlantic Ocean, he became an advocate of stewardship and environmental protection.)

34

Brushing

Brushing removes branches, bushes, vines, fallen trees, and other vegetation to maintain a clear travel corridor of sufficient width and height to allow trail users to pass without difficulty. Brushing tools include loppers, bush saws, clippers, and pole saws. The following guidelines will enable volunteers to brush a travel corridor so that it looks as natural as possible.

- Cut bushes flush with the ground to avoid leaving a stump that might trip a hiker. Cut branches close to tree trunks to avoid leaving "hat racks" that might snag clothing, packs, horses, or people.

- Undercut tree branches by sawing through about one-third of their diameter from underneath, then complete the cut from above. That will prevent the falling branch from stripping the bark from living trees.

- Scatter brush and branches out of view of the trail. Cut brush and pruned branches that lie flat on the ground will decompose quickly. Do not leave piles of brush that might attract harmful insects.

Brushing and limbing for a hiking trail

Maintaining Drainage Structures

Many hillside trails deter erosion with embedded *water bars* that divert rainwater and snowmelt from the tread. Built from large rocks, logs, or lumber, water bars should be placed with enough care to withstand hard use by hikers and horses while still accomplishing their task.

Silt building up behind a water bar can render it useless. Using a shovel, mattock, Pulaski, or even the heel of your hiking boot, scrape away the silt and restore the shape of the drainage slope so that the water bar will be effective again. Where necessary, replace rotted logs and reset loose rocks.

Maintaining Tread

A common trail concern is silt buildup on the inside edge of the tread (where it is called *slough*) and the outside edge *(berm)*. Slough and berm narrow the tread, making passage more difficult. Water trapped between slough and berm can cause erosion as it flows along the trail.

Mattocks, Pulaskis, shovels, and rakes are effective tools for removing compacted slough and berm. Loosened silt can fill in ruts along the trail or be scattered over a wide area beyond the trail.

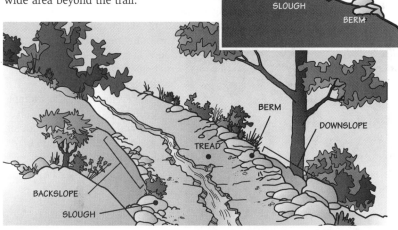

Compaction of the tread can create a berm on the outside edge. Rainwater running from the backslope to the downslope of a trail may deposit silt on the tread. Removing this slough and berm can restore a trail's proper appearance.

"We should know the Great Spirit is within all things: the trees, the grasses, the rivers, the mountains, and the four-legged and winged peoples."

—Black Elk (1863–1950), Oglala Sioux holy man

This restored wetland near Jackson Hole, Wyoming, provides good habitat for fish and other wildlife.

Restoration, Revegetation, and Habitat Improvement

Lakeshores, stream banks, trails, campsites, meadows, alpine tundra—all environments that humans use extensively will show signs of erosion and vegetation loss. The encroachment of nonnative vegetation also threatens many ecosystems vital to wildlife. Progress in repairing damaged sites is often slow, but groups serious about revegetation and restoration will see dramatic long-term changes.

A trail 3 feet wide represents nearly a quarter-acre of bare ground per mile.

Revegetation is the art of reintroducing plant communities to areas where vegetation growth has been discouraged. Revegetation improves an area's appearance, protects it from erosion, and enhances it as an inviting wildlife habitat. Sowing grass seed on mine tailings is a good example of a revegetation project.

Restoration is an attempt to heal the land by returning it to its natural integrity. In addition to sowing seed, restoration of mine tailings might include contouring the terrain and bringing in topsoil.

3 feet

It might not be possible to restore a site to its condition before being disturbed by human activity. For example, a climax forest that has been cleared away cannot be recreated even if volunteers were to devote the rest of their lives to it. However, they can recreate the early stages of such a forest so that natural processes can move forward. Restoration gives an area a jump start on recovery, allowing the land a better chance to heal.

Erasing Inappropriate Trails and Campsites

Little will grow where the weight of many footsteps has compacted the tread's soil, so an inviting trail emerges. By concentrating use on the trail rather than on the surrounding environment, impact is limited to the tread. A planned trail is a sacrifice zone that we accept because it makes travel easier and it limits human impact to the pathway.

Problems arise when people stray from designated trails and, by trampling vegetation and compacting soil in other areas, create *social trails*. Many land managers try to solve that problem by selecting one route through an area, enhancing a single trail for everyone to follow, and then erasing the social trails.

Likewise, heavily used campsites often are so barren of vegetation that more camping on them will cause little further damage. Resource managers often encourage people to continue using those campsites to protect the surrounding vegetation. However, where there are too many campsites or when campsites appear in inappropriate places, it might be wise to close certain sites and restore them as much as possible.

With guidance from restoration experts and land managers, volunteer groups create visual barriers to discourage people from camping where they shouldn't. Loosening compacted soil and transplanting vegetation creates conditions that will help damaged areas recover much of their natural diversity and appearance.

Steps in Restoration and Revegetation

As with any conservation project, land managers and group leaders should do some careful planning before volunteers arrive at a restoration site. The planning process will help determine attainable goals and increase the environmental education opportunities for everyone.

Study the Area

Determine the causes and extent of the environmental damage at a site, then develop a coherent, overall plan to deal with it. Consider the soil type, annual precipitation, length and timing of the growing season, and plant communities native to the area, as well as the amount of time volunteers are willing to dedicate to improving the site.

Provide Options for Human Activity

Areas often become damaged because people use them. Efforts to restore vegetation will not be very effective if visitors continue to trample and compact repaired sites. Providing attractive alternative routes and campsites will help persuade people to avoid areas undergoing restoration.

Loosen Compacted Soil

When many people walk in the same area, their weight compacts the soil, collapsing tiny air pockets, hardening the ground, and driving out earthworms, small insects, and other creatures that enrich the soil as decomposers and aerators. Tiny root ends can no longer push through the compressed earth. Mycelia, bacteria, and other microscopic organisms essential to vegetation health might also be unable to survive.

The first step in restoring closed campsites and abandoned trails is to loosen the top 6 inches of compacted soil using shovels, garden tools, Pulaskis, and picks. Loosened soil is an inviting bed for seeds drifting in from surrounding vegetation. Scattering leaves on the disturbed area creates mulch that can protect seedlings from drying out.

Install Barriers and Camouflage

Among the most satisfying aspects of a restoration project is developing natural-looking visual barriers to discourage people from entering an area. That can give plants the time they need to become reestablished. If people can't see through a site, they are not likely to walk through it, and they will not be tempted to pitch tents there if stones and clumps of thorny bushes are covering the ground.

Restoration experts can show you how to install logs and rocks, transplant prickly native species, and then step back to examine what you have done. Can you make it look more natural? Let your efforts spill over into undisturbed areas to erase the boundary between a restored zone and the natural environment around it.

The same holds true in closing trails. Rather than simply throwing armloads of brush on the tread and ending up with an eyesore of woody debris, blend rocks and brush into the visual background to block the trail but not attract undue attention.

Transplanting

Transplanting bushes, clumps of grass, and saplings into loosened soil speeds the healing of a restoration site, but its success depends upon a project crew's knowledge of local vegetation, proper planting times and methods, and a commitment to the ongoing care of the area.

The best time to transplant usually is autumn, when vegetation is becoming dormant and will be less affected by the shock of being moved. In spring and summer, transplanting can stress plants, especially when most of their energy is going into producing flowers, seed, and roots.

Transplanted grass can thrive in new locations. Select native species from adjacent areas so that the vegetation taking root in a restored area will be the same as what was there before the damage occurred. Take plants from areas that are similar to the restoration area in terrain and amount of sunlight. If shaded plants from a moist forest floor are moved to the edge of a dry, sunnier meadow, for example, they are not likely to survive.

Before you dig up a plant, prepare the hole that will receive it by pouring in some water and perhaps a mixture of mulch and a natural fertilizer such as fish meal. Carefully remove the plant from its original location and immediately transplant it. Remove dead, damaged, and crowded limbs to shape the tree and reduce the transplanting shock to the roots. The less time fragile roots are exposed to the air, the less likely they will be to dry out. Give the transplant plenty of water after replanting. Depending on climate and weather patterns, it might require a few more irrigations in the days or weeks that follow.

34

Weed Control

Among the more labor-intensive challenges facing many land managers is limiting the spread of weeds. A weed is any unwanted plant. Land management agencies often approach a weed problem with a four-step plan:

Prevention—educating the public on ways to avoid transporting weed seeds from one area to another

Removal—removing weeds from an area

Restoration—helping native vegetation reestablish itself

Monitoring—diligently seeking and eliminating new weed growth

With their numbers and enthusiasm, volunteer groups can help with all four steps of weed control. Assisted by land managers, the group's plan to effectively deal with weeds in an area will clearly identify the plants to be removed and the most efficient removal methods. Considerations for a weed-removal plan include the following.

- Identify the plant. If in doubt, don't pull it out.

- Pull weeds at the right time of year, ideally before they produce and disperse their seed.

- Wear long-sleeved shirts, long pants, and gloves when working with weeds that have thorns or sap that can irritate the skin.

- Pull small infestations of weeds by hand, especially when a noxious plant has first been detected in an area. Hand pulling also is a good alternative in sites where herbicides and mechanical removal methods cannot be used.

- If weeds have deep root systems that cannot be pulled out by hand, try cutting them flush with the ground or using shovels, Pulaskis, and other tools to dig them out.

- Land managers will direct you in the best ways to dispose of the weeds you remove.

For more on weeds, see the chapter titled "Plants."

Canada thistle, Cirsium arvense, *is a troublesome perennial weed throughout the United States.*

A South Dakota rancher discusses grazing management techniques with a conservationist from the National Resources Conservation Service.

Lifelong Stewardship

Stewardship is an obvious extension of trek adventures. In fact, caring for the environment can be an adventure that lasts a lifetime and ranges wherever our travels take us. As with other outdoor skills, the more we practice active stewardship, the more easily we can find what needs to be done and the means to achieve our goals. That serves not only the well-being of the land, but also the betterment of ourselves in our appreciation, enjoyment, and protection of natural resources.

"The nation behaves well if it treats the natural resources as assets which it must turn over to the next generation increased, and not impaired in value."

—Theodore Roosevelt, United States president, 1900–1908

Credits

Acknowledgments

The Boy Scouts of America gratefully acknowledges the contributions of the following people for their help in preparing the *Fieldbook,* 4th edition.

- Members of the *Fieldbook* task force: Edward A. Pease, chairman; Riley Berg; Timothy Brox; Hab Butler; David L. Caffey, Ed.D.; Jim Cheatham; Brian Herren; Katherine Knuth; Jeff Marion, Ph.D.; Richards Miller; Arthur H. Mittelstaedt Jr., Ed.D.; Chris J. Moon; William E. Murray, J.D.; Wells M. Stephensen; Gary M. Stolz, Ph.D.; Thomas R. Welch, M.D.; Luke Wolfe

- Members of the Camping task force: James E. Blair, chairman; James H. Bean; Robert C. Canfield; Jim Erwin; Phil A. Gilmer; Eric Hiser; Marshall Hollis; William J. Kane; C. Mont Mahoney; Edwin B. Morrison, M.D.; Edward A. Pease; Gene Schnell; David Shows, Ph.D.; Chuck Wimberly; Darrell Winn

- National office advisory team: David J. Ross, Doug Smith, George D. Trosko, James B. Wilson Jr., Dan Buckhout

- Members of the BSA's Conservation Committee, including John Baughman, chairman; R. Max Peterson, former chairman; Tim Beaty; Doug Blankinship; Ken Carter; Ora Dixon; Don Hansen; Earl W. Hower; Tom Leverman; Bud Pidgeon Jr., Ph.D.; Jim Poole; Randy L. Rutan; and George E. Tabb Jr.

- Scouts and Scouters throughout the nation who participated in focus groups, photography efforts, and manuscript reviews

The BSA also is grateful for the invaluable manuscript reviews and spirited expert opinions of the following contributors.

Mark Anderson
Van F. Anderson, Ph.D.
Tony Aretz
Ross Bash
Susan Bates, N.P.
David Bell
Jerry Bernard
Craig Birkby, M.D.
Jeff Birkby
Lloyd Chapman
Jack Chowning
Joe Clay
Kent Clement
Joseph Cornell
Donna Cunningham
Tim Cunningham
Jim Davidson
Jamie Dickinson
Jack K. Drury
Tim Evans
Vince Ferri
William W. Forgey, M.D.
Don Gale
Jim Goodbar
Rick Goodman
Paul Green, M.D.
Paul Hansen
Kelly Hartsell
Jeff Hohensee
Dara Houdek
Linda Hughes
Cliff Jacobson
Stewart Jacobson
Benn Jelsema
Kerry Jones
Rick Kearney
Ben Lawhon
Thomas Levermann
Tom Lutyens
Don MacDonald
Vernon Mangold Sr., Ph.D.

David R. McClurg
Janet McKinnon
Tedd Mitchell, M.D.
James H. Moss, J.D.
Forrest Muire
Carol Munch
Bruce Newell
Doug Palmer
Pamela Paulding
Jeffrey Pellegrino
Max Peterson
Scott Peterson, Ph.D.
Terry Pogue
Gina Ramos
Scott Reid
Jason Richards
Bob Ricklefs
Tony Rosenberger
Vicki Sakata, M.D.
Debra Salt
Jay A. Satz
Bill Schoonmaker
William Shiner, Ph.D.
Terry Shocke
David P. Sinish
Mike Smith
Robert Sousa
Dennis St. Jean
C. William Steele
Dan Stiles
Charlie Thorpe
Jon Tierney
Buck Tilton
Chuck Treadway
Vish Unnitan, M.D.
Mark C. Wagstaff
Bruce Walcutt
Sam Wampler
Cathy Weil
Gary Williams
Stephen Zimmer

National Office Publishing Team

Project director
David R. Bates, Boy Scout
Division, BSA

**Senior account executive/
publishing manager**
Maria C. Dahl, Custom
Communication Division, BSA

Author
Robert C. Birkby, Eagle Scout,
mountaineer, and former
director of Conservation at
Philmont Scout Ranch

Editor/copy editors
Karen W. Webb, Winston Webb
Editorial Services

Beth McPherson, Custom
Communication Division, BSA

Proofreaders
Karen M. Kraft, Custom
Communication Division, BSA

Amy Thomte, Custom
Communication Division, BSA

Concept designer/senior designer
Julie Moore, Custom
Communication Division, BSA

Design manager
Laura E. Humphries, Henderson
Humphries Design

Designer/illustrator
Linda Hightower, Hightower
Print & Web Design

Design assistant
Ann Winkler, Wink Design

Imaging manager
Melinda VanLone, Custom
Communication Division, BSA

Imaging specialists
Jessica Birchard, Custom
Communication Division, BSA

Roxane Galassini, Custom
Communication Division, BSA

Marcie Rodriguez, Custom
Communication Division, BSA

Senior prepress specialist
Joanne Padier, Custom
Communication Division, BSA

Prepress specialists
Candace Blaylock
Isabel Wood

Print coordinator
Kimberly Kailey, Custom
Communication Division, BSA

Illustrator
John McDearmon, John
McDearmon Illustration & Design

Photography manager
Michael Roytek, Custom
Communication Division, BSA

Photo/production assistant
Kellie Pence, Custom
Communication Division, BSA

Photo file technician
Christy Batchelor, Custom
Communication Division, BSA

Indexing
Julie Grady, Grady
Editorial Services

Webmaster
Jim Shamlin, Custom
Communication Division, BSA

Archive manager
Dorothy Edwards, Custom
Communication Division, BSA

Editorial assistant
Adryn Shackelford, Custom
Communication Division, BSA

Photo and Illustration Credits

Cover

BSA file *(flag on spine)*

Diamar Interactive Portfolios *(background)*

Getty Images *(center and right)*

Brian Payne *(left)*

Inside Front Cover

BSA file *(logo, second, and fourth)*

Randy Piland *(fifth)*

Steve Seeger *(third)*

Scott Stenjem *(first)*

Inside Back Cover

BSA file *(logo, second, fourth, and fifth)*

Roy Jansen *(first)*

Scott Stenjem *(third)*

Section Icons

BSA file *(Leadership and Trek Preparation, and Leaving No Trace)*

©2001 Comstock Images Inc. *(Appreciating Our Environment and Trek Adventures)*

Introduction

BSA file—pages vii *(left and bottom)*, viii *(leaves and patches)*, and ix *(patch and top right)*

©2001 Comstock Images Inc.—pages viii *(compass)* and ix *(center)*

Diamar Interactive Portfolios—page vii *(background)*

Vince Heptig—page ix *(bottom)*

Brian Payne—pages vii *(center)*, viii *(center right and bottom left)*, and ix *(top left)*

©Photos.com—page vi

Randy Piland—page viii *(top right)*

Chapter 1

Anatomy Visual Media Group, *http://www.avmg.co.uk*—page 4

BSA file—pages x–1, 6 *(top)*, 8, and 10

Vince Heptig—pages 6 *(bottom)* and 7

Brian Payne—pages 5 and 9

Steve Seeger—page 2

Chapter 2

BSA file—pages 17 and 20

Vince Heptig—page 12

Roy Jansen—page 21

Brian Payne—page 16

Randy Piland—pages 15, 19, and 22

Doug Wilson—page 23

Chapter 3

Jack Brown—page 26

BSA file—pages 24, 27, 28 *(both)*, 29 *(both)*, 30, 31 *(all)*, 32 *(both)*, 33 *(center, right, and bottom)*, 34 *(all)*, 35 *(all)*, 36 *(all)*, 37 *(all)*, 38 *(all)*, 39 *(both)*, 40 *(all)*, and 41

Christian Michaels—page 33 *(left)*

Randy Piland—page 25

Chapter 4

Dan Bryant—page 49 *(bottom right)*

BSA file—pages 46 *(all)*, 47, 48 *(all)*, and 49 *(top, center, and bottom left)*

Frederic Remington Art Museum, Ogdensburg, New York; courtesy—page 50

Daniel Giles—page 53

National Park Service—page 45

Randy Piland—pages 42 and 44

Chapter 5

BSA file—pages 62, 66, 68, and 69

Dynamic Graphics; ©Photos.com; and Julie Moore *(photo illustration)*—page 63 *(top)*

Brian Payne—pages 56 and 58

Getty Images—pages 61 and 63 *(bottom)*

©Photos.com—pages 59, 60 *(top)*, and 64

Randy Piland—page 70

U.S. Department of Agriculture, Agricultural Resource Service—page 60 *(bottom)*

Chapter 6

Scott Bauer/U.S. Department of Agriculture, Agricultural Resource Service—page 91 *(both center)*

Dan Bryant—page 90

BSA file—pages 74, 78 *(both)*, 80, 81, 82, 85, 89 *(center)*, and 95

Hansell F. Cross, Georgia State University; image 0001048, *http://www.forestryimages.com*—page 91 *(bottom)*

Daniel Giles—page 76

Kitty Kohout/The Morton Arboretum, Lisle, Illinois; courtesy—page 89 *(bottom left)*

John McDearmon—pages 86 *(both)* and 91 *(top left and top right)*

The Morton Arboretum, Lisle, Illinois; courtesy—page 89 *(bottom right)*

Brian Payne—pages 77 and 83

©Photos.com—pages 72, 84, 88 *(both)*, 92 *(both)*, 93, and 94 *(both)*

Randy Piland—pages 79 and 89 *(top)*

Chapter 7

BSA file—pages 98, 99, 100, 101, 102, 103, 104, 105, and 109 *(both)*

©1998 Comstock Images Inc.—pages 96–97

Brian Payne—pages 106, 107, and 108

Chapter 8

BSA file—pages 110, 111, 113 *(all)*, 114, and 117 *(top)*

John McDearmon—page 119 *(both)*

Brian Payne—page 112

Randy Piland—pages 116 and 117 *(bottom)*

Scott Stenjem—page 115

Chapter 9

Dan Bryant—pages 125 and 129 *(both)*

BSA file—pages 121, 126, 127 *(both)*, 128, and 130 *(both)*

©Corbis—page 122 *(third)*

Getty Images—page 122 *(top, second, and bottom)*

Randy Piland—pages 120, 123, 124, and 131

Chapter 10

BSA file—pages 133, 140, 142 *(bottom)*, and 143

Brian Payne—pages 134, 135, 136, 141, and 142 *(top)*

Randy Piland—pages 132 and 137

USDA Forest Service, courtesy—page 138

Chapter 11

Dan Bryant—pages 151 *(top)*, 158 *(top)*, 164 *(top)*, and 167 *(top)*

Dan Bryant and Julie Moore *(photo illustration)*—page 167 *(bottom)*

BSA file—pages 146, 148, 149 *(both)*, 150, 151 *(center and bottom)*, 152 *(both)*, 157 *(bottom)*, 158 *(center and bottom)*, 159, 163 *(bottom)*, 165 *(both)*, and 166

Doug Knutson—page 163 *(top)*

John McDearmon—pages 155
(both), 160 (bottom), and 162

Christian Michaels—page 164
(bottom)

Omega Studios—page 160 (top)

Brian Payne—pages 144–145, 153
(bottom), and 169

Randy Piland—pages 157 (top),
161, and 168

Scott Stenjem—page 153 (top)

Chapter 12

Dan Bryant—page 184 (bottom)

BSA file—pages 180, 181 (both),
184 (top), 185 (top), 188 (bottom
left), 190, and 191 (both)

BSA file and U.S. Geological Survey
(photo illustration)—page 188
(bottom right)

©2001 Comstock Images Inc. and
Julie Moore (photo illustration)—
page 182

Linda Hightower—page 188

John McDearmon—page 173 (all)

John McDearmon and Linda
Hightower—page 187

Brian Payne—pages 172, 185
(bottom), and 189

Randy Piland—pages 170 and 186

U.S. Geological Survey—pages 174
(all), 175, 176, 177, and 183

Chapter 13

BSA file—pages 196, 197 (all), 202
(all), 212 (all), and 215 (bottom)

John McDearmon—pages 195, 198
(top), 203 (both), 204 (top and
center), 206 (both), 207 (both),
208, and 209 (both)

John McDearmon and Julie Moore
(photo illustration)—page 204
(bottom)

Brian Payne—pages 192, 194, 198
(bottom), 199, 200 (bottom),
201 (both), 205, 210 (both), 211,
and 214

Brian Payne, BSA file, and Julie
Moore (photo illustration)—
pages 200 (top) and 213

Chapter 14

Scott Bauer/U.S. Department of
Agriculture, Agricultural
Resource Service—page 223
(bottom)

BSA file—page 222 (foreground, both)

John McDearmon—page 218

Julie Moore—page 222 (labels)

Brian Payne—pages 216, 219, 221,
223 (top), 224 (bottom), and
225 (both)

©Photos.com—page 222
(background, both)

Randy Piland—pages 220 and
224 (top)

Chapter 15

Dan Bryant—pages 228 and
229 (bottom)

BSA file—pages 226, 231, 235,
and 239 (both)

John Fulton—page 230

John McDearmon—page 234
(bottom)

Omega Studios—page 229 (top)

Randy Piland—pages 232 (all),
233 (both), 234 (top), 236
(both), 237, and 238

Chapter 16

Dan Bryant—pages 243 (top and
center) and 245 (bottom)

BSA file—pages 244, 245 (both top),
and 258 (bottom)

Gene Daniels—page 258 (top)

Vince Heptig—pages 242 and 257

John McDearmon—pages 247
(both), 248 (bottom), 249
(bottom), 251 (all), 252 (all),
and 254 (all)

Brian Payne—pages 240 and
248 (top)

Randy Piland—pages 243 *(bottom)*, 246, 249 *(top)*, 250, 253 *(all)*, 255, and 256

Chapter 17

Dan Bryant—pages 267 *(all)* and 279

BSA file—pages 262 *(bottom)*, 263 *(top)*, 265 *(all)*, 276 *(both)*, and 277 *(all)*

Gene Daniels—page 263 *(bottom both)*

John McDearmon—pages 264 *(bottom illustrations)*, 266 *(top)*, 270 *(both)*, 271 *(all)*, 272 *(all)*, 273, and 274 *(all)*

Frank McMahon and Julie Moore *(photo illustration)*—page 260

©Photos.com and Julie Moore *(photo illustration)*—page 266 *(bottom left)*

Randy Piland—pages 262 *(top)*, 264 *(top)*, 266 *(bottom right)*, 268, 269, 275, and 278 *(right)*

Steve Seeger—page 278 *(left)*

Chapter 18

Dan Bryant—page 285 *(all)*

BSA file—pages 282 *(top and bottom)*, 283, 298, and 303 *(top)*

John McDearmon—pages 289 *(bottom)*, 290 *(all)*, 291 *(all)*, 292 *(both)*, 294 *(both)*, 295 *(all)*, 296 *(both)*, 297 *(all)*, 301 *(both)*, and 302

National Oceanic and Atmospheric Administration—page 282 *(center)*

Outdoor Adventure River Specialists, courtesy—page 300 *(bottom)*

Randy Piland—pages 280, 284, 286 *(both)*, 287 *(all)*, 288 *(all)*, 289 *(top)*, 293, 299 *(both)*, 300 *(top)*, and 303 *(bottom)*

Chapter 19

BSA file—pages 306, 311 *(top)*, 313 *(both)*, and 318

John McDearmon—pages 307, 308 *(all)*, 309, 311 *(bottom)*, 312, 314, and 315

Brian Payne—page 319

Randy Piland—pages 304, 310, 316, and 317 *(all)*

Chapter 20

Bicycles 2 Go (E-mail: ColtonEnterprises@comcast.net) —page 323 *(bottom)*

BSA file—pages 322 *(bottom)*, 324 *(all)*, 325 *(both)*, 329, 330 *(bottom)*, 331 *(bottom)*, 333 *(both)*, 334, 335 *(all)*, and 336 *(both)*

Darrell Byers—page 328 *(top three)*

Dynamic Graphics—page 331 *(top)*

Vince Heptig—page 337 *(top)*

David Metz/http://www.metzbicyclemuseum.com, courtesy— page 323 *(center)*

Brian Payne—pages 320, 322 *(top)*, 323 *(top)*, 326, 328 *(bottom)*, 330 *(top)*, 332, and 337 *(bottom)*

Doug Wilson—page 327

Chapter 21

Dan Bryant—pages 341 and 342 *(both)*

BSA file—pages 339 *(bottom)*, 340 *(top)*, and 353 *(top)*

R. B. Dole/U.S. Geological Survey— page 347 *(top)*

John McDearmon—pages 340 *(bottom)* and 349 *(bottom)*

Brian Payne—pages 338, 343 *(all)*, 344 *(bottom six)*, 345 *(top and center)*, 346 *(all)*, 347 *(bottom)*, 349 *(top)*, 350, 351, and 352 *(both)*

©Photos.com—pages 344 *(top)*, 345 *(bottom)*, 348, and 353 *(bottom)*

Chapter 22

Dan Bryant—page 369 *(top three)*

BSA file—pages 356 *(both)*, 357 *(all)*, 358 *(all)*, 359, 367, 369 *(bottom two)*, and 370 *(bottom)*

BSA file and Julie Moore *(photo illustration)*—page 354

Brian Payne—pages 355, 360, 361 *(all)*, 362 *(all)*, 363 *(both)*, 364 *(all)*, 365 *(both)*, 368, 370 *(top)*, 371, and 372

©Photos.com—page 366

Chapter 23

BSA file—pages 374, 376, 377, 378, 379 *(bottom)*, 381, 386, and 391

Kass Kastnig—page 390

Brian Payne—pages 379 *(top)*, 380 *(both)*, 382, 384, 387 *(both)*, 388, and 389 *(both)*

Randy Piland—pages 383 and 385

Scott Stenjem—page 375

Chapter 24

Dan Bryant—page 399 *(bottom)*

Scott Goldsmith—pages 394 and 399 *(top)*

Keith A. Harris, courtesy—pages 397 and 401 *(bottom)*

John McDearmon and Julie Moore—page 402

National Park Service—pages 395 and 396

Randy Piland—pages 392, 400, and 401 *(top)*

Chapter 25

Dan Bryant—pages 412 *(center two)*, 413 *(bottom three)*, 414 *(top)*, and 419 *(top)*

BSA file—pages 406 *(bottom)* and 417

Gene Daniels—page 404

Daniel Giles—pages 408, 412 *(top)*, and 420 *(top)*

John McDearmon—pages 407, 409 *(both)*, 410 *(both)*, 411 *(all)*, 414 *(bottom left and bottom right)*, 415 *(bottom three)*, 416 *(all)*, 418 *(all)*, and 419 *(bottom three)*

Brian Payne—pages 415 *(top)* and 420 *(bottom)*

Randy Piland—page 406 *(top)*

Steve Seeger—pages 412 *(bottom)* and 413 *(top)*

Scott Stenjem—page 421

Chapter 26

Linda Hightower—page 432

John McDearmon—pages 430 *(left)* and 435 *(right)*

Julie Moore—pages 428 and 434

Brian Payne—pages 422, 426, 429, 430 *(right)*, 431, 433, 435 *(left)*, 436, and 437

Chapter 27

©DigitalVision® Ltd.—page 447

©Dynamic Graphics Inc.—page 442

Dennis Eilers/U.S. Department of Agriculture, National Resources Conservation Service—page 448 *(inset)*

©1999 EyeWire Inc.—pages 450–451 *(ram and eagle)*

John McDearmon—pages 444, 445, and 446

National Park Service—pages 438–439, and 450–451 *(arches)*

©Photos.com—pages 448 *(right)*, and 450–451 *(forest, bear, flowers, and waterfall)*

©Photos.com and Julie Moore—page 440

Steve Seeger—page 443

U.S. Fish and Wildlife Service—pages 450–451 *(fish)*

Chapter 28

Robert S. S. Baden-Powell/
National Scouting Museum—
page 456 *(top)*

Karen Bollinger/U.S. Fish and
Wildlife Service—page 463
(top left)

BSA file—pages 454 *(bottom)*, 455,
456 *(center)*, 458, and 462 *(top)*

John McDearmon—page 465 *(top)*

National Park Service—pages 460
and 465 *(bottom)*

Brian Payne—pages 454 *(top)* and
459 *(all)*

Brian Payne, ©Photos.com, and
Julie Moore *(photo illustration)*—
page 461

©Photos.com—pages 452, 462
(bottom), and 463 *(top right,
center, and bottom)*

Randy Piland—page 456 *(bottom)*

Steve Seeger—page 453

U.S. Fish and Wildlife Service—
page 457 *(both)*

Chapter 29

BSA file—page 472 *(top and right)*

BSA file, Julie Moore, and Linda
Hightower *(photo illustration)*—
page 471 *(all)*

Julie Moore—page 468

National Aeronautics and Space
Administration, courtesy—page
475 *(left)*

National Park Service—pages 466,
475 *(right)*, and 476

National Park Service, Julie Moore,
and Linda Hightower *(photo
illustration)*—page 470 *(bottom)*

Ron Nichols/U.S. Department of
Agriculture, National Resources
Conservation Service—page 474

Brian Payne—page 477

©Photos.com—pages 472 *(left six)*
and 473 *(all)*

J. G. Rosen, Julie Moore, and Linda
Hightower *(photo illustration)*—
page 470 *(top)*

Chapter 30

BSA file—page 490

©2001 Comstock Images Inc. and
Julie Moore—page 483

Vince Heptig—page 484

Joanne Padier and Julie Moore—
page 480 *(bottom)*

Julie Moore—page 481

National Oceanic and Atmospheric
Administration—pages 485,
486 *(all)*, 487 *(bottom)*, and
489 *(insets)*

©Photos.com—pages 478, 487 *(top)*,
and 488

©Photos.com, Joanne Padier, and
Julie Moore *(photo illustration)*—
page 480 *(bottom center)*

©2003 WFAA–TV Co.—page 489 *(top)*

Chapter 31

Jennifer Anderson/U.S. Department
of Agriculture, National
Resources Conservation Service
(PLANTS Database)—page 496

Scott Bauer/U.S. Department of
Agriculture, Agricultural
Resource Service—page 516
(bottom)

BSA file—pages 499 *(top)*, 507 *(top)*,
and 512 *(top)*

BSA file, ©Photos.com, and Julie
Moore *(photo illustration)*—
page 511 *(top)*

Bureau of Land Management,
courtesy—page 498

Michael Clayton and the Plant
Teaching Collections at the
University of Wisconsin,
Madison—page 502 *(bottom left)*

Bill Cook, Michigan State University; *http://www.forestryimages.com*— image 1219256 *(page 505 center, third)*, image 1219194 *(page 506, bark)*, image 1218013 *(page 510, third row, left)*, image 1218017 *(page 510, third row, right)*, image 1218070 *(page 510, fourth)*, image 1219077 *(page 514, top left)*, and image 1219109 *(page 514, center left)*

Carl Dennis, Auburn University; image 1203071, *http://www.forestryimages.com*— page 515 *(second)*

Peggy Greb/U.S. Department of Agriculture, Agricultural Resource Service—page 517 *(bottom)*

Gerald J. Lenhard, Louisiana State University; image 0014005, *http://www.forestryimages.com*— page 511 *(bottom)*

Louisiana State Archives; image 0014201, *http://www. forestryimages.com*—page 506 *(acorn)*

John McDearmon and Julie Moore— page 501

Julie Moore—pages 508 *(bottom)* and 512 *(bottom)*

©Photos.com—pages 492, 494, 495 *(all)*, 496 *(top)*, 497 *(all)*, 499 *(bottom)*, 500 *(both)*, 502 *(top)*, 503 *(all)*, 505 *(top two, center left, and bottom set)*, 506 *(leaf and tree)*, 507 *(center and bottom)*, 508 *(top and center)*, 512 *(center)*, 514 *(walnut and bottom)*, 516 *(first, second, and third)*, and 517 *(top)*

Dave Powell, USDA Forest Service; image 0806060, *http://www.forestryimages.com*— page 510 *(bottom)*

©Realworld Imagery Inc.—pages 504 *(all)*, 509 *(all)*, and 513 *(all)*

Jim Stasz/U.S. Department of Agriculture, National Resources Conservation Service (PLANTS Database)—page 499 *(second)*

University of Michigan Herbarium, courtesy—page 502 *(bottom right)*

U.S. Department of Agriculture, Agricultural Resource Service— page 505 *(second row, center)*

U.S. Department of Agriculture, Agricultural Resource Service, Poisonous Research Laboratory—page 499 *(third)*

U.S. Department of Agriculture, Natural Resources Conservation Service—page 515 *(third)*

Paul Wray, Iowa State University; *http://www.forestryimages.com*— image 0008142 *(page 510, first)*, image 0008196 *(page 510, second)*, image 0008210 *(page 514, top right)*, image 0008195 *(page 515, first)*, image 0008440 *(page 515, fourth)*, image 0008438 *(page 515, fifth)*, and image 0008181 *(page 516, fourth)*

Chapter 32

Erwin and Peggy Bauer/U.S. Fish and Wildlife Service—page 539 *(bottom)*

©2001 Brand X Pictures—pages 534 *(center)*, 535 *(bottom)*, and 536 *(bottom)*

BSA file—page 521 *(bottom)*

Irwin W. Cole/U.S. Department of Agriculture, National Resources Conservation Service—page 526 *(background)*

©Digital Vision® Ltd.—pages 535 *(top and center)* and 536 *(top)*

©1999 EyeWire Inc.—page 518

Peggy Greb/U.S. Department of Agriculture, Agricultural Resource Service—page 537 *(bottom)*

John McDearmon—page 524 *(bottom)*

National Oceanic and Atmospheric Administration, Office of Response and Restoration—page 540 *(both)*

©Photos.com—pages 519, 520, 521 *(top)*, 522, 523 *(top)*, 524 *(top)*, 525 *(both)*, 526 *(both insets)*, 527 *(bottom)*, 528, 529 *(third and fourth)*, 530 *(right)*, 532 *(bottom)*, 533 *(both)*, 536 *(second and third)*, 537 *(top)*, 539 *(top and center)*, and 541

Randy Piland—page 529 *(second)*

Jerry Poppenhouse—page 529 *(first)*

Rocky Mountain National Park, National Park Service—page 523 *(bottom)*

SeaWorld Adventure Park, San Antonio, Texas; courtesy—page 530

Steve Seeger—pages 531 *(top)* and 534 *(bottom)*

©2003 Texas Parks and Wildlife, courtesy—page 532 *(top)*

U.S. Fish and Wildlife Service—pages 527 *(top)*, 534 *(top)*, and 538

Zoological Society of San Diego—page 531 *(bottom)*

Chapter 33

BSA file—page 544 *(both)*

©Digital Vision Inc.—pages 545, 546, and 556 *(bottom)*

Dynamic Graphics; Laura E. Humphries/Henderson Humphries Design; and Julie Moore *(photo illustration)*—page 550

Linda Hightower—pages 547 and 553

John McDearmon—pages 548, 554, 555 *(both)*, and 556 *(top)*

Johnny Horne/*The Fayetteville (NC) Observer*, *http://www.fayettevillenc.com*; and Laura E. Humphries/Henderson Humphries Design *(photo illustration)*—page 549

©Photos.com—page 542

©Photos.com; Laura E. Humphries/Henderson Humphries Design; and Julie Moore *(photo illustration)*—page 552

T. A. Rector, and I. P. Dell'Antonio/NAOA/AURA/NSF, courtesy—page 557

Chapter 34

Eric Bakke—page 573

BSA file—pages 560 *(bottom)*, 561, 562, 563, 564 *(inset)*, 565, 566 *(both)*, 567, 569 *(top)*, 570 *(bottom)*, 571, and 572

BSA file, Brian Payne, and Julie Moore *(photo illustration)*—page 564 *(top)*

Peggy Greb/U.S. Department of Agriculture, Agricultural Resource Service—page 574

Roy Jansen—page 558

Tim McCabe/U.S. Department of Agriculture, National Resources Conservation Service—page 570 *(top)*

John McDearmon and Julie Moore—pages 568 and 569 *(bottom)*

Julie Moore—page 569 *(center)*

Bob Nichols/U.S. Department of Agriculture, National Resources Conservation Service—page 560 *(top)*

U.S. Department of Agriculture, National Resources Conservation Service—page 576 *(top)*

U.S. Fish and Wildlife Service—page 576 *(bottom)*

Index

BSA file *(all)*

Index

C